Praise for Beth Macy's

FACTORY MAN

One of the year's best books

*New York Times, Christian Science Monitor,
Publishers Weekly,* Goodreads, and Barnes & Noble

Winner of the 2013 J. Anthony Lukas Work-in-Progress Award

"*Factory Man* is in a class with other runaway debuts like Laura Hillenbrand's *Seabiscuit* and Katherine Boo's *Behind the Beautiful Forevers:* These nonfiction narratives are more stirring and dramatic than most novels. And Ms. Macy writes so vigorously that she hooks you instantly. You won't be putting this book down."
— Janet Maslin, *New York Times*

"A truly remarkable work of researched narrative nonfiction, one that probes every corner of its topic and values every subject who has something to say.... *Factory Man* leaves you feeling better for having read it."
— Lucas Mann, *San Francisco Chronicle*

"Macy brings to the story a keen understanding of life among factory workers....At its best, *Factory Man* traces the intertwined stories of a family, business, and town: the complex, paternalistic relationships, the shared secrets, the vexed bonds of interdependence. Macy writes movingly about what happens when workers in these factory towns face not only closing factories and skyrocketing unemployment but the loss of their community identity."
— Kate Tuttle, *Boston Globe*

"Nonfiction storytelling at its finest....*Factory Man* does what the best business books should: It delivers a heavily researched, highly entertaining story, at the end of which you realize you've learned something....This is a great American story, the kind that we don't read often enough."

—Bryan Burrough, *New York Times*

"An educational, fascinating reading adventure....A moving book about the loss of American jobs—one of the most vital issues of this century."

—Steve Weinberg, *Dallas Morning News*

"The author's brightly written, richly detailed narrative not only illuminates globalization and the issue of offshoring, but succeeds brilliantly in conveying the human costs borne by low-income people displaced from a way of life....A masterly feat of reporting."

—*Kirkus Reviews*

"Macy's down-to-earth writing style and abundance of personal stories from manufacturing's beleaguered front lines make her work a stirring critique of globalization."

—Carl Hays, *Booklist*

"The unlikely hero of *Factory Man* is a determined, ornery, and absolutely indomitable...businessman. He's the head of a family furniture company and damned if he's going to be pushed around. Beth Macy has given us an inspiring and engaging tale for our times, but not the expected one."

—Alex S. Jones, Pulitzer Prize–winning author of *Losing the News: The Future of the News That Feeds Democracy*

"A feat of reporting....There's a big generous heart at the center of this book, and it's hard not to compare *Factory Man* to the seminal nonfiction work of Tracy Kidder or even the storytelling that made David Simon's *The Wire* one of the best TV shows ever....*Factory Man* is a valuable American story, and one of the best books I've read this year."

—Elisabeth Donnelly, *Flavorwire*

"Macy's passion and enthusiasm are palpable on every page.... She makes a complex, now universal story understandable."
—Mimi Swartz, *New York Times Book Review*

"The epic struggle of Virginia furniture manufacturer John Bassett III to save his business has given crackerjack reporter Beth Macy the book she was born to write. Longtime champion of the downtrodden and the working American, Macy brings globalization to a human scale, giving a real voice and a recognizable face to everyone involved, from factory worker to government official to Chinese importer. Brilliant writing and thorough reporting combine to make *Factory Man* an exciting, fast-paced account of a quintessentially American story that affects us all."
—Lee Smith, author of *Guests on Earth*

"Beth Macy sees twists and subtleties that other journalists can't see, and she writes about the world around her with grit, honesty, and remarkable grace. She has a police detective's diligence and determination, a poet's way with words, and a born storyteller's gift for spot-on narrative."
—Martin Clark, author of *The Legal Limit*

"*Factory Man* deserves to be read by anyone wanting to wrap their head around the present-day dynamics and politics of globalization. Macy's book is an important read."
—Shawn Donnan, *Financial Times*

"Boisterous.... *Factory Man* is a Big Tale of a Big Man doing Big Things, and a rebuke to those who would declare American manufacturing dead."
—Earl Pike, *Cleveland Plain Dealer*

"Spirited, meticulously researched, and well written.... A page-turning tale that covers the company's history, family squabbles, and the black-sheep son who rescued the company through pluck, persistence, and political wrangling."
—Margaret Jaworski, *Success*

"A remarkable work.... Rarely, if ever, have I read a piece of book journalism that was more painstakingly researched or more compellingly transferred to the printed page.... It's as much about people as it is about bedroom suites and international commerce, and that human touch imbues it with the flesh and heart that sets it apart from most nonfiction."
— Jeff DeBell, *Roanoke Times*

"A deeply nuanced portrayal of the effects of globalization on a single company.... Exhaustively researched."
—Chris Serres, *Minneapolis Star Tribune*

"John Bassett's story has everything. An extraordinary dynasty, a relevant and inspiring message, and one of the best heroes I've read about in years. It works on every level, from the most personal betrayal to the realities of the global economy, from the struggle of one worker in a small Appalachian town to the future of our culture as a whole. Part of me wishes I'd found John Bassett III, because this is powerful stuff, but it's obvious the story is in excellent hands with Beth Macy. Sometimes the right writer comes along with the right story at the right time. This is clearly that book."
—Bret Witter, author of *Dewey* and *Until Tuesday*

"In a compelling and meticulously researched narrative, Macy follows the story from the Blue Ridge Mountains to China and Indonesia, chronicling John Bassett's tireless work to revive his company, and with it, an American town."
—Jamie Gnazzo, *Garden & Gun*

"I find myself deeply sympathic to Macy's essential point, which is that globalization inflicts a great deal of suffering on millions of people, something the news media should do a better job of acknowledging and the government should do a better job of mitigating."
—Joe Nocera, *New York Times*

"A triumph. . . . Get *Factory Man* and take your time with it. It's a big ol' delicious toasted sandwich of a book."

—Kurt Rheinheimer, *The Roanoker*

"This superbly detailed, exquisitely crafted story is as finely put together as some of that American furniture still being made in Virginia."

—Vick Mickunas, *Dayton Daily News*

"I've been reading Beth Macy for years. She is a great American writer. She sees everything, all the precious detail. A few years back, as the world was collapsing around us, she did a story on the temp who was answering phones at a hotline for those in financial hot water. The temp was this immense hero in all these ways that nobody else would have ever recognized. Of course, Macy never called her a hero. She just let the story do the work."

—Roland Lazenby, author of *Michael Jordan*

FACTORY MAN

FACTORY MAN

How One Furniture Maker Battled Offshoring,
Stayed Local—and Helped Save an American Town

BETH MACY

BACK BAY BOOKS
Little, Brown and Company
New York Boston London

Back Bay Books / Little, Brown and Company
Hachette Book Group
1290 Avenue of the Americas, New York, NY 10104
littlebrown.com

Originally published in hardcover by Little, Brown and Company, July 2014
First Back Bay paperback edition, June 2015

Back Bay Books is an imprint of Little, Brown and Company, a division of
Hachette Book Group, Inc. The Back Bay Books name and logo are trademarks of
Hachette Book Group, Inc.

The publisher is not responsible for websites (or their content) that are not owned
by the publisher.

The Hachette Speakers Bureau provides a wide range of authors for speaking
events. To find out more, go to hachettespeakersbureau.com or call
(866) 376-6591.

Natasha Tretheway interview reprinted by permission of *Garden & Gun*.
"We Can't Make It Here" lyrics courtesy of James McMurtry.
"Furniture Factory Blues" lyrics quoted by permission of Eddie Bond.
"RFD Parade" lyrics written by and quoted by permission of Russ Ashburn.
Family tree by Andrew Svec / Courtesy of *The Roanoke Times*.

ISBN 978-0-316-23143-5 (hc) / 978-0-316-23141-1 (pb)
LCCN 2014937343

10 9 8 7 6 5 4 3 2 1

RRD-C

Printed in the United States of America

For all the world's factory workers, past and present, and especially for my long-ago factory mom, Sarah Macy Slack, whose airplane lights I still imagine I can glimpse, up among the stars

*Black cat, white cat, all that matters
is that it catches mice.*
—TENG HSIAO-P'ING

Contents

Family Tree

A Virginia Furniture Dynasty

Most of Virginia's furniture companies were launched with the help of patriarch John D. Bassett Sr., who created his own competition while at the same time maintaining a thread of control. Intertwining his corporate babies with the family tree, he helped spawn such companies as Bassett, Hooker, Stanley, Vaughan, and Vaughan-Bassett—and generations of family fortune. (This diagram shows the progression of the business through the family.)

Charles Columbus Bassett
- Business partner with John. Married Roxie Hundley, sister of his brother's wife, Pocahontas Hundley.

John D. Bassett's brother

John D. Bassett
1866–1965
Married Pocahontas Hundley.
- Founded Bassett Furniture Company with his brother Charles and a brother-in-law in 1902.

Mabel Hooker
Married Clyde Hooker.
- Clyde Hooker founded Hooker Furniture in 1924.

Avis Weaver
Married R. E. Weaver.
- R. E. Weaver founded Weaver Mirror in 1932.

John Edwin "Ed" Bassett
- Ed Bassett ran Bassett Furniture from 1966 to 1979.

John D. Bassett's children

Blanche Vaughan
Married T. G. Vaughan.
- T. G. Vaughan founded Vaughan Furniture in Galax, Virginia, in 1923.

Bunyan Vaughan
Brother of T. G. Vaughan.
- Bunyan Vaughan founded Vaughan-Bassett Furniture in 1919.

John D. Bassett Jr.
Doug Bassett was the CEO of Bassett Furniture from 1960 to 1966. He was also the chairman of Bassett-Walker Knitting.

Anne Stanley
Married T. B. Stanley.
T. B. Stanley founded Stanley Furniture in 1924.

William "Bill" Bassett
Bill Bassett ran W. M. Bassett Furniture; it later merged with Bassett Furniture.

Fred Stanley
Nephew of T. B. Stanley. Fred Stanley founded Pulaski Furniture in 1955.

Minnie Lane
Married B. B. Lane.
B. B. Lane was chairman of Lane Furniture.

Jane Spilman
Married Bob Spilman.
Bob Spilman was CEO of Bassett Furniture from 1979 to 1997.

Bob Spilman

John D. Bassett III
Married Patricia Vaughan Exum Bassett, great-granddaughter of Mary Jane Hundley Burge, sister of Pocahontas Hundley and the granddaughter of Bunyan Vaughan. John Bassett III was a manager of Bassett Furniture from 1962 to 1982 and came to Vaughan-Bassett in 1983. He has been chairman since 2007.

Rob Spilman
Son of Jane and Bob Spilman. CEO of Bassett Furniture since 2000.

Doug Bassett
President of Vaughan-Bassett.

Wyatt Bassett
CEO of Vaughan-Bassett.

Frances Vaughan Bassett Poole
Board member of Vaughan-Bassett.

• = Furniture manufacturing company created.

FACTORY MAN

The Dusty Road to Dalian

John D. Bassett III was snaking his way through the sooty streets of rural northern China on a three-day fact-finding mission. It was 2002, and the third-generation Virginia furniture maker was gathering ammunition for an epic battle to keep the sawdust in his factory flying. He was close to the border of North Korea, on the hunt for a dresser built in the style of a nineteenth-century French monarch. If he could find the man who'd made that damn Louis Philippe, he might just save his business.

Back at Vaughan-Bassett, his factory in Galax, line workers had already deconstructed the dresser piece by piece and proved that the one hundred dollars the Chinese were wholesaling it for was far less than the cost of the materials—a violation of World Trade Organization laws. The sticker on the back read *Dalian, China,* and now here he was, some eight thousand miles away from his Blue Ridge Mountains, trying to pinpoint the source of the cheap chest of drawers.

It was November and snowy. The car creaked with every icy pothole it hit.

Word had already reached him through a friendly translator a few months earlier: There was a factory owner in the hinterlands, a hundred miles outside of Dalian, who'd been bragging that he was going to bring the Bassett furniture family down.

If they were going to war, Bassett told his son Wyatt, their family needed to heed Napoleon's advice: Know your enemy.

Today, for once in his life, JBIII sat silent. The car lurched along northward, farther into the remote province of Liaoning.

The first time John Bassett visited an Asian factory was in 1984, and it was only after dinner and way too many drinks that an elderly factory owner in Taiwan revealed his real opinion of American business leaders. The man was so candid that at first, his own interpreter clammed up, refusing to translate his words.

The Taiwanese businessman had negotiated plenty of deals with Europeans and South Americans, but he'd never met people quite like the Americans.

What do you mean? JBIII pressed.

I have figured you guys out, the translator finally relayed.

Tell me.

If the price is right, you will do *anything*. We have never seen people before who are this greedy—or this naive.

The Americans were not only knocking one another over in a stampede to import the cheapest furniture they could but they were also ignoring the fact that they were jeopardizing their own factories back home by teaching their Asian competitors every nuance of the American furniture-making trade.

When we get on top, the man said, don't expect us to be dumb enough to do for you what you've been dumb enough to do for us.

It would take many more trips to Asia before it became clear to JBIII what the Taiwanese furniture maker meant. During that time, two events helped ensure China would indeed get on top: China's admission into the WTO, and the great exodus of 160 million rural Chinese to the cities—the largest migration in human history.

It would take the hundred-dollar dresser and getting eyeball-to-eyeball with the man behind it before JBIII fully understood the battle he was about to enter. The rules of war had changed—drastically—and cowboy capitalism seemed to be the only rule of international trade.

It was cold inside the factory where Bassett finally met with business-man and Communist Party official He YunFeng in northern China in November 2002. The workers' breath froze in little puffs of vapor. The Chinese furniture magnate looked him "in the damn eye," Bassett recalled. Then he said something that raised the hair on the back of the Virginian's neck.

He YunFeng would be happy to provide Bassett with the dressers at a fraction of what they cost to make, a feat Bassett knew would not be possible without Chinese government subsidies. All Bassett had to do in return, He YunFeng said, was close his own factories.

Close his factories? John Bassett pictured the whole lot of his hard-charging forebears turning en masse in their graves. He thought of his 1,730 workers—plainspoken mountain types, many of whom had fol-lowed their parents and grandparents into the factories—standing in unemployment lines instead of assembly lines. He thought of the smokestacks that for a century had borne his family's name and of the legacy he wanted to leave his kids.

Back at home, he felt alone in the industry, with only his two sons and his scrappy little factories. He was the last American furniture maker willing to raise hell about what was happening. If he could prove the Chinese were selling the product below the cost of the materials, if he could prove their factories were buoyed by Communist government subsidies in an illegal price dump designed to drive American compa-nies out of business, then his company just might survive. If he could convince a majority of his industry to join him in persuading the U.S. Department of Commerce and the U.S. International Trade Commis-sion of the truth, maybe the entire industry could be saved.

But those were big ifs, with potentially huge pitfalls. Surely he would be scorned by both his longtime customers and his competitors.

He'd be ridiculed by the handful of families that had ruled the fifty-billion-dollar industry, as well as some members of his own family, who were too busy closing down factories—and cashing their checks—to protect their furniture-making legacy.

He'd be ostracized for trying to stop the flood of furniture jobs from America, for striking back against the one-percenters who were about to move damn near all their plants to Asia and tear the heart out of the Blue Ridge region he loved.

From the taverns of Virginia to the halls of power in Washington, DC; from the factory floor to the back roads of Liaoning, China, where he would uncover a great lie at the heart of globalization, John Bassett was going to war.

PART I

1

The Tipoff

What were all them little people doing at work today?

—Bassett Furniture line worker on the presence
of Taiwanese factory managers

O nce in a reporter's career, if one is very lucky, a person like John D. Bassett III comes along. JBIII is inspirational. He's brash. He's a sawdust-covered good old boy from rural Virginia, a larger-than-life rule breaker who for more than a decade has stood almost single-handedly against the outflow of furniture jobs from America.

"He's an asshole!" more than one of his competitors barked when they heard I was writing a book about globalization with JBIII as a main character. Over the course of researching this book, over the course of hearing his many lectures and listening to him evade my questions by telling me the same stories over and over, there were times that I agreed.

I first heard about him in Rocky Mount, Virginia, about half an hour from my home in Roanoke, while eating breakfast with my neighbor and good friend Joel Shepherd. Joel owns Virginia Furniture Market, a Rocky Mount retail establishment that began thriving at the same time the import boom hit. Right now as I type, I'm sitting in a paisley recliner that my husband and I still fight over because it's the

comfiest seat in our 1926 American foursquare. I remember Joel showing it to me in his store, rocking it back and forth. Despite what I might
have heard about made-in-China furniture, he told me, a swarm of
high-school wrestlers could pin one another on this chair and it would
not fall apart. With the friendly-neighbor discount, I bought it for a
hundred and sixty bucks.

I had invited Joel to breakfast to pick his brain. I was working on a
Roanoke Times series on the impact of globalization on southwest Virginia's company towns, articles inspired by the work of freelance photographer Jared Soares, who'd been making the hourlong trek from
Roanoke to Martinsville three times a week for more than a year. His
photos were gritty and moving: church services and tattoo artists; a
textile-plant conveyor belt converted for use in a food bank; a disabled
minister named Leonard whiling away the time in his kitchen in the
middle of the afternoon. The people of Martinsville and Henry County,
Virginia, were refreshingly open about what had happened to them,
Jared told me, and he'd long wondered why our newspaper didn't do
more to document the effects of globalization in our mountainous corner of the world.

Not that many other media outlets had done any better. According
to a 2009 Pew Research Center survey, the gravest economic crisis since
the Great Depression was largely being covered from the top down, primarily from the perspective of big business and the Obama administration. The percentage of economy stories that featured ordinary people
and displaced workers? Just 2 percent. If the people of Henry County
wanted their stories to be heard, Jared and I were going to have to help.

It would be up to writers and photographers like us to paint the long-
view picture of what had happened when, one after another, the textile
and then the furniture factories closed and set up shop instead in Mexico, China, and Vietnam, where workers were paid a fraction of what
the American laborers were earning. In the Henry County region
alone, some twenty thousand people had lost their jobs.

In the early 1960s, Martinsville was Virginia's manufacturing powerhouse, known for being home to more millionaires per capita than
anywhere else in the country. But by 2009, one-fifth of the town's labor
force was unemployed, and many of the millionaires had fled for cheer-
ier landscapes. Henry County was now the capital of long-term unemployment, with Virginia's highest rate for nine of the past eleven years.

A week before my breakfast with Joel, an empty Bassett Furniture
plant had burned to the ground. Police arrested Silas Crane, a thirty-
four-year-old Henry County man who'd been trying to salvage the
factory's copper electrical casings to sell on the black market but
instead had sparked an electrical fire. His burns were visible in his
police mug shot. I'd heard many similar stories, as some of the desperate moved from the unemployment rolls to the crime rosters. A stranger
approached one woman I know outside a CVS pharmacy and offered
her a hundred dollars if she'd sign for the purchase of the cold medicine pseudoephedrine—the main ingredient used to make metham-
phetamine.

Most people, though, were scraping by in legal ways—babysitting,
growing their own food, working part-time at Walmart. The director
of an area food pantry told me that he could divine what people used to
do for work by their disfigurements: The women who'd been bent over
sewing machines all day making sweatshirts had humps on their backs.
The men who culled lumber were missing fingers. "We're the last, last,
last resort, to come stand in line and get a box of old food," he said.

But, Joel explained, there was this feisty old man in Galax, a small
town about seventy miles away from Rocky Mount, who'd managed to
buck the trend. He was from the family that had once run the largest
furniture-making operation in the world, Bassett Furniture Industries.
His name was John D. Bassett III, and, yes, he was from *that* Bassett
family—the name inscribed on the back of so many American headboards and dressers; the name often stamped on the bedroom suite
behind door number three on *Let's Make a Deal*. The story of how he
fought against the tides of globalization was full of legal cunning,

political intrigue, and, judging from what Joel told me about Bassett's Asian competitors, some serious cowboy grit.

As Joel explained over a plate of sausage biscuits and gravy that morning, imitating the patriarch's booming voice and cringe-inducing chutzpah: "The 'fucking Chi-Comms' were not going to tell *him* how to make furniture!"

But there was another, even juicier element to the story. John Bassett was no longer living in the eponymous company town of Bassett, Virginia. He'd been booted out of his family's business by a domineering relative. Three decades later, the family squabble turned corporate coup still had local tongues wagging with talk of a living-room fight scene (some say it was the front porch), a rescue-squad call, and, my favorite detail: John Bassett tipping the ambulance driver a hundred bucks not to tell anybody that he'd had his battered brother-in-law hauled away, like something out of *Dynasty.*

But was any of it true? And what did the family infighting have to do with John Bassett giving the middle finger to the lure of easy money overseas?

Plenty, it would turn out. But peeling that onion would take me more than a year. It would have me burning up U.S. Route 58, the curvy mountain road that meanders through the former company towns just north of the Virginia–North Carolina line, where it hits you why the people of Henry County have come to call what happened "the 58 virus."

It would send me across the Blue Ridge to John Bassett's billowing smokestacks in Galax; to the International Home Furnishings Market in High Point, North Carolina, to meet a crop of young MBAs and marketing execs in their skinny suits and aggressive glasses; and, on the advice of laid-off Stanley Furniture worker Wanda Perdue, to Surabaya, Indonesia, where much of the world's wooden bedroom furniture is now made.

I first met Wanda in early 2012 outside a community college computer lab, where she came for regular tutoring in math. She was fifty-eight years old, cobbling together a living by working part-time at Walmart and hoping to land a full-time position as soon as she got her associate's degree in office administration. Her one splurge was buying Luck's pinto beans, the only non-store-brand food she allowed herself.

The farthest she'd been from home was a trip to Myrtle Beach she'd taken three years before. It was her first time seeing the ocean — at the age of fifty-five.

"I want you to see what they do in Indonesia and explain to me why we can't do that here no more," she said.

Fair enough, I thought.

Joel and I were sitting in a landscape of rusted silos and vacant factories. Weeds sprouted through cracks in empty parking lots. Across the street from us was the shell of Lane Furniture, another defunct furniture maker that, like Stanley, had family connections to Bassett. In the 1920s, Edward Lane pushed the notion that every teenage girl in America needed to store her trousseau in a hope chest made of protective cedarwood, a safe place to keep her hopes and household accessories until she landed the man of her dreams. By the time soldiers returned from World War II, the cedar chest was ubiquitous, a must-have in the starter kit for a suburban home. *"It's the Real Love-Gift," Say America's Most Romantic Sweethearts,* proclaimed a 1948 ad featuring Audie Murphy, the decorated combat soldier and movie star.

Joel pointed to the silk mills where his aunts had once worked, now closed, every one of them: the victims of what economists call "creative destruction." The lost jobs and vanishing industries that resulted from the ratification of the North American Free Trade Agreement in 1994 and China's joining the World Trade Organization in 2001 were necessary outcomes, the theory goes. Over time, society becomes richer and more productive, and citizens across the globe benefit from higher living standards.

Thomas L. Friedman devotes nearly all 639 pages of *The World Is Flat* to the benefits of globalization, noting that it saved American consumers roughly $600 billion, extended more capital to businesses to invest in new innovations, and helped the Federal Reserve hold interest rates down, which in turn gave Americans a chance to buy or refinance homes.

Or as Joel put it, reminding me of my hundred-and-sixty-dollar recliner: "We've all enjoyed the benefits of falling prices. A person can get far more value for [her] furniture dollar now than she could thirty years ago." Not to mention that globalization has improved the standard of living among factory workers in China, Vietnam, and Indonesia, people who used to toil in rice paddies and farm fields.

The car put the carriage makers out of work, just like the Internet hurt mail carriers and many of my own newspaper colleagues—one of the reasons my newspaper shrank its core coverage area and no longer has a Henry County beat.

But as the daughter of a displaced factory worker, I wondered about the dinghies being sunk by globalization's rising tide. I questioned why the unemployment stories rarely quoted the displaced workers or mentioned the fact that many folks in the corporate offices had simply switched jobs from factory bosses to global-sourcing managers. They were *still there, still fabulously employed,* some hauling in seven-figure salaries. When the big guys weren't off traveling the globe, their cars were among the few left in the company parking lots.

In small towns across America, the front-page stories about escalating drug crime and lower test scores seemed somehow linked to the page 3 briefs on deaths in faraway garment factories. But that connection was hard to define—and even harder to report on—given the complex Spirograph of interlooping supply chains, impotent regulators, and press-avoiding CEOs.

No one, it seemed, was minding the back room of this new global store.

My first memory: Riding with an older sister to pick up my mom from work at Grimes, the aircraft-lighting factory in Urbana, Ohio. Mom worked the graveyard shift when the economy was good. When it wasn't, she waitressed — badly, she said — and watched other people's kids. At Grimes, she sat with other women at long tables in a cavernous, dimly lit room, tucked into a row of Quonset huts. They soldered strobe lights for airplanes. When she got home, she used to pay me a quarter to rub her throbbing neck.

I remember pointing to airplanes passing by overhead and saying to my friends, "See that light? My mom *made* that." So what if the lights Mom soldered were fixed to military transport planes, not those passenger jets I pointed out. My mom's handiwork was stellar. You could see it up there, right near the stars.

The Vietnam War ended, and it would be a long economic slog in Urbana before the aircraft lighting workers benefited from a thirteen-million-dollar contract to make searchlights for Black Hawk helicopters, in 2012, some fifteen years after the heirs of inventor Warren "Old Man" Grimes cashed out. Honeywell International now runs Urbana's aerospace lighting operations in modern facilities staffed by about half the number of assembly workers it once employed. The company that used to be the town's sugar daddy now employs about 650, down from 1,300 at its peak, with much of the production accomplished via circuit cards and high-tech machinery rather then hand labor. One of my high-school buddies helps manage the outsourced engineers—via video teleconferencing—in Bangalore, India, where they're paid one quarter of what their American counterparts earn.

Throughout my childhood, my dad nursed his psychological wounds from World War II in VFW and American Legion halls. He was a housepainter by trade, but in my shame, I saw him as the serially unemployed town drunk. He didn't attend my band concerts or my softball games or even my high-school graduation—lapses that seem almost criminal to me now that I have kids. But that's the way it was, and since I didn't know any different, it didn't keep me awake at night. The best thing he provided was access to a doting grandmother: his mom, who lived next door, taught me to read when I was four, and kept a roof over our heads (she owned our house).

* * *

We weren't victims of globalization. But, like the blue-collar folks I interviewed in Bassett and Galax who followed their parents and grandparents to the assembly lines, we didn't have a lot of options beyond high school. I managed to get to college thanks to the nudging of wonderful teachers and friends (and friends' parents), federally funded Pell Grants, work-study jobs, and scholarships. My older brother edged his way into the middle class through grit and brains. A high-school dropout with moderate epilepsy, he progressed through a series of car-safety jobs until he landed at a major automotive research-and-development center in Raymond, Ohio, where he designs crash-test fixtures. By the time I graduated from college and got my first newspaper job, he was making more than twice my salary.

A few years back, a group of researchers at the University of Virginia invited him to share the details of his work. My brother, with his GED and a few community college courses under his belt, was summoned to Mr. Jefferson's University to tell those PhDs what he'd put together by way of experience and elbow grease. Not long ago his company gave him a bonus for inventing a new process that saved it thousands of dollars. He's been lucky to get to use his innate intelligence despite his lack of a formal degree. "It's no big deal," he tells me when I brag about his ability to make or fix not just cars but *anything*. "Mostly it's just common sense."

The moment I heard there was a company owner who had actually taken on big business *and* the People's Republic of China, I knew I had to find out who John Bassett was. He had not only kept his small factory going but somehow managed to turn it into the largest wooden-bedroom-furniture factory in America.

I got on the highway to Galax to meet the Southern patriarch, then seventy-four, at his Vaughan-Bassett Furniture Company. I'd already mapped out his insanely twisted family tree at the Virginia Room of the Roanoke City Library, already called around to get the real scoop about his long-simmering family feud. I'd already interviewed several

Henry County textile and furniture workers who were laid off not long after Taiwanese managers showed up to take pictures of the Virginia assembly lines so they could copy them back home.

One woman described her mom hobbling home from work, her knees shot from decades of standing on concrete floors, and wondering aloud, "What were all them little people doing at work today?"

I already knew that JBIII (as I began to refer to him) was grooming his middle-aged sons, Wyatt and Doug, to take over. Both had returned home after business school to help save the family company. I'd heard, too, that he'd cut their salaries when the recession hit rather than lay off more line workers, and he personally stopped pulling a paycheck during the leanest years.

One rainy afternoon, a furniture-store owner in nearby Collinsville described for me how globalization had taken a 70 percent bite out of his business, a store that used to be frequented by people who worked in the Henry County textile and furniture plants. Delano Thomasson's father had worked down the road from Bassett at Stanley Furniture, in Stanley-town, and his mother down another road at Fieldcrest, a sprawling textile plant started by Chicago-based Marshall Field's—and now the site of a weekly community food bank. (In the ladies' room of the Fieldale Café, a meat-and-three diner frequented by retirees, a framed photograph proudly displays what put this town on the map: a stack of Fieldcrest towels.)

Bassett Furniture was no longer made in Bassett, Delano explained in his Southern drawl as rain plinked into metal buckets set down to protect the sofas and bedroom suites (pronounced "suits" in Southern furniture lingo). "With his determination, John Bassett probably would have kept some of Bassett Furniture factories going if he could've kept the company."

I should have made up a shorthand for that statement the first time I heard it. I've interviewed scores of people since then who've said essentially the same thing.

Delano knew all about JBIII's covert mission to Dalian, China, and he had his own version of the evil-brother-in-law yarn—the story of the man who'd elbowed JBIII out of the CEO job at Bassett Furniture, the company John Bassett III had been reared to run. But would any of the Bassetts open up to me about those things? Would JBIII reveal what it felt like to be the family black sheep with a dresser-size chip on his shoulder? Would he tell me the real story of how he'd fought the Chinese? If he wouldn't, would the people who grew up under the thumb of the family that ran the company town be bold enough to spill the beans?

"You don't even realize what kind of spiderweb you've got going," said Bassett Furniture's longtime corporate pilot, a man who worked for years under John Bassett's brother-in-law and nemesis, Bob Spilman. "*War and Peace* will seem like a ten-cent novel compared to your spiderweb. But lucky for you, the scorpion is already dead," he added, referring to Spilman, the Bassett CEO who could be equally brilliant and biting.

JBIII comes from an imposing family of multimillionaires whose ancestors signed the Magna Carta and who maintain a persistent but unspoken code that, no matter what, one should always keep the family secrets where they belong: in the family closet. What secrets would he tell me, the daughter of a former factory worker?

I relate better to people like Octavia Witcher, a fifty-five-year-old displaced Stanley Furniture worker who gave me her elderly mother's phone number as a contact, because her own phone was about to be turned off. And to people like divorced former Tultex worker Mary Redd, who described trying to raise her fourteen-year-old daughter alone, working the only job she could find — as a thirty-hour-a-week receptionist, with no benefits. When she told me that, I recalled receiving full financial aid for college because my mom, widowed by that time, made just eight thousand dollars a year test-driving cars for a Honda subcontractor.

When Mary recounted running into the former Tultex CEO at a party she was helping cater for Martinsville's elite, what she said to him literally made me gasp: "If Tultex were to open back up today and the only way I could get there would be to crawl on my belly like a snake, I would do it."

* * *

John Bassett grew up with chauffeurs, vacation homes, and prep schools. I was the longshot and the underdog, but fortunately for me, John Bassett was too, whether he was ready to admit it to a reporter or not.

With any luck at all, he would help me explain this circuitous piece of American history, from its hardwood forests to its executive boardrooms; from handsaws and planing tools to smartphones and Skype; from the oak logs that sailed from the port of Norfolk, Virginia, to Asia and then returned, months later, in the form of dressers and beds.

2

The Original Outsourcer

Someday I'll buy and sell you.

—J.D. Bassett Sr. to his father,
John Henry Bassett

To understand JBIII, you have to understand where he comes from, a place where everywhere he looked, he saw his name: on the WELCOME TO BASSETT sign, the bank, the library, the school, and the myriad company smokestacks that rose high above the town. Born into a family of brash, industrious people who weren't afraid of hard work—as long as their pockets were getting lined—he was named for his grandfather John David Bassett Sr., or J.D., as the town's founder and patriarch was known. If you worked for him, and most people did, you called him "Mr. J.D."

But before there was a company called Bassett, there was a place called Bassett, and before it was called that, it was just red clay and foothills, a nowhere spot from a time when people named things for exactly what they were.

Horsepasture is where this story begins.

To the families who lived in Horsepasture, the Smith River dominated everything. It floated tobacco to market on bateaux. Its floods made soil-enriching silt, grist for fertile bottomland, and bumper crops of corn and tobacco. With its flat, low, and deceptively slow current, it would become one of Virginia's best trout-fishing streams. It froze in winter, gave cooling relief in summer, and by and by, it unleashed its might.

And on the day of JBIII's birth, the Smith River nearly ruined everything.

John Bassett III was born during the epic flood of 1937. Town Creek, from the county to the north, had spilled over its banks, and the Smith soon followed suit. It had been a good summer. The future Yankees' star Phil Rizzuto had just pounded out eighty-eight hits and turned nearly as many double plays, leading his minor-league team, the Bassett Furnituremakers, to the Bi-State League title. People were feeling good about the bustling little company town, and JBIII's grandfather Mr. J.D. felt especially good. He liked to buy ice cream and peanuts for kids at baseball games, and he could afford to, with six humming factories that sent freight cars laden with Bassett furniture all over the country.

Then, overnight, everything changed. After several hours of rain, Mr. J.D. saw the river rushing. His chauffeur ran him from one end of town to the other while he barked orders and warned people to seek higher ground. In the worst flood to hit in a century, the Smith steeped the railroad tracks and made kindling out of the town's swinging suspension bridges, which were owned by Bassett Furniture, like most everything else.

Water flowed through the first-floor windows of the town's Riverside Hotel. Drenched phone lines and highways were rendered useless. The people who worked in the Bassett Furniture plants climbed the hills and watched everything that wasn't fastened down float away, even the cows.

It was a dramatic backdrop for the entrance of the third John Bassett, a flood of near biblical proportions that had people wondering, decades later, if it prophesied his exit from the town. His parents already had three girls, and the entire family had been praying for a boy. An heir. Someone who would one day run the growing furniture dynasty.

Days before John Bassett III was due to enter the world, a different chauffeur had driven his mother sixty miles south to a hospital in Winston-Salem, North Carolina. Labor had come so swiftly with her last baby that the girl had been born at home. With this birth, the parents wanted to be cautious, especially with the river rising.

The flood was so bad that the Red Cross pitched tents on the hills. People sat atop railroad cars to inspect the rising waters as silt poured into their company-owned homes. Yet another Bassett family chauffeur was dispatched to pick up Mr. J.D.'s son, John D. Bassett Jr. — or Mr. Doug, as he was known — so he could check on the drenched factories while his wife was away giving birth. Despite the devastation — it took the factory equipment days to dry out — Mr. J.D. could at least take some comfort in the arrival of a third-generation heir.

Along with Mr. J.D., the Smith River ruled Bassett, Virginia, or at least the ten-mile stretch of it that bisected the smoky little unincorporated town. In a grainy photograph of the flood, four young men standing in knee-deep water pose for the camera, two of them clad in bib overalls, the typical factory worker's uniform. The three white men in the picture are playful, clearly enjoying the rare day off. The lone black man is standing slightly apart, straight as a pine, his arms folded and one hand clutching a hat. Very likely he was descended from Henry County slaves. Most black people there were.

"Race is entwined with everything down there," a Roanoke historian and race scholar warned me repeatedly as I set out to understand the Henry County of JBIII's youth.

"You'll run up against some raw truths," said the Virginia folklorist Joe Wilson, named a Living Legend by the Library of Congress for his study of Appalachian history and culture. Wilson reminded me that relationships between the races, and the complexities of one dominating the other, have been an evolving part of American history for four centuries and counting.

In a county known for a tobacco industry propped up by nearly five thousand slaves—it was said you could walk the thirty miles from Danville to Martinsville and never leave plantation land owned by the Samuel Hairston family—there are 486 Hairston descendants currently listed in the Martinsville–Henry County phone book, and nearly all are black. (The white Hairstons pronounce the name *"Haawr*-ston," Gladys Hairston, a young African American, told me, chuckling.)

Slavery may have been long past by the time the furniture makers hit the scene, but its Jim Crow legacy was very much intact. The plantation mind-set was palpable in the factories and in the homes of the well-to-do, and it was key in the development of Bassett Furniture.

My friend Joel, the furniture retailer, has a copy of his family's land grant framed on the wall of his country home in Rocky Mount; next to it is the last will and testament of the home's original owner designating which family member would inherit which slaves. In Joel's backyard, there's a family cemetery with granite headstones. At the edge of the property sits a cemetery for the family's slaves, marked by periwinkle and fieldstones.

Henry County lies just over the next ridge. It's named for the Revolutionary War orator Patrick Henry, Virginia's first governor after the country won its independence and the owner of Henry County's Leatherwood, a ten-thousand-acre tobacco plantation flanked by the Blue Ridge Mountains to the west and the North Carolina foothills to the south. The region was settled by frontier folk and wealthy planters who were sent west to nab land, much of it courtesy of grants from King George III. The red-clay soil was perfect for tobacco growing, especially if one owned slaves to work the labor-intensive crop.

Topography drove demographics; tobacco stopped at the foot of the mountains, so that's largely where black migration stopped, too. An hour away, in mountainous Roanoke, the much younger city where I live, today's black population is 28 percent. But in the Henry County seat of Martinsville, African Americans make up nearly half the population.

When the great migration drove six million Southern blacks to work in cities in the Northeast, Midwest, and West, many in Virginia's Piedmont chose not to leave home. Thanks to people like the Bassetts, there was plenty of work to be had in mill towns across the South. Tobacco, textile, and furniture plants in the Virginia and North Carolina Piedmont helped the descendants of slaves avoid the hopelessness of the sharecropping system embedded farther South. Then, as now, there were few unions to protect them in these Southern right-to-work states, but at least they finally had paying jobs.

Long before he built his empire, J.D. Bassett knew his fortunes rested outside the family farm, which had to be cultivated by hired help or by the owners' hands. He was born in 1866, the year after the Civil War ended, descended from a long line of prominent Bassetts. William Bassett sailed from the Isle of Wight aboard the *Fortune* in 1621, built one of the original forts at Jamestown, and filled it with books he'd carted from his English home. His descendants included Revolutionary War captains and westward pioneers.

The first Bassett to stake a claim in Henry County was Nathaniel Bassett, a Revolutionary War captain who'd had the good luck to be deeded a 791-acre land grant from King George III in 1773. That property begat more wealth and property, and his son, Burwell, bought land from war hero Colonel George Hairston, Burwell's wife's uncle, a member of the county's most prominent family, and the largest slaveholder in Virginia, which was the largest slaveholding state in the Union.

In the official family narrative, the furniture founder claimed his father, John Henry Bassett, owned eighty-eight slaves before the war. He "had lived the life of Reilly just like the other young gentlemen of his time, visiting around among the neighbors," J.D. told an interviewer in 1939. But 1860 census records show that was not the case; Alexander Bassett, Nathaniel's grandson and John Henry's father, was a tobacco farmer with real estate and personal property valued at $14,300, but he had only twenty slaves, ages six months to thirty-nine years.

"Even the myth of how many slaves they had wasn't right!" the historian John Kern ranted, warning me to check and double-check everything I got from the family and corporate archives.

While Alexander's oldest son, Woodson, owned nine slaves, J.D.'s father, John Henry, owned just two boys, ages fourteen and eight. He relied mainly on family hands, claiming ownership of two horses, five milk cows, three sheep, seven swine, and considerable stores of wheat, rye, oats, corn, and tobacco.

J.D.'s mother, Nancy Spencer Bassett, was thought to be the brainy and driven one; John Henry, a Civil War veteran turned gentleman farmer, "sat around and grinned a lot," said Spencer Morten, who married into the family in 1949 and became a company executive. A former journalist, Morten was eighty-nine when we first met, but his memory was razor sharp. And after sitting on the family's periphery for so many decades, he was ready to describe all the dramas he'd witnessed in the boardrooms, in the factories—and behind the scenes at family dinners.

John Henry was ill prepared for Reconstruction. He had general knowledge of farming and had ridden horses across his estate, but the social whirl of antebellum life had taken precedence over learning to reap profits from his land. Now, he mostly walked, routinely visiting his brother, who lived eight miles away. After his wife died, John Henry walked to court a woman who lived two miles down the road. He was eighty-five at the time, and his daughters weren't pleased at all, often sending a relative or friend to fetch him home.

That's a story you'll find more than once in this family saga, with one generation after another running a critical eye over potential spouses—the aristocracy's number one tool for protecting the family fortune. The women may not have held titles to the businesses or the land, but they had subtle ways of exerting power.

After the war, much of the South was in chaos, and those who had been prosperous before it were now land-rich and cash-poor. John Henry's sons had little choice but to work. They took care of horses and cattle, cut wood, and harvested crops, which they sent to market with the help of former slaves turned farmhands. J.D., the oldest, quickly emerged as their leader.

As a granddaughter would gush much later: "Could these adversities have planted the seed of ambition to succeed and make something of his life?"

J.D.'s first job off the farm was pinhooking, or speculating, on tobacco. He bought the crop directly from the farmers, then sold it at auction in Martinsville, which was fast becoming the plug-tobacco capital of the world. Tobacco was second only to moonshining, the county's other big cash-making enterprise.

He worked twelve-hour days, and he was good with people. When it came time to marry, he didn't chase the daughter of a wealthy landowner. He went after his former teacher, who was just three years his senior and every bit as hardworking. With his wife, Pocahontas, he started a small grocery on the family farm along the Smith River.

Chickens sold for eight cents apiece, a pair of shoes for fifty cents. Miss Pokey, as she was called, minded the store while J.D. hopped onto a mule-driven carriage and sold their goods on the road. Other than the family home place, the store was the first building erected in the area, and before long it housed the first post office. In need of a postmark, "the government agent asked what we would name the post office," J.D. recalled. Not so modestly, he told the agent, "My name is Bassett, so why not call it Bassett?"

The location was ripe for expansion, with the rushing Smith River right there to generate power, not to mention all of J.D.'s inherited land along the Blue Ridge foothills. After the war, the extended Bassett clan owned 21,197 acres in Henry County, most of it thickly forested with walnut, oak, maple, hickory, and other valuable trees.

The fledgling Norfolk and Western Railway was building a new line, called the Punkin Vine, from Winston-Salem, North Carolina, to Roanoke, Virginia. And J.D., itching to help restore his family's fortune, dreamed of getting a sawmill up and running before the new tracks being laid reached Henry County, the halfway point between the two stations. The wheeling and dealing commenced: to persuade the railroaders to run their tracks through Bassett instead of Ferrum Summit, just north of his family's farm, as was originally planned, J.D. offered them free right-of-way through his property. One account has him secretly traveling on horseback to meet with the railway president to convince him to change the route. In another version, memorialized in a romanticized woodcut print that was part of the company's thirtieth-anniversary promotion, a twenty-one-year-old J.D. wearing a dapper three-piece suit called on the railway president in his office.

We do know he promised that railroad construction workers could rent rooms in the back of his store at a low rate, a business model that would become part of his family's philosophy: offering incentives to the other guy is a good idea, as long as you end up getting more from him in return.

Already a commanding presence at six two and two hundred pounds, young J.D. kept a cigar in his hand or in his suit jacket pocket, hoping it would make him seem older than his years. When he wasn't working, he was thinking constantly about ways to reap benefits from the new transportation boom. He rearranged the store as a gathering place, stocking it with goods for not only the usual farmers and townsfolk but also the railroad men, engineers, and workers who would do most of their trading at the store. He would make it their store—and make their money his, even during the panic of 1893. Customers came in as late as midnight, and J.D. was usually the last in town to go to bed.

J.D. had more cash on hand than most people in Horsepasture, and, as storekeeper, he was privy to the financial affairs of his neighbors; if he paid attention, he was privy to their private affairs too. So the young J.D. Bassett became friend, adviser, creditor, and commissary general of some one hundred folks, including the railroaders.

But he wanted to be more than an innkeeper and merchandiser. He wanted to sell the N&W wood for its bridge timbers and railroad ties. To pull off the sawmilling that would require, he needed more than moxie. Before he could become *Mr.* J.D., what he needed most was cash.

The first time I met Spencer Morten, at the Bassett Historical Center, he brought along a yellowed newspaper clipping that explained the genesis of that critical cash infusion. It described how "Uncle Billy" Law had saved J.D.'s hide after J.D.'s own father turned him down for a business loan. A few years earlier, J.D.'s pinhooking partner in Martinsville had swindled him. Together they'd earned what was considered a bundle at the time — $450 — but when J.D. went to the bank to withdraw his share, he found that his partner had absconded with the haul. He owed his innkeepers six dollars for room and board, and, tail between his legs, he'd gone to his father and asked him to loan him the money.

John Henry refused to give him a loan and instead made his son dig out the season's potato crop and sell that to pay off his debt.

When his father refused him a loan again, this time for the sawmill, family tensions flared.

"Someday I'll buy and sell you," J.D. snapped.

Bassett blood may have been thicker than Smith River water, but not by much. J.D. traveled to neighboring Patrick County and borrowed the money from his wealthy uncle William J. Law instead.

Not long ago, at a cousins' gathering of third-generation multimillionaires in Hobe Sound on Florida's Jupiter Island, where several Bassett relatives, including John Bassett III, winter in neighboring homes, Spencer Morten offered a toast to Billy Law. Few had even heard of Uncle Billy, and none of them seemed to care about his role in the family fortune.

"Spoiled brats," Spencer fumed, later, to his wife.

By the time the iron horse of the Punkin Vine first rattled the floors of Bassett Mercantile, in 1892, J.D. had paid his uncle back, with interest, from his sawmill proceeds. The train rolled past the fledgling town of Bassett atop oak ties made in the Bassett sawmill. J.D. then set about wheedling the railroad into building a depot across the tracks from his store.

Several people in town told me in hushed tones — as if protecting a century-old secret — that J.D. sold the railroad buyer lumber and then, the next day, sold him some of the same pieces *again*. Purchased lumber was marked with whitewash at the ends of the logs, but J.D. simply sawed off the painted part and then, the next day, trotted out the same pieces of wood. If the buyer had actually gotten out of his carriage to look at the wood himself, he might have noticed the scam. A century later, JBIII still abides by that old Bassett Furniture principle, insisting that every piece of lumber delivered to his factory be counted by a lumberyard employee.

J.D. may have been a country boy educated in a one-room school, but he had the sense to marry a brainy woman. When J.D.'s first sawmill partner disappeared from town with a chunk of the profits, just as the pinhooker had done, J.D. tasked Miss Pokey with handling the books. He also made a vow that would both enrich and complicate things for his extended clan: the Bassett company would henceforth be a purely *family* affair.

While photographs show a formal Mr. J.D. sporting a mustache, bow tie, and derby hat, Miss Pokey was rarely seen without an apron. With hammer and nails stuffed in her apron pocket, she didn't mind measuring lumber or tacking down a loose floorboard. The town of Bassett was little more than a building, a river, and a set of train tracks flanked by dirt roads. People traveled mainly by wagon, and when the rains pushed the Smith out of its banks, the carriages were often bogged down in mud and dependent on mules to pull them out.

Once the rail line was built, J.D. took his horse and carriage on the road to rustle up new customers, selling his timber to casket companies and small furniture factories from High Point, North Carolina, to Lynchburg, Virginia. For a time he and his brother C.C. built and sold caskets themselves. He told an interviewer in 1958 that he had routinely split four hundred rails a day and was not above polishing shoes or making communion wine for churches when business was slow.

The big daddies of furniture-making were still in places with large immigrant populations, such as Grand Rapids, Michigan, and Jamestown, New York; the recently arrived craftsmen turned out high-quality designs in the traditions of Sheraton and Duncan Phyfe. J.D. would take off for points north and be gone for weeks, selling the furniture manufacturers on the value of Henry County hardwood—and poking around their factories.

The official version of what happened next, printed in the Bassett Furniture corporate history, has Mr. J.D. outplaying the factory owners in Grand Rapids in 1902 to bring the heart of American furniture-making to the South. Most people say the scheme was actually hatched by his wife. "Miss Pokey had a good business mind, and she'd tell him what to buy and what not to buy," said Bassett librarian Pat Ross, whose grandmother knew the woman well.

The story goes that the couple had ridden the train to a factory in Michigan. While her husband was making his lumber pitch, Miss Pokey coyly asked a secretary for a tour of the plant, during which she took copious mental notes. "I think we can do this ourselves," she said to her husband on their way out of town.

At the time, the Southern economy was still recovering from the Civil War, and the Bassetts knew little about making furniture—or "fu-ni-cha," as they pronounced it then and still do now. But the savings in freight alone would give them an edge over the Northern manufacturers. They had plentiful Henry County woods on Bassett-owned lands — and lots of small-time farmers, sharecroppers, and moonshiners eager to come out of the hills and escape pauperism. Why not make the furniture in the same place they milled the lumber?

The industry had already shifted from New England to Michigan, and now it was coming to the South, predominantly to small towns in Virginia, North Carolina, and Tennessee. Nearly a century before the first container of furniture was shipped from China to the United States, J.D. Bassett joined the flow of entrepreneurs hoping to capitalize on cheap, hungry labor and all those tree-stocked hills.

A handful of North Carolina sawmillers in Lenoir and High Point had already proved it could be done. "There was a lot of fine timber in those days," J.D. recalled, but no real roads yet for moving it out. "We had to go by horseback any distance at all."

In one photograph, J.D. sits astride his horse in front of the old family home place, a surprisingly ramshackle affair. The house was clapboard with crooked posts supporting the front porch, which held a lone, wobbly-looking chair. Wearing a rumpled suit and tie, he poses with his teenage daughter, Anne, on the horse next to him.

Hardwoods dot the foothills in this sepia-toned scenic backdrop — though some are chopped and lie scattered on the ground.

Down the hill, out of the camera's view, sat the seeds of the family's growing fortune.

J.D. had built a factory in his front yard.

He'd mapped it out first in a drawing, based on the Northern factories he'd been selling to, showing everything from the rough end, where the lumber was measured and cut, to the finishing room. Then he called a meeting of his sawmill partners — his brothers, C.C. and Sam, and his brother-in-law Reed Stone. Smoke would coil from boiler chimneys and steam would hiss from vents, he told them. Imagine the quiet wilderness filled with the slapping of leather belts on flywheels and the screeching of saws.

Careful management would be vital, and salesmanship was so important that he would personally see to that himself. He asked his brothers to "abandon the foolishness of sawing all our good timber and shipping it north" and instead visualize trains loaded down with Bassett beds and Bassett dressers.

From day one, he was the self-appointed brains and boss of the operation. He once ordered his brother-in-law to "run down there" and fetch him some supplies.

"Aye, God, J.D., I'll walk but I'll not run," Reed Stone replied, in what became a long-standing family retort.

The year was 1902. Cuba had just broken from Spain, Teddy Roosevelt became the first president to ride in a motorcar, and J.D. Bassett was about to build himself a company—as well as a proper town.

Together, the four men begged, borrowed, and scraped up $27,500. The first Bassett factory began a stone's throw from the post office in a two-and-a-half-story wooden shed next to the river, a site the people of Bassett still refer to as Old Town. Horsepasture was now far out *thataway*—in the Henry County foothills—as the Industrial Revolution arrived and began shaping the narrow riverside town.

The men employed fifty workers at the start, Scots-Irish mountain men and black sharecroppers, rugged farmers and moonshiners, all of whom were happy to work for five cents an hour. Like most refugees, the first generation of Southern mill hands were known for their patience. Desperate to feed their families, they brought with them an individualism nurtured by solitary life on small farms—a trait that would make them putty in company owners' hands, especially when union organizers came to town. (They may not have loved their bosses, but they trusted them more than they trusted the outsiders.)

They had lived in coves, distant from the cash economy. Now they traveled to work on foot, carrying lanterns in the predawn, some from as far as eight miles away. For one hundred dollars, J.D. hired a traveling furniture designer he'd met in Grand Rapids to develop blueprints, beginning with bedroom furniture because that was simplest to make. Built of Henry County oak, the beds wholesaled for $1.50 and were Victorian in design. When the first piece of furniture came off the new Bassett Furniture Company line—a chest of drawers with a carved mirror held up by ornate curvy arms—it sold for $4.75.

Never one to hide his light under a bushel, J.D. began to imagine that one day he just might swipe Grand Rapids' "Furniture City" nickname. He talked it over constantly with his wife.

As people moved away from the extended-family farms and built homes in cities and towns, the demand for mass-produced furniture soared. By 1905, just three years after forming the company, Bassett Furniture was entirely debt-free, partly because J.D. was paying himself only seventy-five dollars a month. By 1907, the town was so full of new arrivals that he opened a bank.

By 1918, he was shipping furniture to every corner of the country as well as Canada. He owned a bank and held stock in several other furniture factories, from Galax, Virginia, to Lexington, North Carolina, all of which allowed him to set aside one million dollars for each of his children, according to Spencer Morten, the equivalent of fifteen million dollars today.

Virginia didn't have the immigrant craftsmen from Germany, Poland, and Lithuania that Grand Rapids claimed. But J.D.'s hardscrabble lot was willing to figure out how to make the basic forms with minimal carvings and overlays. When special knowledge was required, J.D. thought nothing of venturing to a competitor's factory and hiring its foremen away. He'd already swiped their ideas; he would steal their people too. By 1924, he had five hundred employees, many of them North Carolina natives.

His goal was nothing less than to establish the South as the dominant furniture-making region in the United States.

If everyone in the family could just get along, there was no telling how far the company would go.

By the time most people switched from driving horses to driving cars, Mr. J.D. had settled on being driven—in his Cadillac—by a chauffeur, first Pete Wade and later James Thompson. When his grown sons teased him in later years about never learning to drive, he shot back, "I pay Pete twenty-five cents an hour to drive me around, and I sit in the passenger seat thinking about how to make more money. If you boys want me to pay you twenty-five cents an hour to drive me around, that would be fine."

Decades later, John Bassett III would grow up thinking of his grandfather's methods as Bassett 101. Cash is power; avoid all but necessary debt. Buy the best machinery and run the hell out of it. Hire smart people who think like you (but not too much), reward the best ones, and work the hell out of them. And by all means, pay somebody else to do your e-mailing and iPad-ing if it frees you up to do the heavy lifting of moneymaking.

Above all, when you see a snake's head, hit it. He liked that problem-solving mantra so much that when someone made him a cross-stitch of it, he hung it on his office wall.

But those strategies were of little concern to the young furniture heir during his first days on the planet, which he spent in another state, far removed from the whining planers and hissing steam of the factory, everything now quieted by the flood. Soon enough, the Smith River would recede to its proper place. The chauffeur would deliver mother and son to their sprawling brick home, enveloped by oaks and perched high on a hill. He'd meet his daddy, his sisters, and the family's faithful servants, Willie and Augusta, who lived above the garage.

The sisters were loved and they knew it. But when Little John finally arrived, it was the happiest day of their father's life. The prince had arrived. Doug Bassett called Mr. J.D. and shouted into the phone, "Papa, I've got a son and he's a boy!" Mr. J.D. was so happy, he offered to pay the hospital bill on the spot. He sent a check for $1,000, along with this letter, written on Bassett Furniture Industries stationery:

My dear Boy:
Grandpop is writing you this letter so you will see it when you are a man. I will not be living when you are grown, but I want to say to you that I am hoping you will do big things, following the pace set by your grandpop and your dad. We are going to expect much bigger things of you than we are able to do, as you are living in a more progressive age....I want you to know that I love you and always will, and expect you to be a great man some day.

Yours,
Grand Daddy
J.D. Bassett

The letter was framed, along with the check, and when the dear boy grew up and entered the family business, he hung it front and center on his office wall.

3

The Town the Daddy Rabbits Built

I was born with a silver spoon in my mouth,
and I had no intention of taking it out.
—John Bassett III

JBIII's first memory: It was a Saturday morning in 1943, and his father, Doug, took him to several Bassett factories to check on operations. W.M. Bassett, the boy's uncle Bill, was now overseeing Bassett Furniture and, with Doug, had come up with the notion of contracting with the Yellow Cab and Coach Company to make wooden truck bodies that would carry weapons for the armed forces. The factories had limped through the Depression without laying anyone off, though salaries and hours were severely cut, and one year, the N&W train car brought employees Virginia hams instead of bonuses. Mr. J.D. had personally surveyed his employees, counting the number of dependents each man had, and he assigned shifts accordingly, making sure each man had enough work to support his family.

But now Bassett was back to running full blast. Six at the time of this visit, towheaded Little John (as the entire town called him) promptly got lost in the maze of whirring routers and band saws. The confident factory-man stride was still decades away, and scared of the noise and unable to find his dad, Little John burst into tears. He was so upset when he was found that a chauffeur was dispatched to drive him back to his family's house on the hill.

It may have taken him a few years to conquer his fear of loud machinery, but the silver spoon fit perfectly from the start. Richmond lawyer Tom Word recalled meeting JBIII at a Boy Scout Jamboree when they were both twelve. "He was the rich man's kid, the person everybody liked to talk about. And he was spoiled beyond belief," Word said. He had the kind of unwavering confidence you get when you live in a town named after and run by your family. And Little John had the same name as his grandpop, who controlled everything for miles around—the cops, the area politicians, the factory workers, the household help.

The Bassetts and the families who owned Martinsville's textile mills were known as the Families—the people who ran things, with tentacles stretching to the state capital, Richmond, and beyond. Since J.D. Bassett owned the land the community was built on, he chose not to incorporate the town of Bassett, preventing the formation of a town council.

Bassett Furniture Industries ran the town of Bassett. It was as simple—and as complicated—as that.

Mr. J.D. even owned a piece of Stanleytown. The unincorporated town just south of Bassett was home to Stanley Furniture, which was founded in 1924 with seed money from Mr. J.D. Here's how the family tree is intertwined with Southern furniture-making: Thomas Bahnson Stanley was an early Bassett Furniture manager who married J.D.'s daughter Anne Pocahontas Bassett. A former bank teller, Stanley had set his sights on marrying well, carving out a piece of the growing furniture pie, and ascending the political ranks, in that order. He'd tried to court C.C. Bassett's daughter Avis, and when that didn't work out, he took up with her cousin Anne.

Besides, it was Mr. J.D. who ruled the company, not his brother

C.C., who was more comfortable at home, in the store, and on the farm. Their roles were clearly delineated as far back as 1926. In a social-club charter I found at the Bassett Historical Center, C.C. listed his occupation as farmer, even though he was a co-owner of the furniture business, while Mr. J.D. asserted much broader authority, writing down *capitalist*.

"T. B. Stanley was the consummate politician," fellow in-law Spencer Morten recalled. In 1929, Stanley built a sprawling Tudor stone mansion on the hillside overlooking his furniture plant, and it was hands-down the grandest structure for miles. He called it Stoneleigh, to reflect the family's connection to British nobility and because it (sort of) echoed his surname. He'd wanted to name his town Stanley, but that name was already taken by another Virginia community. "He didn't like that they had to put *town* on the end of it when Bassett was just Bassett, not Bassett-town or Bassett-ville," said Ward Armstrong, a lawyer whose father ran a veneer-making subsidiary of Stanley.

Uncle Bonce, as the Bassett children called Thomas Stanley, was a U.S. congressman from 1947 to 1953 and the governor of Virginia for four years after that. When Queen Elizabeth II and Prince Philip visited Virginia in 1957 to commemorate the 350th anniversary of the founding of Jamestown, Governor Stanley—who had already sent the queen miniature sets of Stanley Furniture for her children—held a reception in her honor. It was a watershed moment for the former bank teller.

Bonce Stanley would be best remembered not for his royal connections but for his allegiance to U.S. senator Harry F. Byrd Sr., the powerful Democrat who controlled Virginia politics for the first half of the twentieth century. On Uncle Bonce's watch, Virginia closed many of its public schools rather than desegregating them as mandated by the Supreme Court, robbing the black children of Prince Edward County of five years of schooling. As Stanley put it during a 1956 press conference, "No public elementary or secondary schools, in which white and colored children are mixed and taught, shall be entitled to and receive any funds from the state treasure." The purpose of this, he insisted, was to protect "the health and welfare of the people."

Uncle Bonce is just one looping branch of the sprawling family/corporate tree. He lived a half mile down a winding road from Mr. J.D.'s oldest son, William McKinley Bassett (Mr. W.M., in company-town parlance), who ran Bassett Furniture after the old man stepped down. Mr. W.M.'s home was somewhat more modest than his brother-in-law's, though still stunning; the brick house, called Eltham, recalled a slightly smaller version of Jefferson's Monticello and had been named for the Bassett ancestral manor near Greenwich, England, called Eltham Palace. The men of the family competed fiercely over everything, from furniture sales to furniture workers. They were even known to argue over the best parking spot in the company lot.

But on weekends, the whole lot of them quail hunted, fished, and golfed together, often inviting along Uncle Clyde, who married into furniture royalty when he wed C.C. Bassett's daughter Mabel.

Confused? So were people in Henry County, who learned not to say anything about the Bassetts to strangers because there was a good chance the person they were gossiping to was somehow related to the extended clan.

J. Clyde Hooker was another early Bassett manager whose later business was helped along by the old man, who lent the Bassett name to the enterprise. In exchange, J. Clyde located his Hooker-Bassett Furniture plant in Martinsville, far enough away from Bassett that the companies wouldn't have to compete for labor, which might have forced wage increases. (The "Bassett" part of the name was later dropped.) Four other early Bassett managers were granted seed money for furniture plants extending from Galax, Virginia, to Lexington, North Carolina—also a safe distance away.

By the time Little John came along, Grandpop was the majority stockholder of seven plants in Bassett and Martinsville and was a major stockholder in six others. He had his own FDIC-insured bank. With three thousand people now living in his namesake town—most of them in company-owned shotgun homes—he was putting a serious dent in the business of his Northern competitors.

He created his own competition, yes. But by intertwining his corporate babies with the family tree, he was also spawning generations of family fortune.

His secret weapon was his succession plan, his reliance on those relentless Bassett genes. As one Bassett competitor, Pulaski Furniture president Bernard "Bunny" Wampler (now retired), told me: "He wasn't a brilliant person, but he was absolutely a genius at picking people who were." Especially from his family.

Mr. W.M. Bassett, his oldest son, turned out to be quieter than he was but just as tenacious. In 1927, W.M. was running the Bassett factories that J.D. had built and named for himself, plants that are still known in town as J.D. No. 1 and J.D. No. 2. His father encouraged rivalries among his plants as well as his children, and there were times when the designer of one company would sneak into the workroom of another in the dead of night to find out what his competitor's new line would be.

The atmosphere was cutthroat, and it gave W.M. ulcers. He was also mad that his father had made Bonce Stanley a company vice president when here he was, Mr. J.D.'s own son, still toiling as a plant manager. So W.M. quit, retreated to the family's enclave in Florida, and plotted his next move.

Within a few months he had secretly joined forces with a Martinsville real estate magnate. Heck Ford knew Craig Furniture in Martinsville was about to go belly-up, and he told W.M. there was a fortune to be made. W.M. was game, but he didn't want the Bassett name associated with the deal, knowing it would drive up the price. So Heck put the deal together in his name and was given 10 percent ownership in the brand-new W.M. Bassett Furniture Company as thanks.

In 1928, W.M. premiered his first line of furniture at a trade show in Chicago—and sold out on the spot. At that point, Mr. J.D. decided to make things right with his oldest son. He was sixty-three years old and finally ready to hand over the reins. If his son would let him buy the profitable W.M. factory and bring it into the fold, Mr. J.D. would put W.M. in charge of a new umbrella corporation called Bassett Furniture Industries, which would allow the company to get better deals on bulk supplies and advertising. By 1929, his son's lone act of revolution, the W.M. Bassett plant, was shipping out $1.5 million in furniture a year.

Whether the old man ever apologized for causing the ulcers isn't known, but W.M. had demonstrated his bona fides in a way that earned his father's respect. To assure that the assets were divvied up fairly, the family hired the accounting firm of Ernst and Ernst to make a certified inventory of each factory's holdings. "Daddy Bill was very sharp," said Spencer Morten, W.M.'s son-in-law and a longtime Bassett Furniture board member. "But the whole thing, all of it, was just rife with nepotism and infighting. If you crossed one of them, you'd better look out."

The umbrella company mushroomed to cover all the furniture basics, including a factory dedicated solely to making chairs. As one local writer boasted, "When demand cannot be met by present facilities, why, just build another plant somewhere along the winding course of the Smith River, equip it with the best procurable machinery, hire additional hundreds of workers, and there you are—without a break in your daily routine."

A few years later, it came to Mr. J.D.'s attention that another competitor was about to go belly-up. That day, he left the bank and met up with W.M. near the railroad tracks. They were going to lunch in the family mansion; Miss Pokey and the maids usually had a four-course lunch prepared, and the sons often talked shop and debated business strategies with Mr. J.D. while they ate.

If Miss Pokey agreed with her sons' business plans, she offered her husband an after-lunch "nap," following which he was generally persuaded to adopt his sons' position. (JBIII told me that story proudly the first time we met, as an example of both male Bassett virility and female Bassett cunning. It was not long before I realized it was also a fine illustration of his two favorite subjects, the first being furniture, the second being sex.)

"Bill, what happens when your liabilities exceed your assets?" Mr. J.D. said en route to lunch that day, fingering his unlit cigar.

"You go broke," W.M. said.

That was what was happening at Ramsey Furniture down the road, a fact Mr. J.D. had just determined inside his bank. So it went that in 1934, Bassett Furniture paid $117,000 for the three-story brick Ramsey plant at auction and then renamed it Bassett Superior Lines, a move that for decades would cement the company's position as the low-cost producer in the lower-priced, promotional range of bedroom furniture.

With W.M. at the helm, Bassett Superior Lines would become one of the most profitable furniture factories in the history of the industry. During World War II, when W.M. got himself named to the War Production Board, he brokered a deal for Bassett to make wooden truck bodies for the military. Fellow board member "Engine Charlie" Wilson, chairman of General Motors, schooled him on the wonders of conveyor belts.

The old Ramsey plant was soon running so fast that folks in Bassett still call it Bassett Speed Lines. "We were making so much furniture so damn fast, I'm telling you, we were *printin'* money," Joe Philpott, Superior's longtime plant manager, told me. By August of 1955, Bassett Superior broke a company record by shipping out more than $1 million in furniture in a single month.

If you had to put your money on one of the many smokestacks proliferating like dandelions throughout the Southern mill towns, Bassett Superior Lines seemed like the best bet.

Bassett Superior Lines. If you said it fast, it sounded like *Bassett Spear Lines*. Which, for decades after, is exactly what it did to nearly every rival in its category.

* * *

From their veranda, J.D. and Miss Pokey kept a careful watch on the smokestacks below, and almost everything else. On the next hillside over sat a mirror image of J.D. and Pokey's house, the home of J.D.'s brother C.C. and his wife, Roxie, who happened to be Miss Pokey's sister. The cofounder brothers each had a private set of cement stairs that gave them direct access to the factories.

All the better to keep an eye on the booming town. Miss Pokey had started out attending a Baptist church in the area, but when the hard-line minister frowned upon her bridge playing—and the fact that the couple liked to drink, in moderation—the Bassetts built a bigger church on a hill next to their Victorian home and hired a more progressive minister to run it.

There's a photograph of the foursome dressed to the nines aboard a Florida fishing boat, the women clutching pocketbooks and fishing poles. In it, J.D. looks nothing like that young man on horseback.

Cigar in mouth and clad in a three-piece suit—while fishing on a boat!—his aspirational phase had long since passed, as had his horse. He could go anywhere he wanted now.

In 1938, Bassett replaced its initial Early American designs with a look that would become its signature: the waterfall. Sharp edges were replaced by curves that were said to spill from the top of a dresser like a waterfall streaming from a high cliff, usually topped off by an ornate circular mirror. Beds had thick posts, and armoires came with decorative, hand-carved flourishes that echoed the waterfall's rolled top. A ten-piece bedroom suite sold for $110.75, and everybody wanted one, it seemed.

To the masses it looked expensive, but it wasn't, especially when veneer construction, aided by Mr. W.M.'s machinery, replaced the finickier and more expensive solid oak. Immigrants landing in New York and New Jersey especially loved the stuff, which taught the Bassetts the importance of keeping up with the buying habits of the public—and hiring the right designers.

The Bassetts' premier designer was the Princeton-educated son of a Prague-born furniture designer. A Renaissance man who spoke three languages and played the cello, Leo Jiranek lived in New York but spent weeks at a stretch camped out in Bassett with his sketchbook and pen. He could knock off a piece of furniture after seeing it just one time, and knocking off furniture was something Bassett and the other moderately priced furniture companies did — and still do — right and left.

The knockoff game went like this: If a higher-end Henredon item sold out, the Bassetts would try to offer a spot-on copy of it for sale — at half the cost — by the next season's furniture trade show. Known simply as Market, the semiannual show was (and still is) the major industry event: manufacturers set up elaborate showrooms to display their latest samples, and retailers walk in, assess the offerings, and decide what to buy for their stores. (The Market eventually migrated from Chicago to High Point, North Carolina, where it remains, though competing trade shows have cropped up in Las Vegas and elsewhere.)

Jiranek also knew exactly how to fend off a patent-infringement lawsuit, which Lane Furniture learned when it sued Bassett in the late 1960s. The lawsuit was ultimately dropped when Jiranek found a near identical copy of the piece in a Philadelphia furniture museum — proving the design had been around for centuries.

For decades, Jiranek figured largely in the company's success, with magazine ads in *Life* and *Look* that proudly touted his designer name. But he would end his career with mixed feelings about the Bassett clan. "They were a group of unsophisticated people who worked hard and made money," Leo's son Bob Jiranek said. "They needed somebody up in New York who could tell them how to market furniture."

During one such trip to New York, the story went, Mr. J.D. proudly bragged to his competitors that he was "the bread in my small town of Bassett."

"Yeah, but up in New York, you're only the damn crumb," one shot back.

In a 1967 *Fortune* magazine issue, a dismissive headline called Bassett, Virginia, "the Town the Daddy Rabbits Built." The story openly mocked the company for its cronyism and its mass-produced, Middle America designs—a backwoods throwback.

> The unincorporated town of Bassett, Virginia, is the headquarters of the world's largest manufacturer of wood furniture. It is also one of the last examples of a dying appendage of industry—the company town dominated by a single family. Employees of Bassett Furniture Industries enter the world in a Bassett-endowed hospital, are educated in the John D. Bassett [high] school, live in Bassett houses, work in one of the six local Bassett plants, deposit their savings in a Bassett bank, and worship at the Pocahontas Bassett Baptist Church.

"It was the feudal system," recalled Sonny Cassady, who grew up poor and fatherless in Bassett with a mother who waitressed at the Main Street Café. That's where Jiranek and two of the company's top salesmen hung out when they waltzed in from New York every spring and fall. His mother, Mary, had beautiful legs, Sonny told me, and she went out dancing with the men nightly in exchange for a twenty-dollar tip at the week's end. "In the spring, she bought me tennis shoes and jeans with that money," he said. "In October, she bought me a coat."

When his mother married his stepfather, a teenage Sonny left to live with the town's cabdriver, Roy Martin, who drove to the Greensboro airport to pick up Jiranek and the New York salesmen. Accompanying Roy on the trips, Sonny learned he wanted nothing to do with factory life. "The rich people lived in castles on the hill, and the rest of us were peasants living in riverside shacks," he said. A football scholarship gave him a college education, and Sonny eventually went into sales, wearing wide-lapelled double-breasted suits just like the ones worn by the New York salesmen. He now owns two merchandise-closeout companies.

*   *   *

Sophisticated or not, the furniture was leaving the riverside factories as quickly as the Bassett Speed Lines employees could load it into the railcars. The Bassetts were making so much money they could now hire decorators to fill their own homes with antiques and high-end pieces made in Grand Rapids.

"We made awful furniture," lamented Jane Bassett Spilman, who owns property in Virginia and North Carolina but does not have a single Bassett Furniture piece in any of her homes. In a 1970 *New York Times* article, she told a reporter, "I'm sort of the Perle Mesta of Bassett," a reference to the Washington socialite.

Fortunately for the Bassett family, the country was growing, and the masses needed places to sit, eat, and sleep. By the time JBIII left for boarding school, in 1952, fifty years after the company was formed, it was selling $33 million in furniture a year and had 3,100 employees. W.M. had talked his father into letting him pump $6 million into factory modernizations to fully capitalize on the postwar prosperity and the new housing boom. Bassett's slogan was "Pioneers in Furniture for the Nation," and its company newspaper was the *Bassett Pioneer*.

The waterfall design—and the hands that planed, sanded, and stained it—had made those poor, unsophisticated Daddy Rabbits rich. The joke, it seemed, was on everybody but them.

4

Hilltop Hierarchy

The Negroes made me.
—J.D. Bassett Sr.

To get to Junior and Mary Thomas's tidy trailer, you turn into the cut between the two dominant hills of Bassett. The hill to the left is where C.C. Bassett lived in his sprawling Victorian mansion, and the hill to the right is where Mr. J.D., his brother, lived in an almost identical home. The Thomases lived down below, like many of the black laborers, along a road that used to be named for George Washington Carver, in a snaky hollow that was home to a thirty-nine-house shanty-town built for the black workers of Bassett Furniture.

There are just fifteen houses there now, and several years ago, when the new 911 road-naming system went into effect, the road's name was changed from Carver Lane to Carson Drive. Both were improvements over what people called the hollow back when it was part of Horsepasture—Snot Holler and Chigger Ridge.

Junior Thomas was born in 1926 in one of the original shacks, now a bank thick with kudzu. He was brought into this world by his grand-mother, a midwife, and raised by a homemaker mom and a dad who worked first in J.D. Bassett's sawmill and later at Old Town, the first

Bassett plant. Junior's father-in-law worked at Bassett Mirror and helped Junior get hired there after he came home from World War II.

For forty years, Junior poured silver nitrate and cut glass for mirrors. When he retired, in 1990, he was making six dollars an hour plus benefits. He's been on call for the Bassett family ever since, occasionally chauffeuring for Spencer Morten and C.C. Bassett's granddaughter Roxann Dillon, who gives him forty dollars at the end of every month — tiding him over until his Social Security check arrives — in exchange for his being available for odd jobs she needs performed. "I never did get weaned away from 'em," Junior said, a sly grin forming on his unwrinkled face.

Reed-thin and agile at eighty-five, he moves gracefully, his tight-cropped silver hair a blur much of the time. He sings like a nightingale, and he rarely eats more than half a sandwich for lunch, believing that sluggishness from overeating and good health don't mix. When I left his house after our first interview, he refilled my water bottle and gave me Nabs for the ride home, then coached me as I navigated his steep curvy driveway across a crumbly narrow bridge so I wouldn't land my car in his front-yard creek. ("Keep going," he directed gently, moving his arms like a traffic cop. "That's right, you got it, that's right.")

Clad in a housecoat and slippers, his wife, Mary, stood on the front porch as I drove away, hollering for me to "Have a blessed day!" After my third visit, they sent me home with a produce basket full of bottled beer. A friend had given it to them after cleaning out someone's estate. "We don't want somebody from church coming by, seeing it, and getting the wrong impression!" Mary said.

Unlike the employees in the whites-only mills in nearby Martinsville and Fieldale, Bassett's workforce was 20 percent black from the very beginning. Bassett Furniture paid its first black workers half of what it paid the white workers, but the company did hire them, and it provided housing, segregated and ramshackle though most of it was. While the white line workers lived in four-room shotgun houses with outhouses that fed directly into the Smith River, most black workers lived in shacks dotting Carver Lane, which angled away from the river and the railroad tracks like a tributary. Their outhouses fed into the woods.

"That was unusual for the time, blacks and whites working together at industrial jobs," historian John Kern said. The Civil War had raged here just four decades before. In many Southern cities, it was illegal for blacks to live in certain neighborhoods, and Jim Crow laws throughout the former Confederacy prevented biracial gatherings in barbershops and baseball parks, at circuses and domino matches.

Black employees knew their salaries weren't equal to the whites' working at Bassett, and the possibility for advancement was nil. But for the most part, they were treated with some dignity, and, relative to other jobs in the segregated South, working conditions were adequate.

Besides, it was better than what the North Carolina furniture makers were offering blacks, which initially was no jobs at all. With most of his Southern competitors hiring only whites, relegating the blacks to sawmilling and sharecropping, Mr. J.D. knew that hiring blacks would yield high dividends. A black employee's pay stub from 1932 showed that for one hundred hours worked, the take-home pay was ten dollars, or ten cents an hour. A white worker made more than double that for the same number of hours. (In later decades, the pay disparity amounted to about five cents an hour for comparable work, sometimes more, according to Kern's research. One table-plant worker he interviewed was earning $1.25 an hour when he quit, in 1963; his white replacement started out at $1.35.)

Blacks had to use separate bathrooms and drinking fountains. But like the Taiwanese and Chinese rice-paddy peasants who would replace them a century later, they were eager to join the cash economy—and to work inside, away from the blazing heat of the tobacco fields. In the southern United States in the early 1900s, hiring black factory workers was unprecedented. None of the industries in nearby Martinsville were hiring blacks—not until 1933, when three black entrepreneurs and a

Jewish mill owner founded Jobbers Pants Company, a sewing plant run out of a former R. J. Reynolds tobacco factory.

In early photos of Bassett employees, the black workers stood together in the back row or sat inside the second-story window frames, their feet dangling. They worked the hottest, dirtiest jobs, usually in the finishing room, where it didn't matter how dark you were: when the whistle blew at the end of the day, everyone was stained with varnish. Many of those who didn't live in Snot Holler/Carver Lane walked or caught the train to a black enclave in nearby Fieldale, recalled rub-room worker Doretha Estes, whose grandfather, parents, and husband worked in the factories or as domestics in the Bassett homes.

Outside the factory walls, Jim Crow brutality loomed in many corners of the 1920s American South. Cabell Finney, one of Estes's uncles, was running late to catch the train to Bassett one morning, so he jumped on a slow-moving train car. As he made his way through the whites-only section to get to the black car in the back, an angry conductor grabbed him and literally kicked him off the train. Killed on impact, Cabell Finney was twenty. His father, George Finney, a minister who worked at Bassett's veneer plant, sued the N&W Railway and won a four-hundred-dollar settlement, according to the family.

Another Finney, George's cousin Ben, later had the nerve to use the whites-only bathroom inside the Bassett plant, where he worked as janitor. "He was self-taught, and he carried himself with dignity and pride," his niece Carolyn Blue said.

When the foreman asked why he went to the white bathroom, Ben Finney told him the "colored [one] was occupied."

"Ben, you know you shouldn't have used that bathroom," the foreman said.

"The last time I checked, shit was shit, and I was not gonna go on myself," Ben replied, and after a moment of awkward silence, the foreman walked away.

"Do you know how bodacious that was at the time?" Carolyn exclaimed after she told me the story.

*   *   *

Talk to people in Bassett today, and most say the company viewed all workers through a paternalistic but pragmatic lens: work hard and show up on time, and management didn't care what color you were. The Bassetts spoke out virulently against unions but never expressed outward racial prejudice in their factories or homes during segregation, many people, black and white, told me. When a service station opened in Bassett in the 1950s, Mr. J.D. was heard to say that the owners "had better hire some blacks if they wanted to stay in business."

When a white doctor who worked for the company refused to treat the black employees, Mr. J.D. told the doctor to pack his bags, according to Naomi Hodge-Muse, Estes's daughter and an NAACP leader. "It's all jaded with the reality of racism, but Mr. Bassett did believe the doctor had to take care of everybody, so it ended up the doctor changed his freakin' mind and stayed," Naomi said.

One of the family's maids, Mary Hunter, trusted the couple so much that she left her estate to them, along with instructions that it be put toward the education of black children. Born during the Civil War or immediately after (census records give conflicting dates), Mary Hunter was badly burned as an infant when her mother left her sitting in front of a fireplace while she fetched water from the well. Despite her crippled feet, she worked hard, ironing the family's clothes and polishing the silver. She often sat in a rocking chair and used it to scoot herself across the floor. When she cooked, she propped herself up on a single crutch. Living in the Bassett family home, Mary Hunter minded the house and helped raise the four children while Miss Pokey worked at the company store.

According to Hodge-Muse and her mother, when Mary Hunter died, in 1940 at the age of seventy-eight, the Bassett family tried to cover her funeral expenses, only to be reminded of the servant's vehement final wishes: It was beneath her dignity to let her employers pay for her burial and headstone; her estate would take care of it.

"I don't remember if it was a hundred dollars or a thousand," Jane Bassett Spilman said of Mary Hunter's estate, adding that the family made sure the county's segregated school for blacks, built in 1956, was named Mary Hunter Elementary. "But I remember her saying, 'You are my family.'"

According to an account written by the school's first principal, John B. Harris, Mr. J.D. visited the school shortly after it opened and explained how Mary Hunter had managed his household "so efficiently and well, how she saved money for his family and herself." Astonishingly, the maid, who had never learned to read or write, had somehow amassed forty thousand dollars. (Her will, however, shows her estate was valued at only $782.64 in cash—suggesting, again, that family lore and the facts weren't always in sync.) The first school in the county to be named for a woman or a black person, Mary Hunter Elementary had an enrollment of 450 students.

Hodge-Muse went on to graduate from high school and college, but it's the alma mater song from Mary Hunter Elementary that has stuck with her, she told me. Then she sang it through twice:

Mary Hunter's gonna shine tonight, Mary Hunter's gonna shine
It will shine with beauty bright on down the line
When the sun goes down and the moon comes out
Mary Hunter's gonna shine.

Jane told me Mary Hunter's story at her horse farm in Manakin-Sabot soon after she had watched the movie *The Help,* the film adaptation of Kathryn Stockett's book of the same name. She was shocked by the way Southern whites demeaned their servants in the film. "The people I knew would never dream of treating their help that way," she said. Jane certainly didn't, according to several of the area's black residents, who recall Jane and her longtime cook sharing a warm relationship. Jane's maid, who died in 2012, was still baking homemade yeast rolls for the family on holidays well into her nineties. Jane also had a house built for her parents' servants, Augusta and Willie Green, a home now owned and occupied by the Greens' daughter.

But Jane seemed not to know of the thinly veiled secrets surrounding some of the men in her extended family—that Estes's mother, a Bassett family cook, wore two girdles at once to keep wandering Bassett hands in check; that there were whispers about the light-skinned black children who grew up in C.C. Bassett's home.

In the Bassett Historical Center, as I photocopied the seventeen-pound Bassett genealogy, a tome written by Mr. J.D.'s granddaughter, a library assistant told me in all sincerity: "She left one of her relatives out."

Talk to the right people long enough, and the worst-kept secret in town emerges again and again. A former Bassett salesman brought up the sexually exploitative practice of sleeping with the servants, common in slavery as well as in Reconstruction and continuing in Bassett, in the most well-known instance, with C.C. Bassett and the family maid. Hodge-Muse was the first of many to reveal the mulatto child's name: Clay Barbour. Naomi's grandmother Dollie Finney was the one who corseted herself with two girdles, and she was there when another servant hollered at Mr. J.D., "John Bassett, you'd screw a black snake if someone would hold its head!" Her frankness sent the old man into such a fit of roaring laughter that he slapped his hat on his leg.

"He didn't get insulted by nothing [servant] women said to him. He was too busy on his journey," Doretha Estes said. "He figured, If I can't get this one, I'll get me another."

Estes, who was eighty-six when I interviewed her, stood to demonstrate the way her girdled mother bent over the dining-room table while serving the family's dinner, using both hands to hold a dish. The way she steeled herself as the inevitable hand began to crawl up her leg, knowing that she couldn't flinch or complain—otherwise a Bassett wife might accuse her of flirtation and, quite possibly, fire her.

Estes told me all this eighteen months after I started reporting this book, during my fifth visit to the house she shares with her daughter. She was initially reluctant to be interviewed, snapping that I had no right to dredge up such uncomfortable things. But finally, having witnessed a lifetime of Bassett family decision-making—and its rippling effects on the community, pro and con—she was ready to talk.

Working for the Bassetts allowed Estes to send her daughter to college, a family first. It allowed her grandfather George Finney to build a three-hundred-dollar home out of chestnut—by lantern, at night, after working in the factory all day. "Look, the truth is, back then, the Bassetts weren't too stingy. It's just so hard now to be fair about it all, but I'm trying."

Her daughter, speaking in her usual impassioned tone, struggled to articulate her own mixed feelings. "They were greedy, yes. They were controlling, yes. But they weren't all evil," Naomi told me, citing the separate black and white recreation centers they built. "As strange as it was, it was a symbiotic relationship," she said, "and I think that biological term actually applies. They were the huge tree that gave life to small vines, and because there were small vines, I'm sitting here in Chatmoss"—a high-end subdivision near Martinsville that is also home to some Bassett descendants.

Henry "Clay" Barbour was born in 1911, lived on Carver Lane, and died a bachelor in a Martinsville nursing home in 1993. In his obituary, his mother is listed as the late Julie Ann Barbour. No father was named, though his employer—the Bassett family—was mentioned. According to census documents, he was a mulatto child who lived in the C.C. Bassett home. Unlike his mother, who never learned to read or write, Clay was literate, though he'd been schooled only through the third grade.

He had an older, mixed-race sister named Lelia—nicknamed Tea—born to Julie a month before C.C.'s wife gave birth to a daughter, Dorothy, in 1909. By 1920, Clay's light-skinned sister Tea was living with a different family, presumably relatives, out in Horsepasture, and it took several visits to Junior and Mary's house before I learned what had happened to her.

"It's quite well known that Mr. Ed Bassett had a half brother who was black," longtime town barber Coy Young said, speaking of Clay Barbour. "They say he was in the same crib [with a Bassett] as a baby." Clay's mother, Julie Barbour, remained in C.C.'s home and was "taken care of" throughout her life, numerous townspeople told me.

But what did that mean, exactly? The last mention I found of Julie was in the 1940 census, ten years after C.C. and Roxie Bassett died in a car accident. She was fifty-five, living in Bassett with C.C.'s daughter Dorothy Rich, and cooking. She made $520 a year, about $150 less than the average furniture worker. Her son, Clay, worked as a driver for a Bassett-owned trucking company and earned $500 a year—about $8,000 today, adjusting for inflation.

When Clay Barbour needed money, he staggered up the steep hill and appeared at the back door of the house he'd been reared in—C.C. Bassett's, by then occupied by Mr. Ed and his wife, Ruby, who shared Clay's weakness for alcohol. She gave Clay money on the back stoop, no questions asked. "The family didn't shun him, but he wasn't invited to dinner either," Coy said. Several people said Ruby Bassett left Clay money in her will, but a search through the Henry County courthouse documents revealed no Barbour beneficiaries named among the white relatives. The Thomases pointed out that Mr. Ed was the Bassett executive who finally got the dirt road where they lived paved, in the 1960s. "Before that we had to drive across the creek three times just to get up the holler," Junior said.

Ruby Bassett was Clay's biggest supporter in the family, Estes recalled. "Clay could go to any store in Bassett and buy anything he wanted, and Miss Ruby would pay for it."

Clay wore the furniture maker's uniform of denim overalls every day of the week, and his light skin and blondish-brown hair gave credence to the rumors everyone talked about—but never within earshot of the Bassetts or the Barbours. Mary Thomas remembered Clay waving to her from the door of the Carver Lane shack where he lived as she walked to school in the morning.

He was friendly, but he drank too much, usually with Hodge-Muse's stepfather, William "Pork Chop" Estes, who was Ruby's chauffeur. The Bassetts accommodated his alcoholism the way one might help out a distant cousin who'd fallen on hard times. They gave him easy factory jobs and the freedom to sleep off hangovers when he needed to, the Thomases said. They tried to promote him to foreman once, but he couldn't handle the responsibility, and it didn't take.

"Clay was caught between two races," recalled Carolyn Blue, a woman whose father and grandfather worked in Bassett factories and who has traced her own lineage back to a Bassett-area plantation called Hordsford, where miscegenation was also common. "Clay was a very tall, slender man, and he could pass for white. It was just like Thomas Jefferson, only this was the twentieth century. . . . But it was the elephant in the room." The Bassetts weren't the only patriarchs who practiced it, she said, citing a textile mogul in the region who also sired children with his maids.

When Carolyn and her sisters arrived at their historically black colleges, friends teased them and called them "redbones" because of their white lineage. "This was 1968 and people were saying to us, 'Y'all must be from Martinsville,' and 'That white man really did a job on y'all,' because most [black] people from Henry County are fair-skinned."

But to college they had gone, thanks to the hard-earned money of their factory-worker parents. "Whether they were nice or not, or whether they slept with the maids, you have to give the Bassetts and the rest of them credit," Blue said. "That work was a viable income for blacks. We were no longer a sharecropping community, and I really appreciate that. It allowed me to go to college."

The Thomases are similarly conflicted about the Bassett family. The industry employed many of their kin, and while they weren't paid as much as their white coworkers, there were times when they benefited from the paternalism that blanketed the town like smoke from the chimney stacks. After years of having no children, Junior and Mary adopted their son, Kim, with help from their Bassett bosses, who not only paid their legal fees but also gave them a brand-new crib for the boy.

I asked what it must have felt like to be Julie Barbour working in the C.C. Bassett home, and this seemed to be a scenario Mary had played out often in her mind. Having picked up extra work cleaning in the homes and offices of some Bassett managers herself, Mary reasoned that Julie must have felt trapped and alone, especially once she had her own children to raise. She doubted Julie was raped outright, but she was probably the victim of a subtler, more long-term form of coercion. Maybe Julie Barbour and C.C. Bassett loved each other—who knows?—but Mary doubted that.

"You would be surprised with these men and how they'll wanna try to molest you," she said. "I have left [cleaning] jobs because I could see they was gettin' fresh. They'll wait till the wife leaves and then be all, 'Come here, I got something to tell you,' [and I'd say,] 'Why couldn't you tell me that while your wife was still here?'

"You see, you have to work until you can get your money and so you just don't say nothing," she said. "They'll do it. You'd be surprised.

"They were *just that slick*."

Junior Thomas remained silent as his wife of sixty-three years spoke, occasionally nodding but mostly staring blankly at the evangelist preaching on his television screen. He nodded when Mary talked about the person she'd worked for the longest, a wealthy woman (not a Bassett) who never paid employer taxes or Social Security taxes. Decades later, a lawyer advised Mary to bring it up with the woman because Mary's Social Security benefits amounted to less than three hundred dollars a month.

So Mary did. "Are you *threatening* me, Mary Thomas?" the woman had said. Reluctantly, she agreed to meet Mary with her "pension," not in her actual home, but down below it, on the other side of the Thomases' cement bridge. Her retirement? An envelope containing a hundred dollars in cash.

The only time Junior raised his voice came near the end of our first two-hour interview.

"We *made* 'em what they had," he boomed.

"We *made* 'em rich."

Mary Elizabeth and Spencer Morten, Mr. J.D.'s granddaughter and her husband, conceded the critical role of African Americans in the making of Bassett Furniture Industries. They quoted from a recorded family interview in which Mr. J.D. himself echoed Junior Thomas's assessment, nearly word for word.

"The Negroes made me," they recalled him saying, pronouncing the word "*nee*-gres."

His competitors to the south were using white labor, and he could cut his overhead by hiring workers who were even cheaper than the Scots-Irish coming in from the countryside. Like the Asian competitors who would take his own descendants to the mat a century later, he knew cheap labor was the key to outmaneuvering his rivals.

"The blacks didn't work harder per se, but they were paid less, and they tended to have the worst jobs," Spencer said, like pouring the nasal-burning silver nitrate on glass at Bassett Mirror, a family-run company Morten headed for decades, and where Junior Thomas spent the bulk of his career. "I'd walk in there and get a headache, but the blacks used to tell me, 'You get used to this.'"

In fact, they said, working amid the fumes seemed to prevent them from catching colds.

But when asked about the genealogy of Clay Barbour, Spencer Morten seemed sincerely incredulous. "A black man who was Uncle Ed's brother and C.C. Bassett's son? I never heard of it." After our meeting, Spencer even called around, questioning blacks and whites alike about the story, wondering why he and his wife seemed to be the last to know.

"Things floated around town through the employees and through the townspeople, and sometimes management was the last to find out," Pat Ross, a town librarian, explained to him and, later, to me.

Bassett was a company town with two distinct narratives: the prevailing one, told by the Families and the local media (owned by friends of the Families), and the whispered one, discussed on front porches and in the bleachers at John D. Bassett High by everyone else.

Pat Ross, who is white, grew up hearing hints of the story, and she can now recite most of the Bassett family tree — even those members who were never written in. Like most people in Bassett, she has her own connection to the early days of the furniture company. Bassett Furniture is, in fact, the reason she exists.

Bassett lured both sets of her grandparents to town in the early 1920s. Her paternal grandfather, J.G. Clay, had been the boiler man for Broyhill Furniture in Lenoir, and word of his skill reached the ear of J.D. Bassett himself. For a few more cents an hour, J.G. would become Bassett's boiler man — a position so hot and so important that he was given two black assistants to carry his wood and coal as well as the rare permission to wear sandals to work. As another incentive for him to leave the North Carolina competition, J.G. and his family were allowed to live in one of the coveted two-story, company-owned homes.

"If you worked for Bassett, you got a house as part of your pay," Pat Ross explained, though rent and electricity were deducted from gross earnings. If you lived in Bassett Heights, along the southern edge of the town, the company even gave you a ride to work, courtesy of a truck called the Old 97. It had a wood-frame room built on its flatbed, complete with open windows and a door, and it was covered in black tar paper.

North Bassett homes shared power with the north Bassett factories, and when J.G. shut down the boiler for the day, the currents surging from the early electrical system caused ripples throughout the community. His wife, Addie, knew when she saw her lights flicker that she had five minutes before her husband would arrive home, five minutes to get her boys to the supper table.

The power company, the doctor, even the police station in the company parking lot—everything was Bassett operated and Bassett owned. Like Rich Uncle Pennybags from the board game Monopoly, Mr. J.D. put everything in town under his purview—especially the community chest.

Pat's other set of grandparents arrived in Bassett the same way the typical white line workers did: They heard there were paying jobs that came with houses, albeit small ones (though nothing as ramshackle as the Carver Lane homes), and the probability of an easier life than the one sawmilling and farming provided in Patrick County, an afternoon's mule ride away. Early white workers lived near the Smith River banks, mostly across the river from the factories, and teamed up in groups of four or five to build boats together, then pooled rides across the Smith. Eventually, they walked to work on company-owned swinging bridges.

"J.D. Bassett was a large man with a large presence," Pat Ross recalled. When relatives of Bassett employees died, he would allow them to be buried in the Bassett family cemetery—not far from his sprawling Victorian home—but on its outskirts, reserving the inner circle for family.

Clay Barbour is buried ten miles away from the Bassett family mausoleum. His final resting place is in Martinsville, in a segregated cemetery named for George Washington Carver. A few years before he died and just after Ruby Bassett's death, his Carver Lane shack was burglarized. Thieves waited till he left the house on a day shortly after the first of the month, knowing his Social Security money was inside (and that his door wouldn't lock), then ransacked the place.

The next day, Naomi Hodge-Muse took him a box of food, some cash, and a lock for his door, with a bar that extended across as extra security.

"Why would you do that, child?" Clay asked her, tears streaming down his face.

"Because God loves you, Mr. Barbour." And because of Pork Chop,

Clay's old drinking buddy. He was her stepfather and the only daddy she'd ever known.

What she didn't say was that she knew, with Ruby Bassett dead, Clay had no one left to turn to.

Clay's only surviving relative is a niece, an eighty-five-year-old widow living in nearby Fieldale. When Junior Thomas and I visited her, she warmly welcomed us into her brick ranch, decorated with pictures of Martin Luther King Jr. and President Barack Obama. She and her husband had lived in Detroit, where he worked for General Motors, but they retired and moved back to Henry County not long after Clay was robbed.

"I don't remember the way I used to," she said when Junior and I gently asked about her family history with the Bassetts. Her mother, who was Clay's older sister, Tea, had a job in Martinsville at Jobbers, the sewing plant. Her father worked for sixty years at Bassett Mirror.

"Mama spent all her time worrying over her brother and her son," she said, both of whom were alcoholics. She produced several photos of her mother, clad in a plaid dress and wearing a beret, with her arm around her much-darker son. When I noted that her mother could have passed for white, she said, "Yeah, she was right white-looking," but she did not acknowledge the miscegenation in her family tree. (Even to friends, she describes her family as simply "mulatto," said Carolyn Blue, whose mother is the woman's friend and contemporary.)

Asked directly if she was related to the Bassetts, she said, "Here lately, I can't remember nothing. I've been suffering so with my legs, it keeps my mind all messed up."

As Junior and I drove off, Junior Thomas observed that the Barbours seemed to live a kind of self-imposed exile. Clay drank his loneliness away, while his niece prospered by marrying a hardworking man and moving far away from Bassett. When she returned home to Henry County, she was an old woman with a foggy memory—and every right in the world to let the uncomfortable facts of her past slip away.

"She know it true," Junior said after we left her smiling at the doorstep. "*Everybody* know it true." Months later, Junior returned to the old woman's house alone— "She'll tell me things she won't tell you"—but she did not want to discuss Bassett genealogy with anyone.

"I asked her if C.C. Bassett was her granddaddy, and she claims she don't know who her granddaddy was." Asked to sign a form granting me permission to request her uncle's and mother's death certificates— though it was unlikely C.C. Bassett's name would have been listed as her father on any official document—she declined. Junior told me she was worried the Bassetts could still, somehow, find a way to take her home away if they wanted to, even though she owns it free and clear.

I'm not in the business of keeping eighty-five-year-old ladies awake at night, so I asked him to relay the message that I would not use her name in this book. (She's hard of hearing and can't talk on the phone.) When I brought up the issue with Hodge-Muse, who traces her own ancestry back to the slave owner Pete Hairston, she wasn't surprised.

"Part of it is shame. And part of it is just pissed, because how dare you have relations with a woman and care nothing about your off-spring? You give them nothing. N-o-t-h-i-n-g. Not a piece of land. Not a piece of money. Not education.

"Why would you acknowledge they're in your family tree when all they did was take out their animalistic lust on your ancestors who had no way of protecting themselves?"

After all these years, I wondered: Did it even matter who Clay Barbour's daddy was? It's a question I wrestled with as I researched the growth of the furniture dynasty, with its roots in Southern plantation history and land grants that helped turn all that lumber into cash.

Does it matter how the powerful treated their employees—whether they paid them a living wage or remembered them in their wills, what they tried to do to them when their wives left for the store?

Does that history matter when a century passes and the workers' descendants are replaced by fax machines, Mandarin-speaking interpreters, and plane tickets to China?

In the end, I believe, these stories are part of a larger one about power and paternalism. Even Mr. J.D. acknowledged it when he said the Negroes *made* him. And having done so, they are part of the foundation on which his family's wealth was built.

The men in the family made the beds. But they never had to lie in them.

Unless they wanted to.

The help was such a critical part of the Bassett family fabric that the extended clan took the servants along to their winter enclave on Hobe Sound, Florida, on the street locals still refer to as Bassett Row. After taking his family to Palm Beach to escape the 1918 flu epidemic, Mr. J.D. decided he liked Florida so much that he bought an entire line of lots in a community called Hobe Sound on Jupiter Island—he said the fishing was better there than in Palm Beach—and gave a parcel to each of his kids.

The Bassetts brought along their cooks and maids, and the mothers took turns arranging tutors for the children. The first time Mary Hunter saw the white Florida sands, she wasn't sure what she was looking at, according to family lore. "Lawdy, Lawdy. Miss Pokey's done fooled me. There ain't nothing here but more snow."

In one set of extended-family pictures from 1945, the entire Virginia furniture-making clan gathered to celebrate the patriarch's birthday. Flanking Mr. J.D. and Miss Pokey is an eight-year-old JBIII, on the right, and one of his cousins, three-year-old Patricia Vaughan Exum, on the left. Patricia's father helped manage a Bassett spinoff in Galax, ninety minutes away, begun in 1919 by her grandfather Bunyan Vaughan. He was a brother of Taylor Vaughan, who had the good fortune to marry Mr. J.D.'s daughter Blanche.

Further twisting the family tree, Miss Pokey's sister was Patricia's great-grandmother, and Miss Pokey was JBIII's grandmother. Taylor Vaughan began Vaughan Furniture in Galax a few years after his brother started Vaughan-Bassett Furniture, both men with the help of start-up cash from Mr. J.D.

None of this would matter except for the fact that decades later, JBIII and his distant cousin Patricia revived another custom of their noble European ancestors — they married each other.

"That's not a marriage, that's a *merger*," some people said. It was meant to be a joke, but, like the circumstances of the boy's dramatic birth, the barb proved prescient.

In one of the old pictures, Little John stands with hands on hips, sporting a cowlick and saddle shoes. He's looking directly at his future wife, whose little-girl panties stick out from under her dress. Later he would joke, "I'm thinking, I better put her in my little black book for twenty years from now." The future governor of Virginia is in the photo, along with Virginia's other furniture-making royalty and most of their offspring, the whole lot flanked by sprawling boxwood shrubs.

Everyone is smiling in the picture — especially the young woman standing directly behind her grandpop Mr. J.D.

Big sister Jane had witnessed the princely reception of her little brother. Before he came along, she was the one who toured the factories on weekends with her daddy. After church at Pocahontas Bassett Baptist, the two of them went next door, kissed the grandparents, and then walked through the plants. She pointed out things that looked amiss, and her dad wrote them down on his steno pad. If dirty rags were left on the finishing-room floor, the fire hazard would be noted on his list. If the lumber was stacked haphazardly, that went on the list too, and come Monday morning, *someone* would pay.

Her father remarked on it. Her uncles noticed it. Her teachers commented on it too.

"If Jane were a boy, she would be the one."

"Jane has the mind of a man."

"If only Jane wore pants…"

Jane was quick-witted, a brainiac, a force to be reckoned with. The whole town knew it. Little John was a firecracker at math, but he struggled with reading and was only average in school. Born a generation later, he might have been labeled learning-disabled. To this day, he reads very slowly. "But even at twelve, thirteen years old, you saw the intensity in him," said Bassett native John McGhee. "He was very cocky, and whatever it was [that kept him from excelling in school], he still worked twice as hard as everybody else."

Jane was more interested in factory operations than any of her male cousins were, and she loved talking shop with her father at the family dinner table. "He used to call me his conscience," she said. Her father, John D. Bassett Jr. (who went by Doug, or—you guessed it—Mr. Doug), preferred banking over manufacturing. When her uncle Bill, W.M. Bassett, passed away, it fell to Mr. Doug to run the entire company, not just the bank.

He confided in daughter Jane, then in her twenties, that he was going to appoint someone else to manage the bank, even though it was his favorite part of the job. To which she replied, "I'm very disappointed in you."

Her face lit up as she recalled the event, and when I asked if she was her father's favorite, she chuckled girlishly and continued the story. "The next morning he called me and said he was sitting in the bank president's office."

It was among her first of many quiet triumphs where the family business was concerned.

PART II

PART II

5

The Cousin Company

When I went to work last morning, well,
the temperature was nice
By the afternoon, oh Lord, you could boil a pot of rice
I had the blues... the furniture factory blues.

—EDDIE BOND (FIDDLER AND FORMER GALAX
FURNITURE WORKER), "FURNITURE FACTORY BLUES"

In Henry County, they used to joke that after you graduated from high school, you went to the University of Bassett. In the Blue Ridge Mountain town of Galax, Virginia, sixty-seven winding miles west of Bassett, the path between the school and the furniture factories was equally direct. Rodney Poe, a third-generation furniture man, remembered Galax High School teachers pointing to the smokestacks from the windows and admonishing, "If you don't turn your homework in, that's where you'll end up."

Furniture-making was tough work everywhere; just ask world-renowned old-time fiddler Eddie Bond, who thought he'd earn a little pocket change one summer at Vaughan Furniture, where his mother worked so long fastening panels onto dresser drawers that her staple-gun finger became permanently arced from it. A coworker on the finishing line perished right in front of his mother after a spark ignited the glaze the woman had inadvertently spilled on her clothes. "Instead of dropping to the floor and rolling over, she ran through the factory," Eddie said, adding that his mother still had nightmares about the death.

Eddie's summer-long stint at Vaughan, sans air-conditioning, convinced him to go to community college to learn how to be a machinist, and that's what he does now, between fiddling gigs, at a Pepsi bottling plant in nearby Wytheville. "I tell you, the furniture factories, they were a blessing and they were a curse. They did provide jobs, which kept food on our table, but you just barely eked out an existence."

As a teenager, he settled for the dollar-store variety of tennis shoes when Nikes became popular; there was no need to even ask for the ones with the swoosh. When his mom, Brenda Faye, finally quit her job in the cabinet room, in 1989, she was making $5.10 an hour. (Federal minimum wage was then $3.35.) She had threatened to quit if they didn't give her a raise, at which point her managers shrugged and let her go.

"Fifteen years, and she hadn't missed a single day of work. And they didn't tell her bye or nothing," Eddie said. "But it's always been hard times here in the mountains for poor people, and you just kinda got used to it."

For generations, the men who ran Bassett and Galax counted on that.

Galax (pronounced "*Gay*-lax") was named not for a founding father of the town but for the evergreen herb that grows in the foothills of the Blue Ridge. To make extra money, mountain folks used to go "galacking," gathering up the shiny evergreen leaves to sell for use in floral arrangements. Some still do, even though it's now considered poaching. Which should tell you something about the independent spirit of the moonshiners, galackers, and sangers (ginseng poachers) who roam these Appalachian hills.

With an elevation of twenty-five hundred feet, the town is surrounded by rolling hills and an ample supply of timber, especially white pine, a band of which runs atop the Blue Ridge. Some of the first Scots-Irish settlers brought fiddles and banjos, and they sang the high lonesome ballads they'd learned from their ancestors in a loud, nasally tone that carried from ridge to ridge.

So Galax became synonymous with furniture and mountain music, drawing people from across the globe to its annual Old Fiddlers' Convention, still going strong today after nearly eighty years. In the 1920s, a quartet named the Hill-Billies got its start in a Galax barbershop, launching a distinctive new sound that swept the nation and came to be called hillbilly music. For decades, furniture workers and textile-mill hands in the region taught one another songs and picked up extra money playing weekend gigs. Both sides of Bond's family worked as mill hands and musicians, and one of his great-uncles played for a string band called the Zero Defects, named as a hat-tip to the cotton mill where they all worked.

Well, if you're young and fancy free, let me give you some advice
You better get your education, don't you ever think twice
Or you'll have the blues… the furniture factory blues.

Galax was not a monument to a single man or company, but its manufacturing roots reach back to Bassett. When Bunyan Vaughan showed up to launch Vaughan-Bassett Furniture in 1919, he was doing it the Bassett way—in another labor market, a butt-numbing carriage ride away from Mr. J.D.'s plants, and with $50,000 in start-up capital from the old man. The enterprise was yet another family affair, the Bassett company's first factory outside Henry County. Bunyan had gotten his start as a Bassett Furniture bookkeeper and worked his way up to plant manager of Bassett's Old Town while his brother, Taylor, went on the road selling Bassett Furniture from western Pennsylvania to Michigan. Taylor was about to do his brother the favor of marrying J.D.'s daughter Blanche, tying the two families together for good.

The old man liked Bunyan. He'd advanced at Bassett through hard work: ten to twelve hours a day during the week and six hours on Saturdays. Bunyan's parents died when he was young, and he'd put himself through National Business College in Roanoke by working summers in the Bassett plant. Mr. J.D.'s son Doug had gone to the same business trade school after his lackluster performance at Washington and Lee University, then an all-male bastion of the Southern elite.

"My father never graduated from W and L because when he came home to visit, my grandfather asked him some questions he couldn't answer," JBIII recalled. "He couldn't add figures fast enough." So Mr. J.D. jerked Mr. Doug out of W&L and sent him to NBC, underscoring an early Bassett code: Coddle neither your employees nor your kids (even if the babies had emerged from the womb with a silver spoon).

When Mr. J.D. heard there was a small cabinet plant for sale in Galax, he and Bunyan went there to negotiate the deal. Bunyan sold his brother one-fifth of his share of the company and hired him on as sales manager. Together, in the backwater boomtown of Galax, they set out to replicate Mr. J.D.'s success.

Vaughan-Bassett Furniture was a minor affair compared to Bassett, with little hope of becoming a household name in the United States, much less in China. It started out making wooden bedroom furniture for the same reason Mr. J.D. had: those items were the easiest. Within four years, Taylor Vaughan had set up his own factory near the railroad tracks down the street and named it Vaughan Furniture, specializing in dining-room furniture. (It was Taylor's son John who was in charge of the company years later when Eddie Bond's mother was allowed to quit rather than given a five-cent bump in pay.)

"They didn't fight for labor back then because the area was growing so fast," said town historian John Nunn, whose grandfather started a mirror plant to supply the furniture makers. The Vaughan brothers chose Galax because the town fathers, a group of prominent landowners who'd formed a real estate company, gave them a deal on the land. As an early Galax promoter wrote: "The town has a very liberal policy and sympathetic attitude to new industries, and will give all possible cooperation and assistance to investors and home seekers."

Unlike Bassett's creators, Galax's founders hired an engineer from Lynchburg to lay out the town, with downtown corner lots selling for $100 to $250 apiece. The region's first settlers weren't plantation operators, as in Henry County. They were small-time farmers, some of whom were Quakers and staunch abolitionists. Unlike Henry County, mountain-ringed Galax never claimed plantations, which is one reason its black population is comparatively small.

From Galax's very inception, there was a tad more to the town than sawdust and smokestacks. Carnation would build a milk plant and Coca-Cola a bottling company, and from its founding in 1905, the small city had its share of maverick cowboys, including Thomas L. Felts, a gun-toting lawyer who dabbled in a whole lot of things, eventually owning a bank and a huge Ford dealership. He was best known for his partnership in the Baldwin-Felts Detective Agency, a crime-busting alliance that grew into one of the South's best-known bandit chasers and union busters.

Most important for the Vaughan brothers and their patriarch sponsor, Galax harbored the three keys to Southern furniture-making: plentiful lumber, railroad tracks to carry the finished beds and chifforobes away, and desperate people eager to join the new industrial economy.

Unlike Bassett, Galax had an elected government, a mayor, and a city council. Scots-Irish settlers set up groceries, hardware stores, and newsstands in the booming town, often living above their stores.

When people migrated to new places, they had to build homes and furnish rooms. So it went that a market for furniture was born, albeit a modest one at first. The furniture factories kept the men busy, and the hosiery plants employed their wives. It was happening in small towns across the Southern Piedmont, from Altavista, Virginia, on down to the North Carolina towns of Lexington, Hickory, and Lenoir. As *Southern Lumberman* magazine recalled of the early 1900s, "There have been thousands of families in the Southern States that have not had a new bedstead, bureau, or set of chairs since the close of the War Between the States."

Because the Southern furniture makers didn't produce high-end furniture like their counterparts in Grand Rapids, they didn't have as much to lose when the Great Depression hit. At the end of World War I, Grand Rapids had claimed seventy-one furniture factories, employing nearly half of that city's workers. But by the 1940s, furniture workers made up just one-sixth of the workforce.

The Southerners helped kill their competition, which was already struggling. The Michigan woods were becoming depleted, for one thing, and unions in the North forced factories to pay higher wages, especially after the automobile industry took off. The original industry pioneers were dying out, a phenomenon encapsulated in a saying I heard often throughout my reporting for this book: "Shirtsleeves to shirtsleeves in three generations." As the theory goes, the third generation of business innovators, the ones who grow up teething on silver spoons, typically turn out to be slackers who fritter the family fortunes away.

In *The City Built on Wood,* Frank E. Ransom argued that J.D. Bassett and his Southern ilk had the Northern manufacturers' high standards—and maybe their snobbery—to thank for their own roaring success. "The making of furniture is a creative art, and one which has not yet been debased in Grand Rapids by wholesale production lines and mechanization," he wrote. "In a period when the principal strategy and tactics of American industry have been concentration and combination, mass production and standardization, the furniture industry of Grand Rapids has remained virtually aloof from this pattern."

In other words, the city that had the audacity to crown itself "the Paris of Furniture Design" chose to bow out gracefully rather than demean itself by employing machinery. In clinging to their craft, the Michigan furniture makers folded like cheap lawn chairs, while the

Southern furniture makers kept on working, a film of machine-flung sawdust coating their glasses.

Mr. J.D.'s business concerns in Galax and Bassett weathered the Depression not through layoffs and plant closings but via meticulous management, staggered shifts with reduced hours, and continuous adaptation to change. Mr. J.D. cut salaries across the board, a fact that sent Naomi Hodge-Muse's proud grandfather George Finney back home to his small Koehler Hollow farm, where he remained for the rest of his life. ("A man don't work for less than a dollar a day," he told his family.)

Bassett Furniture retiree Howard White recalled his family moving to Bassett in 1930, after his father had been laid off from a Statesville, North Carolina, furniture plant, where he'd operated a motorized spindle carver. "Plants in Hickory and Lenoir were closing during the Depression, so a lot of people came up to Bassett because Bassett was still running. Bassett was always careful with its money, not extravagant," said White, who worked for the company from 1939 until he retired, in 1986. "If you bought a load of lumber, you counted and made sure you got exactly what you paid for. You looked after things."

Over in Galax, Bunyan Vaughan was adopting the same strategies. He may have started out as a Bassett Furniture bookkeeper, but he developed what people in the industry call having "sawdust in his veins." When his brother died unexpectedly, in 1940, Bunyan continued to run Vaughan-Bassett and took over Vaughan Furniture too. He sent his daughters off to boarding school, just as the other first-generation furniture makers had done. When his daughter Frances married U.S. Army Air Corps pilot Wyatt Exum, he set his son-in-law up in business, following the familiar model of Mr. J.D.

Wyatt was a natural at sales and had a photographic memory for numbers. He had movie-star good looks and a death-defying war tale that became the basis for a 1948 film featuring Robert Stack. In September 1944, his squadron was tasked with destroying the Nazi rail lines in Hungary. A fellow fighter pilot's blast backfired, knocking out the cooling system of his plane, and the man was forced to make a belly landing deep in enemy territory. From the air, Wyatt watched it unfold in his single-seat plane, prompting a radio discussion among the pilots about what to do. Above all, their commanders had instructed them, they should not let any of the American planes, with their brand-new radar and communications technology, fall into enemy hands.

Pilot be damned, the protocol went. *Blow the sucker up.*

"We gotta go get that boy," Wyatt told the other pilots in the air, in defiance of the protocol.

"Ex, I don't know, wait a minute," a major said.

By the time the major looked back, Ex was gone. Braving heavy ground fire, he landed his single-seater P-51, scooped up his buddy, threw him over his shoulders, and carried him piggyback on the return ride to Allied territory. The mission was taught in subsequent P-51 pilot-training classes, and Ex, although unsure at first whether he was going to be court-martialed or acclaimed a hero, was awarded a Silver Star.

Ex found a hero's welcome awaiting him in Galax, along with a sales job at Vaughan-Bassett Furniture, his father-in-law's plant. When the second generation became old enough to take over the Galax plants, Bunyan's other son-in-law, Buck Higgins, became president of the company, and Bunyan retired to his farm, where he raised purebred Herefords and spent afternoons with his beloved granddaughter, Ex's little girl, Pat. Unlike Mr. J.D., he did not spend his retirement stopping in at the factories every day to make sure the lumber was collated and counted just so.

Belonging to both branches of the furniture dynasty, that little girl was often asked over the years to compare Bassett and Galax. When I brought up the topic not long ago, Pat Bassett's answer seemed rehearsed but genuine. "In Bassett, business was an end unto itself. The people in Bassett were *obsessed*, almost manic about making furniture. But in Galax, the furniture business was a means to an end. It gave you a nice life. It gave people jobs. But you didn't let it take over the whole world."

By the time Ex and his buddies returned from the war, Grand Rapids was no longer the Paris of furniture design—or of anything else. The baby boom was starting, setting Bassett up to become the largest furniture maker in the world, a feat the smaller, laid-back Galax factories could only dream of.

On the other side of the globe, America's former ally China would soon fall under the spell of Mao Tse-tung, making few rural peasants think of sending their children into the cities to work. Capitalism was his enemy; private farming was prohibited, and counterrevolutionaries who opposed collectivization were persecuted as Mao attempted to end dependence on agriculture and make China a world power, no matter the human costs. In Shanghai, some residents avoided the sidewalks so they wouldn't be hit by people committing suicide by jumping from tall buildings.

Little John read about it in the mornings as he delivered the *Roanoke Times*—his first nonfactory job—to his neighbors. Soon after, he started sorting lumber and learning the intricacies of factory work, and when his supervisor gave him a raise, he bragged about it during a family lunch. His father didn't say a word but headed directly to the boy's foreman after lunch and had him rescind the raise.

"Mr. Doug wanted him to know: He wasn't gonna get any preferential treatment because of his last name," said Bassett native John McGhee, who later worked for Mr. Doug. "He was gonna have to earn every inch of what he got. And Bassett beat the hell outta you no matter who you were or department you worked in. *Nobody* was coddled."

The young heir dreamed of the adventures awaiting him and longed to leave the stifling confines of his family's town. In 1952, he finally got his wish. His parents sent him away to Riverside Military Academy, where he would learn to be disciplined—yes, sir; no, sir—and to never ever let things slide. He no longer had servants to pick up his clothes or polish his shoes, and he got his first taste of living someplace where his name—and his family—didn't dominate everything. He loved it.

His sisters began discussing the woman he might one day marry, and his father had his rise to the throne of Bassett Furniture all plotted out.

The Smith River was even tamed, thanks to a fourteen-million-dollar dam-building project funded by the federal government and secured by none other than J.D. Bassett's son-in-law T.B. Stanley (Uncle Bonce), then a congressman.

There was plenty of time for Bassett's youngest heir to rise up and, as his grandpop hoped, do big things. Little John followed in Mr. Doug's footsteps to Washington and Lee University, where he became a popular member of the Kappa Alpha fraternity. He was known for being wild, loud, and competitive, at times insufferably so. Fortunately for his frat brothers, he was also handy with machinery. Having spent most of his teenage summers measuring lumber and tinkering with equipment at the J.D. plant, JBIII knew how to repurpose the Kappa Alpha house's basement soda machine so that it sold beer instead of Coca-Cola, and at the same markup as furniture—double the wholesale price.

"He took the spinning wheel out and just stacked the beer in there, and from then on he was keeper of the beer," recalled fraternity brother and family friend Nelson Teague, now a retired Roanoke urologist. "He didn't need the money; he was obviously not on scholarship at W and L. But he has always been shrewd and innovative—it's in his Bassett genes."

His connections came in handy freshman year when Uncle Bonce, then the governor of Virginia, was called upon to introduce the current Kentucky senator and former vice president Alben Barkley at W&L's mock presidential convention. A quadrennial campaign-season event, the convention is a long-standing W&L tradition that simulates a presidential nominating convention, and it attracts national attention because of its uncanny track record for correctly predicting who a party's presidential nominee will be.

In the sweltering college gym that day, JBIII sat in the front row next to his aunt as Barkley delivered an impassioned speech. "I would rather be a servant in the house of the Lord than to sit in the seats of the mighty," Barkley said to loud applause.

Then he had a heart attack, collapsed, and, almost immediately, died.

It was a sobering moment that drew national press. It came on the heels of several days of convention festivities, including a parade in which states and territories were represented by floats. Some of JBIII's classmates had drawn the Virgin Islands dominion, which they chose to illustrate not by building a float but by borrowing a pair of convertibles from a local Chevy dealer and filling them with students from nearby women's colleges.

VIRGIN read a large sign on the first car, followed by a tiny ISLANDS sign on the second.

Barkley had roared when the float passed him, but the convention merriment was now jarringly halted. Barkley's wife asked Uncle Bonce to make arrangements to have the senator's body transported to Washington from the local mortuary where it had been taken. And the governor asked his nephew to get him to that funeral home.

"Uncle Bonce, I can tell you where the ABC [liquor] store is. But I have no idea where the undertaker is," JBIII said. With a state trooper escort, they found their way, finally, to the funeral home, where the governor banged repeatedly on its locked door. "Whoever's in there, this is Thomas B. Stanley, the governor of Virginia, and I need to speak to you," he barked.

The undertaker did his best to appear lugubrious, JBIII remembered. "But in his wildest imagination he never thought he'd have the vice president of the United States in his shop. He was trying not to smile because, after all, this was a very sad time."

In the limousine on the way back to W&L, Bonce looked at his nephew and, with a half grin, said, "That man enjoys his work, doesn't he?"

* * *

I accompanied JBIII on a February 2013 visit to address a W&L business-journalism class. It was an important moment to him, a chance to show the academics that he was no longer the wild man he had been decades before — though he did wear a pink tie embossed with tiny hula dancers (they were visible only when you saw them up close). He pointed out his old fraternity house, the field where he'd gone parking with girls visiting from Hollins College and Sweet Briar, and — of course — the liquor store. He brought along his executive assistant, Sheila Key, and a young IT employee who advanced the slides on his PowerPoint presentation. "I don't iPad! I have people who iPad!" he told me once, discarding technology in favor of his grandfather's favorite activity: thinking up new ways for his company to make cash.

At W&L, Little John had majored in business administration, excelled in partying, and gotten grades just good enough to avoid having his father yank him out of his collegiate reverie the way Mr. Doug's own father had done to him. (One semester, though, Mr. Doug did take away John's car as punishment until his grades improved.)

"I can assure you I was not Phi Beta Kappa. I got out, okay?" He still reads slowly — waking up before five a.m. so he has time to scan five newspapers for international and business news in front of his kitchen fireplace. But what he reads, he remembers, especially numbers. And especially those numbers that represent cash, such as figures from long-ago balance sheets I heard him recite to the dollar, with astonishing accuracy, time and time again. He forgot many conversations we had, frequently repeated himself, and several times told me to read business books or articles that I had initially recommended to *him*. But when dollars were involved, he gave the same figures every time, and his numbers always checked out.

When he graduated from Washington and Lee, in 1959, the headstrong heir did something nobody expected: He went as far away from Bassett, Virginia, as he could. He imagined it would be his last chance. He joined the army and relished the opportunity to have his butt chewed out by someone whose name wasn't Bassett. In fact, chances were good that his commanding officers didn't even know what Bassett Furniture was. Or care!

He took a page from the cowboys in Galax, and for the next three years he found his own work, finally, on top of an army tank. The factories, the town, and the family squabbles—all that would be waiting for him.

Far away in Europe, "Nobody could get their arms around me," he recalled.

6

Company Man

They used to say of Mr. J.D., "The old fool dyes his hair."
People in Bassett were tough. The long knives were
usually out.

—Spencer Morten

A lot happened while Little John was away guarding the German border and proving to himself that he was a fighter and a patriot, a person who could rise to the rank of first lieutenant by merit rather than by his name. Mr. W.M., his CEO uncle, had just spent seven million dollars to modernize Bassett Furniture Industries, doubling the size of many of the plants. When his competitors copied him and added conveyor systems of their own, W.M. went a step further to lower his overhead: Using leftover sawdust and coal, he made his own power for the factories and the five hundred Bassett-owned homes. Then he sold the excess power he made back to the power company and used the profits to pay the street sweeper and town police.

"Gentlemen, get out your smelling salts," W.M. told his regional salesmen gathered for the Chicago Furniture Market, beaming beneath his trademark fedora. The salesmen had brought him pictures of what the competitors were selling, thanks to intelligence gathered by friends from a third-party retailing organization. Designer Leo Jiranek was there with his sketchbook and Bassett's sample man, the person who turned the drawings into wooden prototypes. W.M. would build the same suite his competitors were selling, and, with Bassett Speed Lines operating at full tilt, he would do it at a price that could not be matched by competitors in the twenty thousand retail stores where Bassett furniture was sold.

With his ulcers long since healed, W.M. was a relentless patriarch— insiders called him the number one Daddy Rabbit of the industry— but he was also gentlemanly and fair. If he asked a question but didn't like the answer an employee gave, he'd cock his head and say, "How's that again?" rather than chew him out on the spot. According to Junior Thomas, he was "real proper-like"—by which he meant, Mr. W.M. did not terrorize the maids.

"We wanted for nothing," recalled Betty Shelton, whose parents worked as W.M.'s chauffeur and cook and who grew up in a house down the hill from Eltham that was owned by W.M.'s family. "They bought our school clothes and things. We ate breakfast at their house every Christmas and were just loaded up with presents. When my brother went to prom the first year, [W.M.'s wife, Gladys] let him take her big crystal punch bowl to Carver School," she said, of the segregation-era high school for blacks.

W.M. Bassett carried a small ledger book in his suit pocket in which he kept up-to-the-minute balances of the factories' accounts, all held at the Bassett bank. "He'd pull out his little book and go, 'Let's see, there's eight over at Bassett Mirror, twelve at Bassett Furniture, and four over at Superior,' and what he was talking about was *millions*," retired Roanoke banker Warner Dalhouse told me.

W.M. could price a piece of furniture in an instant, calculating material costs, the overhead, and the profit margin in his head. He knew almost every BFI employee by name, and he knew the names of many of their children too. Reared in the Mr. J.D. mold, he wore a suit every day, as well as a pair of severe, black-framed glasses. He chain-smoked Lucky Strikes and frequently strode around the factories with his left hand tucked in the pocket of his suit jacket.

"He had absolutely no personal ego," said Jerome Neff, a sales representative who worked alongside his father, also a Bassett salesman, the first twenty years of his career. "W.M.'s greatest joy was at the close of the day in the showrooms at Market in New York or Chicago.

"He'd break out a bottle, and the old salesmen would have a few drinks, and he loved that because they were his boys."

Having learned the industry from the bottom up starting on day one, W.M. had sorted his share of lumber as a child, and he is included in the first known picture of the sawmillers turned Bassett Furniture workers, taken in 1902, sporting holey knickers and crooked bangs. A wide-eyed eight-year-old perched on a jumble of boards, he's surrounded by a cast of characters who look like they could have tumbled out of the reels of *Bonnie and Clyde*. He learned deal-making from the same wily sawmillers who'd taken that railroad lumber buyer for a ride.

When the Teamsters threatened to unionize Bassett Trucking in 1945, it was W.M. who engineered an end run designed to keep them as far away from his furniture workers as possible. He organized a merger of Bassett's trucking operations, housed near the J.D. plants, with another trucking company owned by an ambitious and stubborn entrepreneur named Roy Stone, then moved the whole setup to Collinsville — eight miles away from the nearest Bassett plant.

A strike threatened to halt Stone's business, but for weeks on end, Stone and his sons personally drove their own trucks rather than give in to the strikers' demands — until the Teamsters grew frustrated and eventually left the region. "He knew the Teamsters would be so distracted in Collinsville they'd leave Bassett alone," Spencer Morten, W.M.'s son-in-law, told me. "It was a strategic move on Daddy Bill's part...very subtle and very quietly handled.

"He didn't want them unionizing the woodworkers. So he distracted them, and when they left, he was tickled."

W.M. worked ten-hour days well into his sixties despite having high blood pressure, which he refused medication for (he called it "dope").

That and the Lucky Strikes were a dangerous combination. While driving back to his Eltham mansion from a weekend getaway in Roanoke in 1960, he blacked out, crashed the car, and died. He was sixty-five.

On the day of W.M.'s funeral, the community closed the stores, factories, and the Henry County Circuit Court. "He was the man who made Bassett what it was, a salesman from the word go and a great financier," said longtime Bassett sales manager Bob Merriman.

With W.M.'s passing, the chairmanship fell to Little John's father, Mr. Doug, who appointed his cousin Ed Bassett (C.C.'s son) to be his number two. By all accounts, he made Mr. Ed feel subordinate, never relinquishing his preferred parking space or the head boardroom chair. "Mr. Doug Bassett used to treat Mr. Ed Bassett like a piece of dog poop, and I don't think Mr. Ed ever forgot it," one Bassett manager told me.

Months after Spencer Morten learned of Clay Barbour's lineage, he told me he'd developed another theory explaining Doug Bassett's shoddy treatment of his cousin Ed. He remembered Ed, his close friend and fishing companion, telling him once in Florida, "Our family's had some chapters we're not proud of, and Doug used it against us." You mean Doug looked down on Mr. Ed because of his black half brother and used that knowledge to his advantage? I asked Spencer. "I think Ed wanted that information kept away from the rest of his family," he said.

Whatever the motivation, that tension was the genesis of a cutthroat succession battle that would play out over decades. Which branch of the family would run the show?

This is the Bassett Furniture Industries that First Lieutenant John Bassett III came home to in 1962, after three years of keeping Western Europe safe from the threat of communism by day and having the time of his life by night. He spoke enough German to get along with the girls, and it had cost him just sixteen cents a gallon to fill up his new favorite toy: a Porsche. "You'd go ski in the Alps and stay in a beautiful room and pay maybe a dollar fifty a day," he recalled. "The Danes were really good-looking. The Swedes were even better-looking, but they're cold."

He was having such a good time that Mr. Doug worried he would reenlist after his tour was over, so he sent Jane and her new husband, Bob Spilman, to Germany to convince him not to.

"Ya gotta come back!" his brother-in-law bellowed, pounding his fist on the table where they sat.

Before the couple returned to Bassett, Jane pulled her brother aside and said, "I don't blame you. I'd stay here too."

He may have missed being part of the Greatest Generation, but JBIII credits everything he knows about leadership to his three years of active duty. Which is why he quotes Churchill at every opportunity. And Patton, especially the line "When in doubt, attack."

"There are certain principles of leadership that people respect," he said. "You can't buy it either. You have to earn it."

When he returned to Bassett Furniture, there was no buying respect from his family, even if his name was John Bassett III. In fact, he would spend the rest of his life trying to earn it.

"You could tell he was loved in the family, but he was in no way revered," said a household servant who watched the succession battle unfold.

The executive offices were on the third floor of the new $1.8 million corporate headquarters in the center of Bassett, a four-story building the locals still call the Taj Mahal, only half jokingly. Mr. Doug had the primo CEO suite in the Taj, JBIII's office was next door, and Mr. Ed's was third in line.

From the very beginning, it was clear: the older guys could dismiss Little John all they wanted, but as far as Mr. Doug was concerned, John Bassett III would one day run the show at Bassett Furniture. The young heir hung the framed letter from Grandpop behind his desk, making the succession a virtual slam dunk; it was not far from a picture of himself astride an army tank.

The army picture was okay with his old man, but a few things JBIII picked up in the army weren't. One was the Porsche he had shipped backed from Germany, a cream-colored convertible with a red interior. It struck his father as showy and un-American. "Doug made him trade it in for a clunky Chevy," Spencer Morten said. The car was so rarefied in 1962 Henry County that the day it went up for sale, three doctors from Martinsville had a bidding war over it.

The other thing that rubbed Mr. Doug wrong—and his wife and daughters too—was the photo JBIII brought back of his busty, blond German girlfriend. People whispered that he intended to marry the woman. At a time of lingering anti-German sentiment, that was a positively *un-American* idea in Bassett, Virginia. When JBIII was in Germany, though, patriotism had proved to be no match for hormones. "He had a really good time with the girls in Germany," Teague, a fraternity brother, told me. "He liked that they were a little freer over there." ("Freer?" JBIII roared, when I told him what Nelson said. "How about just *free?*")

But a fräulein would never do for a Bassett man. Several years before, the family had helped arrange Jane's marriage. From a North Carolina textile family, Bob Spilman had gone to North Carolina State University with Jane's cousin, John Vaughan, of the Galax family branch. Bob was in John Vaughan's wedding, which Jane missed because she was vacationing in Europe. By the time the family threw a party for him, Jane was dating a young lawyer in Richmond and working for a bank. She didn't want to attend, but her father called and said it would be rude not to, she recalled.

That party would forever change the fate of Bassett Furniture and John Bassett III. Not to mention the Richmond lawyer, who would soon be toast. Bernard "Bunny" Wampler, Spilman's fraternity brother at North Carolina State, remembers the party well. "Spilman walks in and says, 'Damn, look at all these rich women! What do you say I go and marry one of 'em?'"

By the time Jane and Bob married, in 1954, Doug Bassett was

suitably impressed with his son-in-law, a hard-charging veteran of the Korean conflict and a former West Point instructor who read the *Wall Street Journal* and traveled regularly to California by plane as a New York–based sales manager for Cannon Mills. "He's on a plane out to California, and Bill and I haven't even been out there yet," he marveled.

JBIII may have started out with the coveted office space, but down the road, in the sales offices of the Bassett Chair plant, Bob Spilman was the one to watch. "When Robert got here, believe me, he was a go-getting somebody," Jane Bassett Spilman said. "And he was a trader like you can't believe. He'd rather save ten dollars in a trade than make a hundred dollars just in a yawn. He liked the challenge of talking people into things. If I were God and I could have put him in the best position he could be in, it would be mergers and acquisitions."

The acquisitions would come later, in spades. For now, Spilman had to prove himself as more than a favored son-in-law. And John Bassett III had to prove himself as more than a Porsche-driving skirt-chaser. His dad put him in charge of quality control, which meant he roamed from plant to plant suggesting improvements and taking notes, just as his father had done. He got to know the different plant managers and was able to study every aspect of furniture-making.

But some perceived him as a tattletale, Little Lord Fauntleroy with a legal pad. When a new plant opened or an employee received a service award, JBIII was happy to get his picture in the *Martinsville Bulletin* or the *Bassett Pioneer,* which didn't earn him points with Mr. Ed in the office next door. Several former managers told me JBIII thought nothing of skipping the chain of command and going directly to his father instead of Ed, whose memory, he would soon learn, was as long and roiling as the Smith River.

JBIII's demeanor was as cocky as it was charismatic. According to Reuben Scott, who reported to him for several years, JBIII's initial factory-man tenure was fraught, fueled by insecurity and a misguided sense of what a Bassett heir was supposed to know and do. Scott recalled him making a costly mistake on an entire order of dressers — a mistake his father berated him for publicly, then insisted he stay late to correct.

"At first you couldn't tell him anything," Scott, now ninety-two, told me from his nursing-home bed in Stanleytown. (Childless and widowed, he was on oxygen the two times I visited him, but he was mentally sharp and thrilled to talk about his factory days.) "He wouldn't ask for help, I guess because he thought he was already supposed to know everything. But he got better."

From his room at the Martinsville hospital, where he spent the last five years of his life, Mr. J.D. kept an eye on his namesake. A chauffeur picked the old man up daily for drives around Henry County so he could check on the bank and the plants, and every year on Mr. J.D.'s birthday, the local newspaper ran a feature on him with a picture. In one, his uniformed chauffeur stands next to the Cadillac while Mr. J.D. and his nurse pose next to the Smith holding a fish he had just caught (well, *someone* caught it). In another, chauffeur James Thompson is handing him a copy of the *Henry County Journal*. The cigar is in Mr. J.D.'s mouth, and the nurse is in the backseat forcing a half smile.

One afternoon, between plant visits, JBIII stopped by the hospital to see his grandfather.

"What time do the factories close, son?" Mr. J.D. wanted to know.

"They close at four," JBIII said.

"And what time is it now?" he asked, pointing to the grandfather clock he'd had hauled up to his hospital room.

It was not even close to four o'clock.

"You go back and go to work, and, when the factories close, *then* you come see your grandfather."

The message was clear: there was no leaving early, even if you were the boss's son, and there was definitely no acting like you were better than the workers on the line, the people who were busy making *you* rich. Mr. J.D. had hammered that into his moody son, Doug, as a child, chiding him during a carriage ride through the town of Bassett.

"What is wrong with you today, boy?" the old man boomed. "We have passed a lot of people on the streets, and you've just sat there like a cigar-store Indian while I have doffed my hat and waved and smiled and nodded on both sides of the street. And you have not even acknowledged anybody."

It wasn't so easy to be the company heir in a small company town. People talked incessantly about your family. And there was always pressure to be the world's largest as well as the world's best. At Spilman's urging, Mr. Ed had recently gotten the company into the upholstery business, buying a plant called Prestige in Newton, North Carolina, which, according to a press release in 1963, made Bassett the "largest manufacturer of wood furniture in the world." A year earlier, the company celebrated its sixtieth anniversary by hanging banners across the town that read $60 THOUSAND TO $60 MILLION IN 60 YEARS. It also laid claim to the world's largest chair, a Duncan Phyfe model that Jiranek designed as a publicity stunt for Curtis Brothers Furniture Company in Washington, DC. It was nineteen feet tall and weighed 4,600 pounds; state patrolmen had to shut down a portion of the highway just to get it trucked to Washington. But that was no problem for Bassett, a company that had friends—as well as relatives, like Uncle Bonce—in high places.

"Discover Bassett..." whispered a short-skirted model in a *Look* magazine ad featuring a bright yellow canopy bed and an avocado-colored upholstered couch made in the company's newly acquired Prestige Furniture. "Bassett Lets You Show Your Style Now," announced an ad in *Reader's Digest* in which a wife crocheted in an avocado-colored chair while her husband and dog slept on dueling plaid couches, his smoking pipe at rest atop a brass-handled coffee table.

The company was advertising in *Life* and *Look* magazines and buying up smaller companies, a strategy that helped it nearly double sales in four years. Thanks to the baby boom, the entire furniture industry was now a four-billion-dollar concern, with furniture receiving the third-largest share of consumer dollars, behind only houses and cars.

The rebels had long since won the Furniture War between the States: of the thirty largest manufacturers, twenty-three were now in the 150-mile furniture belt stretching from Bassett to Lenoir.

Mr. J.D. had carved a multimillion-dollar empire out of cornfields and foothills, and the pressure was on his heirs to keep up the exponential growth. No one gave a thought to the Bretton Woods Agreements that had been negotiated among Allied nations in 1944, or the General Agreement on Tariffs and Trade (GATT) that followed in 1947, establishing the international trading system and setting up a sequence of global trade negotiations designed to lower trade barriers on a "mutually advantageous basis" between the countries involved.

Doug and Bill hadn't yet landed in California, after all, much less in China, where Mao Tse-tung spent much of the 1960s building state-owned factories, after banning private enterprise and foreign investments, and initiating the Cultural Revolution to keep the naysayers grindingly in check, starving and executing millions in the process. "We took the furniture, pots, and pans we had in our house, and all our neighbors did likewise," said a teacher in rural Shanghai, speaking of Mao's Great Leap Forward. "We put everything in a big fire and melted down all the metal" for use in government-directed infrastructure projects.

China would modernize using the principles of diligence and frugality, Mao wrote in his *Little Red Book* manifesto, first published in 1964. "Nor will it be legitimate to relax if, fifty years later, modernization is realized on a mass scale," Mao proclaimed.

From Beijing to Bassett, no one was relaxing, especially not JBIII, who'd been smart to take the postcollege time-out from the business. His father was strict and, occasionally, erratic. Managers recalled Mr. Doug entering the boardroom and barking to his cousin Mr. Ed, "Get the hell out of my seat!"

Barber Coy Young remembered Mr. Doug chewing John out on the sidewalk in front of Bassett headquarters for the whole town to see.

W.M. Bassett had paid for the stress with ulcers and high blood pressure, while Doug was known to have his first cocktail not long after his postlunch nap. "Doug maybe expected too much of his own abilities, and that took him to drink," Spencer Morten said.

To encourage the young men in his family to get along better, Doug suggested they join forces to form a new subsidiary of Bassett Furniture, a plastics supplier called Dominion Ornamental that made frames for Bassett Mirror. Morten ran the company, which was jointly owned by several of the third-generation heirs, including Spilman and John. The venture made the men a bundle, but it was not the family healer it was intended to be.

For one thing, Spilman would not defer to anyone, repeatedly going over Morten's and the other directors' heads, even negotiating the final details of the company's sale to Libby Owens Ford three years later. Each director walked away with $800,000 from an initial investment of $35,000. "And no one's thanked me yet," said Spencer Morten, still happy with the windfall but sore that his power was usurped.

Spilman's moneymaking instincts were right on, as usual. But "he was a real asshole about it," Morten said.

During our third interview, Spencer Morten invited me to touch the bump on the crown of his head. He got it the first time he knocked heads with a Bassett. He was a World War II medic, a Midwesterner by birth. And when the army weapons carrier he was riding in crashed, he hit his head on the carrier's Bassett Furniture–made frame.

Morten was not born into the family fortune he now shares with his wife, Mary Elizabeth Bassett Morten, whom he dotes on, with assistance from the help, at their homes in Bassett and Hobe Sound.

When he showed up in Martinsville to work for the newspaper, he carried a single suitcase. He met his wife at a bridge game arranged by the sister of Mr. Doug's wife. Mary Elizabeth and Spencer married at Eltham, after which Mr. W.M. installed Spencer in management at Bassett Mirror, where he worked for fifty years. For twenty-seven of those years, he represented his wife's family's considerable Bassett stock holdings as a member of the Bassett Furniture Industries board, and, believe me, he knows where the bodies are buried — even the ones along the edge of the family cemetery. During several interviews, he spoke animatedly and with surprising candor, as if he'd been waiting sixty years for someone to come along and ask him how it all felt. A former reporter, he even helped me track down long-gone employees and household servants.

It was Spencer, in fact, who first told me how Mr. Doug finally disposed of his son's fräulein, in a scene that must have broken the young heir's heart. Mr. Doug had heard she was flying in with her mother to visit John, much to the Bassett family's chagrin. To head them off, Doug dispatched Leo Jiranek, the company's signature designer, to meet them when their plane landed in New York. Jiranek dutifully treated them to lunch at his favorite place, the Princeton Club, then put them on the next plane to Germany, explaining that JBIII had changed his mind about the woman.

"But that's a chapter John does not want to talk about," Spencer warned me. Jiranek's son Bob said the same thing.

Sure enough, when I broached the subject with JBIII, he snapped, "Girlfriend in Germany? I'm not gonna tell you about that."

There are very few topics that John Bassett III won't discuss, but after spending the better part of two years interviewing him, I'd apparently landed on one. He changed the subject, talking about the first apartment he shared with Pat, his wife of fifty years, a run-down duplex that was spitting distance from the train tracks in Bassett. "This wasn't about being affluent. It was about settling down, and going to work, and being successful. I mean, don't make it complicated.

"You knew what was expected of you, and [the workers] knew what was expected of them. Got it?"

Got it. Subject dismissed. According to the Bassetts, it was the simplest story in the world.

7

Lineage and Love

*There is nobody in the world that can take care
of a woman like another woman.*

—JBIII

The women in the family waited until they reached the Galax city limits to give Little John the news: he was about to meet the woman of his dreams. It was September 1962. The occasion was the funeral of Vaughan-Bassett Furniture Company founder Bunyan Vaughan, and the entire Bassett clan was paying its respects to a fellow industry leader. Bunyan Vaughan was related by marriage to the Bassetts, and his company was related to them, too, having been started with Bassett money.

The women had ample experience in matters of love and money. Mr. J.D. was a nonagenarian widower now, with steady companionship provided by his chauffeur and his full-time nurse, who was in her sixties. The daughters and granddaughters had had a *lot* to say about that, having called a family meeting to share the news that someone had found Grandpop very happily *sleeping* with his nurse. The women were aghast, worried she would lay claim to the family fortune, though there was scant evidence to suggest that the nurse had anything other than caretaking and companionship in mind.

The Bassett men, however, had an entirely different response than their wives. The two were fooling around. It was mutual, nobody was getting hurt.

"You women be quiet," Mr. J.D.'s Galax grandson George Vaughan snapped. "What we need to do is find out how the hell he's pulling it off!"

Ultimately, the women prevailed, moving Mr. J.D. to the hospital in Martinsville, where he spent his final years. With more eyes on him, the theory went, the hanky-panky would stop, and the fortune would be safe. "There is nobody in the world that can take care of a woman like another woman," JBIII recalled, shaking his head. "Men who don't understand that are stupid."

The women were now immersed in finding Little John a mate. Every sister was in charge of picking somebody, and Pat Vaughan Exum had gotten letters from Jane about him. Pat was a student at Jane's alma mater, Hollins College, an old liberal arts finishing school for the elite daughters of the South—the Hollie Collies, they were nicknamed. It was the kind of college to which young women were (and still are) encouraged to bring their horses. (Back in the antebellum era, they were even invited to bring their slaves.)

Pat was related to Miss Pokey—her great-grandmother was the matriarch's sister, making her a fourth cousin to Little John. She was also the granddaughter of Bunyan Vaughan, a position that entwined her lineage as well as her stock holdings with the Bassett corporate/family tree.

"Put on your lipstick," Pat's mother told her at the start of the funeral reception, held at the Vaughan family estate. "They have brought John Bassett up here to meet you."

John stood silent as Jane asked Pat all the questions, firing-line-style, without missing a beat. What year was she at Hollins? What was her phone number? What were the rules these days on leaving campus for a date? "She was all over it," Pat recalled.

Mourners lined the room, and they all fell silent as people strained to listen in when the two finally spoke. JBIII told Pat he was sorry about her grandfather and got her number, and then everyone commenced talking again. Years later, he would recall of his future wife's figure, "That girl could put some wrinkles in a blouse."

Two weeks later, they went on their first date. He didn't want to risk asking her for a weekend date, in case she was already busy, so he proposed a Wednesday-night dinner instead. They courted twice a week for nearly a year, dining regularly at an exclusive Roanoke club where his parents were members.

And though Wyatt Exum wished his daughter would stay and finish college, Pat said her mother could see how much they were in love, and she urged the couple on. Pat earned her "Mrs." degree instead and never looked back, she insisted. A music major "with no discernible talent," as she put it, chuckling, she saved herself the embarrassment of the dreaded senior piano recital by dropping out after her junior year.

The bride wore her mother's satin wedding gown designed with an oval neckline of rose-point lace, an elongated basque, and a shirred skirt ending in a court train, according to the wedding announcement. Spencer Morten recalled Mr. Doug leaning toward him at the reception and saying: "Good for John. He's got him a good American car and now a good American woman, a Baptist even!"

The kissing cousins have learned to ward off jokes by beating observers to the punch line. "We're so inbred around here, our family tree is a palm," their son J. Doug Bassett IV deadpanned. When my story about John Bassett ran in the *Roanoke Times,* their daughter, Fran, wrote to thank me for explaining, finally, exactly how her parents were related. She'd never before understood.

The couple honeymooned in Hawaii, then set up house in the modest Bassett apartment within hollering distance of the factories. The windows rattled when the trains passed.

They were a long way from their golf-course mansion in a gated Florida community, decades from claiming Tiger Woods as a neighbor. It was 1963, and the young couple had little concern for China, where Mao Tse-tung was declaring, "Communism is not love! Communism is a hammer we use to destroy our enemies!"

Mr. and Mrs. John Bassett III had also yet to hear of a Chinese force of nature named Larry Moh, a Wharton School grad who had just launched a parquet-flooring company in Hong Kong and whose ideas—heaven help the Southern furniture makers toiling away in the Taj Mahal—would one day threaten to transform the South's humming factories into stagnant piles of bricks.

Pat Vaughan Exum Bassett settled into the hilltop hierarchy, where moneymaking was the rule and her in-laws called the shots. At the Taj Mahal, her father-in-law, Mr. Doug, delegated most of the factory details to Bob Spilman and Mr. Ed—especially during the winter, when he usually retreated to Hobe Sound. He was more consumed with finance and furniture design than manufacturing. Mr. Doug phoned his nephew-in-law Spencer Morten at home late one night, announced himself as J.D. Bassett Jr., and barked that he wanted a complete report on Bassett Mirror's finances by nine thirty the next morning. Spencer stayed up till midnight compiling it—only to have Doug brush it off with a cursory "Looks like you guys are doing well."

Doug had been drinking when he phoned, Spencer explained, and he'd forgotten all about his call. By the next morning he was preoccupied with arranging his afternoon tee time at the Bassett Country Club, where he took an avid interest in the maintenance of the course, regularly dispatching a truckload of factory workers to the club to help—a habit that still inspires fury in several long-retired plant managers when they think about it.

Underlings could tell how their mornings would go by how loudly Mr. Doug's foot sounded when it landed on the wooden step outside his office. If a manager spent too long in the bathroom, he might counsel him to take the *Wall Street Journal* into the stall. If the manager was going to waste company time, he should at least be thinking while he did it. If supervisors wanted to change a supplier for their sandpaper, they had to run it by Mr. Doug first, or risk infuriating him by souring some long-standing backroom deal the family had made.

Doug's best friend and confidant was his next-door neighbor and cocktail-hour buddy Whit Sales, the man who ran the Bassett-owned Blue Ridge Hardware. Whit and his wife, Virginia, couldn't have children, and they treated Doug Bassett's four as their own. The relationship was complicated and symbiotic, like a lot of things in Bassett, with Sales proving himself a reliable surrogate—and an extra set of company eyes—but always deferring to Doug.

This extended to hiring decisions, from the corporate office right on down to the person sweeping up at night. When Henry County native Joe Philpott returned home after college in 1955, he landed a job working for Sales—only to have Sales rescind the offer after discovering that Mr. Doug wanted Joe to learn the management ropes at Bassett instead. (Doug was incensed when he found out during one happy hour that Sales had nabbed him first, and Sales quickly set about undoing the deed.) The furniture job paid Joe considerably less than what Sales had offered. So, to make up for it, Doug dropped by the plants every couple of months, tapped Joe on the shoulder, and told him his salary had just been upped.

That the Bassett rule was arbitrary, completely at the whim of whichever Bassett was calling the shots, was both the best thing and the worst thing about working in a company town. Since there was no town council, churches and service clubs were left to organize civic projects. Mr. Doug ran the school board and the country club, while Mr. Ed was keeper of the Kiwanis. Doug's branch of the family held the reins of Pocahontas Bassett Baptist, while Ed's controlled the Methodist church. Nobody passed Go without the family's blessing.

To outsiders, the extended-family hierarchy seemed equally fraught. When cousin Bonce Stanley was governor, Mr. Ed used to call ahead before church on Sundays to see if the governor was in town. If Bonce was in Richmond, Ed went to church. If the governor was in Henry County, Ed stayed home. He resented the idea of having to stand when the governor—who was not only his cousin by marriage but also his furniture competitor—entered the sanctuary.

Like most newcomers, John D. Bassett High football coach Colbert "Mick" Micklem did not receive a memo on the way things worked when he moved to Bassett, in 1961. Mick had planned to put the proceeds from the season's first football game toward new equipment, but he quickly learned the Kiwanis Club had dibs on the money. Mr. Ed made sure the game sold out by requiring his furniture salesmen to buy tickets by mail, despite the fact that they were scattered across the United States and couldn't have attended the game even if they'd wanted to. Tackle dummies for the team had to be ordered through the family-owned Blue Ridge Hardware too—or neighbor Sales might complain to Mr. Doug.

"The county owned the school, but the family owned everything from one foot around it. Everything, even the sports fields, belonged to Bassett Furniture Industries," Mick told me. The exception was the smattering of independently owned stores, including a furniture store—which sold Bassett Furniture, of course.

But paternalism could also be beneficial, as it was when Mick and his wife went to the First National Bank of Bassett to apply for a seven-thousand-dollar loan to buy their first home. The bank manager he met with said he'd have to talk to the board and would get back to him, at which point chairman Doug Bassett popped in the bank doors, and he happened to be in a good mood. "Hello, Coach! What do these fine folks want?" he asked his manager.

"They want a loan."

"Well, give it to 'em. They're good folks!" He didn't even ask how much the loan was for. When a Bassett deemed you fine folks, the deal was done.

Mr. Doug kept the tightest rein on Little John, whom he considered brilliant but undisciplined. It was okay that Little John wasn't the humblest of people, but he should have the courtesy to at least *act* like he was.

"Motivation by intimidation," Mick told me. "That was the motto back in those days." The most important thing was always, Are the factories running full-time? Are we selling more furniture now than we did last month?

That relentlessness became an enduring legacy of Mr. J.D., who lived to be ninety-eight years old. He was seventeen months shy of the century mark and $17 million shy of hitting $100 million in sales at the time of his death, in February 1965. He died in his room at the Martinsville General Hospital, where his family had moved him, not just because they wanted to put some space between the old man and the nurse-girlfriend but also because he'd let his Victorian house on the hill fall into disrepair. "Miss Pokey said J.D. was too stingy and wouldn't let her spend the money, so it was just never fixed up," said a neighbor whose grandparents were close friends and original investors in the company.

Barber Coy Young recalled seeing the old man being chauffeured around town in his black Cadillac, and he remembered with great clarity meeting the man when he was a teenager. Coy was playing baseball with his friends near Mr. J.D.'s home, when he tiptoed into his garden to fetch an errant ball, nearly running into Mr. J.D., who'd stopped by his house to pick vegetables.

"Come here, boy, and help me." He beckoned to Coy, then tapped his cane on the cucumber he wanted him to pick. He wore bedroom slippers and pajamas, and he carried his trademark unlit cigar. And even though Coy was scared of the ghostly-seeming grump, he thought it was a little bit pitiful when the old man said, "They tell me I'm a millionaire, and I don't even have a suit of clothes!"

In her pressed uniform and stiff white shoes, his last nurse — not the amorous one — just about killed herself looking out for him at the hospital and on his daily outings, Young said. "He was one of those who got meaner the older he got. He thought he was staying at the hospital for free because he'd donated a lot of money to it earlier. But the family was paying for it." (Mr. Doug was a hospital trustee.)

According to the inventory of his estate, at the time of his death he had $6.3 million in assets (about $48 million in today's dollars), including sizable stock holdings in the myriad furniture companies he'd founded and in tobacco, coal, railroads, oil, and automobile companies. His children inherited it all, except for some bequests. He left sixteen thousand dollars to his longtime maid Gracie Wade, the one who succeeded Mary Hunter. He also left ten thousand dollars to his personal secretary, who'd told a reporter once that she'd been too busy working for the industries to ever get married.

His nurse got three thousand dollars. According to a handwritten note he filed with his will documents, Mr. J.D. had originally promised to leave her eight thousand but he wanted the money he'd lent her in 1959—to pay for her husband's hospital costs and burial expenses—to be deducted from the initial promised gift.

He left his personal home and surrounding land to the Pocahontas Bassett Baptist Church. If the building ever ceased to be a church, he noted in wobbly cursive, then it should be given over to the "benefit of the white citizens of the Bassett community" to become a community center and a "playground for white youth."

Area journalists poured on the love in numerous newspaper editorials, like this sweeping tribute:

> Unlocked and still free of the shrouds of the casket and tightly secured walls of the burial vault, the heritage of an indomitable will hovered, as it will through the ages, along the factory-lined banks of the Smith River; the products of a spirit of conquest and great strength rumble by train and truck into every corner of the nation and to marketplaces throughout the world.

A little more than a year after Mr. J.D.'s death, Mr. Doug was diagnosed with end-stage spine and neck cancer. The announcement was a total shocker, and it heralded a succession issue that would haunt Mr. Doug's only son and threaten to sever both business and family ties for decades.

Few people understood why, at the age of sixty-five, Mr. Doug had a major change of heart. Few could explain why, on his deathbed in the hospital, he called in some members of the Bassett Furniture board to announce a change in succession: now, upon Mr. Doug's death, cousin Ed would move up to chairman of the board, and Bob Spilman, the hotshot son-in-law, would become Ed Bassett's number two.

"But what about John?" asked Spencer Morten, board member and in-law.

"John will be handling my estate," Doug said.

Mary Elizabeth Morten, one of the largest Bassett stockholders at the time, said she never understood why Doug chose his son-in-law over his own son. But Spencer has a memory of his uncle's final hour: As Spencer walked into Mr. Doug's room, he passed Jane Bassett Spilman walking out. The favorite child. The one Doug called his conscience. The daughter who had arranged her brother's marriage.

The one with the mind of a man, as her father liked to brag.

After Spencer offered that missing piece of the family saga, I remembered the furniture store I visited when I began chasing this tale. Amid the bucketfuls of plunking rain, owner Delano Thomasson had shared a critical piece of information that few members of the Bassett family were willing to reveal. It resulted in both the worst thing that ever happened to John Bassett III and, though it would take him decades to understand it, the best.

The last-minute double-cross stung him and it humbled him and ultimately, it made one helluva fighter out of Little John.

"It's real simple," Delano told me. "Jane hugged Papa and got her man the job."

PART III

PART III

8

Navigating the New Landscape

We used to wonder why she spent so much time at the
college picking out bathroom fixtures.
—ANNA LOGAN LAWSON ON JANE BASSETT SPILMAN

While Mr. Ed managed the town's affairs via the company and the Kiwanis Club, which he ruled with an iron fist, Bob Spilman stuck to business and rarely mixed with the townspeople. He frequently asked barber Coy Young to cut his hair early in the morning, before the shop opened, so he wouldn't be seen. He joined neither the church started by C.C. Bassett (Methodist) nor the one started by J.D. (Baptist). Though he was originally from North Carolina, the nephew of a prominent textile manufacturer, Spilman had arrived in Bassett by way of the Connecticut suburbs of New York City. He thought that, socially, Bassett was Death Valley—and he said so, loudly, more than once.

Though Jane may have secured his future as company president, Spilman thought it would look wimpy to have his wife conspicuously involved in company affairs. In the corporate world of the 1960s, that just wasn't done. Company officers suggested he appoint Jane to the

Bassett board, but "I knew it would be a cold day in hell before that happened," Jane said.

I knew Jane had relished talking about the factories with her father so I asked whether her husband at least shared what was happening at the Taj Mahal with her over dinner. "I wish you hadn't asked me that question," she said, and she seemed genuinely stung. "But the answer is no. And it used to break...my...heart."

Jane exerted her power in other ways. She had a new clubhouse built for the Bassett Country Club and appointed herself head of town beautification, concerning herself with such details as the color of paint on the company homes and store facades and how frequently the streets were cleaned and the grass along the highways mowed. She became the first woman to chair the board of her alma mater, Hollins College, where she's remembered as a driven, but cheerful, powerhouse.

A diminutive blonde with stick-straight posture, she wore navy blue suits with brass buttons to board meetings and ran roughshod over fund-raising protocols, faculty input, and presidential search committees. Her phone conversations were purposeful and direct, always ending with a breezy "Do be of good cheer!"

The gorgeous new Wyndham Robertson Library on campus? She nailed the ask for that one, charming Wyndham's billionaire brother, Julian Robertson, and securing three million dollars toward the fourteen-million-dollar project in a single visit. She even chose the architect for the project, all the better to ensure it matched the other traditional brick squares on campus and suited her vision to a tee.

Bill Young, Bassett's retired corporate communications director, recalled Jane sealing the deal on a two-million-dollar donation to Hollins from a Bassett board member—during a single fifteen-minute car ride. She was efficient, if imperious, in her role, once discarding a lesbian board-member nominee for the Hollins board because "she's not our kind," according to fellow board member Anna Logan Lawson, and concerning herself with every detail of an alumni-quarters renovation, down to picking out the faucets.

"But when the students met with her, she really spoke to them as a powerful woman who could get stuff done," added Lawson, an anthropologist and Roanoke-area civic leader. "She was strong and she looked good, and she was in their corner. I admired her and everything she did for Hollins, but I would not want to be her."

Jane had already proven — to the world — that she was not afraid to ruffle feathers. An otolaryngologist friend had recognized Jane's firebrand qualities after she'd founded a residential facility for juvenile offenders as an alternative to jail in Martinsville, a feat that garnered statewide press in the 1970s. The doctor encouraged her to join the board of Gallaudet University, and within four years, she had risen to chair. But at the federally funded liberal arts college for the deaf in Washington, DC, her leadership style was viewed as "unenlightened" and autocratic. Some professors criticized her "plantation mentality" and described the entire board as a bastion of paternalism toward the hearing-impaired. Asked why she had not bothered to learn sign language in her six years of serving on the board, Jane explained that "my efforts and my time would be best directed in areas where others couldn't perform, like the budget."

In 1988, when the board hired a hearing president over two deaf finalists, the students shut down the college, took to the streets, and marched with signs that said SPILMAN, LEARN TO SIGN: "I RESIGN!" They burned Jane and the president she'd hired in effigy and called for their immediate resignations.

For eight days, Jane refused to bow to their demands and was quoted as saying, "Deaf people are not ready to function in a hearing world." That quote became the spark that mobilized the international deaf community, which called the protest the "Selma of the deaf."

Though she said later she'd been misunderstood by an interpreter and, consequently, misquoted, Jane did resign the following week, conceding that her presence on the board had become "an obstacle to healing."

Back in Bassett, she told a *Roanoke Times* reporter that just a few weeks earlier, she had been fund-raising for Gallaudet in New York, where a potential donor told her the university suffered from not being well-known.

"Lord knows, there's nobody who hasn't heard of Gallaudet University" now, she said. Wistfully, she swore that she had not uttered the offending quote — though "it probably will be on my gravestone." She held her head high and kept her cheerfulness in check.

Had Jane been born a decade later, Lawson said, "I think she would have had a much different, probably much happier, life. She would have run Bassett Industries. There's no question in my mind."

Though she never said it directly, Jane described herself in a way that implied she was a victim of the Southern patriarchy. But behind the scenes, according to dozens of people I interviewed, an entirely different narrative emerged. She had claimed that there were no discussions of the factory at the dinner table, but most people I talked to insisted that Jane maintained a firm grip on the company tiller throughout her husband's tenure. "Jane was Bob's personal board of directors," a former Bassett vice president, Howard Altizer, said.

Observers could tell they were fond of each other. "But you could also tell there was an ongoing tension about who's the final word here," Warner Dalhouse, the banker, recalled. "Jane wasn't gonna let Bob totally use up her authority as a Bassett.

"All the Bassetts were tough, but Bob Spilman was more Bassett than the Bassetts," he added. Perhaps even more Bassett than Jane.

Although barber Coy Young has his doubts about that. "Kiss my foot that she was wounded!" he said when I told him how she described being cut out of business discussions. "Listen, when she went into the barbershop or the bank, you knew she was there. She'd go into a beauty parlor and order lobster on the phone in front of everybody, showing you she had the capability."

Young remembered counseling a distraught Bassett shipping supervisor named Cosmo after watching Bob Spilman cuss him out publicly in the barbershop one morning. Cosmo had been put in the middle of an argument between Bob and Jane having to do with furniture they'd collected to give to their children. It was a disagreement about which kid got which piece, and Cosmo had sided with Jane.

Coy tried not to react as Bob cursed Cosmo, but he felt the display was childish and inappropriate. Then Cosmo dragged Coy into the dispute, asking him, in front of Spilman, to weigh in.

"Cosmo, when Bob gets through cussing you out, it's over," Coy told him. "But if you had crossed Jane, it would never be over. You did what you had to do."

After which Spilman grumped, "Coy, cut my goddamn hair."

Spilman was the one who hung a sign behind his desk proclaiming himself THE MEANEST SON OF A BITCH IN THE VALLEY. When he needed a ride to High Point for Market business, he called up the Henry County sheriff and told him to send over a deputy to drive him there.

Spilman was also the one who stood by the elevators of the Taj Mahal and said "Good afternoon" to people who dared to show up for work at 8:02 a.m., just two minutes late. And Spilman was the one who sent the company jet to fetch plant manager Joe Philpott from his family vacation at the beach when personnel issues arose that called for a deft, diplomatic touch Spilman wasn't capable of providing. Twice.

But behind the scenes, according to most people I spoke to, Jane was the mover of the family chess pieces, knighting her husband and later her son, Rob, and relegating her brother, Little John, to pawn. "John was on the board, but from the very beginning after their father's death, he was cut out of all decision-making," said Altizer, who worked for the company from 1965 to 1980. When John suggested ideas for improving plant efficiency, he was openly brushed off by Spilman, who didn't believe in spending money on expensive new machinery. "Do the best with what you have," he was fond of telling plant managers—and if you could cut costs by 5 percent, even better.

In the community at large, the little people had to walk a tightrope, recalled industry veteran John McGhee. "You couldn't show too much love and affection for Bob and Jane because that would piss off" the C.C. Bassett side. "And if you were like me, you probably felt like John Bassett would be the heir apparent when Bob relinquished the board chairman or the presidency." And yet there seemed to be no love lost between Spilman and Little John, so who knew?

Not long after Spilman became president of Bassett, conglomerates such as Mead and Burlington Industries decided the furniture industry was ripe for diversification, and, seeing profits in furniture, they started buying up companies.

Bassett's balance sheet was the envy of the industry, and the company was still the largest single-name-brand furniture company in the United States. It was averaging a 17 percent return on invested capital and more than 8 percent on sales, and by the mid-1980s, it had $65 million in cash and almost no debt, which gave Spilman the flexibility to make big acquisitions. The company was publicly held but tightly controlled by managers and relatives—that is, the appointees of Spilman and Jane.

Rather than modernize the Bassett factories, Spilman began acquiring others to beef up sales. As he told an interviewer in 2005, "We bought so many damn plants it takes a long time to remember them all."

"Bob was a good pitchman behind the scenes," said Colbert Micklem, a Bassett salesman of that era. "He loved to handle the money and look for ways to purchase things and grow his industry. But he did nothing to improve the efficiency of the plants."

A reporter for *Fortune* had visited the town in 1967, and the resulting article chided Bassett and the other Southern furniture makers for their "Rube Goldberg assembly-line techniques," calling their mass-produced furniture "uniformly uninspired and often downright ugly."

But when Little John suggested a design change, it was usually dismissed outright. More than once, Spilman prohibited John from flying on the company airplane, even after John's suitcase was packed and he was ready to board. Mr. Ed griped that "Little John is just plain smart"—and not in a good way. In fact, several people told me that Spilman, Jane, and Ed quietly promulgated the notion throughout the industry that John Bassett wasn't smart or "sophisticated" enough to become CEO of a furniture company as large as Bassett. As Bunny Wampler put it, "John was always trying to tell Spilman what to do, but Spilman was a lot smarter and wouldn't listen to him. So he just wanted to get John out of his hair."

John was, after all, ten years younger than Spilman, who was already a vice president when John returned to Bassett. Just twenty-eight when his father died, John knew he didn't have the management experience to run the company. But he believed that if he held tight and learned the ropes, playing the good soldier and biding his time, the presidency would one day be his.

When he returned home from Germany and repeatedly went over Mr. Ed's head, he had no idea he was playing into the Spilmans' hands. "John should've respected Ed more than he did," Spencer Morten said. He alienated Morten, too, when he brought a furniture buyer from Norfolk into Dominion Ornamental, the plant Mr. Doug had set up to make the boys play nice. John was running the J.D. plants at the time and thought nothing of taking the furniture buyer to Dominion, run by Morten, and committing the ultimate sin: shutting it down (temporarily) to show the visitor how it worked. He was doing something worse than showing off; he was slowing the production line. JBIII disputes that account and says that shutting down an operating assembly line is anathema to him, then and now.

Several Spilman friends, relatives, and industry insiders who asked not to be named said Mr. Ed and Spilman cut a secret deal within minutes of Doug Bassett's funeral. If Spilman promised never to fire Ed Bassett's manager sons, Eddie and Charles, Ed would retain his spot as chairman of the board, but Spilman would run the daily operations—and do whatever he wanted with the brassy young heir.

"Ed could not stand Little John Bassett," one family friend said. "And Spilman sucked up to Ed because he had to."

"It was all about survival," one relative told me. "If John's father had lived longer, Uncle Ed would have never had a shot at running the whole thing." John surely would have been promoted over Spilman, the relative added. "But Ed mucked everything up."

In the 1967 *Fortune* magazine photo spread, John is already on the periphery. CEO Ed stands in the middle of his management team, his foot perched casually on the railroad track that intersects the company town. He's flanked by his son Charles and his confidant Bob Spilman—while John grins at the photo's edge.

The article called Ed a blunt advocate of paternalism, describing the $1.5 million the company had just spent to build two recreation centers, one for blacks and one for whites. "We have to keep the people happy, although I must say it was easier to do in the days before television and cheap transportation," Ed told the magazine, which described the family's style of living and management as belonging to a "bygone day."

And *Fortune* didn't know the half of it.

At Jane Spilman's home in central Virginia, horse country, on the Charlottesville side of Richmond, photographs of children and grandchildren were arranged neatly on bureaus. Bob Spilman was present in a few of them, but most of the photos he was in featured his prize possession, a sport-fishing yacht he named *Sawdust*.

Sure, he had a woodworking shop in all three of his homes, and once he used his shop to construct a nineteen-foot dory (with the help of a company sample maker), which he launched at a party—in his swimming pool. But if you asked any of the thousands of people who worked the Bassett assembly lines, they would tell you: He did not have sawdust in his veins.

I visited eighty-two-year-old Howard Hodges at the Fork Mountain Rest Home to talk about the thirty-eight years he'd worked at Bassett, and Hodges said Spilman rarely toured the plants. But when employees had problems with their managers, they were encouraged to snitch on them by writing directly to Spilman via a form the company referred to as the hotline.

"Most people were scared of Mr. Spilman, but he was always good to me," said Hodges, wearing a robe, undershirt tank, and sweatpants. He sat on the side of his twin bed, which dwarfed the tiny room, with its worn linoleum floors and cinder-block walls. His wife, Myrtle, died in 1973 in a car wreck; they were carpooling to work at the Bassett Chair plant with some other employees to save gas money, and the driver hit a pothole, lost control, and crashed into an embankment. "Lord, I have missed that woman," he said.

His goal had been to work until he turned eighty, but his doctor made him retire in 2000 at age seventy. Twelve years earlier, he'd had a heart attack at work but refused to leave his planing machine until his foreman forced him to see the company nurse—twenty minutes into his attack.

He has fond memories of working for JBIII in the J.D. plants, John's first plant-manager job. He stopped by Howard's machine regularly to check on the planer, telling him to keep up the good work. Like his father and his uncle Bill before him, John knew most of his employees by name. His workplace philosophy was that direct communication was preferable to snitching: "If you want to find out how a machine is doing, don't go to the foreman. Go to the man who's running it," Hodges recalled John telling him.

Decades later, John Bassett III will say very little about how his relatives treated him in the family business. More than once, he bit my head off for asking. After my three-hour interview with Jane, though, he wanted to find out everything she'd said. A newspaper article I had written about him a few months earlier prompted him to thank me because it led to the first honest discussion the two had had in decades. Now he was curious. "What else did Jane say? What did she say about me?"

I was surprised to be dragged into the family drama, with John pressing me to tell him exactly what his sister said, and Jane implying to me that they'd both been the victims of her husband's domineering personality. "Robert was terrible to John. Terrible!" she said.

Their relationship seemed devoid of the affection I'd witnessed in Junior and Mary Thomas's modest trailer, watching them interact with their grandson and hearing them tell departing visitors, "Have a blessed day!"

When I told JBIII that Jane claimed she'd stood up for him with Spilman—that "John was unaware of how far I went to bat for him"—he nodded and admitted, "That's probably true." He hadn't known Spilman withheld details about the factories from Jane and refused to put her on the board. It was also news that Jane felt she'd had to choose her husband over her brother if she wanted her marriage to last.

"Bob was very pedantic," John said in a rare unguarded moment. "He'd give you a job and then he'd try to micromanage how you did it. He'd tell you to go to New York, then call back to ask what plane you were taking, what airport you were leaving from. He wanted to control every little thing."

And that's all he would divulge at that point about the man who would dominate the narrative of his career and, ultimately, his family. Nearly three years after Spilman's death, John Bassett told me I could interview anyone I wanted to. But if I was looking for more on his brother-in-law—and the humiliation John suffered at his hands—he was not going to be the one to give it to me.

9

Sweet Ole Bob (SOB)

*He got a lot of enjoyment out of people being
afraid of him.*

—BILL YOUNG, RETIRED BASSETT FURNITURE
CORPORATE COMMUNICATIONS DIRECTOR

In 1972, the company hired Frank Snyder to be its first in-house lawyer. Like Spilman, a former army paratrooper and ROTC student at NC State, Snyder was an ex-military guy who was vigilant about workplace punctuality and impeccably shined shoes. During Snyder's first decade on the job at Bassett, the two tough-guy veterans bonded like glue to plywood.

Snyder was initially tasked with handling a delicate legal case. Some workers had complained to the Equal Employment Opportunity Commission that blacks and women weren't getting a fair shake at Bassett, resulting in a lawsuit. In fact, eight years after Title VII of the Civil Rights Act of 1964 required employers to halt discrimination, Bassett Furniture's thirteen plants, now operating in several Southern states, were still largely segregated.

Sanding- and cabinet-room employees were all white, but the spray rooms—the dirtiest part of furniture-making—were operated entirely by black men. Black women handled the rub rooms, where workers wiped off the excess spray by hand. It wasn't dangerous as long as there was proper ventilation, and workers wore masks and gloves. Women weren't allowed to run machines, which put them at an unfair wage differential since machine operators typically earned more than those working the line.

Before Snyder came on board, Bassett's legal affairs had always been handled by lawyer and top Virginia legislator A.L. Philpott, with his Main Street office just down the street from the Taj Mahal and his entwined Henry County family connections weaving several generations back. Having aligned himself with Bonce Stanley and the other Virginia segregationists, Philpott had been in no hurry to see the Civil Rights Act followed to the letter at Bassett. One of the first stories I heard about racial tension in the region, in fact, involved a brief run-in between A.L. Philpott and Doretha's husband, William "Pork Chop" Estes, the chauffeur of Ruby Bassett, Mr. Ed's wife.

Estes was out with his stepdaughter Naomi Hodge-Muse, a chemistry major home visiting her folks from historically black Virginia Union College, when they ran into the legendary state legislator, whom Estes knew through the Bassetts. Estes politely stopped Philpott on the street to introduce him to Naomi but was cut off with a stern "Boy, I don't have time for you today."

"All he wanted was to introduce me and say, 'This my li'l girl. She in college,'" said Naomi, slipping into Pork Chop's dialect. She's in her early sixties now, retired from a management job at Miller Brewing in nearby Eden, North Carolina, and likes to joke that she was the first in her family to make alcohol and "do it legal!" The widow of the banker who ran Martinsville's first black-owned savings and loan, she lives comfortably in Chatmoss, the upper-middle-class community named for one of the largest tobacco plantations in the area—not far from where her great-great-grandmother Amy Finney once toiled as a slave. She organized the Christmas parade float for her local branch of the NAACP in 2011—and shook her head when the city of Martinsville bestowed the honor of best float on the Sons of the Confederacy. "And they don't understand why people stay mad!" she fumed.

The memory of her stepfather being dismissed by A.L. Philpott still brings tears to her eyes. He was so ashamed by the incident that he never spoke of it again. The following year, when the family fell short on tuition, Naomi dropped out for a semester to work at a competing furniture factory in the region. The man who fed the ripsaw spit tobacco juice on her feet to intimidate her, and a manager threatened daily to rape her during lunch. She knew if she told her stepfather, a World War II combat veteran, he'd do something about it that would end in his arrest. She confided in her grandmother instead. A maid for the Bassetts—the one who wore two girdles at once—Dollie Finney had sparked young Naomi's interest in chemistry when she bought a science-fair kit for her on layaway in 1964. That was the beginning of a string of science-fair projects that eventually earned Naomi a college scholarship. She was the first in her family to go.

"I ain't never let no man put his hands on me, save [when] I wanted him to," her grandmother told her. "You take care of your business."

The next day, the ninety-seven-pound firebrand tucked a switchblade into the back of her jeans on her way to work. This time when the supervisor cornered her and threatened to take her out behind the lumber stack, Naomi whipped out her knife. She demonstrated the movement for me at a quiet sidewalk café in Martinsville on a crisp fall day in 2011, the anger still palpable some four decades later. Her hand shook, and her eyes were blazing. The foreman had backed down immediately, swearing that he'd only been kidding. "That's when I learned that being timid didn't get you a damn thing," she said.

But Naomi still shudders to think how her life would have played out had her blade pierced his white skin.

Her grandmother's double-girdling may have been more prudent. But Naomi started working in the 1970s, when the great changes sweeping the nation were finally reaching this remote corner of smokestacks and red-clay earth.

It was race relations and the war in Vietnam that consumed most Americans when President Richard Nixon made the bold, historic

move of meeting with Chairman Mao Tse-tung in 1972, thawing relations with the People's Republic of China for the first time in twenty-
five years. "This was the week that changed the world," Nixon declared
after leaving behind an American redwood sapling as a symbol of
mutual peace, prosperity, and international trade.

Spilman had more immediate concerns than China on his mind. Up in
his office at the Taj Mahal, he ordered Frank Snyder to bring the company into EEOC compliance and make the lawsuit go away, echoing
the mandate of Mr. Ed Bassett, who didn't want to experience the
indignity of being chewed out by a federal judge again. Decades earlier,
Ed had borne the brunt of a legal lashing when Bassett was found to
have sixteen-year-olds on its payroll, a violation of child-labor laws.
(Like his relatives before him, Ed had started working in the factories
at fourteen and didn't understand what the big deal was—but the federal government felt differently.)

Ed didn't like the idea of paying a full-time staff lawyer, though,
and Snyder recalled arriving at his office at 7:20 a.m.—long before
most corporate lawyers were on duty—just to show Ed that he could
keep up with any Bassett. One morning, Ed appeared at Snyder's door,
stretched his arms authoritatively against both sides of his door frame,
and sighed. "Tell me again, what is it you do?" he asked.

Mr. Ed was the originator of the great Henry County adage that
John Bassett would go on to adopt: "When you see a snake's head, hit
it." Ed was also the subject of an even more colorful regional phrase:
"Mr. Ed didn't cull up and down the Smith River." The first time I
heard it—from a group of Vaughan-Bassett salesmen who worked for
Bassett in the 1960s—I had to get them to spell the word to be clear.

C-u-l-l. In the furniture industry, it's a term that refers to sorting—
culling—the bad lumber from the good. Only in Mr. Ed's case, the
reference was not to wood but to women—secretaries and other companions whom he met with at his private retreat, a cabin in the Henry
County woods. Several retired Bassett office workers I interviewed

could still quote from the sex-talk-laden "business letters" Ed dictated to his company secretary (and mistress). The men routinely swiped the tapes from her desk and passed them around for a laugh. Once, in fact, W.M.'s secretary volunteered to type up the letters for Mr. Ed's secretary when she was out sick, and when she discovered the content covered a lot more than baby-crib sales, she transcribed them and then forwarded the transcriptions, word for word, to W.M. "He was going to fire Ed, but they were reorganizing the sales force at the time, and he couldn't afford to do it without him," said Reuben "Scotty" Scott, longtime manager of the J.D. plants.

According to several industry insiders, "Mr. Ed didn't cull up and down the Smith River" meant that when it came to women, he didn't sort the bad from the good. He'd cavort with anyone. They also said he wasn't the only higher-up to act like that either, adding that several managers routinely cheated on their wives.

It was *Mad Men* in the mountains.

With moonshine instead of martinis.

Some managers competed to see who could bang the new company nurse or the new hire in advertising first, and at least one senior manager contracted gonorrhea. (He quietly arranged for his wife to get treatment after making the family doctor promise not to disclose the real reason she had to be on the antibiotic.)

Spilman didn't participate in it, multiple people told me. But he was eager to hear every lascivious detail. In 2005, he lamented in an American Furniture Hall of Fame oral-history interview that he missed the old ways of doing business: "You've got so many things you can do and can't do legally—age restrictions, sexual remarks. Techniques are entirely different than they were in my really active years," he said.

Managers were so brazen that a female buyer from J.C. Penney once turned the corner during a tour of a Bassett factory to see two people going at it during their lunch break.

The buyer deadpanned to a colleague, "Are they doing a cutting?"—the production term for a single order of a particular suite.

"The joke at Bassett was, you had to stand in line on the Smith River banks sometimes to get a spot at lunch," Bob Merriman told me.

One out-of-town supplier was so shocked by the language and lewdness that he joked that all men in Bassett were afflicted with the Smith River Twitch.

But Mr. Ed was all business when it came to sales, arriving at work before seven every morning to run the prior day's numbers. He encouraged sales managers to hound the salesmen working under them. "Send them a telegram or write a letter or call, or do all three!" sales manager Mick Micklem recalled him shouting. "Keep the pressure on these guys every single day. We've got thousands of people depending on us in these factories for their livelihoods, and we've gotta keep 'em working."

Mr. Ed was so tenacious, JBIII said, that he once dispatched the company's lumber buyer to the Mississippi Delta to buy lumber during an industrywide shortage, and when the man returned empty-handed, Mr. Ed was steamed.

"Did you get my lumber, Charlie?"

"No, sir."

"Why not?"

"Because the sawmillers would've had to wade out chest-high into the swamps to cut it," Charlie explained.

"Charlie, there's no water in the swamp," Mr. Ed persisted, squinting his already deep-set eyes.

"But there is, sir," Charlie said.

"Charlie," Mr. Ed repeated, enunciating each syllable, *"there's no water in the swamp."*

So Charlie went back to the Delta with Mr. Ed's permission to beg, borrow, or overpay the sawmillers — whatever it took — to bring some lumber back.

If Mr. Ed needed wood, then there was simply no water in the swamp.

* * *

Snyder said it took him one week to figure out the corporate/family hierarchy: "Doug Bassett had given Ed Bassett a beating, and when Ed took over, he passed the beatings on to Bob Spilman, who passed all the static on to John."

The truth was, Spilman was an equal-opportunity beater — tough on everyone who worked for him, from his company pilot to, eventually, his own son. He was honest, loyal to the people who mattered to him, and he *culled*, which meant he was faithful, if not exactly tender, to his wife.

"He'd sit at the table on Christmas Day, and I could strangle him, but he'd say, 'Oh, I wish I heard the factory whistles blow,'" Jane said.

"He thought Christmas was a great waste of time," his son, Rob, told me.

It was Jane, in fact, who came up with the pointedly ironic nickname Sweet Ole Bob. SOB for short.

If Mr. Ed was leery of going in front of a federal judge again, then Spilman would see to it that Snyder set things right in the factories. The blacks could have their civil rights for all he cared, as long as the unions steered clear of Bassett. Spilman's allegiance was to his pact with Mr. Ed and their mutual goal to keep Little John marginalized.

Snyder toured each of the company's plants, explaining how they all were going to adhere to the Civil Rights Act and the new EEOC rules. In the two J.D. plants John managed, the sanding room was staffed by white men, most of them relatives of two extended families who had been laboring for generations in that department. The families sent their elders into John's office to throw down the gauntlet: they weren't going to tolerate working with "any goddamn niggers," as Snyder recalled them saying.

To which John calmly replied, "If that's your feeling, then you can leave right now because this is the way it's gonna be."

"I always respected John after that," Snyder said.

On the surface John seemed impervious to the bullying of his uncle and brother-in-law, an attitude that gradually earned him the respect of those who used to discount him as an entitled spoiled brat. When Spilman showed up at his desk in the factory, he made John stand up and give him his chair. Then he'd sit down in his tailor-made suit and put his feet up on John's desk—while John stood and listened.

He paid no attention when Spilman told his inner circle, "My brother-in-law is still a child. He's the most immature person I've ever seen."

John didn't complain either when Spilman refused to pay for production-incentive bonuses. John simply paid for them himself, ordering lobsters flown in from Maine and steaks brought in from Kansas City; throwing three-thousand-dollar parties (featuring pigs roasting on spits) to reward his factory supervisors for upping the company's profits; and handing out gold *#1* tiepins he'd had commissioned and Swiss army knives. One retiree told me that John once took the supervisors to a strip club in Roanoke as a reward.

"Bob should have offered [the incentives] to the other plant managers," John said. "I could afford it, but the others couldn't." Besides, what JBIII paid out was pocket change compared to the hundreds of thousands of dollars' worth of pure profit the company made when it produced a hundred and twenty dressers an hour instead of a hundred.

He used his money as a motivator again when he couldn't convince his plant foremen to keep the factory as clean as he wanted. He called up a chocolate manufacturer an hour away and asked if the company could deliver an order the same day he placed it. Then he wrote a letter to the wife of each supervisor saying, If your husband's department is clean by the time we shut down for Christmas, he will bring you home a box of chocolates made fresh that very morning. "The next Friday, you could eat off the floor of any department!" he told me, beaming at the memory. Chocolate—and the promise of what came after it at home later, if the guys were lucky—was a better motivator than intimidation.

Once, when he surpassed the allotted budget on a screwdriver order,

Spilman had the money docked from his pay. "You didn't get my permission!" he barked. Weeks later, Bill Brammer, the company's chief financial officer and an old family friend, reimbursed John without Spilman's knowledge.

It was a lonely spot to be in, with his father gone and Mr. Ed and Spilman eager to shove him aside. "When others only want their sons to do well, it hardens you," he said. "But at some point you quit feeling sorry for yourself and say, How am I gonna get this job done?"

Publicly, he handled Spilman's treatment well. "But privately I think it was always in his craw," said Howard Altizer, a vice president who rented a house on the Spilman property that was equidistant from the couple's elegant Dutch Colonial home and the mother-in-law cottage they built for Jane and John's mother, Lucy, after Mr. Doug's death.

It was a great perch from which to observe the family members, and observe them he did, noting the way Bob and Jane rarely socialized with others in the family except Jane's mother, whose affections "they seemed to claim at the expense of John," Altizer said. "In a small community like that, you'd think all the Bassetts and their relatives running the [competitor] factories would be thick as thieves, but they were not."

While John didn't seem to be revered in the family, he was admired in the greater community, said Carolyn Blue, who babysat for Pat and John Bassett's three children in the late 1960s. Carolyn's father and grandfather had worked in the Bassett plants, and from her perspective — spending hours inside the young couple's grand house on Riverside Drive, the one they bought when the apartment became too small — John and Pat Bassett reminded her of a young JFK and Jackie, going to parties and staying out late and calling the Bassett taxi driver, Roy Martin, to take the babysitter home.

Pat was adventurous and fun, not blinking when she had to drive her Jeep up the steep back road to pick up Carolyn, the rocks flying in her wake, and not caring when Franny, her youngest, drew on the walls. Pat complained when Carolyn called her Mrs. Bassett, insisting that Carolyn call her the less formal Miss Pat.

"Can I be candid?" Carolyn asked me. "I just didn't like that.... Why not just [let me] call her Pat? But I liked her and respected her immensely. She was lighthearted and very generous with me. She gave me tons of very nice clothes and jewelry."

One time during a party at Pat and John's house, Carolyn was glued to *Star Trek* and didn't notice when little Fran made a paste of laundry powder and slathered it all over her face.

"Oh God, your parents are gonna kill me!" Carolyn shrieked.

"It'll be all right, Care-non," the toddler reassured her. And it was.

JBIII experienced no such warmth at work—and neither did anyone else. Spilman ruled the growing corporation as if he were a general, the kind who flies into a rage at the sight of a private's dirty shoes. He controlled every aspect of the business, down to deciding who rode which elevator. No one in the corporate office was permitted to spend more than three hundred dollars (it was later upped to five hundred) unless Spilman personally approved the purchase. He chose the furniture suites the company would premiere every six months at Market. He decided which factories made which suites. He gathered his inner circle in his office after lunch every day to play gin rummy and poker—and so he could gather intel on what was going on elsewhere in the company. Without, of course, inviting his brother-in-law.

"They were throwing hundred-dollar bills around!" Snyder said of the games, which continued on the corporate jet during business trips.

"We used to say, all the decisions made in this company are made in that damn poker game," recalled former Bassett sales manager Bob Merriman. "If you got rid of the poker game, the company might really take off!" If they were on the plane and still playing poker or gin rummy just before the landing, Spilman would order his pilot to circle around the city until the game was over—especially if he was winning.

Junior Thomas, the retired mirror-plant worker, nearly spit when I brought up Bob Spilman's name, calling him a "wicked, wicked man!" Thomas had business on the third floor of the Taj Mahal one day when

Spilman was in charge, and he couldn't help hear him berating employees from down the hall. "He cussing them folks around there like he *owned* 'em," he said. Spilman once threatened to remove W.M. Bassett's name from the town community center sign when Bassett Mirror, run by W.M.'s son-in-law, reduced its annual donation to the center during an economic downturn.

No one was spared his fevered scoldings, longtime managers said. His closest confidant was the longtime Superior Lines plant manager Joe Philpott, whose factory churned out $600,000 to $1.2 million in furniture profits—*a month*—during the company's heyday. Philpott got so mad at Spilman once that he threw his keys, accidentally piercing the company oil portrait of Mr. Doug. "I called him Sweet Ole Bob... and he'd call me one too. God, we'd go at it," Philpott said, grinning.

The feisty, expletive-dropping plant boss was one of the few managers who did battle with Spilman on a daily basis. He not only lived to tell the tale but actually liked the man, warts and all. Spilman even sent him to Harvard once, a semester-long executive-training program run by Harvard Business School. "He was trying to refine me a little, but it didn't take," Philpott said.

One time, showing off a new product at High Point, Philpott pointed out the piece's "bifocal doors," at which Spilman erupted: "Goddamn! I spent all this money sending him to Harvard, and he can't even pronounce *bifold!*"

But when Philpott's mother-in-law died while he was at Harvard, Spilman dispatched the corporate jet to ferry him home for the funeral. When Spilman heard about a Martinsville woman who needed lifesaving surgery that was available only in New Haven, Connecticut, he quietly had the plane fly her up there and bring her home. He ordered the company treasurer to donate twenty-five thousand dollars in company funds for the renovation of a rural black church, though he was infuriated later when he learned the minister, a Bassett Mirror Company employee, had given it away to "some sisters who'd fallen on hard times," Philpott recalled, chuckling at his boss's fury.

Joe Philpott was among the handful of Bassett bigwigs I visited who actually deigned to have Bassett Furniture in their homes. Built on family land a stone's throw from the center of his own family's even older company town, the once-thriving sawmill community of Philpott, his brick house featured a dining-room suite and various other pieces made at Bassett during his career.

His family had not fared as well as the Bassetts financially, but they were equally entwined in the region's good-old-boy network, especially when it came to Joe's cousin A.L. Philpott, the powerful legislator. "I loved every one of them, but I have never known a Bassett who couldn't give you a good ass-chewing," he said.

When Joe and I met in the summer of 2012, he had just returned from a vacation in France and had garden produce spilling from his kitchen counters, so much that he sent me home with a bag of cucumbers and a to-go cup of iced tea. In an accent that was more Johnny Cash twang than Andy Griffith gentleman—and speech peppered with the word *damn*, which he used like a comma—Joe Philpott described midcentury furniture-making as cutthroat and fun, and so all-consuming that he once calculated that, given all the time he spent there, his salary came to about sixty-five cents an hour.

Stanley Furniture may have paid more than Bassett, as did the Hooker and American plants in Martinsville. But Bassett gave a bonus twice a year, at Christmas and on the Fourth of July. (At Christmas in 1970, the top bonus for line workers with at least twenty years of service was $490.) As the barber Coy Young put it, "It was the old sharecropper mentality, like you were being paid four hundred one-dollar bills, and you'd never seen that much money in your life."

Bassett managers understood the factory-man mentality to a tee. And the higher-ups got hefty bonuses, Philpott said, adding that his last semiannual bonus before he retired, in 1999, came to $65,000. He was supervising thirteen Bassett factories at the time, including two in Georgia and five in North Carolina.

Spilman and Philpott sometimes went on factory-buying excursions together, once drinking an entire bottle of scotch while the company's tee-totaling financial officer did the driving. Spilman relished competing with other furniture companies, especially Stanley, though he was happy to team up with the cousin competitors when it came to keeping wages down. "We had a secret pact," whispered Philpott, who worked for Bassett from 1955 to 1999. They tried not to hire each other's workers—meaning a Bassett employee wouldn't be able to leave and work for a slightly higher wage at Stanley, and vice versa. Back then, unemployment was low, and it was hard to find and keep good labor. Several dozen former mill workers from Henry County told me that, as late as the mid-1990s, it was possible to quit one job in the morning and have another one lined up by noon.

Labor was such a premium in the 1970s that Bassett actually trucked in work-release convicts from a prison in Rustburg every day. They were paid the same rate as the regular workers, though part of the money went to the state for their room and board. "About the middle of the 1990s, the godsend happened with Mexicans," Spilman recounted to an interviewer in 2005. At a Bassett-owned upholstery plant in Los Angeles, there was a concentration of Hispanics, and they didn't get along as well with black workers as Hispanics did in Henry County. "Every family had a patriot," Spilman said, probably meaning a *patriarch* or *patron*. "If you needed someone in the sewing room, you'd tell this patriot and hire who he brought in the next day. We didn't know if they were legal or illegal. But now, you better have them legal," he added, referring to growing enforcement of immigration laws.

Competing furniture makers protected their mutual interests too. Coy Young recalled that during a short-lived union presence at Stanley in the early 1970s, when workers were striking for higher wages, Stanley surreptitiously trucked the lumber out to be made into furniture three miles down the road at Bassett. "Don't believe a word about the rivalry between the two," he told me. "When it came to unions, Bassett was in there helping them any way they could because they didn't want the unions anywhere near *their* plants." Spilman confirmed that scenario himself in the same 2005 interview.

Under Spilman, the bottom line ruled, with furniture designed and churned out at a breakneck pace. Though his degree and training had been in textiles, Spilman learned the ins and outs of furniture-making "faster than anybody I've ever known," said Reuben Scott, who worked for Bassett from 1937 to 1986. "He'd make you feel worthless as a plug nickel, but the truth is, the man was a genius."

His forte was always sales, said James Riddle, a former Bassett regional sales manager who's now CEO of Lifestyle, an importing company. "Bob could walk down Main Street of High Point or Main Street of New York, and he could either be selling Bibles or popcorn or Tootsie Rolls, and everybody that would walk by would wanna buy it," Riddle said. "John Bassett always wants to give you his reply before you complete your sentence, which is a talent in itself. But Bob was truly the born salesman of the two."

At times, he was even humble about it. When strangers asked Spilman how he got into the furniture business, he liked to deadpan: "Married a Bassett."

The humor extended—sort of—to his competitors, whom he sliced verbally, like a band saw through hearts of pine. Sales manager Joe Meadors, another member of Spilman's inner circle, recalled copying a suite made by Dixie Furniture, based in Lexington, North Carolina, down to its brass-detailed corners. Spilman and Dixie's CEO, Smith Young, were archrivals. People in the industry called Young the "Spilman of North Carolina," and not in a complimentary way. Once, when Young was in the hospital for an emergency appendectomy, Spilman sent him a telegram saying *Please don't die because then I'll be the biggest son of a bitch in the furniture industry.* After which another competitor wired: *By a vote of 7 to 5, your directors have just voted they hope you make it.*

Spilman had designer Leo Jiranek copy one of Young's suites, called Arrival, while Philpott was left to figure out how the company could produce it and sell it for sixty dollars less than Dixie was charging but still make a profit. "We knocked it off, cold as hell!" Meadors told me.

As an added tweak, Bassett named its suite Departure—then

mailed a copy of the suite price list to rival Young, who wrote back: *Thanks for the publicity you've given my new suite. Since this photograph went out, my sales have really picked up.*

Of all the people I interviewed about Bob Spilman—including his own wife and son—no one stood up for him more than his top sales executive, Joe Meadors. Spilman had hired him not long after buying a car from him at the dealership where Meadors worked in the early 1960s. Under Spilman's tenure, Bassett became so profitable that when Meadors retired, he was able to build a spacious lakefront home in the affluent bedroom community of Smith Mountain Lake (it's also furnished with Bassett Furniture). He still owns property in Bassett, but with its long-standing double-digit unemployment rates since the factories began shutting down, he's had trouble renting it out.

The first time I spoke to Meadors, when I called to set up an interview, he started defending Spilman, praising him as a loyal boss. Asked for examples, he said he'd have to think about it. When I arrived at his house a few days later, he held a list of points he wanted to make about Spilman, including two stories about his loyalty. One involved a Bassett employee whose wife, also an employee, was convicted of embezzling from the company. After the story hit the newspaper, the man went to Spilman's office to announce he was turning in his resignation.

"Why are *you* quitting?" Spilman barked.

"You know, my wife took that money."

"Yeah, did you take any of it?"

"No, sir."

"Did you know she was taking it?"

"No, sir."

"Well, get your ass back downstairs and go to work," Spilman told him, and that was the last that was said about his wife.

Loyalty example number two was equally telling, even though it eventually backfired. Mauri Hammack, the corporate pilot, was practicing his landings at the airport one day when he forgot to put his landing gear down, badly scraping the belly of the plane.

"You *what?*" Spilman boomed into the phone when Hammack reported what he'd done. The other managers had been begging Spilman to fire him for months, calling his flying methods risky and unorthodox. As head of sales, Meadors thought it was important to coddle the company's top-dog customers such as Sears, J.C. Penney, and Levitz Furniture, not risk their executives' lives. Meadors also wanted him fired.

Mauri took unnecessary risks with the retail executives on board, Meadors argued, landing in the fog, for instance. Once he'd inexplicably picked up a snake on a Georgia runway and carted it back to Virginia in a paper sack, unbeknownst to all but Spilman, who spotted the bag moving — not far from his head.

"Old Bob chewed his ass out for that one. But you have to admit, Mauri was a strange guy," another Bassett executive, Sherwood Robertson, said.

Still, Meadors pointed out proudly, out of a sense of loyalty, Spilman refused to fire Hammack even after he'd done twenty thousand dollars' worth of damage by skid-landing the company's $850,000, ten-passenger King Air prop jet.

Now in his eighties, Hammack still flies recreationally and spends a lot of time reuniting fellow veterans who served at RAF Burtonwood, a British air force base. Spilman was so irritated with Hammack after the belly scrape that eventually he had him evaluated by a psychiatrist, who determined, after five sessions, that he suffered from — *surprise!* — an abusive boss, according to Hammack. He said he was eventually forced to choose between quitting and being fired.

The incident that led the psychiatrist to the diagnosis? A few years before, Hammack was landing in Palwaukee, a small airport outside Chicago, in icy conditions. He chose to land on a short runway into the wind, avoiding the crosswinds that were bedeviling the longer runway typically favored by pilots. A Chicago salesman who was an amateur pilot heard about the landing after Spilman griped that they'd been so perilously close to trees that he'd been able to see a deer. The salesman convinced Spilman that Hammack's landing was fraught, though Hammack insists it was the prudent choice.

Just before boarding the return flight, Spilman lit into Hammack, barking, "You were trying to kill me!"

Hammack then made the mistake of asking the obvious. "Have you been drinking, Bob?"

Spilman's face turned instantly red, and before Hammack could register what was happening, he felt a sharp pain in his thigh, "like someone took a baseball bat and hit me with it," he said. Spilman had hauled off and kicked him, full force, in the leg.

Hammack was so stunned, he walked away.

He thought about getting a taxi to O'Hare and walking out on the men, the job, his bully of a boss. But with a wife and five children, and jobs scarce during the mid-1970s recession, he stayed — and has regretted that choice ever since. "Spilman could do anything to me from then on because he'd already proven he'd broken me."

Hammack said he didn't feel safe for the rest of his tenure at Bassett. Spilman continued berating him, though he never touched him again. "Bob was a chameleon," Hammack said. "He had charisma and a very brilliant mind. But he could change his color anytime."

At one trade show, Bassett was doing the annual courtesy of bestowing upon the reigning Miss Virginia a complimentary bedroom suite, and Spilman greeted the beauty queen with warmth. But the second Miss Virginia, her chaperone, and the cameras left, the affability ended.

He turned to his public relations man Bill Young and harrumphed: "Are we gonna give that bitch another free bedroom suite?" Young chuckled at the memory. He said he enjoyed driving his boss places, even though the second Spilman got out of the car, he complained loudly to anyone within earshot about Young's driving. "It's like he couldn't help himself," Young said. Being mean was part of his shtick.

"I have no idea what made him like that, whether it was his childhood or what," Young told me. "But I don't think he was as tough as he pretended to be."

* * *

Spilman's parents divorced when he was young—after his father abandoned the family for another woman—and Spilman grew up with a wealthy uncle, C.V. Henkel, who sent him away to military school. "He had a tough deal growing up," his son, Rob, said. "His dad was a jerk. And I think that affected him. Dad was just always a 'Don't tread on me' kinda guy. Growing up, we went at it, hammer and tong, for a number of years."

Henkel called his nephew Bob "Sonny," a childhood nickname that grated on him as an adult. Spencer Morten recalled traveling to Newton, North Carolina, with Spilman and other board members. They had invited the county supervisors and other dignitaries to dinner to convince them to close a road they wanted to use for Prestige, Bassett's upholstery plant. Henkel, a former state senator, had gone to the trouble of inviting North Carolina senator Sam Ervin, who attended the event at Henkel's request. (Not long after, Ervin went on to chair the Senate Watergate Committee.)

"Sonny, you made a big mistake tonight," Henkel told his nephew. "Senator Ervin turns down three hundred speaking engagements a year, and you didn't even acknowledge him in your remarks tonight."

After Morten and the other board members returned to their hotel rooms, they could hear Spilman berating his uncle—at a fevered screech—for criticizing him in front of his board. It was embarrassing to everyone within earshot, and Morten recalled feeling a mixture of pity and dread for all involved, including himself. "I think he probably felt abandoned by his dad," he said. "But he was so conniving and so clever. It really was a shame he married into the family."

By the early 1970s, the post–World War II economic boom was officially kaput. The recession of 1973 to 1975 was characterized as stagflation, a double whammy of high unemployment and high inflation. An oil crisis loomed, with filling-station lines and OPEC headlines. In the winter of 1977, Jimmy Carter urged Americans to turn their thermostats down.

Spilman was still acquiring new properties — a case-goods plant in Dublin, Georgia; a kids' furniture plant in Hickory, North Carolina — and spending millions on national advertising, including a prime-time television show hosted by E. G. Marshall that featured grand estates across the country, from Jefferson's Monticello to FDR's Hyde Park to the Hearst Castle. With thirty-four plants in thirteen states, the company now had more than six thousand employees. One 1970 commercial featured Vicki Lawrence from *The Carol Burnett Show* as Goldilocks shopping with the three bears at a store filled with Bassett Furniture, the message being that Bassett was affordable for all, from sophisticated city dwellers to suburban families to rugged mountaineers.

The company still had loads of cash in the bank, as was the Bassett way — upwards of $100 million — and Spilman aggressively managed every penny of it. "He'd get the plant managers to reduce costs by five percent in a month, and then they'd come back and report how hard it was, how they were down to skin and bones," Snyder, the company lawyer, said. They weren't laying people off, but they were working the employees faster and the equipment harder and longer.

It was frustrating for everybody, especially JBIII, who pestered his brother-in-law boss constantly for new equipment. "He would wear the shit out of Spilman till he got what he wanted approved," recalled Reuben Scott, who was JBIII's number two at the J.D. plants. "He'd wear him down."

Spilman's goal at that point was to get himself placed squarely among the captains of industry by adding more plants, with the hope of snagging Bassett a slot in the Fortune 500. As an added bonus to himself, he hatched a new plan for the troublesome Little John.

By 1972, he had acquired two aging furniture plants in Mount Airy, North Carolina. The factories were small, inefficient, and located in a floodplain, so Spilman tapped into the cash reserves to construct a brand-new, four-hundred-thousand-square-foot plant, and he sent JBIII down to check on the progress every week.

It dawned on him how nice it was having his brother-in-law gone.

None of his nagging him for new equipment. No more challenging his authority with end runs around the spending cap.

Spilman merged the two companies into one and named it National Mount Airy Furniture Company. It would specialize in high-end furniture, something Bassett had never made. Just to break even, the company would have to increase its annual output from the $5 million the two smaller companies had been producing to $15 million.

Spencer Morten told me that some of Spilman's fellow board members gave him a hard time about the money he spent building the megaplant. According to Morten, Spilman called John Bassett into his office and said, "Someday you'll be sitting in this chair as president, and I need you to go down there and turn this thing around, get it profitable. We're taking gas from the directors."

Throughout his career at Bassett, JBIII referred to this Spilman tactic as the "sunshine pump." The technique commenced with disingenuous praise that made it seem as if a manager was getting a raise or a promotion when really Spilman was just asking him to do more with less. "He'd pump yo' ass full of sunshine, but in about two months all the sunshine would leak out and you were no different than you were before," JBIII said.

The high-end-furniture niche was on the upswing, and Spilman wanted to prove his company could play ball with the likes of Henredon, Baker, and Bernhardt. Or so the story went.

"On one hand, Bob gave his brother-in-law a wonderful opportunity to show what he could do," said furniture-industry analyst Jerry Epperson. "But several of the [Bassett] board members I knew were saying, 'On the surface it sounded great—until we got into it.'

"I remember thinking, you're patting a guy on his back with a knife. And you've done it in such a way that you've made it look like a favor."

Little John would be down in Mount Airy for at least two years. And chances were good, the way Sweet Ole Bob saw it, that the sunshine would all leak out.

10

The Mount Airy Ploy

Bob thought John would hang himself.
And he just about did.

—Reuben "Scotty" Scott, Bassett plant manager

The first time I traveled to Mount Airy, North Carolina, the hometown of actor Andy Griffith and the place that inspired his popular television show, I felt like a big-city outsider—a reporter from Raleigh, say, traveling to profile the good people of Mayberry and trying to steer clear of Sheriff Andy's jail. Goober and Gomer were long gone from the town immortalized by its native son, but every other storefront on the picturesque Mount Airy Main Street was an homage to them and the other characters from the show, which still ranks among the most widely watched TV programs in syndication. The furniture factories closed long before my 2012 visit, but the business of being the real Mayberry was still very much intact.

Deejay Brent Carrick had asked me to do a call-in radio show at the offices of WPAQ, the one-story brick AM radio station known the world over as the tiny titan of Appalachian string-band music. Carrick played scratchy old vinyl recordings made by the textile and furniture hands who came together on weekends to create some of the nation's first country music. I'd discuss the research I was doing for this book and, with any luck, listeners would call in to talk about what it had been like to work at the brand-new National Mount Airy plant in 1974.

People didn't just call; they actually drove up to see me at the little station on the kudzu-covered hill, two of them bringing gifts. They said hello to the WPAQ secretary, then sauntered across creaky wood floors, past piles of old radio equipment from the 1940s, and straight into the studio—while we were on air.

"Hey, Russ!" Brent called out in the middle of introducing one song. Old-time music fans, some as far away as Scotland, listened in via WPAQ740.com; my husband listened in from Roanoke and couldn't wait to tease me about my clipped Midwestern accent turning as thick and sugary as Aunt Bea's sweet tea.

Ruth Phillips called to tell me that her husband, Crawford, had worked in the cabinet room of National Mount Airy (and its predecessor, Mount Airy Furniture) for forty-five years, earning six dollars an hour by the time he retired in 1985. Her father, Doc Reece, had worked at the Mount Airy Chair Company and National Desk plants ahead of him, including a stint with a very young Andy Griffith, with whom he traded knives during sack lunches of butter beans and ham-stuffed biscuits. "Daddy said he made out better on the knife swap, but then again, Andy went to college and came out a whole lot better in the long run."

That's a fact. Halfway through the show, unemployed singer-songwriter Russ Ashburn drove up to give me a copy of the song he wrote not long after Bassett closed its National Mount Airy plant in 2005. Called "RFD Parade," the CD cover featured a picture of Russ standing in front of an American flag and holding a handwritten sign that said NAFTA IS NOT NICE.

We used to have a lot of jobs around our little town
We made furniture and socks and shirts
Good times were all around
Here comes NAFTA, it'll help us is what they say
So let's give a cheer for progress, hip-hip hooray.

Russ helped construct the National Mount Airy plant for John Bassett in the early 1970s. Soon after, he remembered, he watched workers run to their cars when their shifts ended. "They wanted to get the heck outta there!"

My third visitor, George Fricke, had similar things to say about the early days of John Bassett's Mount Airy tenure. "Low pay and bad conditions," he told me. "It was a terrible place to work."

But my favorite insight into John's Mount Airy assignment came later, courtesy of Bassett High's former football coach Colbert "Mick" Micklem, who recalled John phoning him from the real Mayberry RFD shortly after arriving there.

"Mick, it's the fourth quarter," John told the old coach. "I'm on my own one-yard line. There's one minute left to play in the game, we're down seven, and somehow they want me to win the damn game."

The two tiny plants Bassett had purchased were bleeding money while the new factory was being built. The old-timers were used to competing against one another, but they struggled to get along when Bassett combined the workforce. And Spilman had tasked him with tripling sales while making high-end furniture, something the company had never before produced.

To complicate matters, the furniture makers in Mount Airy were real craftsmen, people who had only recently stopped employing the old bench-made building process. Rather than using conveyor belts and Henry Ford–style assembly lines, these guys worked at half the speed of the line workers in Bassett, and they rarely used standard interchangeable parts.

Until Bassett bought the companies, a customer could mail in a picture of a piece of furniture he saw in a magazine and designate the color he wanted, and the old companies would actually complete the order—even if it was just a single chair. Like their furniture-making predecessors in Grand Rapids, they took pride in it too.

Back in Bassett, W.M. Bassett had done away with those methods *before* World War II. As far as John Bassett was concerned, the workers in Mount Airy were fifty years behind the times. They were change-resistant, undisciplined, and spoiled. Most of them were also debt-free and owned orchards on the side and thought nothing of taking off work when peach- and apple-picking season hit. "They are very independent mountain peo- ple who will just tell you to go to hell and walk out!" said Eddie Wall, a retired Bassett manager who worked in Mount Airy.

Unemployment was low, which meant that if workers didn't like the way their bosses treated them, they could quit and easily nab another job. By the time JBIII turned up, morale was lower than a snake's butt in a wagon rut.

The workers had no idea the old companies had been bleeding money. They didn't realize the customer base for their high-end tables and chairs had eroded when the plants, failing to modernize, could not produce the volume the retailers were demanding. Profits had gone into shareholders' pockets instead of into updated machinery. If John Bassett had his druthers, he would have bought a bigger, better-run company to start with, one with a more loyal customer base. "But Bob never called me up and said, 'What is your opinion?' He said, 'I want you to go run these things,'" JBIII told me.

As he recalled, "When your wagon's in a ditch with a broken wheel, and you've been sent out there by yourself, you try everything you can think of." He instituted the legal-pad method of management his father had used, only the young heir never knocked off midday for a round of golf, much less a scotch. To get the new plant up and running, his wife told me, "John worked nineteen hours a day"—one time for forty-five days straight. He thought, read, and talked about furniture twenty-four hours a day, including in his sleep.

His plant manager and number two man, Duke Taylor, remem- bered going on a business trip with him and developing a new empathy for what it must be like to be Mrs. John Bassett. "He went to bed talk- ing furniture and he woke up talking furniture, and I finally had to say, 'I'm getting tired of hearing that!'" Duke said.

The legal pad got his full attention at 6:00 a.m., after he read the

New York Times and the *Wall Street Journal*. There were sometimes as many as three hundred problems he needed to address, but if he focused on the top seven or eight things he needed to do that day—after the two or three things he *had* to do—gradually, he made a dent.

Some of the items on the list involved cajoling Spilman into approving five-hundred-dollar-plus purchases or getting him to send supervisors from the Henry County plants to train Mount Airy people to operate the new machinery. But his biggest challenge was changing the mind-set of his stubborn crew: he had to convince line workers who knew him only from his famous (but mass-market) furniture name that he had more than money invested in the operation.

"Bob gave him the plant to do something with, and then wouldn't give him the money to do it," recalled Sherwood Robertson, who operated the National Mount Airy plant several years after John Bassett. "Bob was very good at watching pennies while dollars fell through the cracks in the floor."

The other problems with National Mount Airy? The new roof leaked every time it rained. The ceilings had been ill designed, built so high that the lights had to hang down a full four feet. "It was ridiculous!" another Bassett plant manager harrumphed. The place was so big that the only way to get it profitable was to run the hell out of the machines...as well as the people operating them. "Bob thought John would hang himself," Reuben Scott, the retired J.D. plant manager, said. "And he just about did."

The workers hated the wholesale changes the mean, young Bassett was thrusting upon them. In hindsight, it was as if he expected them to go from using a rotary-dial phone to designing iPhone apps overnight. Pat Bassett even heard about it at the hairdresser, when another woman in the shop complained that this new furniture big shot in town was ruining her husband's life. "Wait a minute, that's my husband you're talking about," Pat said, bringing the gossip session to a halt.

The key was to get the workers to have the same amount of pride in their work as they'd had back in the bench-made days, when craftsmanship and elegance trumped production goals. "He needed them to believe that they could do it the conveyor way and have that same amount of pride"—even though they were now doing the exact same thing every day, with fewer mistakes and a higher output, "all words that made Spilman salivate," company lawyer Frank Snyder recalled.

As Pat Bassett remembered it, John had been so worried about what Spilman would do in Bassett with him gone that he asked her to stay behind to keep an ear to the ground. "I said no. You are not going away to the war," she said. "You are going seventy miles away, and I'm coming!"

She wasn't the only one put in the middle. Spilman dispatched Bassett sales manager Bob Merriman to Mount Airy to head its sales force—as well as to spy. "Get one thing straight," Spilman told him. "You don't work for my brother-in-law. You work for me."

"Bob, I don't want that kind of situation," Merriman said.

"I don't care. Anything he tells you to do, you don't do it without coming to me first."

Merriman drove straight to Mount Airy to report what Spilman had said. "Here's my dilemma. He's got me in the middle, but I want to work for you both."

To which John replied, "Just do what he tells you—and keep me up-to-date on everything he says." Forced to be a double agent, Merriman was now the one getting ulcers.

Early in the overhaul, John lost his cool when he spotted one line worker sitting atop a bucket to do his work. He hadn't realized in the new plant configuration that the worker had to be down that low to do the required floor-level detailing. John assumed he was lazy, and that kind of behavior was anathema back in Bassett, where no one ever sat down on the job. In Bassett, you could be so dehydrated that your fingers wrinkled, but you still didn't sit down. Why, the company kept salt tablets right next to the drinking fountains for your electrolyte replenishment! It was no wonder Howard Hodges kept working twenty minutes into his on-the-job heart attack before anyone thought to send him to the nurse.

JBIII got so mad when he saw the worker sitting down that he kicked the bucket out from under him, sending him sprawling onto the floor.

The story spread across Mount Airy, over the mountains, and all the way back to Bassett—a display of temper that surely made Bob Spilman grin. But John did something that night that Spilman would never have entertained the thought of: He went to the man's house, apologized, and begged him to come back to work.

If Spilman revered authority and dollar signs, John revered respect.

He did other things that endeared him, gradually, to the Mount Airy workers. He personally unloaded veneer when the company fell behind on orders. He stood atop the new conveyor belts and gave speeches about the company's finances and goals. "He told 'em how we were going to survive, and eventually people actually mended together and started doing what he said," Duke Taylor said. "But a lot of people still didn't like him because he was so aggressive. He'd call manager meetings for six a.m. And everybody knew he was this silver-spooned Bassett and definitely not one of us."

Taylor remembered when a Bassett textile plant cofounded by J.D. Bassett decades earlier was sold, which meant an eight-figure sum was dumped into the heir's lap—in a single day. That was not something that happened to regular folks in Mount Airy, not even to Andy Griffith.

Gradually, though, the distance between JBIII and Spilman began to work in the Mount Airy employees' favor, as John tried to insulate the plant from Spilman's tyrannical whims, with varying degrees of success. To boost sales, Spilman would order the Mount Airy factory to help the other Bassett plants make midlevel furniture for J.C. Penney, Bassett's largest customer, at the same time it was still making the higher-end stuff. "You couldn't turn those people off and on like that," Taylor said.

But Mount Airy was the place where some managers were finally let in on the secret to getting along with Sweet Ole Bob: You could never let him think that you needed him more than he needed you. Sherwood Robertson, the Mount Airy manager who's now a furniture consultant, said he figured that out the moment Spilman let it slip that he knew exactly how much money Robertson had in his personal trust account, held in a Martinsville bank. He then had the nerve to suggest that Robertson invest the seven-figure sum in Bassett stock instead. (He declined.)

That was the moment Robertson became one of the few people amid the Bassett higher-ups brave enough to make unilateral factory decisions. He arranged an advertising deal that he knew Spilman wouldn't have sanctioned, and he premiered the industry's first suite of Louis Philippe bedroom furniture at High Point, a suite that Spilman had considered so "goddamn ugly" that he'd ordered it hauled out of the showroom. It later became National Mount Airy's bestselling suite and an industry favorite, as well as a major weapon in John Bassett's assault on his Chinese competitors.

Robertson just happened to have what most employees at Bassett didn't—enough money that he could take Bob Spilman or leave him. A second key to getting along with Sweet Ole Bob was perhaps even more important: Spilman knew that Robertson could leave any time he wanted.

John Bassett had at least as much cash in the bank as Robertson, but what he didn't have was the satisfaction of doing what his father and grandfather before him had done: run Bassett Furniture Industries. And that was Spilman's ace.

There was no way to turn back the clock.

No way to make Mr. Doug return from the grave and safeguard his son's position in the company.

There was no denying it: Not only had Spilman beaten JBIII to the CEO desk, but it seemed he was not ever going to clear a space for him at the top, no matter how much he matured, how much productivity he inspired, or how many days in a row he worked.

After two years at Mount Airy, John had proved to the board of directors that he could take a giant new facility and make it profitable. "He introduced some of the most beautiful and creative products I've ever seen," said the furniture analyst Jerry Epperson, including a massive rolltop desk made of twenty-six pieces of solid oak that Epperson still uses in his Richmond office.

More important, John had proved that he could recognize top-notch talent, even in the quirkiest of places, a skill that would prove handier than he knew. With Taylor's help, he'd recruited Linda McMillian in a Rose's five-and-dime store—she was taking a popcorn machine apart—and put her on the path to becoming arguably the best furniture engineer in the United States. She had popcorn grease up to her elbows and no mechanical training at the time, but she worked hard and could do complex geometry in her head—as long as you let her chain-smoke all day long and didn't make her talk to anyone.

Back in Bassett, he would have been laughed at just for interviewing such an eccentric maverick. How would a ninety-pound woman command the respect of the foremen and line workers?

But back home, it was finally starting to dawn on John Bassett III, the possibilities were no longer what they had once seemed, even if your name was on the smokestacks.

By 1977, when Pat and John tromped the seventy miles back to Bassett with their three young kids, the message had become even clearer. Spilman had rearranged the furniture on the third floor of the Taj Mahal. The design had Spilman and his secretary occupying two spaces, including John's former office—the one where he'd hung the letter from his grandpop Mr. J.D. that said he hoped he'd do big things. Spilman had cleverly designed the floor plan so that to get to board chairman Mr. Ed's corner office, you had to walk through *his* office first. Lawyer Snyder's office was up there too, along with the head of finance's.

But there was no longer room for Little John. Spilman had located the National Mount Airy corporate office in a shared open-air space inside a former clothing store, down the street from Bassett headquarters. "He had a telephone but no secretary and about twenty square feet of space," Spencer Morten told me. "That was humiliating."

JBIII had moved his family to another state for three years, and when he returned to his hometown, he was not expecting a victory parade, but he did expect something even rarer in Bassett—a little acknowledgment that he'd just won one squeaker of a game. Instead, he got nothing; even the framed letter from his grandfather had been taken down from the wall.

11

The Family Elbow

*There was definitely a pre-1982 Bob Spilman
and a post-1982 Bob Spilman. After Ed Bassett left,
his body language, his gestures, everything
about him became more aggressive.*

—Frank Snyder, Bassett corporate lawyer

Spilman soon found himself occupied with worries far more serious than his cocky brother-in-law. Overseas competitors were beginning to bore holes in the furniture market.

Mao's successor, Teng Hsiao-p'ing, was forging his brand-new "socialist market economy" and opening China up to foreign investment, global markets, and limited private competition. "To get rich is glorious" became his mantra, the slogan credited with launching China's path to capitalism. Entrepreneurs in Taiwan and Hong Kong were particularly keen to cash in. If they couldn't sell much to the impoverished Chinese, why couldn't they use its disciplined labor pool to manufacture products for sale elsewhere in the world?

In July 1978, the Hong Kong–based Taiping Handbag Factory opened China's first foreign-owned plant in the city of Dongguan. Workers processed materials from Hong Kong into finished purses, then shipped them to Hong Kong for sale around the world, a business model that would go on to be copied by thousands of companies. Powerfully, if gradually, China was dismantling its old commune system and setting up shop. Purses would be followed by shoes, bags, garments, and suitcases in an export rush that elevated China's foreign trade to $20.6 billion by the end of 1978. Furniture was bigger and bulkier than purses, yes, but it was not impossible to ship, especially items that could be broken down easily into parts, such as end tables (called occasional tables) and chairs.

By 1980, the Chinese government had set up four special economic zones, places where it could experiment with entrepreneurial concepts, including allowing foreign investment and offering tax incentives. Within another decade, Chinese exports would break $100 billion.

In the early 1980s, Spilman vented his feelings about Far Eastern competition in a speech he gave before a banquet of furniture manufacturers, including some Asian businessmen. "I was looking at a list, and I see you're letting the damn slant-eyes in this business too," he said of the foreign competition, causing some in the audience to shrink into their chairs. In 1985, after watching the company's income slip 4 percent, he told his shareholders in a prescient speech that, while he didn't welcome U.S. government intervention, some form of parity was needed, or American-made occasional tables would soon become extinct.

His wife, Jane, recalled the first time a New York businessman suggested that Bassett begin importing from Pacific Rim countries, which were exporting occasional tables and chairs that broke down neatly into parts for reassembly in the United States.

"I can't do that," Spilman said. "The people who live here, this is their livelihood. If I close these plants, they'll have no jobs. Most have no other marketable skills and no high-school degrees. What will happen to them?"

Jane got goose bumps listening to the investment banker's reply. Her stomach sank. "I will sit back and wait," he told Spilman. "It will happen. You may not want it to happen, but you will be forced into this position."

She remembered her father, a second-generation furniture maker, discussing globalization in the early 1960s, back when South Korea and Japan began exporting radios, TVs, and automotive parts. Mr. Doug was sure that furniture would be immune to offshoring because, he argued, its weight and bulk would make the cost of shipping prohibitive. Jane had begun to wonder about that when she heard the retailers at Macy's and J.C. Penney in California — the first American region to be socked by the Asian imports — talking about how great the new furniture looked.

Spilman ordered his salesmen to ship some of the new Chinese cocktail-table imports to Bassett, then had his sample men make duplicates of the pieces and price out the parts. "And our costs, not adding any profit whatsoever, were appreciably higher than what the furniture was we were trying to compete against in California," Jane recalled, still incredulous. "What do you do?"

Spilman understood that the retailers would pocket even more profit if they sold a higher volume of the imported goods — especially if the stuff was 20 to 30 percent cheaper than the American-made items — and it dawned on him that if the retailers cut out the middlemen altogether and went directly to the Asian manufacturers, they wouldn't need Bassett Furniture at all.

The first time Spilman toured a Chinese factory, in 1979, the lack of safety precautions stunned him, Jane said. The plants were crowded, many had dirt floors, and most of the workers were crammed together into tiny dormitory rooms. As one shift ended, a tired worker would slide into bed — moments after his replacement had awakened in that same bed and left for work. It wasn't quite Bassett, Virginia, circa 1902, where families moved in from the countryside, some carrying lanterns in the predawn as they walked to work. The typical Chinese migrant arrived alone via one-way bus or train ticket, camped out in a dorm, and sent money to his or her family back in the rural countryside.

As chairman of the Virginia Port Authority, Spilman "knew very well the size of those ships and containers, and he knew that the statement my father had made forty years ago was absolutely ridiculous," Jane said. "The Asians could ship anything in the world they wanted to ship, and when he saw the size of those factories—huge plants on giant campuses—he knew it was no longer a threat. It was a real disaster knocking at our door."

And guess which furniture company Asian factories knocked off more than any other?

"You didn't copy the also-rans," furniture industry analyst Epperson told me. "You went after Bassett."

The first importers designing furniture solely for American customers were based predominantly in Hong Kong and Taiwan. Throughout the 1980s, they approached Spilman and other furniture CEOs, promising to deliver Bassett quality for 20 to 30 percent less than it cost them to make it domestically—and that included freight costs. As the Americans considered their options, they allowed the importers to tour their factories, though some things were still considered sacred: the Taiwanese were never permitted to tour the company's cash cow, Bassett Superior Lines, which churned out two hundred nightstands an hour.

Back in the early 1980s, most of the Taiwanese exporters were novices at furniture-making, especially where the finishing process was concerned. But how long that would last was anybody's guess. U.S. furniture workers were averaging $5.25 an hour, while the Taiwanese made $1.40 an hour, and the Chinese labored for 35 cents. The Far East may not have had the machinery or the lightning-fast conveyor belts that Bassett Speed Lines did, but when it came to throwing labor at a problem, no one worked harder, longer, or cheaper than the Chinese.

It was a delicate time for the American furniture makers, especially Sweet Ole Bob, even if he did still run the number one wooden furniture company in the world, with record sales of $301 million in 1981 and $25.1 million in profits. And even if he had gotten himself elected to several Fortune 500 company boards and to the councils of prestigious institutions—including colleges and coal corporations, banks, and an insurance company. And even if he was chairman of the Virginia Port Authority, a job that had earned him the nickname "Nuclear Bob," in honor of his one-man protest against New Zealand. (When the island nation refused to allow the U.S. Navy's nuclear ships to enter its harbors in 1984, Spilman stopped buying New Zealand lumber for use in Bassett furniture. "I just got tired of this country being kicked around," he told *Virginia Business* magazine.)

To complicate matters at the Taj Mahal, the company was being hammered with new lawsuits and a storm of bad publicity: Children were dying in Bassett-made cribs. An Early American–style model called Candlelite had been designed to mirror the bed in a popular adult-bedroom suite, a perfect replica of the headboard, with cutouts near the finial posts, only in miniature. What the designer hadn't taken into account was the risk of a toddler getting his head trapped inside the hollowed-out space between the finial and the headboard. Another design, a bamboo crib called Mandalay, had a similar flaw. Children had gotten their heads caught in the cut-outs. A child would panic and try desperately to extricate himself, yanking backward to the point of exhaustion. As he slumped forward on the crib's edge, he choked to death.

Rather than recall the cribs, Spilman ordered production halted and sent out modification kits to retailers, who passed them along free to Candlelite customers—the ones they could locate, anyway. (With the Mandalay model, the finials could simply be unscrewed, which removed the danger.) The kit included a piece of wood that had to be affixed to the headboard with a screwdriver and drill. "I said, 'Gee, Bob, not everybody has a drill at home,'" board member Spencer Morten said. "And he told me to shut up."

A couple of the cases were bogus, as Bassett lawyer Frank Snyder discovered when pediatric forensic specialists figured out that one baby hadn't died from suffocation at all but from blunt trauma to the head. In another case, a coroner determined the cause of death had been pneumonia, not choking as was alleged. According to a Consumer Product Safety Commission investigation, Snyder was concerned that Bassett was vulnerable to "crazy people" who might learn of the problems with the cribs and try to exploit the situation for financial gain. "He believes that such people may abuse their children and then contrive to set up accidents using Bassett cribs," an investigator noted.

By the time syndicated columnist Jack Anderson wrote about the crib deaths in 1980, six infants had died—including one in suburban Detroit whose relative was a secretary for the retailer where the crib was purchased but who had failed to pass the modification kit on to the child's parents. The repair packet sat unopened in the relative's car trunk as the little girl died slowly from the compression of blood vessels in her neck.

A child in Greenville, South Carolina, languished on life support for seventeen months before dying—the same week Bassett agreed to pay her parents $416,000 in an out-of-court liability settlement.

Anderson's column was a stinging rebuke. It lambasted Bassett for failing to notify the CPSC as required by law, resulting in a $175,000 civil fine. Anderson also hammered "the true insensitivity of the corporate brass," as he put it, showing a back-and-forth between Snyder and a customer who tried to warn the company about the problem, reporting that his daughter's head had been twice stuck (without injury) in a Bassett crib. "Such a situation could have proved fatal," the father, Richard Ball, had written to Snyder in 1976.

Snyder pointed out that Bassett cribs complied with all federal regulations and added: "I suggest that you have over-reacted to the experience of your child. Certainly, the suggestion [of possible fatality] magnifies the incident out of reasonable proportion."

When Spilman read the column, he asked his lawyer, "Good God, Snyder, did you actually say that?"

It was a nail-biting time. And heartbreaking. A pall was cast over each of the factories every time another Bassett-crib death was reported. "It weighed a lot on Bob," his friend Bunny Wampler said.

In hindsight, Snyder regrets his handling of the ordeal. He personally tried to track each of the thousand-plus cribs sold between 1974 and 1977 to ensure that each customer had a kit.

But some retailers kept poor records, especially those who were paid in cash, and the twelve thousand posters the company sent out to its three thousand crib retailers weren't seen by customers unless they happened to return to the store. (The CPSC estimated that most of the Candlelite cribs ultimately were not modified, a claim Snyder still firmly disputes.)

The company also voluntarily sent out warning posters to pediatricians across the United States for display in their waiting rooms, and in 1980 the CPSC required Bassett to take the unprecedented step of sending hazard notifications by mail to every parent in America who had a child twenty-one months or younger. The mailing was sent to four million parents and was estimated by CPSC to cost the company $1 million. Bassett also agreed to purchase half-page ads in *TV Guide* and *Family Circle* magazines to warn consumers of the potential hazard, as well as to offer a five-dollar reward to anyone identifying a crib in which the hazard had not been fixed.

The repair kits were beyond the skill set of many parents, Snyder conceded. "No wonder they scalded my butt," he said. "We should have just replaced the cribs immediately. In hindsight, I know now it was stupid." And though most of the lawsuits were bona fide cases resulting from the design flaw, "You had to investigate them all," he said, adding undue strife to already grieving families. All told, nine deaths were found to be associated with the cribs, and, eventually, Bassett paid out $800,000 in settlements.

Snyder, a fit eighty-four and healthy enough to work his hobby farm, met me at the McDonald's in Bassett Forks, a strip-mall cluster of fast-food restaurants and gas stations near the confluence of Martinsville and Bassett. It's where he has coffee regularly with other retired furniture men, and where he frequently spouts his goal of living a long life. He wants to spite Bob Spilman, who refused to pay Snyder's pension after he retired and went to work for a competitor, since, Spilman argued, it violated a noncompete clause in Snyder's contract.

Snyder went to court to fight back but ended up settling for getting his retirement reinstated after he realized the case would cost him a fortune in legal fees. He gave up his job at Pulaski Furniture—which made curio cabinets, and therefore wasn't a substantial competitor to Bassett, Snyder argued. He told me he still avoids fatty foods and eats predominantly vegetables and healthy grains and nuts, adhering to the alkaline diet, believing that it wards off cancer and other diseases.

"By God, I pray every day that Bassett stays in existence so they'll have to pay me my retirement till I'm a hundred and ten," he said.

Snyder said Spilman supported his work throughout the crib ordeal. But by the time Mr. Ed announced his retirement, at the end of 1981, his boss had begun to change—for the worse—as Spilman retained his presidency and also nabbed Ed's position as chairman of the board. Without Ed on hand to serve as a check and balance, Spilman not only physically claimed most of the executive floor but also became the absolute center of the corporate wheel, with all spokes feeding directly to him, giving him a near omnipotent amount of power, Snyder said. Information went directly to Spilman, but very little flowed back out. And JBIII was nowhere near the inner hub.

The home furnishings industry praised Spilman's demanding demeanor and "hands-on" attitude, naming him the top chief executive in the business in 1981. Bassett was still the biggest-volume furniture producer under a single name, with thirty-five plants in fourteen states and seven thousand employees.

Fifty-four at the time, Spilman was described as being charming and gracious one minute and profane and impatient the next. "His curiosity is boundless," one reporter wrote. "Spilman, his colleagues say, has *got* to know."

The worst thing Snyder ever witnessed Spilman do during that time? He had a salesman flown in from California so he could talk to him face to face—or rather, face to feet. With his underlings flanking him, Spilman removed his loafers, put his stocking feet on the edge of the boardroom table, and told the man he was fired.

Another time, Spilman learned that his yacht captain had accidentally been paid twice. When the captain refused to send the second check back, thinking he deserved a bonus, Spilman sent Snyder to Manteo, North Carolina, to threaten a lawsuit. "About something that amounted to fifty or sixty bucks," Snyder huffed. "That trip costs five times what that check was worth, and it embarrassed the hell outta me."

Spilman sometimes invited a select group of plant managers to join him on the yacht, according to manager Eddie Wall, who, like John Bassett, was not an invited member of the fishing or gin-rummy inner circle. "They said he was just another guy on that boat, very nice and gracious, except for one thing: He always made his visitors swab the deck and clean up at the end!"

No one in Bassett seems to know exactly what put John Bassett over the edge in December 1982. Maybe he got tired of the cubicle with no secretary or of having to ask for approval for every new screwdriver set he ordered. Maybe, as Spilman's close friend and competitor Bunny Wampler believes, Pat Bassett finally put her foot down and said, Enough's enough.

"Hell, they're both millionaires!" Wampler said. "What do they need that crap for? So Pat says, 'We're going to Galax,' and that's that. The women are always smarter than the men anyhow; don't you know that?"

One other popular theory: With the board of directors clearly cowed by Spilman and Spilman's son, Rob Jr., now ascending the ranks, maybe reality set in and John realized the Bassett presidency never would be his. "John would get so mad at Spilman, but Spilman just ignored him, like he didn't even exist," Wampler recalled. "For somebody like John Bassett, that was the worst thing you could do."

The Spilman-JBIII rivalry is widely rumored to have culminated in a fistfight, the news of which filtered down, in its usual manner, throughout the Henry County hollows and hillsides. The regular people in Bassett—the line workers and librarians, the barbers and beauticians—tell the story so convincingly that it's now just accepted community lore, like Mr. Ed's inability to cull up and down the Smith or Mr. J.D.'s selling the railroad the same lumber twice. As Junior Thomas put it, "Bob Spilman and John Bassett didn't trade no horses," which is a Henry County way of saying: They hated each other's guts.

"Little John like to have killed him. That's true!" Junior said.

The most reliable source I ferreted out on the subject was eighty-five-year-old rescue-squad volunteer Claude Cobler. "All I can say is, Bob Spilman didn't come back to work for a few days; he had a black eye," Cobler said. Asked if he was the ambulance driver who nabbed the hundred-dollar bill—the rumored tip John Bassett handed over to keep him quiet about hauling Spilman to the hospital—Cobler shrieked, "I am not going there!

"Listen, everybody in town knew when it happened, but we never did talk about it," he told me. "You just don't say anything negative about people giving you anything you want." Cobler had often called upon John's mom, Lucy Bassett, for support of the volunteer rescue squad in Bassett, and, relishing her patrician role in the community, she never once refused to write a check.

Three decades later, Cobler conceded that he was the ambulance driver called to the scene. Friends of Spilman claim they never heard of Spilman getting punched by John Bassett, so I'm left to wonder whether it's another part of the *Upstairs Downstairs* narrative in which the ones below stairs don't provide information to the ones above—like Spencer Morten not knowing the complete family tree.

"I don't know about a fistfight, and I think I'd remember if that happened," said Joe Meadors, Spilman's senior vice president for marketing. Retired plant manager Howard White, who still refers to his boss as Mr. Spilman, was so offended by the notion that he snapped, "If you can't say something nice, you shouldn't put it in your book."

As for John Bassett III, he firmly and repeatedly denied getting into fisticuffs with his brother-in-law. They didn't trade horses, sure, and family relations were forever strained. But blood was never spilled, he insisted.

So, for the record, JBIII will go to his grave denying that he laid out his brother-in-law in late 1982, shortly before he turned in his resignation at Bassett Furniture Industries. The two had a mild shoving incident one time, he said, but no one ever threw a punch.

The day Little John resigned from the company he was born to inherit, he said to his brother-in-law, "I might end up a failure, but I'm not going to my grave being known as J.D. Bassett's grandson, or Doug Bassett's son, or Bob Spilman's brother-in-law.

"I am not somebody else's surrogate."

JBIII departed Bassett to work for the company that his grandfather and his wife's grandfather had founded in Galax, Virginia, in 1919. According to *Home Furnishings Daily,* Vaughan-Bassett Furniture Company was making a fraction of what Bassett produced in a bad year—in 1982, it sold $22.8 million to Bassett's more than $300 million—but the move would finally allow John "to fulfill his ambition of becoming a furniture president."

Spilman was not available when a reporter called for comment. But when he accepted his brother-in-law's resignation from the position of vice president and from the Bassett board of directors, he told him not to bother returning to his office to collect his things. Somebody would pack up the would-be heir's belongings for him—including the framed letter from Grandpop—and bring them to his house. Those big things his grandfather hoped he would achieve? The only guarantee now was that he would not be doing them in his namesake town.

* * *

Things were unusually quiet in the Spilman household at dinner that Christmas. Pat and John spent Christmas with their children at their Florida home, as they typically did, while John's mother, Lucy, spent the day with Jane and Bob. Practically the only noise came from the maid, Gracie Wade, who'd worked for the Bassett family fifty-some years, beginning with Mr. J.D.

Gracie was then in her seventies. A retired widow living on Carver Lane, she grew flowers and vegetables, and when her roof needed patching, she took care of the repairs herself. It was her tradition, by choice, to serve the family's dinner on Christmas Day. She'd helped raise Little John and, after his father's death, went to work for John and Pat, who accommodated her favorite chore—ironing—by adding a small ironing room onto their house, with a sign that said GRACIE'S OFFICE outside the door. She was a terrible laundress, Pat Bassett recalled fondly, regularly shrinking clothes. But her position in the extended family was absolute. (Her husband, Pete, was Mr. J.D.'s longtime chauffeur.)

In fact, shortly after Mr. Doug's death, Lucy called Pat and John to tell them that Gracie was on her way to work for "Mr. John," as she called him, because she worked only for Bassett men. "Get ready!" Lucy warned them.

Of all the people interwoven with the family/corporate tree, of all the millionaires and smokestack magnates, the only one willing to question John Bassett's exit from the company he'd been born to inherit was the elderly family maid.

No one seated at the Spilman dinner table wanted to upset John's mother, Lucy, by discussing what was on everybody's mind. But Gracie didn't care. She was tired of propriety trumping family, tired of them trying to mask their true characters behind some pretentious veneer.

A Bassett quitting Bassett? She didn't like it one bit. She muttered to herself as she served the meal.

"It ain't right," she said.

PART IV

PART IV

12

Schooling the Chinese

A businessman setting up shop in Hong Kong
finds low taxes, no foolish government interferences... a
government leaning over to encourage him to
make as much money as he can. He finds, blessed
discovery, no politics.

—*ECONOMIST*, 1977

It took a Chinese native living in Taiwan and educated at the University of Pennsylvania's Wharton School to figure out how to capitalize on the new importing landscape. As a young man, Larry Moh had fled Communist China under Mao with his family, later marrying into a wealthy Taiwanese family and gaining two well-educated brothers-in-law: Ronald Zung, who had an MBA from Harvard, and his brother, Laurence Zung, who held a PhD in chemistry.

There was a hotel boom in Hong Kong in the mid-1970s, part of an industrialization wave that was bringing hordes of American businessmen to East Asia. China's growth was still modest, an exception in Asia at the time, with just 17 percent of its population living in cities (compared to half its population today). The so-called Asian tigers—Japan, South Korea, Taiwan, Singapore, the Philippines, and Hong

Kong—were already roaring, providing China with strong examples of economic possibility from every side.

But under the iron fist of Chairman Mao, China remained poor, agrarian, and isolated, partly by choice and partly as the result of an American embargo against China that had been in place until 1972. China was at the beginning of what Marx called the "primitive accumulation of capital," during which the bulk of a population moved from working land to working under smokestacks in cities and towns. China's evolution from farm-based to factory-based economy was half a century behind the American South's, although China would undergo the transition in a much shorter time under Teng Hsiao-p'ing's market-economy quest.

Larry Moh understood that Asia was ripe for industrialization, and with his new furniture company, Hong Kong Teakworks, he and his brothers-in-law borrowed $80,000 and positioned themselves to take full advantage. Brother-in-law Ronald was sent to North Carolina State University to learn the ins and outs of furniture manufacturing, and brother-in-law Laurence was dispatched to find furniture-grade lumber the company could use in Asia—other than the prized but expensive native teak—so it wouldn't have to import hardwood from the United States.

Rubberwood was plentiful in nearby Malaysia, where it was grown in groves and tapped for latex, like American maples are for syrup. Rubberwood sap went into the making of tires, condoms, and rubber gloves, and when the sap became too thick to extract—typically when the trees reached their midtwenties—the trees were usually felled. With its high sulfur content, rubberwood attracted bugs, and the two countries where it was most prevalent—Malaysia and Indonesia—were humid, causing mold and insect problems. The trees decayed so quickly once felled that rubberwood turned to Jell-O in as little as ten days. Once a rubberwood tree no longer produced latex, it was deemed unharvestable, and burned.

Until Laurence Zung came along and figured out how to turn

garbage into gold. "You had to be one step ahead of the bug," he said. When he applied the correct concentration of a chemical called penta-chloride to the raw rubberwood, he found he could repel the insects without staining the wood. Hong Kong Teakworks could then use that rubberwood in furniture-making, with results akin to hardwoods grown in the American South.

The lumber would be free, regulations in Hong Kong were minimal, and labor costs were next to nothing. In 1975, an Asian production worker made seventy-six cents an hour against an American factory worker's $6.36.

So Larry Moh and his brothers-in-law built a factory on two floors of a Hong Kong high-rise and set out to expand the Asian furniture offerings far past the usual wicker and rattan. With urban space at a premium, the high-rise didn't allow for the typical loading-dock setup, so they installed ramps inside the building, allowing delivery trucks to get to and from the higher-level floors.

They started out with hotel furniture, using a wider design to fit the heftier shapes of American business travelers. "You had all this trade building up, with big Americans going over there who didn't like the smaller, Asian-styled furniture," analyst Jerry Epperson said.

Making American-size hotel furniture was a natural beginning for Moh and his brothers-in-law, and hotel owners embraced it because they could charge more for the larger rooms that housed the furniture. But a question soon dawned on Larry Moh: Why couldn't he build furniture in Asia and sell it in American stores, just like the carmakers in Japan were doing?

Within a few years, Moh's company, now called Universal Furniture, had factories in Hong Kong, Singapore, and Taiwan. And he learned something it would take the American businessmen years to figure out: Culture mattered. While Laurence handled the science and Ronald focused on business, Moh was a master at navigating the welter of values and ethnicities within his factory walls. In multicultural Singapore, skin color played an important role in the hierarchy, just as it had in Bassett before the antidiscrimination reforms. The darkest people, those of Indian descent, were tasked with the finishing- and rub-room work. The native Malaysians handled the rough end, where the lumber was culled and cut to size, while the Chinese did the intricate veneer work and carving.

Moh knew that the people doing the tailing—handing off items from one department to the next—were especially key. The person tailing from the rough end to the carving had to be able to speak Mandarin so he could talk to the Chinese carvers, and the person handing off to the Indian finishers had to be comfortable communicating with them.

"They all had to eat separately because the food requirements were very different, and you couldn't mix any of the three," Epperson said. "Larry understood all that. He also knew how to shift production where it needed to be because of changing labor or tax rates or a political issue. He was knowledgeable about every aspect of it."

The Italians and Koreans had long exported furniture from their countries to their immigrant cousins in the United States, but Moh was the first to export furniture from Asia to Middle America. "From a visual point of view, it was identical to what we were buying here," Epperson said. It was basically Bassett Furniture—less, of course, 20 to 30 percent the cost.

So it went that Larry Moh became the first Asian to clobber the Southern furniture makers exactly the way they'd punched the guys in Grand Rapids a century before—with free hardwood and dirt-cheap labor. And the most surprising thing of all? Moh was so proper and polite, practically Southern in the way he went about conducting his business, that the Americans taught him exactly how to do it.

The worry Spilman had been harboring ever since his first trip to China soon proved valid: It wasn't long before Broyhill and other companies selling imports had Bassett's prices beaten, which meant that Spilman had to import too, just to stay competitive. Imports "will be with us forever," Spilman predicted.

Dining-room furniture became the next category, after occasional tables, to fall to imports, and by 1986, the domino effect had led to some bankruptcies. Seventeen American furniture factories closed that year.

"All the expertise we'd developed over the years and all the wonderful finishes and veneer work and carvings — we had to teach the Asians how to do it so they could provide us with more product," explained Michael K. Dugan, a former Henredon Furniture executive and a retired business professor.

"The problem is, once that process starts, there's no stopping it."

Joe Meadors can tell the story of globalization just by looking at the furniture in his room. Pointing to an ornate Bassett cocktail table, the company's retired vice president of marketing recalled when Larry Moh started selling ones just like it — for less than what it cost Bassett to buy the lumber.

Moh's dining-room table, china hutch, and four chairs? "Man, he'd come in with that suite, and it was so ornate and so cheap, you couldn't touch it," Meadors said. Moh's factories produced the parts and panels, fitted them into boxes, then shipped them, unassembled, to one of the five Universal assembly plants Moh had built across the United States. A comparable Bassett dining-room suite would wholesale for $999 (and retail for double that), but Moh's version was substantially more decorative, and it wholesaled for two hundred dollars less. "The overall quality wasn't quite as good at first, especially some of the finishes. But they could do much more than we could with ornate tops and fancy veneers," Meadors said.

The American consumer ate it up, especially the price. One of Universal's especially popular dining-room suites featured beautifully ornate French-style legs, which required considerable hand labor to produce. Meadors recalls the Jewish retailers who were big Bassett customers in New York, New Jersey, and Miami referring to Moh's furniture as pure *punim* — Yiddish for "beautiful face."

To compete against Universal and the growing throng of smaller importers, a Bassett plant manager in Dublin, Georgia, designed a bedroom suite the company could wholesale for $399, called a Shotgun Special. Buck Gale was a Bassett native with deep manufacturing roots whom Spilman had transferred in 1983 to run two struggling plants in Georgia. He was such a good engineer that when John Bassett left Bassett to go to Galax, he tried his best to lure Buck to come work for him. A second-generation furniture maker—his father had been a manager for both Stanley and Bassett—Buck had studied business at the College of William and Mary, and his line workers were totally devoted to him. He was also one of the few managers who defied Spilman on a regular basis, giving unapproved bonuses to managers and premiering his cheap new suites at the High Point Market even when Spilman refused to let him put Bassett hangtags on them.

Spilman may not have cared for Buck's renegade ways, but he was not about to let his brother-in-law abscond with his best plant manager. "He actually sent my wife and me to Williamsburg, to hide out in the woods for a week, to keep John from being able to get in touch with me," Buck recalled. Spilman plied Buck with a raise, a bonus, and a retirement pension that was hard to say no to, and it was aimed directly at John Bassett: it came with a clause that stated Buck could never, ever work for a competitor, not even in retirement.

The genius of Buck's so-called Shotgun Specials was the way he engineered them for efficiency: With minimal effort, the factories could change out the front of the headboard or chest to give the suites a flair of Mediterranean, contemporary, or Early American design. He lifted his methods from kitchen-cabinet manufacturers, reorganizing his factory layout around worker pods, or cells, and rearranging the work flow from the rough end to finishing. The old furniture axiom "You lose money at the saws" wasn't true for Buck's plant. He'd figured out how to maximize his yield by introducing finger joints—a joinery method in which short pieces are glued together to reduce the amount of culled lumber. "It was a damn no-brainer, but Spilman said no because his big idea was he wanted to start going higher end, from making Fords to Mercedes. But that's a hard thing to do overnight," Buck told me.

Buck also wanted to adopt a finishing system called KD—short for *knockdown*—which called for spray-painting the components, then shipping them to the consumer for assembly. KD furniture would go on to turn the Swedish-based IKEA into a powerhouse. But Spilman didn't want to spend the money to upgrade his finishing rooms, even though Dublin was by then the company's best-performing plant, with Buck's lean manufacturing practices firmly in place.

"Everything I did, it was all about: What's the least amount of materials? The least amount of labor? The least amount of overhead?" Buck said. "When we went to that kitchen-cabinet-type construction, I tell you, the process was so damn fast, we could've eaten 'em alive.

"But what we did in Dublin, it was like we hit a single and just stood there on first base," he went on. The company stopped trying to keep the factories running five and a half days a week—something Bassett had always prided itself on doing. That had long been the company-town mentality, even when they were only breaking even to do it, even when Hooker and American and Stanley were sending their workers home before the workweek was up. "Bassett used to be just hell-bent and determined to keep the plants running, even during hard times." One of Mr. J.D.'s favorite sayings, passed down through his heirs, had always been: "The money we make isn't made in the office. It's made in the factories."

By the late 1980s, the office had taken on a more prominent role, as fax machines, travel agents to coordinate trips to Asia, and translators became key to the importing operation. "The only thing we ever talked about in our meetings anymore," Buck said, "was margins."

Spilman achieved his dream of hitting the Fortune 500 in 1987 and 1988, but it was anticlimactic. Bassett was still the largest single-name-brand furniture company in the United States, with sales in 1985 of

$408 million and 8,400 employees working in fifty-seven plants in fifteen states. But with foreigners crowding into an already shrinking number of retailer showrooms, American manufacturers had 40 percent less display space than they'd had a decade before.

Mid- to higher-end furniture lines, including Kincaid, Stanley, and Lane Furniture, had cashed out or fallen prey to corporate raiders—Bonce Stanley's descendants had sold out to the Mead Corporation in 1969, a move that resulted in a succession of five company presidents in the 1970s and four separate owners in the 1980s. It was a far cry from the 1950s, when three-quarters of the furniture industry had been controlled by a handful of families in Virginia and North Carolina.

Now, instead of investing their profits in new machinery, many of the megacorporations were paying off leveraged-buyout debts, said Dugan, who chronicled the corporate infighting in his 2009 book *The Furniture Wars: How America Lost a Fifty Billion Dollar Industry*. The outsiders were Northern-based, mostly, companies with made-up marketing names—Interco, Masco, and the like—rather than family names.

From their faraway corporate perches, these executives aimed to teach the slow-drawling Southerners new ways of merchandising and marketing, reaping giant profits for all. They bought out family owners of profitable businesses in an industry they knew nothing about, promising to leave the local management alone except when they felt their financial expertise was required. The honeymoon ended when the profits had been milked to meet a corporation's earnings targets, and usually after management had demeaned the local guys and sapped initiative on the factory floor. When the conglomerates sold or spun off their acquisitions, citing "poor performance" or "failure to meet profit goals," the businesses parted ways for good.

"They didn't have sawdust in their veins, they had sawdust in their *brains*," Dugan told me. "You had all these outsiders taking over so much of the industry and basically bankrupting it."

According to Dugan, the villains were the outsiders, who didn't understand that making wood furniture wasn't something they could profit from overnight, and the victims—of their own self-inflicted wounds—were the Southern insiders, who were too change-resistant to modernize. "The bigger public companies had the hardest time trying to compete with Asia because they move slowly, with management that's far removed from the battlefield," Dugan said.

Most of them were so busy fighting each other, he argued, they paid scant attention to the mild-mannered importers invading their turf.

Following the corporate acquisitions of Stanley, Lane, and American, Bassett was rumored to be the target of a takeover. But Spilman said he believed the raiders were mainly pursuing medium- to high-end furniture makers, not moderately priced Bassett. One saving grace was Bassett's $65 million in cash reserves, which was there thanks partly to all those decades of hyperfrugal management by the second-generation Misters W.M., Doug, and Ed. "Spilman made sure the company had a balance sheet like Fort Knox, and he did a great job protecting the brand," said Paul Fulton, who was a board member at the time.

While the family had its share of internal battles, it maintained a sizable cadre of stockholders and corporate executives in its third generation who still cared more about furniture-making than cashing out. (Granted, they were already pretty rich.)

Two hours south of Bassett, in furniture-rich Hudson, North Carolina, Steve Kincaid, the third-generation operator of Kincaid Furniture, not only had to adapt to his extended family voting to sell out in 1979 but also had to fend off two hostile corporate takeovers in the 1980s—first from LADD Furniture, then from Nortech Systems, a conglomerate that also owned Stanley Furniture at the time. Surrounded by a bevy of Goldman Sachs investment bankers representing the company in New York in 1988, Kincaid, who was still running several factories for the company, had a simple question: How much was all this takeover-quashing going to cost?

At least two million, came the reply, and worse: Goldman Sachs needed him to pay a retainer of $465,000 by the next day.

"I said, 'I need to go call my dad!'" Kincaid, then in his forties, recalled, shaking his head.

At the same time, he was dealing with a divorce, a dying brother (who was also a business partner), and the Larry Mohs of the industry, by then termed, in the Southern furniture makers' minds, the *Asian invasion*. With its twelve factories and four-thousand-plus workers, Kincaid was eventually purchased in 1989 by the recliner giant La-Z-Boy, and again Steve Kincaid stayed on. This time he became senior vice president in charge of case goods and upholstery operations, making him a rare veteran of all three battles in the furniture wars — the family, the corporate conglomerates, and globalization.

The moment an import first made the hair on Kincaid's neck stand up? One of the company's bestselling items had long been its $220 Queen Anne dining-room chair; on a good day, the company churned out twelve hundred of them. When Kincaid noticed sales shrinking by the month, he took a closer look at Larry Moh and his importing ilk and discovered why: They were selling the same Queen Anne that Kincaid sold, only the Asian competitors sold it — even more embellished — for $50. Then $39.

"Our business started going south because we were not a value, so I went over there, and I toured their factories and I knew: We had to start importing chairs. There's just no way we could keep doing it here and compete," he said, even though his American plant was highly modernized, from its automated rough end to its state-of-the-art finishing operations.

For Bassett, for Stanley, and for Kincaid, the American-made chairs were the first items to fall victim to globalization. Time would soon tell what items would be flattened next under the weight of the Asian invaders — and which factories would fall.

At the Taj Mahal, the bigwigs were told to keep quiet. Spilman plotted his move like it was the invasion of Normandy. He even named the covert scheme Operation Blackhawk, a battle that would take place on the worn oak floors where Bassett Furniture had manufactured its first headboards and chests of drawers. Old Town, the original Bassett Furniture Industries factory, was closing. And true to form, Spilman wanted to make sure no one who actually worked there knew about it until he was ready to tell them.

Furniture sales had been flat throughout the industry, with 1989 sales down 1.5 percent from the previous year. The era of conspicuous consumption was coming to a close. One retail analyst said he'd found that most consumers preferred "to spend their money creating interesting lives for themselves and their children, on things like entertainment and vacations." Closing Old Town represented a change in Bassett's strategies, Spilman explained to his board, adding that the company was upgrading its designs to compete in a higher-priced market.

Spilman told stockholders, "Bassett has stuck to its knitting... while most furniture manufacturers have entered the consolidation frenzy and bought up other players via borrowed money." What he didn't mention was that he was investing in bonds for the company that paid 20 percent interest instead of investing in his own plants via upgraded machinery. What he didn't say was that Bassett hadn't gotten to where it was through buying bonds and using old equipment but by investing in its own industry.

In Henry County lingo, Bassett Furniture forgot who brung 'em to the dance.

"By that point, Bob was more interested in being on the boards of places like Bank of America than actually running a furniture company," said Tom Word, a Richmond attorney who represented the Spilmans and other furniture executives related to the family. "He wasn't going into the factories very often. He preferred to summon people to his office."

When Old Town closed, many of its four hundred workers were shifted to the six remaining plants in the area, as was much of the machinery. Members of the public were invited to stop by and take a commemorative brick from the premier storied plant. Later, laborers who'd once worked in the factories were hired to chunk off mortar from the building's bricks, which were sold to a British company. Which eventually shipped them to New Orleans, where they were used in the construction of townhouses.

Not one person quoted in a *Roanoke Times* story mentioned the real culprit behind the closing of Old Town: all the chairs and occasional tables arriving in containers at the Norfolk port, some of them trucked in willy-nilly, with chair arms in one shipment and chair legs in the next. No one quoted the middle-aged line workers who'd been going home for supper and wondering aloud, "What were all them little people doing at work today?" and "Why are they taking snapshots of everything we do?" None of the executives came right out and stated the obvious: that the sooner the "little people" learned how to craft Bassett Furniture in Asia, the sooner the local jobs would be offshored and the locals' positions deemed redundant.

Bassett was importing 8 to 10 percent of its inventory, but visits from Virginia to Taiwan and Hong Kong were picking up. Sales had declined for three years in a row, and tempers were flaring. Reuben Scott recalled Spilman showing one of his Asian visitors how he did his pricing: he looked at a new line, priced out the parts in his head, and, within a few seconds, calculated exactly how much the company should charge for the suite and what the margin would be. He'd often humiliate his plant managers in the process, Scott said. "He'd take my [pricing] sheets, tear 'em in half, and throw 'em on the floor and go, 'You're *crazy!*' "

While Spilman stormed around showing everyone who was boss in Bassett, Larry Moh plotted his next move. The center of Moh's operation was still Taiwan, but wages were rapidly rising there, and Moh had had the chessboard savvy to quietly spread the work around East Asia, with plants now in ten countries. With annual sales of $500 million, Universal was now the industry's fourth-largest company.

The Berlin Wall had just fallen, and the red tiger would soon leap into capitalism's fray. Over in Galax, John Bassett had left one enemy camp and had no idea he was about to be thrust into another. He was on his own now, charged with turning around a struggling and much smaller enterprise—and navigating a new minefield of family dynamics.

Thanks to the roaring success of Larry Moh and others, John Bassett had a hunch that it would not be long before he'd find himself staring down the barrel of a Communist government–backed competitor, and he'd be doing it at very close range: from inside his own factory walls.

The Dalian dresser was still two decades away, but already JBIII sensed the ground shifting beneath him, beneath the entire industry. If his little factory in the foothills stood any chance at all of surviving, everything about it would have to change. .

13

Bird-Doggin'
the Backwaters

*A good bird dog understands that the game has to be
between the hunter and the dog. The dog doesn't run out
by herself and leave the hunter a half mile behind.
She knows exactly how you get the bird.*

—JOHN BASSETT III

Decades before John Bassett made his way over the mountains to Galax, he hiked into the Henry County foothills with his Browning Sweet 16 shotgun and his English pointer, Cindy. They were quail hunting, a sport long enjoyed by Bassett men and their wealthy companions—well before Vice President Dick Cheney made a caricature of it in 2006 by shooting his hunting buddy in the face.

Cindy had always been a decent pointer. She could find and flush out quail from the heaviest of brush. But on every outing, when John shot down the birds, the dog refused to retrieve. He called in a dog-trainer friend, who brought along his beloved Llewellin setter Jill, arguably the best bird dog in the Appalachians.

John and his wife, Pat, were already among the nation's champion skeet shooters. They'd earned top honors individually and as a hunting pair. When you're married to a workaholic who spends most of his time thinking and talking about furniture, Pat said, it's helpful if you pursue the same hobbies. So she became a golfer, a skeet shooter, and a hunter of quail and grouse, and by all accounts, she matched her husband putt for putt and bird for bird. ("She was a little petite woman, but she'd pull out that big gun and shoot the crap outta that thing," said their babysitter Carolyn Blue, who traveled the skeet-shooting circuit with them.)

Cindy was not so enamored of the sporting life, though, especially retrieving. So John, the trainer, and their two dogs spent Saturdays trying to hone her instincts until finally they landed on the right strategy: The dogs flushed out the birds; the men shot the birds down. But when it came time to retrieve the prey, Jill sprang forward by instinct while the men kept laid-back Cindy tethered to her leash. Hour after hour, Jill was rewarded with praise for each bird she handed them while Cindy watched it all unfold, unable to move. Before long, she grew antsy.

By late afternoon, Cindy figured out exactly what she was missing and whined desperately to be put in the game. Every time Jill bolted for another bird, Cindy yanked hard to be freed.

The first time they let her go, the men kept Jill behind, tethered to the leash. Cindy was now not only a pointer but a retriever too. It went exactly as the trainer had planned.

Jealousy was a powerful motivator, and not just for dogs. When John begged to buy Jill from the trainer, he refused to sell. After three years, John finally got her, but only because he waited till she was almost at death's door. After nursing her back from a life-threatening case of mange and paying a whopper of a vet bill, he'd learned the power of patience and of waiting a competitor out. Though her tail tip remained forever hairless from the mange, Jill was a friend and hunting companion so devoted to him that for years she slept underneath his Ford Bronco to indicate she was always ready to hunt.

When John Bassett told me the story of Cindy and Jill, I understood perfectly what he was trying to convey: his powerful, if one-sided, vision of teamwork. He gave the orders. And because Jill trusted him for saving her life, she listened and loyally obeyed, which he then rewarded. And the cycle continued, leading to rewards for all, especially the man in charge.

John Bassett's likeness is rendered in an almost life-size oil painting that hangs in the parlor of his sprawling stone Tudor home in Roaring Gap, North Carolina, with views that stretch from Buffalo Mountain, near Floyd, Virginia, to Winston-Salem, a hundred miles south. Perched along the spine of the Blue Ridge Mountains, the community is so exclusive that the first time I turned onto its main thoroughfare, the road on my GPS vanished.

"And that's just the way we like it," John Bassett said.

The portrait, painted in 1969, shows a blond, thirty-two-year-old JBIII with his left arm around Jill and his right hand clutching his Browning. In the background, Cindy pants happily, as if waiting to spring forward and fetch him another bird. Mounted on the opposite wall of the room is a fan made of feathers from grouse Jill helped him nab, and looking out the window, you can see Jill's headstone protruding from the well-manicured lawn between the mansion and its three-bedroom guesthouse.

The first time I visited John and Pat Bassett's home, he spent twenty minutes telling me about Jill, a dog that had died nearly three decades before. It took one year and several visits to his factory before I understood what a mangy dog had to do with manufacturing—not to mention fighting the Chinese.

Cindy and Jill are minor characters in the trajectory of John Bassett's career, but when you examine the scenario facing him at the Galax factory, where he landed in 1983—the worn-down workforce, the festering feud roiling yet another branch of the family tree—it all circles back to the dogs. John Bassett went after the notion of putting Vaughan-Bassett on the furniture-making map with the cunning and persistence of a hunter on the prowl.

But this time he couldn't simply buy—or ass-chew—his way into a position of authority with the fifteen hundred Vaughan-Bassett line workers, as his forebears had done in Bassett. He had to bird-dog it—one department, one dresser, one sawdust-covered worker at a time.

But how to motivate a lackadaisical management team? And what to do with all the antiquated machinery, some of which had been purchased used—in 1954? When JBIII arrived at Vaughan-Bassett, it consisted of the Galax plant and a sister factory in Elkin, North Carolina, and together they produced a measly $28 million in annual sales with after-tax losses of $200,000. "The quality had gone to hell," said Tom Word, a Richmond lawyer and longtime Vaughan-Bassett board member. "Some suppliers wouldn't do business with them because they were behind on their bills. The designs weren't very exciting, and customers were returning stuff all the time." Quality was such a problem that several retailers had dropped Vaughan-Bassett from their showrooms.

Further complicating matters was the fact that C.W. "Buck" Higgins, Pat's uncle and the company president, was not as ready to retire as he had hinted back when Little John was sweating his Spilman demotion to the cubicle and wanted out of Bassett. Two decades his nephew's senior, Higgins named John plant manager instead of president and kept the top post for himself.

"I have never known a furniture man to retire well," Pat Bassett said.

John made inroads where he could, investing $317,000 of his personal money in company stock the first year, which he used to pay off company bills. He negotiated new contracts with suppliers, eventually buying in bulk to get a discount, which explains why you can't drive two blocks in Galax today without spotting one of the company's myriad thirty-foot stacks of lumber. He also hoards lumber before the winter months because bad weather can halt work in the sawmills. It's the same reason he tops off the gas tank of his bought-used 2007 Lexus every morning on his way to work—at Hess, the cheapest gas station in town. If you're not thinking ahead, you might find yourself stranded. ("What a curious man," said his wife of the gas-routine time-suck.)

To purchase new machinery, he loaned the company money from his personal fortune and convinced his boss to let him take out loans on behalf of the business, eventually saddling it with $18 million in debt, a move that made Higgins nervous. The Galax furniture factories had never been run with the drive—or the risk-taking—the Bassetts employed. "The family lived out of the business," John said. "They were comfortable, but they didn't drive the damn thing to the best it could be."

Hope Antonoff, a longtime sales rep for Mid-Atlantic Furniture, was so frustrated with the company's service—delayed orders, poor quality, and the old-boy mentality that resulted in her being treated like "some little girl"—that her company was planning to stop carrying the Vaughan-Bassett line. But when her boss heard that John Bassett was coming to Galax, he told her, "There's no way we're leaving now."

Jere Neff had worked for Bassett Furniture from 1948 to 1969, and years after his departure from the company, he watched with interest the elbowing-out of John courtesy of Spilman and Mr. Ed. He'd seen John build the National Mount Airy plant into something the company could be proud of, only to be thanked with a humiliating homecoming in Bassett.

Neff knew that John was as detail-oriented as his uncle W.M., the one who'd transformed Bassett from a backwoods sawmilling operation into the largest maker of wood furniture in the world.

"John is more like W.M. than he was his own father," Neff said. More important, "I knew John Bassett could sell ice to an Eskimo," Neff said, adding that John was also willing to fly to Miami at a moment's notice if his presence meant helping a rep close a six-figure sales deal.

After John's humiliation during the Spilman years, Neff had a hunch that conditions were just about perfect for a forty-five-year-old family black sheep.

Neff told Antonoff, "We are hitching our wagon to that man's star."

* * *

Higgins may have held the reins, but he knew when to remove himself from his nephew's path — especially where the details of the factory were concerned. John took his foremen to machinery shows, equipping them all with walkie-talkies (in the pre–cell phone era) so they could reach him if they spotted something he might want to buy.

"He ran a lathe. He ran a band saw," retired sales manager Bob Merriman told me. "He wanted them to see how it ought to be done." As the new equipment began rolling in, JBIII moved his desk from the Vaughan-Bassett offices and plunked it in the center of the machine room, between the rough end and the finishing department, something no plant manager had ever done.

People calling on the phone could barely hear him because of the roaring routers in the background, which is partly why he wears hearing aids today. Among my favorite moments of reporting this book was when he called me during my two-week residency at the Virginia Center for the Creative Arts. The writer in the studio next to me was working on a memoir about his two years of solitude in the Vermont woods. He got so mad about my loud discussions with JBIII that he banged repeatedly on our thin mutual wall. Artist-colony studio silence and interviews of partially deaf furniture guys did not mix, I learned.

There was a new sheriff in town, and John wanted all fifteen hundred workers to know he was *watching* them. He pored over every number the bean counters produced, examined the course of each component traversing the conveyor line. The employees were so scared of him at the beginning that secretary Sheila Key agreed to be his assistant on a trial basis only. "The time he spent in the office felt totally different" from the time he spent elsewhere in the company, she recalled. "People were terrified of him."

Like his grandfather before him, John knew the money wasn't made in the office; it was made in the factory. Occasionally, an ass had to be chewed to drive home that point. "He was really sweating the labor,"

Spencer Morten, a former board member of Vaughan-Bassett, told me. "John Bassett stayed on top of everything, including how many screws they needed to be putting in per minute."

To really get the factory humming, John knew, Vaughan-Bassett needed to recruit his old superintendent from National Mount Airy to the team. Duke Taylor could be difficult—higher-ups at Bassett had thought about firing Duke for years, but they feared he might actually hurt someone if they did. "The best thing I can say about Duke is, he may have been a curmudgeon, but the man could not make a bad piece of furniture," Merriman said. "He could make it out of Popsicle sticks if he had to and still make money."

Duke was downright fanatical about accuracy, and as far as John Bassett was concerned, that made him the prize bird dog of furniture-making.

The 1983 Vaughan-Bassett annual report tells the story. Orders were so slow that the factory was operating only half-time. The company was competing with its cousins at the other end of Chestnut Creek, Vaughan Furniture Company, almost double the size of Vaughan-Bassett. The plant was bleeding money.

And damn if John didn't leave Bassett after two decades of family infighting and land in the center of more family drama, some of it courtesy of Spilman. Spilman had gone to college with John Vaughan, and he'd been badmouthing Little John to Vaughan and his friends in Galax for years. "Look, John Vaughan and John Bassett were first cousins, and yet when John Bassett moved to Galax and John Vaughan had parties, Pat and John were never invited," Bunny Wampler explained, even though Pat was closely related to the Vaughans. (Pat's mother was the daughter of Vaughan-Bassett founder Bunyan Vaughan, and the two companies' boards had long been interconnected.) "Does that tell you something?"

When Pat and John declined to buy a home in Galax, with John commuting forty minutes across the state line from Roaring Gap, word filtered down that the Bassetts thought they were too good to live in Galax—a charge Pat and John vehemently deny. As one industry insider put it: "In the old days, the furniture families had been very, very reserved and modest and community-oriented. They lived in mansions, but they did not portray themselves as being above the people. The criticism you always heard of John Bassett was that he was full of himself, that he was too self-promoting."

John Bassett may have come across as arrogant to the power-wielding families in Galax, but he was too busy working to notice. Though the couple initially rented a house in town to see if they might want to buy in Galax, the absence of invitations from the extended family made it clear that blood was not thicker than water as far as Galax furniture-making was concerned. "They weren't that nice to us," Pat said, referring to their Higgins and Vaughan cousins.

Another Galax executive blamed faulty cocktail chatter for the rift: A false rumor had spread featuring John Bassett declaring that he "would rule Galax someday," offending the Vaughan cousins to no end, although it was actually a Martinsville stockbroker who'd made the prediction.

So Pat and John retreated to their home in Roaring Gap, where they were already entrenched in the supper-club circuit and there was no need to call friends on Wednesday to set up a Saturday golf game. At the Roaring Gap clubhouse, built by Hanes Corporation magnates in the early 1900s, there was a standing game every Saturday afternoon, a match in which John Bassett frequently excelled. And nary a player referred to him as Little John.

The Vaughans had visions of one day buying Vaughan-Bassett themselves, and more than one industry exec told me that John Bassett's arrival in Galax destroyed their dream of running the whole town. Just as he was not asked to join the gin-rummy fests on the Bassett corporate jet, John Bassett was not invited to be part of the Galax "knothole gang," the phrase for chummy furniture execs who liked to golf, hunt, and party together.

When one of the first things John Bassett did was raise wages on his factory floor, Morten recalled, Vaughan president George Vaughan sped over to the factory in his Cadillac Fleetwood and shouted at him, "Boy, you are in Vaughan country now! You can't go raising wages without checking with me first!"

Vaughan sales executive John McGhee recalled warning George and John Vaughan, "This guy's gonna be a powerhouse," when John Bassett moved to town. But like many in the industry, the Vaughans underestimated him at every turn. A few years younger than JBIII, McGhee had grown up in Bassett and had watched John navigate every challenge thrown his way. He'd watched his father chew him out on the sidewalk and jerk away his raise. He'd watched him compete on the golf course and in the classroom, and he knew that what John lacked in natural talent, he made up for in resolve:

Flood or not, there was never any water in the swamp.

"From the time we were twelve, thirteen years old, I just saw the intensity. Whatever it was, he worked twice as hard as anybody else," said McGhee, who shared that insight with his bosses at Vaughan.

"They got mad at me for even saying it," McGhee said.

Galax natives speak warmly — but carefully, as if still intimidated — about the Vaughan family's influence on the town. The family contributed generously to major community projects, including the hospital and library, and George Vaughan successfully lobbied for the construction of a four-lane highway, which buttressed development by connecting Galax to the nearby interstate and allowing trucks easy passage to and from the factories.

He got the road approved by inviting members of the state highway commission, of which he was a member, to meet in Galax while the Old Fiddlers' Convention was going on — when traffic congestion was at its peak. "He brought them up here and wined them and dined them out at his house, and every afternoon, when the factories let out, he managed to have them there on that [old] road between here and the convention," George's brother, John Vaughan, recalled.

After three days of battling the fiddlers and factory workers in their cars, the commission voted for the funds to build the highway.

George's younger brother and the CEO after him, John Vaughan "was a good man who looked after the town," said police chief Rick Clark. When one longtime employee at Vaughan was going to lose his health insurance because he couldn't work, John Vaughan couldn't convince the insurance company to see things his way. But he did allow the man to sit in a lawn chair in the factory and punch in and out, extending both his salary and his benefits.

"People here are extremely loyal and want to work hard," said Jill Burcham, a Galax minister and social worker whose family ran a textile factory in nearby Independence. "But that spirit was sometimes taken advantage of. When John Bassett arrived, it was time for the monopoly of a few controlling the town to change."

While the Vaughans were dreaming of expansion and Spilman was busy forgetting who'd brought him to the dance, John Bassett set out to do in Galax what he'd witnessed in Bassett: get the best equipment and the best workers and run the hell out of them.

There was just one problem with nabbing Duke Taylor, the headstrong plant manager who was a work-flow fanatic: Taylor still worked for Spilman. When another of John Bassett's first moves was putting Vaughan-Bassett's own longtime plant superintendent on a short leash, word reached the higher-ups at Bassett that the Vaughan-Bassett superintendent was looking for work, and they invited him to Bassett for an interview.

John was just about to fire him, and it turned out Bassett Furniture didn't want him either. Call it what it was — ethical hairsplitting — but John Bassett viewed the superintendent's interview in Bassett as the opening salvo in what would become a decades-long battle for the region's best furniture workers and managers.

His allegiance to the smokestacks that bore his name was now officially ended. He hired Duke.

As Meadors, the longtime Bassett sales executive, remembered it: "He picked us like a chicken!"

As he was packing up his things on his last day of work at Bassett, Duke recalled manager Joe Philpott warning him: "John Bassett's crazy. He'll never make it."

"You watch him," Duke shot back. "He knows more than all y'all."

So Duke came to Vaughan-Bassett and, eventually, so did many of National Mount Airy's finest workers. For a time, John loaned Duke a company car, a Cadillac he could fill with employees for the forty-five-minute commute. "We hired all the good people I had trained in Mount Airy," Duke said. "Spilman got so mad that he threatened to sue us. But that was like an elephant jumping on a peanut. John died laughing and said, 'Let him sue.'"

The jockeying went on for years. At least two of Joe Philpott's family vacations were interrupted by a furious Spilman ordering him to fly home on the company plane to lure back an employee John had poached. Once, Philpott spotted John Bassett grinning in front of the Bassett bank, like a bad penny whose circulation could not be stopped.

That time, he'd swiped a manager from the Bassett Chair plant for the Vaughan-Bassett plant in Elkin. When Philpott upped the ante by offering the man more money, it turned out John had already sealed the deal by arranging a second job—for the man's wife.

If only John could nab Linda McMillian, the Mount Airy product engineer they'd discovered years earlier with popcorn butter up to her elbows in the middle of a Rose's five-and-dime. John had been in Galax a week before he realized he needed Duke Taylor to get the factory humming. "I had to get Duke, then Duke had to get Linda. That was the key to everything," he said.

Buck Higgins told him the struggling factory had no business hiring a product engineer. Drawing out the parts had always been the job of the superintendent. Schematics for furniture components were maintained as actual wooden patterns rather than drawings, and they were stacked willy-nilly around the plant. "There were pieces of board everywhere," Linda recalled.

Buck was hesitant to believe that some never-married ninety-pound eccentric was the answer to the company's quality issues. Linda didn't really like people or computers, keeping to herself in the upstairs of the plant with her schematics and advanced math. "She don't get along with people too good; she's got a temper," Duke said. "But she has a photographic memory, and there is honestly no mistake on the factory floor she can't correct if you just leave her alone to do it."

She set her own schedule, arriving at four thirty every morning and leaving by two thirty in the afternoon — to avoid working with others, yes, and also to be home for her mentally handicapped sister, Diddy, before the sitter had to leave.

To prove to Buck that Linda was worth her salary, John and Duke paid her out of their own pockets for several weeks. They reconfigured the finishing room carefully, changing it, but not so much that they lost all the important grandfathered EPA permits. They bulldozed the old lumberyard that was always turning to mush when it rained and rebuilt it with a sturdier shale base. John worked Duke so hard — calling him at all hours of the night and on weekends — that Duke had his home telephone number changed and refused to give him the new one.

Buck Higgins finally relented when he understood how good Linda was, and he put her on the payroll. Linda was the only employee allowed to smoke in her office, in a facility chock-full of flammable materials that forbids cigarette smoking inside and out.

Buck told Duke, "John goes by the golden rule."

"What's that, Buck?"

"John's got the gold, and John wants to rule!"

14

Selling the Masses

Sell to the classes, eat with the masses.
Sell to the masses, eat with the classes.
—Henry Ford

They were making progress, albeit too slowly for JBIII. If he really wanted to see the company take off, he needed to bird-dog a new venture into being. He'd create new gold by opening a factory he'd start from scratch in Sumter, South Carolina, with a plant he could run without interference from his wife's uncle as a subsidiary of Vaughan-Bassett. And he'd do it the cheapest way he could—by gluing paper designs onto pressboard.

The Asians had yet to venture into paper-on-particleboard bedroom furniture, which would be popular with Heilig-Meyers, then on the cusp of becoming the nation's largest furniture retailer.

Some people in the industry called it *glit*, a combination of *glue* and *hold it together.*

Others mocked the word, calling it an amalgam of what the product really was: *glue* and *shit.*

JBIII practically stole the old Williams Furniture Company in Sumter, a one-million-square-foot facility, and here's how he did it: The conglomerates had finally realized they couldn't make furniture using the same principles they used to make paper or bathroom faucets. It was time for Georgia Pacific and the like to cut and run. In 1983, Wall Street investment banker Webb Turner had decided he wanted a change from the frenetic pace of New York, and he developed a fondness for furniture, thinking that if everyone else was cashing out, maybe he could profit by stepping in. Turner paid Georgia Pacific an estimated $16 million for the old Williams plant in 1983, then made the critical mistake of bringing in managers from up north—in a deeply Southern town known for its Civil War heritage. He acquired plants in Jamestown, New York, and Batesville, Indiana, then shelled out $60 million for the Burlington Furniture Division. It went bankrupt within the year, and the old Williams factory followed suit.

John Bassett's assault on Sumter was not one of a Yankee interloper but of a lone black sheep with deep pockets. He paid $4 million for the factory in 1987, one-quarter of what Turner had paid just four years before, and he assembled the deal as a three-way venture, calling it V-B/Williams. He used his own family money to buy a third of the company under the name Fivemost Corporation, shorthand for "the five most important people": Pat and John and their children, Doug, Wyatt, and Fran.

Vaughan-Bassett bought another third (partially with money he loaned it), and he sweet-talked a group of local patrons, who were loyal to the town and duly impressed by John's promise to put four hundred unemployed furniture workers back on the payroll, into paying the rest. They included a finishing-supply-company manager, a propane-company owner, and a lawyer, as well as some heirs of the original Williams company founders.

"He knew that coming into a different town in a different state, you can have all kinds of issues," said Sumter plant superintendent Garet Bosiger. "But if you have local people with ownership, all of a sudden people are more willing to work with you."

John Bassett knew it was good business to be courteous in Sumter—at least in public—especially after the carpetbagger treatment the town had experienced with Turner. He charmed the locals with his country-club etiquette and knowledge of Southern history, especially the Civil War. "He comes across as a very earnest person," said ninety-seven-year-old Ross McKenzie, a Sumter native who put $25,000 into the venture. "Not only was he a good businessman, he was very well-mannered."

JBIII? The man who had once interrogated Garet Bosiger so fiercely—because he thought Garet was looking for work elsewhere (he wasn't)—that Garet could no longer bear to maintain eye contact, which only fueled JBIII's fury?

"I like a man to look me in the eye!" JBIII barked.

"Sometimes I look away because I can't take it anymore," Garet replied. "Just tell me what you want me to do. But don't talk to me like a dog."

He'd lured Garet to Sumter from a competitor with the promise of company stock options. Now among the legions of JBIII managers who consider him a mentor and father figure, Garet later started his own furniture-supply factory with ample advice from John as well as a low-interest loan from him. The two of them cobbled together a mutually rewarding deal for Vaughan-Bassett to buy drawer sides from Garet's Appomattox River Manufacturing Company, based in Keysville, Virginia.

Like many of John's loyal lieutenants, Garet would take a bullet for the man. But he would not wish to be his son.

Launching a factory from scratch with just three security guards and a personnel manager made for the loneliest time of John Bassett's career. In Mount Airy, he may have had to dodge Spilman, but at least he had upper-level managers in the company's finance and legal departments on call. "In Sumter, I had to be everything," he said. "The banks weren't loaning me another dime, and I had invested millions such that I could easily go broke if this thing didn't fly.

"This wasn't some hypothetical case at Harvard Business School. My feet were in the stirrups!"

Garet Bosiger's wife, Martha, predicted V-B/Williams would be a moneymaking venture, and true enough, within sixty days of producing its first glit-furniture piece, the company was profitable. Martha predicted it, just as the spouse of every other manager reporting to John Bassett grew to intimately understand that there is still no one in the industry who works harder or longer hours.

They know it with every peal of his signature refrain: the telephone ring.

He calls on Christmas morning. *Make sure the dry kiln is turned on so we don't ruin that stack of wood.*

He calls at 1:30 a.m. *That cabinet-room foreman giving us trouble all these months? Well, I've just decided. He's got to go.*

He calls on your vacation, and if you dare object, he reasons: *If I'm calling you, then I'm working too!*

He calls on Saturday when you're mowing the lawn—and if you can't get to the phone in time, he'll accuse you later of screening your calls.

At precisely 9:15 every New Year's Day, he calls the previous year's top salesperson and asks, *What have you sold for me this year?*

He calls occasionally to share a dirty joke; nothing too bawdy, just something a frat guy from the 1950s would tell.

He calls from the phone next to the *toilet* in one of the bathrooms of his Roaring Gap home.

He calls from his car—though he still isn't sure what button to press if you call him on his cell.

He calls from his bed at New York's Hospital for Special Surgery. Still slurring from anesthesia after a foot operation, he's thought of one more thing he wants to recount: The story of Apollo 13, the way those astronauts and the men in Houston worked night and day to fix the botched equipment so no one would die. The way they refused to accept failure and did not yield and *Guess what, America! They prevailed because they worked hard and smart. And so can you!*

He's practically in tears when he calls after learning that more people at Stanley Furniture will soon lose their jobs. He prefaces the conversation with *This is off the record, this is off o' everything. This is just us girls.*

He calls. And calls. And calls. Never identifies himself; never has to. With that deep baritone drawl and that entitled sense of timing, who else would it be?

He called Garet so often in the early days of getting the Sumter plant running — usually at 5:30 in the morning and again at 10:30 at night — that Garet's wife finally grabbed the phone.

"Are you trying to cut Garet out of all his sex life?" Martha shouted.

John Bassett laughed so hard at that one, he actually gave Garet a night or two off. Still, his personal rule for the telephone is simple, comprehensive, and not open for discussion: "I don't call Gentiles on Easter weekend or Jews on Yom Kippur."

Any other time, when he feels the need to lecture or tell a dirty joke or describe an idea that has just occurred to him, he calls.

The design calls in Sumter were among the most colorful. The V-B/Williams beds came with mirrors glued to the headboards. Some were papered in fake marble. An entertainment center called Good Vibrations came with your choice of fake marble, fake wood, or mirrors, and it had compartments for a television and a stereo, as well as a rack for shot glasses and a bottle of, say, Courvoisier, like something from "The Ladies' Man," that old *Saturday Night Live* sketch.

One dresser was so wobbly that the plant manager had to put it on skis. "It was actually a shim, with two pieces of wood to make the dresser stable enough that it wouldn't tip over, but it was just like a person wearing skis," recalled Bob Merriman, Vaughan-Bassett's longtime sales chief and a board member of V-B/Williams.

The Larry Mohs of the industry were now drilling the wood-furniture market, but John's new Sumter plant could do an end run around them with a cheaper alternative to their solid wood and veneers. The marketing-friendly term was *MDF*, for "medium-density fiberboard." It was also called borax. But critics still called it glit.

MDF was marketed as promotional furniture—in furniture-retail lingo, *promotional* refers to the cheapest items in a company's line. It was sold, usually via credit, in low-end discount stores such as Heilig-Meyers. A V-B/Williams bedroom suite wholesaled for $300, which was about $300 less than the veneer-based products the company made in Galax and $700 less than the solid wood furniture coming out of its Elkin plant.

The target customer lived far away from places like Roaring Gap, but John saw promise in marketing low-priced furniture. Because it attracted an entirely different customer base than he was used to, John called his salespeople together to brainstorm. "We've got to sit down and figure out what the ethnics and the low-income people are buying, because that's what we've got to sell," he said.

They journeyed to stores in the middle of slums in Chicago, Los Angeles, and New York. Harlem customers particularly loved the stuff. Buck Higgins, still the Vaughan-Bassett CEO, had never been to places like that before and had no intention of lingering. In one Los Angeles neighborhood, his rental car overheated, and he panicked. "My God, we'll get killed down here in this barrio! They'll take our pocketbooks and our shoes!"

Buck told John and Merriman to fetch water for the radiator, after which they sped out of there in a scene that still cracks Merriman up. "But you know what?" he said. "The more blue-collar they were, the better John got along with them. Besides, he'd been at [mass-market] Bassett for so long, it's not like he expected to be dealing with Harvard graduates anyway."

Garet Bosiger, reared on a Virginia tobacco farm that didn't have running water till he was ten years old, was shocked the first time he went on one of the company's design trips, as they were called. He went to Heilig-Meyers's offices in Richmond with John's son Wyatt, who had just joined the retailer, and stood back as a pompous buyer berated and belittled Wyatt for selling inferior furniture. More even-keeled than his father and Garet both, Wyatt said nothing—he'd worked for the man out of college and knew he enjoyed intimidating salesmen.

"I'd like to get that guy in a dark alley one night and teach him some manners," Garet told John in Sumter after recounting the episode.

"You're the dumbest guy I've ever talked to," John shot back. "Don't you know the best way to get revenge?"

"What's that?"

"You take their money!"

Garet and I both grew up in houses where the furniture was bought used or picked up along the side of the road. We bonded over our past poverty one rainy fall day in 2012, and we cracked up as he recounted JBIII's eccentricities and the social blunders he made courtesy of his silver-spoon upbringing. There was the time he bragged about the $100,000 he'd just made via a single phone call to his stockbroker. A recession loomed, but, as John said happily to Garet, "Thank God people are still buying cigarettes, Co'-Cola, and beer!"

Another time, John asked his plant manager how things were going at home. Garet told him that he and his wife were buying a house in Sumter and navigating the mortgage-application process.

"What interest rates are they offering?" John wanted to know.

"Nine percent."

"Well, tell 'em you're not gonna do it! Tell 'em you're offering seven, and they can take it or leave it!"

Garet had to laugh. His boss understood the nuances of operating a business, from factory depreciation to EPA regulations to arcane tax codes. He read the *Economist* every week!

But he'd never taken out a mortgage in his life.

* * *

John related remarkably well to most of the four hundred line workers in Sumter, a predominantly black workforce that had been unionized during the Williams tenure. He'd had a chance to buy the plant a few years before Turner bought it, but he hadn't wanted the hassle or added expense of the union. Sumter wages were 10 percent lower than Galax wages, which were already 5 percent below the industry average. And by closing the plant the year before, Turner had done JBIII the huge favor of eliminating the union presence.

Now unemployment was rising, and people were eager to get to work. "He was very adamant with the workers that if the union ever came back in, he would shut the plant down," Sumter controller Ellen Hill recalled. "If they had a problem, they were supposed to come tell him; the line of communication was always open."

We can help you better than some union organizer "who lives off in Timbuktu," he told them. If a worker or manager had any problem at all, he wanted to know about it before it reached critical mass. "Come on, guys, at least bring me a live body to revive!" he told them. "Don't bring me a corpse!"

He presented himself casually to the workers, wearing his trademark sweat-stained golf cap, khakis, and a tattered sweater vest (usually embroidered with the logo of one of his exclusive golf clubs). His clothes were not showy—half blue-blood prep and half cheapskate. By the end of the day, they were usually layered with sawdust, as if he'd stepped out of an Orvis catalog from twenty years back and had yet to locate a shower or washing machine.

"He never wore a suit and tie, and you got the sense he never exploited his position," said Sumter maintenance man Roger Plock. "But people knew he was the boss."

A month after V-B/Williams premiered its first line, the backlog for orders was so long they had to take the line off the market for a while. "The one thing about glit?" Merriman said. "It may have been tacky as hell, but it was profitable."

By the time John sold V-B/Williams to Vaughan-Bassett and merged the two companies together, in 1998, the Sumter plant was valued at $33 million. Not bad for wobbly beds and mirrors held together by glue and you know what.

With Sumter up and running, John began spending most of his time in Galax. Buck Higgins was about to retire, so Pat and John could finally stretch their wings. At the High Point Market, Pat Bassett wined and dined retailers in a house the company rented during the semiannual show, and orders swelled. A talented cook who spared neither expense nor butter — one signature dish was deep-fried chicken Kiev — Pat was deemed by John to be the Perle Mesta of Roaring Gap, just as Jane had nicknamed herself in Bassett. He even hung up signs that said PERLE'S PLACE in their house.

Pat carefully assembled each night's guest list to avoid conflicts among competing buyers. She hired professional chefs to help her cater and made sure no glass went unfilled. The parties occasionally got so wild that she had a Breathalyzer on hand to test people before they left. Not many passed.

"We were a little company, probably the least expected to survive," John said. "So we did anything we could think of to entice customers." Between Pat and Sumter and all that bird-dogging John did inside the factories and out on the road, Vaughan-Bassett sales had nearly quadrupled, to $79 million, five years after his arrival.

But it was the Sumter plant turnaround more than any of the others that buoyed him. "I realized I was J.D. Bassett's grandson and Doug Bassett's son. And I was even Bob Spilman's brother-in-law. But guess what? This time, *I* did it. And that creates confidence that you're just as good as the next guy out there."

Duke Taylor had Vaughan-Bassett humming, and Bob Merriman had permission to go after the best salesmen in the industry. The guys at Bassett were unhappy, Merriman recalled. "Working for Bassett had always been like being in the FBI. You had to do it their way." He contacted every one of them, chicken-picking his way through Bassett's reps in Chicago, New York, and California.

Over drinks that Christmas, Spilman gave John hell for poaching his salesmen, telling him, "I've got to figure out a way to keep you and Bob Merriman from pissing in my tent. Y'all are hiring too many of my people."

To which John responded, "They came to us."

That was true, but only in a hairsplitting way. The two men had poached so many of each other's employees—hiding at least one of them in the woods!—that people in the industry had long since stopped keeping count.

Of graver concern, had anyone been paying attention, were the latest sets of containers trickling in from China. They held solid wood furniture that was about to retail, astonishingly, for the same low price as the glit.

On December 8, 1993, President Bill Clinton signed NAFTA into law. The trade pact would eliminate virtually all tariffs and trade restrictions among the United States, Canada, and Mexico. As he signed it, Clinton said he hoped the agreement would encourage other countries to work toward a broader world. In Mexico, NAFTA was greeted with a mixture of excitement and dread. Some Mexican businessmen worried about the end of the traditional siesta, as the hard-charging, American-style business pace threatened to put a dent in two-hour lunches and naps.

But as discussions about trade deals between NAFTA partners and China began to grab headlines, no one brought up the Asian work culture or the pace. In a 1994 Gallup poll, 68 percent of the Chinese population said that "work hard and get rich" was their overarching personal philosophy of life.

JBIII knew all about what Larry Moh had accomplished in Taiwan, Singapore, and Hong Kong. He followed the progress when Moh made his strategic opening salvo in China, in a coastal area outside Beijing called Tianjin.

"When Larry went into China, he had really done his homework," the industry analyst Jerry Epperson said. He began by sending letters of introduction to the head of the Communist Party in that particular province. He followed up by sending formal letters of reference and bank statements to show that he wasn't just talking—he had money to invest.

Then, following the custom in China, Moh made a sustained show of sincerity and purpose. For three consecutive weeks, Moh arrived for a Monday appointment with the Communist Party official—only to sit in the waiting room for days at a stretch. "As a foreign investor back then in China, you had to get all these different permits," recalled Larry Moh's son, Michael. "You had to meet with many different mayors and secretaries and explain, over and over, how you're going to improve the economy in that particular locale."

Moh understood that he couldn't send an underling to wait there. It had to be the senior-most person in the business. He also knew that his factories would have to be situated facing a certain direction. Feng shui, the belief that positioning objects can affect energy flow, remains popular in this superstition-rich country, and Moh himself was a believer. Likewise, to maximize good luck and fortune, the factory had to open on a carefully chosen date.

Moh also knew that China needed people like him as much as he needed its workforce. The Chinese government realized it had to globalize in order to improve the standard of living among its masses. It didn't want Westernization so much as restoration of the party's legitimacy after Mao, and that could be achieved through economic growth. Any Western culture that seeped in was purely incidental, aggressively discouraged, and occasionally snuffed out. China was still a decade away from formally joining the World Trade Organization, and the entrepreneurialism during Moh's ascent became so unrestrained that observers the world over called it cowboy capitalism.

The underlying strategy was not so different from the one in Bassett, Virginia, circa 1902: cheap labor, efficient production, and minimal government interference. Laurence Zung, Moh's brother-in-law and business partner, remembered the two of them slicing through boiler permits in Singapore, ignoring permits for sawmilling rubber trees in Malaysia—"Before they even find out we're in there cutting, we're already gone," he said, chuckling—and breezily renegotiating land contracts in Taiwan.

"In the Oriental custom," Zung said, "when people know each other and trust each other, things go so much faster" than in the more strictly regulated United States. "Larry is very good at mingling with people, and the thing I admire most about him? He has guts. He will do a lot of things which I doubt I will ever try to do on my own." (Though Moh died in 2002, his brother-in-law still speaks of him in the present tense.)

The gutsiest thing he did, in Zung's opinion, was figure out how to skip the American manufacturers entirely and sell directly to retailers, a strategy that threatened to make the very existence of the American manufacturers moot. But it involved taking some belly-churning financial risks.

Previously, when the company sold furniture to American manufacturers, it was paid the moment the merchandise was placed in the shipping container. With Moh's new scheme, the money would not be transferred until the merchandise arrived in America, and Zung was nervous about funding the enterprise during the three to four months it would take to ship, assemble, and place the items in U.S. stores. But Moh had a hunch that bigger profits awaited if they brought in an investor and changed everything up. He found a sugar daddy in the Matson Navigation Company, an American shipping concern with substantial holdings in Hawaiian sugar plantations and an eagerness to invest in the Far East. (The company was launched in 1882, when Captain William Matson sailed his three-masted schooner from San Francisco to Hilo, Hawaii, carrying merchandise and food supplies.)

"To really make it big, we had to get the money to finance our inventory," Zung told me. After seven years, Zung and Moh bought their shares back from Alexander and Baldwin, Matson's parent company, then took the company public.

By the time he sold Universal to Masco in 1989 for $480 million, Moh was a master of globalization. He had four factories in Taiwan; two plants each in China, Singapore, and Malaysia; and one each in Hong Kong, Thailand, and Indonesia. The company also maintained assembly, sales, and marketing offices in Sweden, Saudi Arabia, and Australia.

"I don't know how he did it, but he always had bright guys working for him here and offshore, and he was somehow able to keep them all from cannibalizing each other," said author and industry watcher Michael Dugan.

One of Moh's acquisitions was BenchCraft, based in New Albany, Mississippi, which owner Hugh McLarty had sold to him in 1987. At that time, Universal was busy acquiring American case goods and upholstery companies alike, many of them based in North Carolina. "Mr. Moh was a man of few words," McLarty said. "He never explained why he did things; he just did what he wanted to do and didn't talk about it much. But he was very respected in the industry, very smart. He knew to grease palms when he needed to.

"People understood," McLarty said. "China was out to run them out of business."

Moh was decisive, focused, and not at all afraid. Colleagues recalled him leading meetings while keeping track of his considerable American stock holdings on a television — out of the corner of his eye. "He made ninety-seven million dollars one day in a single trade," said Richard Bennington, a High Point University professor who regularly courted Moh as a donor for the college's home-furnishings program.

But Moh didn't brag about his money, or his achievements. Moh endowed generous scholarships in his wife's name at both High Point and Wharton, his graduate-school alma mater. When Bennington asked him to contribute $50,000 to help the college raise the $500,000 needed to construct a new furniture-program building, Moh gifted the entire amount. "He didn't want anything named for him," Bennington said, adding that Moh had the building named for the editor of *Furniture/Today*.

"He was a very fierce competitor, but he was very humble about it and very quiet, which is why you won't find much written about him."

Now the owner of a nursing-home chain based near Chicago, his brother-in-law was happy to fill in some details. Too many look at globalization and miss the nuances of the story, Zung argued. He and Moh took the American furniture makers down several notches, granted, but they didn't manage that by cheap Asian labor alone.

"We approached it totally differently than the U.S. manufacturers," Zung said. They did it by targeting volume and efficiency through reverse-engineering and factory streamlining. Once a chair was designed, Zung adapted the blueprint to fit basic settings on his machines, which were geared to reduce assembly-line downtime. Consumer choices were also whittled down with regard to size and finish. The pieces were made in Asia, then shipped to assembly plants strategically stationed in Japan, Canada, Sweden, Saudi Arabia, Wales, Australia, and the United States. The focus was to push out the largest volume in the shortest amount of time and, most important, at the cheapest price.

This was furniture, after all, not cars. Few people looked at the bottom of a chair to see where it was made.

Certainly not the masses, Zung knew, reciting almost exactly the same Henry Ford–ism spouted by John Bassett and his glit-making lieutenants. "My slogan is always, 'Sell to the masses, live with the classes,'" Zung said.

PART V

15

The Storm Before the Tsunami

If it's made north of the Mason-Dixon Line,
it's a furniture set. If it's made south of the
Mason-Dixon Line, it's a furniture suite.
And if it's made in China, it's junk.
—MARC SCHEWEL, CEO OF SCHEWELS FURNITURE

It formed over the eastern Atlantic near the Cape Verde Islands on September 9, 1989. It weakened after killing thirty-four people in the Caribbean, then surprised everyone by regrouping and landing with a vengeance at Charleston Harbor. It killed twenty-seven in South Carolina, rendered a hundred thousand homeless, and caused ten billion dollars in damage. When the tail end of Hurricane Hugo sailed toward the ridge at Roaring Gap, the bedroom windows on Pat and John Bassett's mountainside manor started buckling.

Pat protested when John made her get out of bed at three in the morning so they could barricade themselves in the kitchen. But after the ninety-mile-an-hour winds finally died down, the couple returned to the bedroom to find giant, jagged pieces of glass stuck in the wall—where their heads would have been.

The damage was nothing compared to what happened in Sumter, though, where winds peaked at 106 miles an hour. The hurricane ripped off the roof of the V-B/Williams factory, along with an attached sprinkler system, sending 350,000 gallons of water rushing into the factory.

If glit had a kryptonite, it was water. The whole lot of it reverted to a soggy mush of paper, sawdust, and glue. The factory's dust collectors, funnel-shaped vacuums that were, ironically, already named cyclones, were toppled. The tall, aluminum contraptions had stood sentinel for decades atop the plant, but now they were splayed out on the ground, dented, smashed, and strewn helter-skelter, like a tea party for giants gone horribly awry.

By the time Buck Higgins, Vaughan-Bassett's elder statesman, reached John by phone to tell him about the damages at the factory— some two million dollars and counting—Buck was in a full-blown panic.

"John, we're wiped out," Buck said. "Wiped out!"

Vaughan-Bassett and investors had sunk millions into the Sumter plant, and they were still on the hook for another $5 million in loans. John had taken care of the arrangements himself—the deal-making with shareholders, the bank loans, even the multiple insurance policies required to keep the banks happy. So he knew what Buck didn't: the company had coverage not just on the building and its equipment but also the inventory *and* the loss of business that would occur as they rebuilt the factory.

"Buck, we've got at least twenty-five million dollars in insurance, don't worry," he told his wife's uncle.

There was a long pause before Buck finally answered.

"John?"

"Yes, Buck."

"Maybe we're not wiped out."

In the patriarchal world of furniture-making, amid the cutthroat spirit that sliced through families and companies like a ripsaw, Little John was almost fifty-two years old and, finally, not so stupid after all.

* * *

Garet Bosiger remembered the first call he took about the hurricane. It was John on the phone—at 6:00 a.m., no surprise—and it was maybe John's tenth phone call already that day. From his Galax office, JBIII had already lined up contractors from Mount Airy. He knew the hurricane hadn't hit his competitors in Henry County and Lenoir, so he needed to move swiftly or risk the other glit makers moving in on his turf.

"Let me tell you something," Garet said. "When things go all to hell, that's when it's like the most fun to him. He's giving instructions, and he's positively gleaming. He's like a general!"

That was the first thing Wyatt Bassett, John's younger son, had noticed about his father when he went to work for him in the middle of the recession of 1990. Wyatt had just spent two years working for Heilig-Meyers, learning the retail end of the industry. The Gulf War was on, unemployment was growing, and gas prices were up—all of which took a toll on buying, especially among the Sumter demographic. Orders dried up within a matter of weeks.

"What I learned from him during that time most distinctly was, you don't panic. It's a waste of time," Wyatt recalled. He also got his first lesson on the importance of knowing your BEP, or break-even point, as it's taught in Economics 101. His father introduced him to the ins and outs of depreciation, demonstrating how a company could show a profit by simply breaking even because of the tax benefit of depreciating, or writing off, purchased factory equipment. He learned his dad's theory on depreciation management: If you don't regularly reinvest the money in new equipment, your company will find itself behind the times on efficiency and, ultimately, not meeting its BEP.

"Guys, we've got to compete like a business, not a country club," John told his managers. Nouveau Bassett could engage in aristocratic frippery if it wanted, but Vaughan-Bassett would be run like the Bassett Furniture of yore—lean, mean, and with very careful oversight.

That especially applied to the sales staff. JBIII personally went on the road with his salesmen, selling furniture the best way he knew how — eyeball-to-eyeball, calling on retailers from San Diego to Miami Beach. They flew coach, with the men booked two to a hotel room. Bob Spilman was still jet-setting around in Bassett Furniture's corporate plane, but John used the excuse of the recession to implement austerity measures and eliminate company cars for good, something he'd long wanted to do.

JBIII took that lean attitude and sharp scrutiny inside the factories as well, meaning the hog got inspected on a regular basis, another of Mr. J.D.'s parsimonious edicts. The hog was the machine that ground scrap wood into smaller chips, which were then burned in the boiler to generate steam for the kilns. "The hog is adequately named because if you don't watch it, it will hog all your profits," Mr. J.D. liked to say, referring to employees who were eager to cover up miscuts and other mistakes by throwing them into the hog to burn their blunders.

"You get what you *in*spect, not what you *ex*pect," John told his managers.

When I asked if the company had ever had a corporate plane, he barked, "Oh *hell* no!" He pointed to his spare second-floor corporate office in Galax, where the command center — his conference table turned desk — is enveloped, cubicle-style, in 1970s-era fake wood paneling and furnished with mismatched desks and chairs, most of them veneer. The arrangement allows him to communicate JBIII-style — that is, loudly and directly. When he wants to know the daily account balance or when he needs his secretary, Sheila, to get someone on the phone for him, he simply hollers around the partial walls, which are papered with posters of golf courses he belongs to, drawings by his grandchildren, and printouts of slightly off-color jokes.

Vaughan-Bassett's corporate offices were designed to be the exact opposite of Bassett's headquarters, with its matching high-backed leather chairs and gilt-framed executive portraits. It was so showy that in the 1980s, the townspeople had stopped referring to it as the Taj Mahal and rechristened it the Ivory Tower.

JBIII had to make some tough choices during the first recession of his corporate presidency: V-B/Williams managers took a 10 percent salary decrease, and one was let go. The line workers' salaries weren't cut, but at the lowest point in 1990, forty laborers were laid off.

John took no salary at all, slept fitfully, and when Sheila tried to hunt him down during lunch once (before cell phones), she had to call all around town. She found him, finally, eating at Rose's five-and-dime—but only after describing him to the waitress as "that guy who wears the white hat and talks to himself all the time."

He was muttering a lot those days, in between ass-chewing and penny-counting. His wife, Pat, said that when she really wanted to know what he was worrying about, she stood outside the shower door and listened to him talk through the conversations he was planning to have that day. He'd already improved Buck Higgins's method of cash-flow management. Fearful of credit, Higgins had long been ordering his accountants to pay the company's bills via checks—only to stash the checks in the company safe until there was money in the banks to cover them. Some checks sat for weeks, others for months. (In Buck's defense, he had not grown up with a family business that kept $80 million or more in the company savings account, as John had.) The company was just barely liquid when JBIII showed up, operating on a four-day workweek and trying to manage a 27 percent decline in profits in 1983, according to the annual report. (A cash snapshot from 1982 shows a cash balance of just $14,229, with stockholder equity at $11.5 million, less than one-tenth its current size.)

As punishment for the company's paying bills late, most of Vaughan-Bassett's suppliers upped their prices. So John established new lines of credit. As the company's bill-paying record improved, he negotiated discounts with suppliers and, ultimately, shifted the BEP in the company's favor.

He did not waste time on political correctness, former personnel manager Tim Prillaman recalled. "When I interviewed with him in the mid-nineties, he asked me not one legal question. It was, 'Who's your mama? Who's your daddy? Who's your mama's mama?'"

Prillaman's grandparents on both sides were bootleggers who'd served time. When he explained his family tree, John brightened. Hell, back in Bassett, John had hired every bootlegger he could find because they worked hard and they were good businessmen—they just happened to be in an illegal business.

"So, you a corn-fed boy, am I right?" JBIII wanted to know.

"Yes, sir, I am!" Prillaman said, and he was hired.

At one point when they were perilously close to the BEP in Sumter, Garet remembered, JBIII wrote a personal check for $300,000 and told the bankers, "If the boys need this, cash it. If they don't, tear it up."

He was already employing a labor-efficiency tool he'd discovered years earlier in Mount Airy and filed away for later use. A distraught wife who worked at an apparel plant had sought John out on her lunch hour and begged him to rehire her husband, whom he'd fired for showing up drunk. John didn't rehire the man, but he did get an idea from the woman after she nearly ran him over in a scramble to get back to work before her lunch break ended.

"Why the frantic rush?" he wanted to know. She told him that each month, as long as she didn't miss any days or clock in late a single time, her factory paid a monthly attendance bonus, which added an extra 6 percent to her pay. But the best part was this: the bonus was written out on a separate check, making it possible for a woman with a penny-pinching husband to hide the extra check without said penny-pincher being any the wiser.

When John implemented the bonus in Sumter (and, later, in Elkin and Galax), absenteeism went down from 5 percent to 2 percent. One line worker thanked him effusively, admitting that she squirreled the bonus away for personal needs.

Panty-hose money, she called it.

John Bassett winked at the panty-hose money all the way to the bank. "People love to work for something," he told me. "You just have to be sure that what you get out of it is more than what they get out of it!"

"By the mid-nineties, a lot of furniture was shifting to China, but we still thought bedroom was immune because of the freight costs," Wyatt Bassett told me. American furniture makers still clung to the belief that beds and dressers were not likely to be offshored because bedroom furniture was bulkier than tables and chairs, didn't break down easily, and involved shipping a lot of air-filled drawers.

Wyatt had grown up grouse hunting with his dad—though he never really enjoyed shooting the birds, his mother said. "He's the one who, whenever we were anywhere with two cars, he always rode home with John and everybody else rode with me. He just really wanted to please him and still does."

JBIII recalls counseling his younger son before an admissions interview with Northwestern University's Kellogg School of Management, then the number one MBA program in the country. Wyatt's grades had been so-so at Washington and Lee—not unlike his father and grandfather before him, he had partied hard—though his GMAT scores were in the 98th percentile.

"At the interview, they're going to ask you if you have anything you want to say," JBIII predicted. What Wyatt should say, advised his father, was this: As a fourth-generation soon-to-be factory manager, Wyatt was probably among the very few applicants destined to run a factory. Chances were even better that he would be the only one headed to Appalachia after graduate school instead of Wall Street.

For the first time in family history, a Bassett would represent himself as an element of group diversity—which, considering the elite Northwestern B-school crowd, he probably was. The professors' heads nodded, the interview went far beyond the allotted time, and the strategy worked. ("With every negotiation in life, ya gotta figure out: What do they want?" JBIII said.)

When Wyatt returned to Galax with his MBA, Vaughan-Bassett was importing some components of its furniture—drawer sides from Russia and Latin America—and Wyatt had already begun traveling to Asia with his dad. The Chinese were getting better at manufacturing all the time. Cheap Chinese furniture no longer meant the Chinese furniture was cheaply made, and the Asian competitors had the economics of production and shipping nailed.

By the time labor rates started to rise in one country, Larry Moh was already eyeing the next cheap market. As his son, Michael Moh, told me, "He always stayed ahead; he was always looking to the next developing market, even if the infrastructure there was poor, and the ways of doing business were more difficult.

"If things were perfect, he knew, you were already too late."

Lucky for Moh and Zung, container lines were building larger and larger ships, driving down the cost per unit. When Zung first joined his brother-in-law's company, in 1972, they paid $1,800 to float a container from Taiwan to the United States. Two decades later, they paid even less—about $1,500 per container. The ships were larger than before, and the Asian factories were now the shipping lines' number one customers, which gave Zung the freedom to negotiate better bulk rates. "We guaranteed them two hundred containers a month one way, and more importantly, we said, 'We can guarantee you another fifty or seventy-five a month coming back the other way,'" Laurence Zung recalled.

The boats that had once returned empty to China now went back laden with lumber—much of it harvested in the Appalachians, not so far from the Smith River banks. Whether that wood would eventually be sawed and lathed into beds and dressers—then shipped right back to Bassett, Stanley, Vaughan-Bassett, and the rest—was the question.

But before that question could be answered, John Bassett found himself staring down the barrel of yet another problem, one that was more familiar than the Asian invaders and every bit as deadly. In 1995,

Vaughan-Bassett premiered a new suite of bedroom furniture called Golden Memories. It was Victorian in design, with ornate carvings and brass drawer pulls. But according to furniture giant Lexington Furniture Industries, the suite did more than simply hearken back to the memory of Queen Victoria. It was a near replica of Lexington's spin on that design, called Victorian Sampler, which had long been Lexington's bread-and-butter suite, generating more than $50 million in annual sales and becoming one of the bestselling furniture groups in the history of the industry.

Vaughan-Bassett employed a thousand people at the time and reported sales of $103 million. Lexington Home Brands, then the nation's largest manufacturer of residential furniture, employed more than five thousand people and had sales of $426 million. And it was owned by Masco Corporation, the multibillion-dollar enterprise that had bought Moh's Universal.

In a federal lawsuit, filed in Greensboro, North Carolina, Lexington claimed Vaughan-Bassett had infringed on its intellectual property, a violation known as trade dress. And true enough, Vaughan-Bassett had bought the Lexington suite, examined every piece of it, and made a near identical copy that sold for two hundred dollars less than the Victorian Sampler. But a company's trade dress could be violated only when the look of its product was so distinctive and well-known that the item itself served as a kind of trademark—like the egg-shaped L'eggs hosiery container or the curvy glass bottle of Coke.

Clever copying skills had long cloaked a dearth of originality in the furniture trade, which had always suffered from a lack of brand loyalty among consumers. The surest bet, then, was to copy something that was already selling well, then sell it for less. As Mr. W.M. Bassett had told his brother, Doug, in 1960, after Lane Furniture filed a similar lawsuit against Bassett over the knocked-off modern table group called Acclaim, "There's no way we can settle. It would nullify our whole design program if we did!"

Besides, unless a piece was boldly contemporary or represented a wholly unprecedented design, chances were good that a clever furniture maker could find something in the annals of furniture history that resembled the newly produced suite—even when that designer had "knocked it off cold," as the saying went. (That's what Leo Jiranek had done in response to the Acclaim lawsuit, finding the original design, from the 1800s, in a Philadelphia museum.) There were usually earlier precedents to be found for any design. But now Lexington was trying to change the game, sending out cease-and-desist letters to competitors premiering designs similar to those for which Lexington already held a patent or a patent pending. The letters were working too; Bassett and several other furniture makers had backed off upon receipt of Lexington's written threat. Vaughan-Bassett had too, initially, tweaking its first version of the Victorian knockoff and reintroducing it with a few changes, including a new name: Remembrances.

Lexington responded with a second threatening letter, saying the suite still violated the company's trade dress and arguing that it had sole authority to bring a design back from history because it had been the first in recent history to do so.

John usually tried to play nice. But by now it had become clear that *somebody* had to take on this multibillion-dollar Goliath, and as John Bassett was wont to think: It might as well be him.

We're going to sue you was the next volley from Lexington's New York lawyers.

Bring it, John Bassett said, and grabbed his two favorite tools: a legal pad and a telephone.

This was John Bassett in the catbird seat: A mostly female jury in a Greensboro courtroom filled with piece after piece of furniture, if not exactly of his making then at least made largely of his design. He smiled as his workers hauled in the items, his leg bouncing up and down in anticipation, as it always does when he's about to do one of his favorite things: lecture.

He would compare and contrast his suite with the Lexington suite and with similar reproductions made by myriad other companies, all of which drew inspiration and detail from one another and from the reign of Queen Victoria, of course.

Asked years later if he'd been nervous, he said, "As a whore in church!" But he masked the perspiration well. The moment the judge gave him permission to walk around the courtroom, roaming from dresser to dresser, John Bassett wasn't just sitting in the catbird's seat. He owned it. In his nearly four decades of practicing law, John's lawyer Warren Zirkle said he has yet to encounter a more impassioned trial witness.

John rubbed a cornice piece with his hands, signaling his love of the materials and the craft. He looked the female jurists in the eye, knowing that women handle the bulk of furniture purchases. He spoke so knowledgeably about his favorite subject that if he hadn't already explained that he'd grown up checking on his family's factories en route to Little League games, they would have intuited it. Jurors could practically smell the sawdust emanating from his sweat.

Then came the folksy drawl, the diphthongs, the preponderance of dropped *g*'s.

"He is very adept at wrapping himself in the red, white, and blue," Zirkle told me. "He used every opportunity he could to tie his argument back to why he felt so strongly about his right to sell this furniture—and why it was in the consumer's best interests for that to be so."

The Lexington lawyers had prepared for a case that enumerated the many ways in which Vaughan-Bassett had ripped off Lexington's design. But Zirkle made that argument moot by countering: We admit we copied it, and we have a right to—not just because the styles were popular in Queen Victoria's time but also because copying ultimately serves the consumer by encouraging competition and therefore lower prices.

The company's other ace in the hole? The weekend before the two-week trial began, Wyatt holed up in his parents' Roaring Gap guest-house poring over Lexington's pending-patent applications. And he noticed something: Lexington's newest catalog featured six collections that included the patent-pending label. But Wyatt had a copy of the company's patent applications, and when he cross-checked, he found that none of the six in question were actually on the patent-pending list.

So Vaughan-Bassett countersued, at which point Lexington argued that its patent-pending labels were simply mistaken. "They thought they could just scare everybody off [from knocking off their designs], then after a year or two claim we had violated their trade dress," John Bassett said.

"They were gonna totally change the business for us, and if they had won, they could have gotten triple damages—well into the millions. It could have broken this company."

The trial lasted ten days and included a surprising witness for the defense—Bob Spilman—who talked about how Bassett Furniture had played the same knockoff game as Vaughan-Bassett, as had everyone else in the mass-market price category. The jury knew it wasn't just a typical brother-in-law testimony when John explained that he'd left Bassett Furniture in 1982 because the company wasn't big enough to hold the both of them.

"Self-preservation is the first law of nature," explained Bob Merriman. "Over the years, Bassett Furniture probably copied more people than anybody I know. Bob pretended like he testified to try to help John, but he was also making sure his ox didn't get gored in this thing."

Spilman testified out of loyalty to Jane and to people like B.C. Vaughan and Buck Higgins, according to Bunny Wampler, the CEO of Pulaski Furniture, who also testified as a witness for Vaughan-Bassett. "All we did was tell the truth—that there is no originality in the furniture business, no matter what anybody says," Wampler said.

In the end, the knockoff tradition prevailed, and Lexington's furniture was deemed not so distinctive as to provoke a trade-dress violation. The jury also decided that Lexington's patent-pending labels were in "reckless disregard for the rights of Vaughan-Bassett" and ordered

Lexington to pay Vaughan-Bassett one dollar in damages, a symbolic victory.

John Bassett had no clue that a much bigger legal battle awaited him, against an opponent that was more hostile than Spilman and worth even more than Masco. It would also thoroughly upend his argument about putting the consumer's dollar first.

But for now, anyway, his company was safe.

•

16

Trouble in the 'Ville

By God, Johnny, this doesn't smell like
springwater to me.
—BOB BRAMMER

Though his uncle's legacy would soon come into play, John didn't know much about the venerable W.M. Bassett. In fact, he remembers only one story about his late uncle Bill.

The families were all at the compound in Hobe Sound, Florida, circa 1946. Mr. J.D.'s house was first in the line, followed by the vacation homes of John's aunt Anne Stanley, his aunt Blanche Vaughan, his uncle Bill, and, finally, his father. Little John was nine years old and so bored that he took to dribbling his basketball up and down the concrete sidewalks and driveways of his relatives' homes in the afternoon—when the head of Bassett Furniture just happened to be taking his nap.

It was pre-air-conditioning, and the windows were open, with white mesh screens to keep the no-see-ums out. He was perfecting his dribble when he heard the raising of a screen in his uncle Bill's bedroom window. A crisp dollar bill appeared, fluttered in the warm breeze, and landed gently near his feet.

Little John picked up the dollar, held it like the secret it was, and knew exactly what it meant. He took his ball and left W.M. Bassett to nap in peace.

The following afternoon, the dribbling commenced again, and the manna from heaven reappeared. No one said a word about the exchange. When on the third day a five-dollar bill floated down before him, Little John knew instinctively what that meant too: No dribbling for a week.

In those days, Bassett kids were blessed with a weekly allowance of one dollar—and Mr. Doug expected his son to save half and not blow the whole thing playing slot machines over in "black town," as most whites called the segregation-era black commercial district.

"How much money do you have left from your allowance, son?" Doug Bassett wanted to know.

John carefully retrieved fifty cents from his pocket.

"That's a good boy, son," Doug said, having no clue about the remaining $3.50 John had stashed in his room—or the fun he'd had playing the slots.

JBIII didn't know his uncle well at all, but he has long relished the memory of that floating dollar bill—not to mention the lesson on what money could do for a clever boy who knew when to talk and when to keep his mouth shut.

As former Bassett vice president Howard Altizer put it, W.M. Bassett was probably the best furniture man in the entire extended clan. "But he's the one Bassett that gets overlooked in the company history because for the thirty years that he ran it there was no sensationalism."

But W.M was soon to experience sensationalism, with his name-sake plant at the center of controversy. Had the men at Bassett Furniture known what was about to hit them, they might have heeded Mr. W.M.'s favorite bit of advice:

"Gentlemen, get out your smelling salts!"

JBIII had never worked with his uncle Bill, though early in his career, during his stint in quality control, he regularly stopped by the plant W.M. Bassett had founded. It was a big factory, four stories high and seven hundred thousand square feet, down a hill from a residential neighborhood in Martinsville and not far from downtown.

It was also possibly, as John Bassett learned soon after the Lexington trial, about to be sold.

He knew the factory had a state-of-the-art finishing room, and, even better, it had retained its environmental permits from earlier years. He knew a buyer wouldn't have to bother with those pesky new EPA regulations; the finishing room at the W.M. plant was grandfathered in under the older, more liberal rules.

JBIII also knew exactly where the sewer line was located because one time back in the 1970s, he'd overseen the building of a new lumberyard on the site—only to have a contractor mistakenly nip the sewer line with his bulldozer. He thought the contractors had hit springwater, but before long, a stench engulfed the town, and it traveled all the way to the DuPont nylon plant, the region's best-paying employer for miles.

John called in Bob Brammer, the head of plant expansions, who sped to the W.M. plant so fast he left a trail of dust in his wake. His hooked nose twitched like a rabbit's the moment he got out of his car. "By God, Johnny, this doesn't smell like springwater to me," he said.

It was two decades later now, and John Bassett could recall exactly where the sewer line was beneath the W.M. plant. "I even knew where the damn springwater was. They weren't gonna fool me with this one."

He knew too that NAFTA was already running roughshod over the workers in the region's textile plants: By 1997, thousands of sewing jobs had moved to Mexico and overseas, and rumors were that the great ship DuPont and the other sweatshirt and textile companies that still employed eleven thousand people in Henry County would soon be sunk.

Bassett had closed its original Old Town factory in 1989, but its remaining Henry County plants were running full steam. Spilman, now nearing retirement, had hit a record sales peak of $510 million in 1994, the same year NAFTA's "giant sucking sound" commenced. But sales were now in decline, owing to the rise of importers who were underselling domestic producers at every turn. "We were always the Fords, and suddenly the retailers started going for the Toyotas...and then the big buyers started bringing in container loads of the stuff," recalled Bassett sales executive Joe Meadors. "We lost a lot of our market share because we were trying to fight off the imports."

The California Public Employees' Retirement System, the largest pension fund in the country and an institutional shareholder in Bassett, put Bassett on its list of ten underperforming companies in 1996 and 1997. CalPERS also submitted a proposal to the company's board to separate the positions of CEO and chairman—a move widely viewed as a jab at Spilman.

Spilman, sixty-nine, was also taking heat from some shareholders for being overly committed to other corporate boards, from coal companies and insurance giants to several colleges and banks. A *Businessweek* story pointed out that five NationsBank directors served on the Bassett Furniture Industries board in a rubber-stamp arrangement that the magazine deemed clubby, incestuous, and "little more than a claque of the CEO's cronies."

"The board acquiesced to Bob Spilman too much," said one longtime member, who asked not to be named.

Mary Elizabeth Morten remembers when the extended family finally decided Bob Spilman needed a not-so-subtle nudge off the CEO chair. Joined by her cousin Tom Stanley, Bonce Stanley's son, the pair leveraged their stock holdings and made the case that it was time for Spilman not just to relinquish his post as president but to step down entirely from the operation.

"Has Mrs. Morten sought legal counsel?" one of the pro-Spilman directors wanted to know.

She might have been retiring and unerringly polite—Mary Elizabeth showed up to our first interview wearing a skirt suit with a matching hat in the style of Jackie Kennedy—but she had very definitely sought legal counsel. "It scared them," her husband, Spencer Morten, recalled. "Mrs. Morten was maybe going to sue them for malfeasance. By this time, Bob was [or had recently been active] on twenty-three different boards, and he had no time to run the company."

By the time Spilman's retirement was official, in August 1997, the company had slid to number seven on *Furniture/Today*'s list of the top twenty-five American manufacturers. Of the eighteen publicly owned companies on the list, only three—including Bassett—performed worse in 1996 than they had in 1995. The company hadn't had a real growth spurt since 1992.

When a *Roanoke Times* reporter called John Bassett for his reaction to the news of his brother-in-law's "retirement" from the company, only an insider would have known John's tongue was firmly in his cheek. "Bob has been one of the more unforgettable people in our industry," he said.

Spilman was praised for overseeing numerous acquisitions and expansions and for his role in organizing the purchase of the International Home Furnishings Center in High Point—the main Market showroom building—to keep the trade show from migrating to Dallas or Atlanta.

Neither the local media nor the trade press carried the real story behind Spilman's departure. "The Jupiter Island crowd, they were displeased" with his performance, Rob said, referring to his relatives. But the family no longer had the stockholding clout to force a retirement, he said, disputing Spencer Morten's account. Rob Spilman said his father and the board mutually conceded that since he was sixty-nine and the company was no longer on the upswing, it was time for him to step down.

Barber Coy Young said word filtered down to the masses in town as it usually did.

"He was still in charge of the port authority," Coy said. Spilman had helped transform it from a place ships passed on their way to Baltimore into one of the busiest ports along the East Coast. He'd personally called on governors for funds and shepherded the reunification of the Norfolk and Hampton Roads ports.

"He was still blowing around town like he always did—as Mr. Spilman, CEO. But you could tell he was wounded.

"The air was definitely out of his sails."

Rob Spilman was named president and chief operating officer, and, if Bob and Jane's succession plan came to fruition, before long Rob would be CEO.

Rob had grown up in Bassett—before he went away to boarding school, anyway—when his family's company was top dog. As a kid attending the High Point Market with his parents in the 1960s, he watched his father and uncles implement an astonishing six-week moratorium on accepting new orders from retailers. Back then, the factories were so busy, they could barely keep up.

Like his uncle John, he learned early on that it wasn't so easy to be an heir apparent. He distinctly remembers a Bassett Elementary teacher going around the room and asking students what they wanted to be when they grew up. When Rob said he wanted to be a lawyer, the teacher said, "You can't do that. You have to run the company."

Some kids resented his family's power and picked on him simply because, as Rob said, "You are who you are, and there's only one of you"—another Bassett heir, another silver spoon.

When he was fourteen, his father picked up the phone and told the manager of Bassett's Arkansas plant, "My son's gonna come live with you for the summer." Neither Rob nor the plant manager had a choice in the matter. "Dad and I fought like cats and dogs," Rob said. "When I was a teenager, he was a black belt ass-chewer....I was dying to get away from Bassett."

After graduating from Vanderbilt and doing a six-year retail stint in Houston, Rob went to work for the family business. It was 1984, a time when Bassett's police force was still operated by the company, and residents still paid their power bills at the Taj Mahal.

With blue eyes and receding blond hair, Rob looks like a younger version of John Bassett. He shares a competitive if somewhat easier relationship with his uncle than his father did—though they don't exactly trade horses either, as Junior Thomas would say. John was among several Bassett relatives who offered his opinion via letter to the Bassett board just before Bob Spilman left, arguing that Rob Spilman was too young to assume the CEO mantle during such rocky times, so soon after the CalPERS kerfuffle and just as the battle over Asian imports was becoming a full-on war.

Rob did fly to Atlanta to interview for the position of Bassett CEO, but he didn't get the job. Not then. He lost out to Paul Fulton, the dean of the University of North Carolina's business school and a twenty-nine-year veteran of Sara Lee Corporation. Fulton had helped pioneer the egg-shaped container for L'eggs panty hose as company president and was known for his shrewd management of company brands that included Hanes, Isotoner, and Jimmy Dean.

"He was an operator's operator, a businessman who... started out as a trainee in a Hanes Hosiery plant and ended up running a global monolith," Rob said admiringly. Fulton was plainspoken, and he dropped F-bombs left and right. Rob was happy to take a backseat to him, he told me, hoping to soak up some of his marketing genius and big-picture acumen. "He's been one of the great influences of my life," Rob said of Fulton, the only person outside the Bassett family to hold the CEO title in its century-plus of operations.

Rob considered Fulton's world more sophisticated than the one the furniture industry hailed from; more modern too. He admired his energy, especially when he told his young CEO in training, "We gotta get some shit done around here."

That shit soon became clear to shareholder Spencer Morten, who paid a visit to Fulton shortly after he took over as CEO. "Our asset-management people said we had too many eggs in one basket [in Bassett Furniture stock], and there's a lot of concern about all the textiles going to Mexico and China," he remembers telling Fulton. "Paul, we're concerned about where the company's going."

"Spencer, I'm not a furniture man, I'm a figure man. If Rob doesn't make money on those plants, I'm gonna close 'em." By 1998, furniture imports accounted for nearly a third of all wood furniture sold in the United States, up from 21 percent five years earlier. At the High Point Market that spring, industry executives told reporters that, wherever possible, they would try to beat their import competitors. But in cases where they couldn't match the price of the competition, they would join them and outsource the furniture instead, developing a "blended strategy," as it soon became known.

But that dual strategy soon blurred as many companies, including JBIII's Vaughan-Bassett, started buying parts and finished furniture from overseas factories and selling it under their own names. The question for each company then became: How far should the importing extend?

Fulton embraced the blended strategy, but he also wanted Bassett to cash in on its brand name, which was a rarity in the industry, one culti-vated from decades of furniture giveaways on *Wheel of Fortune* and copious ads in *Reader's Digest, Life,* and *Look.*

Inspired by the Ethan Allen chain, in 1994 Rob had introduced the Bassett Direct Plus concept, gallery stores across the nation that sold only Bassett Furniture. It had been tough getting his dad on board at first. Rob had to get the store architect to bill him for the plans five times in five-hundred-dollar increments, which by then was the classic company circumvention around any purchase that exceeded the Bob Spilman spending cap.

But when he called his dad the weekend after Thanksgiving to tell him how much one store in Mississippi had sold that day— $70,000—his dad saw the wisdom in retailing.

"Goddamn," Spilman said. "You be in my office Monday morn-ing." He wanted more stores. There were eighteen of them by the time Spilman retired in 1997, with plans to open thirty-three more—and add accessories—the following year.

Fulton vowed to take Bassett Direct to the next level, even though it meant the company would alienate many longtime retail customers, who would now be its competitors. Among his first moves was to hire Bain and Company, the umbrella group of the private-equity firm that Mitt Romney cofounded, to analyze and validate his retail strategy via interviewing store managers and franchisees.

"Bassett has got lightning in a bottle here, and they don't even know it," according to Bain's glowing report.

The sea change was controversial, not just with retailers but also with board members and industry insiders. "Fulton came in and thought, *My God, we can't make it on manufacturing anymore; we've gotta go vertical and start importing things we can sell in our own stores,*" said Dave Phillips, an investor based in High Point and part owner of the Market buildings where the showrooms are housed. (Phillips was on the board of Vaughan-Bassett until 2006, when President George W. Bush appointed him to be the U.S. ambassador to Estonia.)

Fulton left it to Rob to sort out the details. During a visit to an Omaha, Nebraska, electronics store that was bursting with energy, Rob told the manager, "This is hip! This is cool!" He tracked down the Seattle-based retail consultant that that store had hired and asked her to remake Bassett too.

It didn't hurt that J'Amy Owens, thirty-eight, was gorgeous — down to her blond highlights, impeccable jewelry, and confident silver tongue. A cover story in *Inc.* magazine praised both her eye for design and her ear for being "well-tuned to the ka-ching of the cash register."

Bassett was a paternalistic throwback compared with her typical clients, which included Nike, Starbucks, and Blockbuster. She began her pitch by telling the male executives that the Bassett conference room they were sitting in had been decorated when the song "Muskrat Love" was a hit, more than two decades before.

With a fast-paced delivery that would have made Don Draper proud, Owens skewered Bassett's corporate culture by presenting a story-board collage of commentary on its factories, offices, and stores: grimy black-and-white smokestacks and white guys in ties sitting in wingback chairs, smoking cigars and drinking scotch. A picture of

Sean Connery. Men who hunted and fished and drove fast cars when their wives let them get away with it—and she didn't even know about the riverside shenanigans of the late Mr. Ed.

In the corner of her board crouched a cartoon of a woman letting out a horror-movie shriek.

Then she dramatically unveiled board number two.

"And this...," she said, pausing for effect, "is your customer."

It was full of pastel colors and smiling women who looked beautiful inside their warm, well-appointed homes.

Rob Spilman got what she was saying immediately: the people who ran Bassett were backwoods Neanderthals, completely out of touch with the customers they were trying to reach.

"Guilty as charged," he said.

The company paid Owens $100,000 to elevate its brand, and, in a 180-degree strategy turn that resonates to this day, the business began a shift toward retail and marketing and, gradually, away from manufacturing. Though the company was importing only 8 to 10 percent of its products at the time, the emphasis on supplying the stores soon reigned supreme.

At Owens's suggestion, the company recruited Janice Hamlin, who'd worked for Disney and Mattel, to become its first vice president of marketing—the company's first female corporate officer. Her job was to enlighten her bosses about what women wanted. Hamlin ran focus groups and hired spokeswomen, including TV pitch people who presented themselves as decorating advisers and encouraged customers to "Let yourself go!"

Cable TV home-decorating host Chris Casson Madden shared her opinions with the furniture designers on everything from table edges (rounded ones are safer for kids) to upholstered sofas (tauter fabric is wrinkle-resistant). Bassett stores were painted in warm earth tones, and fresh-baked cookies were set out for browsers in an effort to quell the anxiety the typical customer felt about making a big-ticket purchase.

The company would no longer sell just to the masses. It would also reach out to middle- and upper-middle-income customers, offering customized upholstery, in-store design centers, and a plethora of imported accessories. Interior designers greeted customers in Ethan Allen's more upscale stores, but Bassett customers were greeted by "idea coordinators" wearing casual clothes and striving for a more approachable look.

Owens also suggested a name change from Bassett Direct (too factory-outlet-sounding, which she felt cheapened the product) to Bassett Home Furnishings, to evoke a higher-end feel. Everything was designed to give the company a softer focus that would be more appealing to women, who made 80 percent of household furniture-buying decisions.

Bassett's transition was so sweeping that it caught the attention of the *Wall Street Journal,* which featured the company — along with the "softer side" peddling of J'Amy Owens and Janice Hamlin — in a front-page story. The new stores won national design awards.

Rob Spilman loved the attention the Daddy Rabbits were finally getting from the sophisticates in New York. With imports slowly taking over the business, he hoped the new strategy would "help the company survive the vagaries of the marketplace, to be more profitable, to utilize our brand," he told me. "Also, it was an insurance policy against losing the J.C. Penney business" — a worry that kept many a Bassett manager up at night because that account alone represented $80 million in annual sales.

At the time, he believed opening the stores might "help save the factories," he said, even though the strategy cost the company thousands of accounts. Mom-and-pop dealers that had been selling Bassett Furniture for decades were no longer allowed to offer the product if they were located within fifty miles of a Bassett store.

The small independent dealers felt duped. "They had good intentions," Mike Micklem, Vaughan-Bassett's Virginia sales rep, said. "But the dealers out in the rural areas and small towns were really hurt. It was like Bassett was forgetting their roots, forgetting who'd gotten them to where they were."

The misters would have turned over in their mausoleums. Mr. Ed had routinely dispersed Bassett reps to every rural corner of the country, demanding they "sell everybody you can sell as long as they can pay their bills."

But the world was changing, and commerce along with it. Time would tell if J'Amy Owens's vision for modernizing Bassett Furniture would go the way of Starbucks, with global outposts and upwards of twenty thousand stores, or the way of Blockbuster, which filed for bankruptcy in 2010.

If this was the "softer side" of selling furniture, the line workers knew they were in for a rough tumble. It was all part of a reorganization to focus the company on the core lines supplying its retail stores.

The old-timers still called COO Rob Spilman "the boy" behind his back, even though he was in his mid-forties, but one of the first unpleasantries he was tasked with wasn't kids' stuff. In May 1997, Rob Spilman stood before news cameras in Martinsville and announced that the W.M. plant was closing, a move that would eliminate four hundred jobs. And there was more bad news: the company's low-end Impact Furniture Division, near Hickory, North Carolina — Bassett's version of glit — would be closing at the same time, followed shortly by Bassett's plant in Booneville, Mississippi.

Fulton hadn't yet started his new job, but he was at the press conference in anticipation of it. "I support this restructuring, the strategic direction that it takes the company," he said. "We intend to perform similar analyses relating to strategy, organizational structure and capital structure after my arrival on August 1."

Months later, Rob Spilman swore that his plan had not been to do away with Bassett's domestic workforce, but he also noted that the company was building a team of fifteen to twenty experts in global trade, particularly in China, where factories with millions of square feet devoted solely to American-style bedroom-furniture production would be up and running within the year.

From the rough end to the rub room, the company's remaining line workers worried that the iceberg had already irreparably marred the ship. Like the chamber orchestra on the *Titanic,* the workers kept on at their jobs because, well, what else could they do? Their friends at Pannill Knitting and Sara Lee Knit Products were already out of work. So were seven hundred DuPont employees, thanks to growing international trade and, to a lesser extent, technological advances that resulted in fewer people running more computer-controlled machinery. (Fueled by NAFTA, Mexico overtook China as the number one clothing exporter to the United States in 1996.)

Henry County's Frances Kissee bounced from one dying factory to the next, holding on as long as she could until the next pink slip appeared. In 1975, right out of high school, Kissee started her working career doing piecework for Sara Lee Knit Products, and she was earning ten dollars an hour plus benefits when it closed in 1994 — not long after Chinese textile managers came and watched her work.

"In the beginning, we used to get truckloads of stuff they'd sewed badly, and we had to redo their mistakes," she recalled. "No one ever said we'd be replaced."

But replaced she was, first in the textile mills, then in the call centers — where it was workers from the Philippines who ultimately nabbed her call-center job at StarTek in 2011. It was her sixth layoff or company closing in eighteen years.

"I like'd to died," Sallie Wells of Bassett told the *Martinsville Bulletin* on the day the W.M. plant closing was announced. She'd spent ten years working in its sanding room. The company had said it would shift most of the workers to other Bassett plants, but the transition grew trickier to pull off because Paul Fulton remained true to his word: he closed any plant that wasn't making money.

At the end of 1997, the company reported $19.6 million in losses on sales of $446.9 million. Between 1997 and 2000, Bassett Furniture went from operating forty-two factories to fourteen.

"We used to brag about how many plants we had," Rob Spilman

said. "But Paul would say, 'I'd like to brag about how *few* plants we have—and how much money we make.'

"Look," Rob added, sighing and sounding not unlike his uncle when annoyed. "Throughout that whole process, in the back of my mind, I didn't know how many factories we would end up with. But I did think the salvation, if we were going to keep any of the factories going at all, was to open a lot of stores and sell the furniture, okay?"

W.M. machine-room operator Ralph Spillman (different spelling, no relation) told the *Martinsville Bulletin* he planned to go into heating and air-conditioning after taking some community college courses paid for by Trade Adjustment Assistance, a federal program that provides training and resources to workers displaced by foreign competition.

But participation in TAA is low—30 percent in Virginia—and the results among blue-collar workers who do participate are uneven, with half earning a fraction of their former pay, and many unable to find work in their designated fields, according to Government Accountability Office studies. Many end up quitting their classes the moment another job becomes available. Spillman took a year's worth of classes, then quit when he found a textile job across the state line in North Carolina, fifteen minutes from his home.

By the time that factory eventually closed, Spillman was on disability. "For my nerves," he told me. "Working in textiles was stressful, and worrying about everything—the closings, how you're going to eat—that has messed a lot of people up."

He recalled employees at the W.M. plant, where his mother and his grandfather had both worked, crying on their last day. The factory closed as most do: not with a final slamming of the doors and hundreds of workers unloosed en masse but gradually, with small, gloomy batches of good-byes. The last pieces of furniture came down the line, and after each department finished its work on the cutting, its employees were let go. That way, the layoff remained orderly, efficient, and true to the bottom line.

* * *

A few months later, as Ralph struggled to adjust to life on unemployment, he was buoyed by a bit of good news. Bassett Furniture had donated the W.M. plant to the City of Martinsville. The company would get a sizable tax write-off from it, and the city would be able to tear down the building and use the site to lure higher-paying employers, preferably in high-tech industries, to the area.

But that wasn't what Ralph considered the good news. This was: John Bassett wanted to buy the old plant from the city and turn it into a modern youth-bedroom-furniture factory that would employ as many as four hundred people. He'd already hired a lawyer to examine the deed to see if there were any restrictions on the gift, knowing the tax write-off was greater when a gift was given free and clear. There weren't.

The possibilities reminded John of his uncle Bill's dollar bills floating down from the window overhead. And he thought, *Why not?*

As John tells it, he and Wyatt paid a visit to Tom Harned, Martinsville's assistant to the city manager. Harned told them the city planned to tear the building down and turn the property into an industrial park.

"Why tear it down when you can sell it to us?" JBIII said. He was willing to pay $5.25 million for the property and guarantee the hiring of two hundred and fifty workers at the start. He was willing to write a check for $20,000 to hold the property; city officials would have it by Monday, the next business day.

Harned was dumbstruck. He recognized his last name but had no idea what Vaughan-Bassett was or why John Bassett seemed to know every square inch of the W.M. plant already, down to the positioning of its sewer line.

"Let me get back to you," Harned said.

News reached Rob Spilman and Paul Fulton that the perennial bad penny had turned up again while the two were at the year-end company retreat at Pinehurst, the North Carolina golf resort. Buck Gale was running the Bassett plants in Georgia at the time, but he had flown to North Carolina for the meeting, and he was sitting near the two executives when an underling whispered to Rob that John Bassett was sniffing around the W.M. factory.

Gale, whose father had once run the W.M. plant, recalled Fulton's response down to the word: "He's just a rich boy trying to get back at us." (In an interview, Fulton, now retired from the corporation but still the Bassett chairman, denied he'd said this and claimed he'd had nothing to do with the W.M. dispute.)

The company plane was dispatched to ferry Joe Philpott and another lieutenant back to Martinsville to run interference on the deal, according to several retired Bassett managers, including Joe Philpott.

"Look, the agreement was when we gave it to the city that it could not be sold to another furniture manufacturer," Philpott said. "It was supposed to be torn down. So my ass had to come home."

Rob Spilman said he knew who the potential buyer was before he heard his uncle's name. The deal didn't smell much like springwater to him either.

According to Rob, John called him the night Rob announced the plant closing to say, "Well, y'all are *finally* doing something." Then he asked his nephew to detail his plans for the remaining Bassett plants: "What are y'all doing with the J.D. plant? How about Macon?" Rob recounted the questions in a cackling impression that made JBIII sound like Foghorn Leghorn (which, honestly, he kind of does).

Rob dismissed the condescending call with a simple thank-you. But now, with John trying to make inroads in *his* labor market, Rob was done with family pleasantries. "John plays by his own set of rules, so I was sure he'd try to take every manager we had and offer 'em more money and further split the diminishing labor pool here," he told me.

Despite all the textile-plant layoffs hitting the news, Rob insisted the furniture labor pool was tight then; that textile workers had never transitioned well to furniture-plant work. "Hell, we were already bus-ing people in from Danville!" he said.

That weekend, Bassett executives circulated a petition opposing the sale of the W.M. plant to Vaughan-Bassett to all the leading citizens in town. "We knew they'd be over there Monday morning to put down their earnest money with the city, so we got there at six in the morning to cut 'em off at the pass," Rob said.

The new finishing room John had wanted so badly, with its grandfa-thered-in permits? His relatives at Bassett made sure he didn't get it. So he bought the hog—the machine that grinds scrap wood into smaller chips—at auction instead, a reminder of his grandfather's advice on getting what you *in*spect, not what you *ex*pect.

But the machinations of Martinsville's good-old-boy network was not some blunder that could be culled from the record like a miscut bed rail thrown into the hog. Most of the line workers in town under-stood what had really happened—that egos and the long-simmering family feud prevented the sale of the W.M. plant to Vaughan-Bassett and, more importantly, the reemployment of four hundred people.

Many of them came to watch when the W.M. Bassett smokestack was toppled and the plant razed the following March—at a cost to taxpayers of $840,000.

Even Howard White, the former W.M. plant manager—the one who'd scolded me not to put anything negative in my book—said he was disappointed and dismayed. White stood there as the cranes and the bulldozers turned the building into bricks and dust.

"Bassett didn't like the idea of having a competitor in town," White recalled, shaking his head. "I couldn't understand them tearing it down; it had a brand-new finishing room.

"There was no point in them doing that, in my opinion."

Mary Elizabeth Morten agreed. She had stood with tears in her eyes and witnessed the toppling of her father's legacy. An old man who'd been a foreman at W.M. noticed her there, walked up, and handed her a keepsake brick.

The following year, 1998, President Bill Clinton touted a national unemployment rate of 4.2 percent, the lowest since 1969. But a few months later, Martinsville posted the highest unemployment rate in Virginia, 15.2 percent — on the same day another apparel plant in that city announced 120 more jobs were going away.

By that time, grass was already growing on the vacant lot that was once the W.M. Bassett Furniture plant, and for fifteen years now, grass it has remained.

17

Stretching Out the Snake

More than a few Chinese friends have quoted to me the proverb fu bu guo san dai *(wealth doesn't make it past three generations) as they wonder how we became so ill-disciplined, distracted and dissolute.*

—JAMES McGREGOR, FORMER CHAIRMAN OF THE
AMERICAN CHAMBER OF COMMERCE IN CHINA

As the branches on Bassett's corporate/family tree were starting to rot from the inside out, China barreled onto the scene with a chain saw in tow. In 2001, when John Bassett heard about the cheapest-of-the-cheap Louis Philippe bedroom suite coming out of Dalian, China—the one clobbering every factory in the business, including even the Taiwanese-owned factories in southern China—he forgot all about his nephew. The suite looked as good as the stuff made by Lexington and Vaughan-Bassett, but the set—dresser, mirror, headboard, and chest of drawers—was wholesaling for just four hundred dollars. No one could figure out how the Chinese were pulling it off. The cheapest version Vaughan-Bassett made cost double that, and the company had already slashed its usual price by two hundred dollars just to get in the same ballpark. If the Chinese had their way, the old "shirtsleeves to shirtsleeves" was about to be proven again.

When Wyatt Bassett first spotted the Dalian importer's catalog sheet in 2002—a photograph of the suite taken in a spare, poorly lit room with *$399* handwritten at the bottom—he was inclined to dismiss it as an outlier. "The first thing your mind does is say, *Well, they're losing money,* so you kinda discard it. You think, *It can't go on forever,*" he told me.

But the Dalian suite went on long enough to steal a sizable chunk of Vaughan-Bassett's market share. It went on long enough to contribute to the meteoric rise in Chinese furniture imports, which had already soared 121 percent, representing half a billion dollars, from 2000 to 2002.

And it put Wyatt's father, now sixty-five but nowhere close to retiring, in one helluva fighting mood.

While he didn't know which factory was making the Chinese suite, John Bassett knew exactly how much money it would cost him to make it in Galax. As he had in similar situations many times before, John bought the suite himself and had it shipped to his factory, whereupon chain-smoking Linda McMillian and her product engineers deconstructed every inch of veneer, hardware, and glue. Linda found the Chinese glue to be of better quality than the American (which had to meet EPA standards) and said the overall construction was "tee-totally different," as she put it, in Galax parlance. "Ours was mortised at the joints, but theirs was kinda...I don't know what you call it. The way they put it together, it looked kinda *stabbed.*"

In his sweat-stained golf hat, John Bassett stood atop a conveyor belt and told his workers he had no intention of closing the factory. But he wanted them to know they were now up against some seriously rock-bottom prices from Dalian. The plants in Sumter and Elkin were getting by, but there had already been layoffs at the new plant in Atkins, Virginia, called Virginia House, a smaller operation that made solid wood bedroom and dinette sets. The company had acquired it in 1998 when business was still good, a year before sales began to dive.

Bassett asked his workers to not only work faster but also suggest ideas for factory-floor improvements. What he didn't want to hear—what he never wants to hear—was the phrase "It *cain't* be done." If something was wrong with a machine and it was slowing production down, the workers should personally let him know.

"The Chinese are not superpeople!" he boomed.

But when the average age of your workforce is forty-six, how much more can you coax out of your employees? A few years earlier, he'd boosted production with an incentive plan that had come to him on Christmas, as if tied with a bow. He phoned his human resources manager on vacation to share the idea.

Thunder and Lightning, he called the concept. To generate excitement among employees, managers posted teasers throughout the plant in anticipation of the big reveal: IT'S COMING.... CAN YOU HEAR THE THUNDER?

It was February in Galax, Virginia. What thunder?

What would possibly get the workers of Galax so fired up that they'd make 210 bedside tables an hour instead of 180?

John Bassett drives a 2007 black Lexus sedan, coffee-stained and bought used as a point of pride. It's hard to picture him roaring through either of his resort communities on a Harley-Davidson.

But a guy in Galax, he knew, would love nothing more than to cruise the hollows of Grayson and Carroll Counties astride a brand-new Harley-Davidson Road Glide. Billed as "the ultimate riding experience" in the company newsletter, the *Vaughan-Bassett Conveyor,* the Road Glide he bought was all cherry red and sparkling chrome, with a lengthened wheelbase and whitewall tires.

"Can you *he-ah* the thunder?" he bellowed as a shipping employee roared into the factory on the bike, and the workers went wild. The *Conveyor* ran pictures of employees who wanted to pose sitting on the bike.

Employees who met weekly goals for attendance, production, and safety were rewarded with tokens. The tokens went into a lottery-style box, complete with a motorized tumbling wheel cobbled together by a maintenance-department worker. At the year's end, the mayor of Galax was called in to draw the winning names, and the whole town was abuzz.

"People were so excited, we had to have a security guard standing by as people put their names in the box," recalled Tim Prillaman, then the human resources manager. "We kept the box in the break room, and we guarded that thing around the clock."

The runner-up got a Lightning, a high-end Browning shotgun — John Bassett's favorite bird-dogging gun. If you won one of the prizes but weren't the shooting or biking type, the company would give you cash instead.

That turned out to be good news for Shirley Blair, a fifty-eight-year-old rub-room worker who'd been worried about job security. She'd heard about the factories nearby that had fallen — Bassett had just closed its veneer plant in Burkeville, Virginia, laying off another 103 workers. Months before the lottery drawing, she'd pulled John aside to tell him that her grown daughter wanted to move her family from a mobile home to a house and needed Shirley to cosign for a portion of the loan. She wasn't asking for money; she just wanted assurance before she signed the note that her job would take her through to retirement. He said he needed some time to think about it. The next day he told her he couldn't make any promises. "But if we ever do close, I promise that you and I will be the last two people working here."

Months later, the mayor drew the Harley winner's name from the bin.

Shirley had signed the loan note for her daughter, and she had worked extra hard. And now, almost by a miracle, it seemed to her, she had the cash to pay off the note.

By the time Shirley retired, things in the American furniture industry were dire. By 2001, no production incentive could compete with dressers as cheap as the ones from Dalian.

The Chinese imports were cutting into everyone's sales. In 2001,

Vaughan-Bassett's sales were down almost 10 percent from 2000. Bassett Furniture sales had also slumped over that same period, by 20.1 percent, as did sales at Furniture Brands International (13.8 percent), Hooker (16.4 percent), La-Z-Boy (5.8 percent), and Stanley (26.6 percent). Dozens of factories had closed in North Carolina and Virginia, including the J.D. Bassett factory where John Bassett had first worked as a plant manager, his old *#1* tiepins now collecting dust in dresser drawers.

He bought some of the factory's joinery equipment at the going-out-of-business auction, which lacked the drama of the W.M. plant ordeal—though he had to scramble to make sure Bassett included a key set of parts that had inadvertently been left out when the machinery was auctioned. ("How did I know [those parts] were missing?" he asked Wyatt on the way home. "Because I'm the one who bought the damn machine in the first place.")

Driving back to Galax, he thought about his place in the industry. He was one of the few third-generation furniture makers still left in it. He had worked for or against Bob Spilman for most of his career, and if that full-contact rivalry had taught him anything, it was this: It's better to think through a problem than it is to panic.

After the W.M. debacle, after the quadrupling of Vaughan-Bassett's annual sales over the past twenty years, even the guys at Bassett had to admit it: John's scrappy little factory was worth worrying about. He was a player now.

China was about to join the World Trade Organization, overtaking Japan as the largest exporter to the United States and establishing most-favored-nation status. In principle, Beijing was agreeing to follow the global rules governing imports, exports, and foreign investment. In principle, it was promising to do business on a level playing field—judging by the two million copies of the Chinese-language edition of the WTO rule book sold after the formal signing of the agreement in December of 2001.

But if John Bassett had his doubts before, the Dalian suite was all the proof he needed that the Asian invasion would soon become his war—not Spilman, who was now seventy-five and splitting his time among his three homes, far removed from the plant closings.

As JBIII told the two-hundred-plus owners of lumber, screw, and trucking companies he gathered together in a rented room of the Galax Elks Lodge on July 30, 2001, he did not intend to go to war with one arm tied behind his back.

Don't panic. It was point number four in a five-point speech he gave called "How to Compete in a Global Market." The speech borrowed from Spencer Johnson's bestselling book *Who Moved My Cheese?*, a parable about four hungry mice who discover that the key to their success is being willing to change and improve continually (point number three).

"He got together all the lumber men and the good-ole-boy sawmillers and the hardware people—guys who were wondering what they were going to do if all the factories closed and there was nobody left to sell to," Merriman recalled. "They weren't a big industry in the scheme of things and they knew, 'Nobody gives a damn about us.'"

Some of the area sawmills had already closed, and several of those remaining, guys who had eight or maybe ten families depending on them for their livelihoods, stood there listening to the self-appointed general, their palms covered with sweat. And they realized: Everything had changed. "They were shaking in their boots," Merriman said. "Some of them were literally in tears."

Garet Bosiger, whose Appomattox River Manufacturing Company sells drawer sides to Vaughan-Basset, left the meeting thinking, *Oh my God, what just happened? I might lose my business.*

Ed Sikes, a sandpaper sales rep, was equally stunned by JBIII's candor—the news that *no one's* job was safe. "You already had friends whose plants were shutting down. It was a house of cards, one plant closing at a time. And it was like a whole culture was being wiped out, people who had known each other and their families for three, four generations," he said. "Eventually, I knew, if I didn't change or diversify, it was gonna get to me too."

So Sikes gradually expanded his business beyond Galax-area furniture to include automotive and construction enterprises across the Southeast. Bosiger diversified by selling drawer sides for kitchen cabinetry, which have to be customized to fit individual houses and are therefore less vulnerable to offshoring.

Bosiger's plant also worked with Vaughan-Bassett, its largest customer, to reverse-engineer the company's own dresser drawers, with the goal of maximizing wood yield and cutting costs. The grooves in the drawer sides and backs were standardized to reduce machine downtime and increase productivity.

JBIII was putting the furniture-industry suppliers on notice: If I can't survive the Asian invasion, you can't either.

JBIII didn't ask the suppliers directly for money, but he did encourage them to cut him a deal. He was coming out with a new, cheaper version of the Louis Philippe—this one priced at $599—but he needed the suppliers to do their part. The new suite would be one of his Barnburners, discount promotions he likened to Kmart's blue-light specials. The Barnburners sold for so little that he barely broke even on them, but they kept the factories running, which was cheaper than running short time—giving workers unpaid days off—and they were critical in protecting the company's market share.

"He'd come at you with, 'Okay, I'm trying to get some volume so we're coming out with a Barnburner, and I need five percent off your parts for this,'" Bosiger said. "He's trying to break even to keep the factories going, but he's also trying to make money by managing the scrap, upping the production, nickel-and-diming every little bit."

Sales reps were forced to lower their commissions from 5 percent to 3 percent. "We sold the shit out of that furniture," Philadelphia-based sales rep Hope Antonoff recalled. "We didn't run a profit, but it kept us open, and in the long run, that makes you money. Because if the plants don't run, you have nothing left."

It was Bassett Furniture 101. Like all the misters before him, JBIII knew how to cut manufacturing corners to get the most out of his wood and lumber. John McGhee said, "When push came to shove, he was just like Mr. W.M. Bassett and Mr. Doug and Mr. Ed Bassett. Only now, he was more Bassett than [the company of] Bassett was."

For inspiration on leadership—point number two on the five-point list—he studied Churchill, whose verbal wizardry he admired. He read and reread Churchill's speech to the House of Commons on May 13, 1940:

> You ask, what is our aim? I can answer in one word: Victory. Victory at all costs—Victory in spite of all terror—Victory, however long and hard the road may be, for without victory there is no survival.

That speech, which he likes to deliver in a British/Appalachian accent, punctuated point number one on his list: If you don't think you'll win, you will lose.

The five-point speech became his personal credo, a populist JBIII version of an MBA. He gave it often, to anyone who'd listen, including to his own board. When a board member suggested Vaughan-Bassett develop a five-year plan, the words cut into John Bassett like a ripsaw. A five-year plan? That was the opposite of the five-point speech. That was the same crap the MBA programs were spouting, the same ideas the free-traders at the publicly traded companies were espousing—the ones who'd noticed that every time they closed a factory, their stock prices went up. The ones who'd awarded themselves multimillion-dollar bonuses at the same time they were putting thousands of people out of work.

Listen, he told his board. Nobody could have predicted the Dalian dresser. "A five-year plan is nothing but an exercise in futility. It's not worth the paper you're writing it on."

What could he offer to keep the company from sinking further into decline? An organization that embodied one of Churchill's favorite words: *alacrity*. "We're gonna be wide receivers here, not linebackers," he told the board. "And we're gonna move with such speed, we're gonna find the hole in the defense and run around the problems. We're gonna give you an organization that's so efficient, mean and lean and well-funded, that I don't need to explain it to some banker who can add two and two but he can't get you from Galax to Roanoke."

John Bassett thought about those cheap Louis Philippes being unloaded on the docks, and then he thought of Mattress Mack, of all people. Jim "Mack" McIngvale was one of the most successful furniture retailers in the industry, a self-made millionaire in Houston who produced memorable but cheesy television commercials — all the while sporting Sansabelt slacks. Mattress Mack was among the first retailers in the country to guarantee same-day home delivery. So the yuppies could prevent the neighbors from knowing they were buying his low-end goods, he had the idea to deliver his furniture in unmarked trucks.

That was the kind of out-of-the-container thinking John Bassett was after. *That* was moving the cheese. It was what he was aiming for when he realized the key to competing with the likes of Dalian was to take advantage of China's biggest disadvantage — the six weeks it takes a container to float across the Pacific. "The Chinese are not superpeople!" he reminded his workers. "They cannot suck the ocean dry!"

So the company would surprise the competition and move with alacrity, Churchill-style: It would adopt a seven-day factory-to-store delivery model called Vaughan Bassett Express, or VBX. Unheard of in the industry, it involved a wholesale change in the way every department operated.

China had swiped the company's number one asset — its low-cost producer status. "You have to hang your hat on something else," Wyatt Bassett explained. "If the nature of the Chinese product was cheap but you're gonna have to wait a long time to get it and it's gonna be very inconsistent, we became the guy that guaranteed you're getting it in a week."

As Wyatt's brother, Doug Bassett, described it: "If a dresser's broken on arrival, you can call us up and, in a heavy Southern accent, we'll [politely arrange to] get it fixed for you. Try getting that from Asia!"

A series of Vaughan-Bassett ads in the trade publication *Furniture/ Today* drove home that point, with a borderline-xenophobic edge. *"Meo wente"* winked a young Asian businessman who gave the A-OK sign with his fingers.

The caption below translated the phrase: "Nooo problem."

"Tired of dealing with broken promises and missed delivery dates?" read the kicker at the bottom of the ad. "We deliver as *promised,* with NO hassles and NO minimums. Vaughan-Bassett Furniture, we mean what we say."

Unlike the Asians, in other words.

Another ad featured a hulking ship laden with hundreds of containers in the middle of the ocean with the caption: "Sure, we can send that repair part out, just tell us what else to put in the container."

A two-page ad made fun of the importers' tendency to deliver all or nothing. On the left-hand side of the page, a buyer stood on the shore looking out on a vast empty ocean; the caption read "No ship." On the right-hand side, the same buyer stood among hundreds of chaotically stacked containers. "Ohhh ship!" read the caption below.

VBX had gotten the attention of the companies who were already importing heavily—especially the company's ads, which the importers decried as insults to the Chinese. But the biggest challenge of launching the speed-delivery program was selling it to the employees, particularly the people in the office. The line workers were happy to help double the company's inventory from $15 million to $30 million to give it more shipping flexibility. More orders meant less short time.

But the credit department, which for decades had taken three to five days to process a new store's order, was another story. John didn't exactly threaten to fire the credit manager, but he did relate the story of

Mattress Mack telling his own credit and delivery people that they had two weeks to figure out how to cut home-delivery time from a month to a day, and if they couldn't do it, Mack would find someone who could.

Vaughan-Bassett's credit manager had the expected reaction when he learned that John wanted the credit on all VBX orders processed not in two weeks but in thirty minutes. He even uttered the forbidden word. "I'm sorry, John, but it *can't* be done."

"Dad taught me, you need to leave the person alone for a little while, let him stew, almost like a grieving process," Wyatt recalled. "Then you go back and say, 'Walk me through this, let's talk about it, let's figure out the bottlenecks.'"

In this case, the bottleneck was eased by a computer program the bosses coaxed out of another department—which simplified the paperwork—and the addition of some temp workers. Deadlines were given and duly noted on the legal pad, and remembering the oft-repeated line of Mr. J.D.—You get what you *in*spect, not what you *ex*pect—employees knew John would personally appear at their desks on deadline day to check.

He coaxed the trucking companies, all independent operators, to move VBX orders to the top of their shipping queues rather than wait their turn at some distribution center in Martinsville or Hickory, as was standard procedure. He did it by giving the truckers something no other furniture factory offered: Vaughan-Bassett, not the individual retailers, would pay the freight fees directly to the trucking companies, and it would do so within a week.

It was more complicated than the panty-hose-money bonuses, but the reasoning was the same: Vaughan-Bassett would, John hoped, ultimately make more money than it paid out.

The biggest hurdle was busting up the bureaucratic logjam—talking dozens of office workers into trying to do something they didn't believe could be done. It was left to Wyatt to figure out how to manage the expanded $15 million inventory cushion so the company never ran low. The company spent $10 million on warehouses to hold the new inventory, buying a defunct retail-outlet warehouse and three shuttered factories—two apparel and one furniture, all closed because of offshoring. The planning, cajoling, and computer coding took six months.

Three months after that, JBIII rolled the idea out to retailers, who were skeptical. It sounded good on paper, especially to the mom-and-pop operations that couldn't afford to order by the container. His claim that it reduced the retailers' financial risk sounded too good to be true too: Stores wouldn't get stuck holding a bunch of closeout inventory, JBIII said, because a business had to pay for only two pieces—one for the showroom and one for the warehouse. Anything that was needed beyond that could be ordered Monday for delivery by the end of the week.

"So, you really think we *cain't* pull it off?" John said, grinning like a cat about to pounce. Then he told them to double-check their invoices. Vaughan-Bassett had already been operating VBX, and for three months.

He'd launched it without notice to give everyone in his office time to work out the kinks—and, of course, for the unbridled glee of telling skeptical dealers, "PS: watch this—we're already doing it."

One shipping-department employee had the task of following up on every single order by phone. "She babysat every little aspect of it because she knew, absolutely, that her name was on John's legal pad," Antonoff said. "She called so much that finally the dealers said, 'Stop bugging us!'"

Another retailer joked that he'd heard the screech of the truck's air brakes the moment he hung up the phone after placing his order. Even better, other retailers asked, "What else of yours can I put in my store?"

Back in Galax, John likened the move to General Robert E. Lee's surprise attack on Chancellorsville. Lee's army was less than half its usual size and yet, in a bold move that further divided his ranks, Lee sent Stonewall Jackson to attack the Union's vulnerable right flank in its own camp. The Union, which misread the dusk-time movements as a retreat, never saw the Confederates coming, in a battle that historians regard as Lee's greatest victory in the Civil War.

Sometimes surprise and cunning trump brute force. Sometimes in business, as in battle, it's best to go against the grain.

Then again, Stonewall Jackson was mortally wounded at Chancellorsville. And come Gettysburg two months later, the Union delivered a crushing defeat.

John had studied it all at his alma mater, where Lee served as college president after the war. ("He sat right there," he told me during a 2013 Washington and Lee University visit, pointing to Robert E. Lee's favorite seat in the campus chapel, to the right of the minister and in the second row.) Civil War buffs consider Lee's tomb, in the basement of the Lee Chapel, to be a shrine. Some plant Confederate flags outside. Some leave coins and carrots at the grave of Lee's horse Traveller, whose bones were buried near the general after they'd been bleached and exhibited—and occasionally vandalized by students, who carved their initials in them for good luck.

The carriage house where Traveller was once stabled is now the university president's garage. Tradition holds that the doors should always be left open so Traveller's ghost can come and go at will.

Tradition, like soldiers and a few third-generation furniture makers, is hard to stamp out in small Southern towns. In recent times, there was a W&L president who kept the garage doors closed, to protect his car. The joke around Lexington went that Traveller had been reincarnated—as a BMW. And that president didn't last long.

Bob Merriman was retiring around the time Vaughan-Bassett introduced VBX, the company's first major return salvo against China's battle to overtake the American bedroom-furniture market. "John will give you a better speech, but Wyatt has computer programs running out of his ears on every situation, and, unlike John, he's very patient," Merriman said. "You've got to be sharp as a tack to oversee all those logistics and not lose your ass by ending up with closeouts."

Wyatt reminds Merriman of Wyatt's grandfather and namesake, Wyatt Exum, the World War II fighter pilot. Exum had a photographic memory and used to wow Merriman by glancing at a string of boxcars, turning his back, and then reciting all the numbers on the passing train.

The younger Wyatt's trick? He can calculate algorithms and returns on investments in his head. He remembers figures quoted on supply invoices eight months after he's seen them. He once casually but breathlessly explained why he'd bought the lowest-priced Honda Acura at the height of the recession: Given that he drives forty thousand miles a year for work, isn't reimbursed, and, figuring in depreciation and gas, he pays under ten cents a mile.

"He can come across as aloof," Merriman said, adding that Wyatt's older brother, Doug, is the friendlier of the two, which was why Doug got tasked with political and media relations. "But Wyatt's by far the sharpest business brain."

In 2000, the company imported 9 percent of the goods it sold—or $1.2 million of its pretax profits—mostly bunk beds from Vietnam, chairs from Malaysia, components from Brazil, and some bedroom- and dining-room suites from Taiwanese-owned factories in southern China. Two years earlier, before the furniture wars were in full swing, the company had even permitted Chinese furniture-factory magnate Samuel Kuo to tour its Galax headquarters, and Kuo's assistant video-taped the entire production line. Kuo, whose Lacquer Craft now owned the Larry Moh–founded Universal, had let Wyatt walk through his Chinese factories, so Vaughan-Bassett responded in kind, though John and his sons insist they didn't realize Kuo's people were taping.

The line workers remember it differently. One longtime sanding-room employee recalled being taped as his department dutifully displayed processes that could be replicated in China. "We even taught 'em how to make it," he told me. "Now, wasn't that dumb?"

The Kuo taping "changed our entire policy to where we no longer allow people to come into our factory," Wyatt said.

They weren't at war—not yet—but they were now in the shoddy Vaughan-Bassett war room contemplating it.

It was under the guise of importing more furniture, in fact, that John sent Wyatt to Dalian in late September 2002. He wanted him to locate the specific factory that made the cheap dresser because, as his friends who grew up along the banks of the Smith River used to say: "You never know how long a snake is till you kill him and stretch him out."

Wyatt would travel with Rose Maner, an industry friend and Taiwanese native who had married an American finishing-supply-company executive. Globalization had brought the Maners together in 1979. She was a waitress, and she'd served drinks to Jim Maner and his American coworkers from Lilly Industries at a nightclub in the industrial city of Kaohsiung, then the furniture capital of Taiwan. "It was love at first sight," Rose recalled.

Soon after the two met, Lilly sent Jim back to Taiwan to launch a finishing plant that would help companies, including Larry Moh's, fine-tune their finishing process. It's a critical step that stymies many novice manufacturers, requiring as many as sixteen coats of finish on high-end pieces. "The first furniture Larry exported from Taiwan had a red, kind of cheesy-looking finish," said Frank Tothill, a retired Lilly executive and Jim's boss at the time.

As American furniture makers flew to check out the possibilities of ordering from the Taiwanese, the fledgling Asian companies flattered them, asking them constantly for advice. Once the Americans became customers, the advice morphed into full-bore instruction, far beyond helping convert inches to centimeters on design sketches. "It just snowballed," Tothill said. "It wasn't that the Asians came over to take our business. We went over there, and, before we knew it, we had *given* it to them."

It was just as the Vaughan-Bassett line workers had predicted back when they were being videotaped. Finishing companies were setting up plants across Asia to support the new furniture factories, as were glue, fixture, veneer, tooling, carton, and machine companies. They were re-creating a supply chain that had taken the Southern furniture makers decades to develop.

Rose soon had tentacles everywhere in the network. In 1984, she married Jim, who was twenty-four years her senior, and for the next fifteen years, she helped him run factory operations for Lilly in both Taiwan and Dongguan. "Rose was his secretary, and of course she was more fluent than he was, and she'd let him know if somebody was pulling his leg," Tothill said. "Our competitors were scared to death of her because they knew she could understand everything they were saying and doing."

The couple's furniture-manufacturing contacts extended all across Asia, where people in the business still warmly call her *lao ban niang*—Mandarin for "the boss's wife."

Rose not only spoke Mandarin and Taiwanese; she was also fluent in furniture lingo, and perhaps most important for Vaughan-Bassett, she harbored no love for mainland China. She'd grown up under martial law in an era when China bullied Taiwan at every turn, from forcing Taiwanese schoolchildren to eschew their native tongue in favor of Mandarin to blocking the country's entry into the United Nations.

In the early 1990s, Rose watched as Taiwanese factories of all kinds rushed to China, chasing free land, cheaper labor, and loose environmental regulations. The move displaced many of her Taiwanese furniture-industry friends, including some who'd once worked for Larry Moh.

With her bubbly personality and disarming disposition, Rose was friends with everyone from Larry Moh—she'd dined with him at one of his three homes in Asia, and Jim and Moh were scotch-drinking buddies—to the laborers on the finishing lines.

But widowed unexpectedly in 1999 at the age of forty-four, Rose sank into a deep depression. She bristled when industry friends suggested she get back into the business, maybe even hire herself out to one of the booming plethora of trading-company agencies based in High Point. The agencies provided offshoring advisers, Asia-savvy people who helped

American companies figure out how to have their products made in Asia by OEMs—original equipment manufacturers—to sell under the American companies' brand names.

Jim Maner, she knew, would have hated the idea. He'd called trade agents "glorified taxi drivers" and recoiled at the high commissions they took from both buyers and manufacturers.

In 2002, John and Wyatt Bassett approached Rose for help, and they couldn't have come at a better time, she told me, using a poster-size map of Asia to describe where they'd sent her. Rose worked as a kind of counteragent—someone who quietly reported to her employers what the agents, American buyers, and Asian factories were up to. She talked to friends about who was doing what, typed up what they said, and e-mailed the reports to Wyatt. She visited factories in Asia as needed. When she had spare time, she even drove to the Galax factory to offer quality-control advice on the finishing lines.

Rose knew people who knew people. And some of those people happened to sell materials to the furniture factories in remote northern China, which was just beginning to boom. Some of the industry insiders even taught the new factories how to set up their finishing lines, just as they had done in Taiwan and, later, in the southern China province of Guangdong.

For the first time in almost three years, Rose was eager, even excited, about something. Attractive, bubbly, and diminutive, she joked to her friends, "I'm with the FBI!"

When Rose and Wyatt ventured into a rapidly industrializing Dalian, a city of six million, their mission was to find the one furniture factory out of dozens that made the cheap Louis Philippe. It was something like Wyatt's twentieth trip to Asia but his first time in China's northern region—the Appalachia of China, where new megahighways intersected with pothole-riddled dirt roads.

If they found the factory, they were to learn as much as they could about the place. Quoting Napoleon, John Bassett said he wanted them to know their enemy—his strengths and weaknesses, his intentions and whereabouts.

"Listen, this is the place that could take us all down," JBIII told Wyatt. "Don't come home until you find it."

It was a Mr. Ed moment: a make-or-break situation where there was simply no water in the swamp.

Rose landed in Dalian a day ahead of Wyatt, and the first thing she did was call a Taiwanese friend working in Shanghai.

"Don't worry, *lao ban niang*," he told his old boss's wife. "I know someone who will take care of everything."

18

The Dalian Dance Card

I heard it was the arrogance of the Chinese that really got John Bassett going. He was in China with 'em and they were braggin' about how they were gonna take over the whole industry.

—Delano Thomasson, Collinsville Furniture Mart owner

Years earlier, on a buying trip to Hong Kong, back when the company was still importing 8 to 10 percent of its goods, Wyatt arrived at his hotel late one night, and when he awoke the next morning, there were twenty phone messages waiting for him from importers and agents who'd been tipped off by people at airport customs and were eager to show him around. Those were the dance-card days of the late 1990s, back when American companies were racing to nab OEM contracts with factories in Asia. Those who couldn't risked becoming wallflowers in globalization's dance.

"The saying was 'The dance card's filling up,'" Wyatt's brother, Doug, told me. "If you didn't sign up with a factory quick, you'd get left out."

By 2002, the dance cards were starting to get tee-totally full, as they say in Galax. Especially the ones in Guangdong, the southern coastal province that was fast becoming China's factory hub. As one executive noted at the fall High Point Market, "I've seen most of the people in this room over in Asia more than here."

If the factory the Americans visited was large, it usually had English-speaking salespeople on-site. If it was Taiwanese owned (and most were), the owners/managers were bilingual and well-versed in doing business with Americans—or at least savvy enough to steer the Virginians and North Carolinians to restaurants that served easily palatable spaghetti Bolognese. "I ate spaghetti all over China because I figure they've been making noodles for two thousand years," Wyatt said.

Furniture imports from China had jumped 121 percent from 2000 to 2002, now capturing as much as 50 percent of the U.S. market in some areas. By 2003, seventy-three thousand jobs had already evaporated from furniture and fixture factories in the United States. Twenty of those shuttered factories were owned by Furniture Brands, the industry giant whose CEO, Mickey Holliman, told *Furniture/Today* that domestic manufacturing was now reserved solely for companies that were "standing on principle."

Tilting at windmills, people in the industry called it.

John Bassett dispatched his Dalian delegation to help him figure out just how far he was willing to tilt into globalization's windmill. Soon, some of his oldest industry friends would be calling him a protectionist.

"Bless him, there goes Don Quixote," they chortled behind his back.

In the spring of 2002, a few months before Wyatt and Rose left for their first trip to Dalian, Wyatt and his dad looked all 334 of the workers at their Atkins plant in the eye and told them they were sorry, but the layoffs hadn't been enough to stem the bleeding. They were closing the factory for good. Virginia House was supposed to have been the Cadillac line of their business, a factory that specialized in high-end solid wood furniture. "The trouble was, solids lost their panache as the imports came in," sales manager Bob Merriman said. "People just didn't wanna pay for it, and the young people coming along liked the Restoration Hardware look better; they didn't care whether it was solid or not."

Looking back, JBIII said, buying Virginia House was probably his biggest strategic mistake. "I don't know, maybe it was hubris," he said. In this battle, the Chinese clearly had him beat.

A thirteen-hour plane ride away, in Shanghai, Larry Moh and his son, Michael, were about to announce their own entrée into the higher-end furniture scene. Larry Moh had promised not to compete in the industry for the ten years following his sale of Universal to Masco in 1989, and now he was back, his entrepreneurialism unfettered by contractual restraints.

He'd spent the past decade developing a fiberboard-and-laminate flooring-supply business, called Plantation Timber Products, based in the southwestern Chinese province of Sichuan, a place even remoter than Dalian. "Labor was less of a factor with this one, which was all about being where the trees were," Michael Moh said in a Skype interview from Shanghai. In the small city of Leshan, the Mohs had provided work for five hundred rural peasants and rare cash for wood for five hundred thousand subsistence farmers, he added.

In the interim, Larry Moh had also made a bundle off a considerable heap of AOL stock. As Tothill, his old supplier buddy, recalled, "He liked to make risky investments, and he was very good at picking them out. He was highly intelligent but also a very emotional man."

In 2002, the Mohs flew a hundred American retailers to Shanghai for the opening of their brand-new Fine Furniture Design and Marketing, a high-end furniture-making and -selling enterprise based in Shanghai with American headquarters in High Point; additional operations across the Middle East, Russia, Australia, and Korea; and forty-five retail stores in China. Having opened just two months before Larry Moh's death from lung cancer at the age of seventy-six, FFDM became the furniture legend's coup de grâce to American competitors like Virginia House. It was also his parting shot to the American furniture makers, who had long dismissed the quality of Chinese imports with the adage "You show me a horse but you deliver a donkey."

Larry Moh had insisted on going out first class, with a plant that boasted 2.5 million square feet and a one-and-a-half-mile-long finishing line. He'd wanted the world to know that China was finished being the poster child for cheap labor, his son said. He did it by educating his factory workers to focus on quality, not just quantity, and this time the furniture would sell solely under *his* company's logo, not OEM-style for Bernhardt, Lexington, or some other American brand. Moh had already intuited that labor rates would increase as the country began making products not just for export but also for its own growing consumer class.

His forecast, as usual, was right. By 2012, FFDM was paying its workers the equivalent of four hundred dollars a month, plus pension and benefits—a tripling of pay in just ten years. "We're constantly evaluating our future," Michael Moh told me in late 2012. "We could move again, absolutely. That's the global phenomenon we're in. As costs go up, you go, 'Where are you going next?'"

Dalian is a seaside city in China's remote northeastern corner, where the Yellow and Bo Hai Seas meet. Once the country's largest trade port, the city was designated a Special Economic Zone in 1984, with the goal of putting people to work. Much of the ensuing industrialization was spurred by Mayor Bo Xilai, who would go on to govern the entire Liaoning Province and, as his stature in the Communist Party grew, become the head of China's Commerce Ministry.

Bo drove the transformation of Dalian, turning it from a drab port city into a showcase of China's rapid economic growth. Before the 2012 political scandal that rocked Beijing and made international news, he was best known for banning motorcycles in Dalian and turning traffic circles into large, lush parks by planting expensive imported grasses.

He transformed the city into a hub of machine manufacturing, petrochemicals, oil refining, and electronics long before the corruption scandal that ended with his wife in jail for murder and his own incarceration for bribery, embezzlement, and abuse of power.

During the initial fact-finding mission to Dalian in 2002, Wyatt and Rose were in Bo's territory, and the Bo-led growth was still in its early stages. The factories they toured looked like something out of Galax, Virginia, circa 1930. They were poorly equipped and inefficiently laid out—one was four stories high and looked like a very old Hampton Inn. "You could tell these factories had been there long before anybody was exporting to the U.S.," Wyatt said. "And now they wanted to get in on it, like the people in the south of China."

They hired a driver and spent the first two days touring five plants, acting like gracious potential buyers while all along scanning each assembly line for the Louis Philippe. Every night, when Wyatt phoned his dad at 9:30 (9:30 a.m. in Virginia) to report that he still hadn't located the dresser, the response was always the same: keep looking.

Rose stayed busy on the phone, calling supplier friends in the finishing industry. One friend referred her to another, who happened to supply a factory called Dalian Huafeng Furniture Company. It was deep in the Liaoning Province, an hour northeast of Dalian in the town of Zhuanghe—fewer than a hundred miles from the North Korean border. *Huafeng* translates to "bright prosperity," Rose knew. Based on what her friend told her, this could be the one.

When they arrived in the small city of Zhuanghe, they found it to be filthy, full of dirt roads and gray cinder-block buildings. For almost two decades, Dalian Huafeng had been making furniture for the Chinese market and exporting to Japan. Its flagship factory was housed in a three-story cinder-block building that employed eight hundred people, Rose said. Not all the workers were squatting near the ground to work on the furniture, as many did in southern China. But some were, as a new conveyor system was only partially built.

NO SPIT! ordered a sign on the stairwell. The building was unheated, and outside, the brisk September winds moaned.

"The people worked slowly—probably because they were so cold," Rose said. "They were like soldiers. No one smiled. The whole place, it was like there was no life in it."

Then Wyatt and Rose spotted a logo on a box in the shipping department that matched the logo on the back of the mystery dresser. Their eyes grew wide, and they looked at each other knowingly but didn't say a word. This was definitely it.

Later, when Wyatt ventured that it didn't look like the factory had enough room to expand fully into the American market, the sales manager suggested they get back in the car for part two of the tour. She had something to show them on the outskirts of Zhuanghe.

Turned out the company was building an entire factory complex dedicated to the American furniture market. Tucked away in the middle of nowhere and surrounded by fields, Rose recalled, "It seemed hidden away like a secret."

For now, the enterprise was dwarfed by a giant billboard promoting the complex that owner He YunFeng intended to build on the site: six different factories, all dedicated to making bedroom furniture for Americans, with a giant warehouse in the middle. They would be modern factories with the same kind of German- and Italian-made equipment John Bassett had installed back in Galax. The billboard stood near the entranceway to the hundred-acre building site, and fanning out from the new construction debris sat neatly stacked piles of timber, some twenty feet tall.

The lumber came from Russia, the sales manager explained. She made no mention of how the wood was logged—by a Russian Mafia–controlled company that was later implicated in an environmental corruption scandal. In 2007, Walmart was criticized for selling baby cribs that had been made from lumber taken from protected Siberian tiger habitats and produced at Dalian Huafeng, according to the nonprofit

Environmental Investigation Agency. (Several months later, Walmart announced it would investigate its suppliers more rigorously and joined the Global Forest & Trade Network.)

Dalian Huafeng would be happy to make samples for Vaughan-Bassett, she told them as they toured the premises and learned more about the company's plan.

Months earlier, there had been a grand-opening ceremony to unveil the plans for what owner He YunFeng was calling the American Furniture Industrial Park. Rose read about the event in newspaper clippings, featuring photos of He YunFeng with Bo Xilai, then the governor of Liaoning. He YunFeng predicted it would "force American domestic furniture manufacturers to close their doors," as he told the government-controlled newspaper the *Liaoning Daily.* The complex would hold twenty-two thousand employees operating thirty different finishing lines with the capacity to ship five thousand containers a month.

Most of the Zhuanghe workers were young men in their twenties, many of them migrants who'd been bused in from northern and western China. They wore uniforms and lived in dormitories that typically housed ten people to a room. They were paid 20 percent less than those working in southern China, where in 2002, workers earned a hundred dollars a month, including meals and housing (compared to the approximately two thousand dollars a month it took to keep an American furniture worker employed).

"If you believed their billboard, they were gonna be the biggest thing in bedroom anywhere," Wyatt said. "The question was, was this what I call a giant-billboard expansion?" He'd seen several promotions like this before in southern China, and when he returned to the sites the following year, the grass was a foot taller and the billboards crumbling. "On one hand, a billboard's a billboard; how seriously do you take it?

"On the other, between their square footage and all that lumber we saw, if these guys had the financing, they were gonna be the most formidable guys ever."

Dalian Huafeng planned to ship one hundred thousand bedroom suites to the United States every month, more than the top four or five U.S. producers combined. The company had piles of lumber sitting nearby to prove it. In the local press, He YunFeng said he'd begun modestly with just ten employees in 1984 but now planned to become "the No. 1 furniture maker in the world." The government would help turn Dalian Huafeng into a furniture-making "superpower," Bo Xilai told a reporter, by helping to *zuodazuoqiang*—"make it powerfully strong."

The moment Wyatt described the project to his father on the phone, John Bassett wanted to see the place for himself. To stretch out this snake, he needed a meeting with He YunFeng.

It was turning into a devil of a year. Profits were tanking, and with the Virginia House closing—which set the company back nearly four million dollars—morale was low at Vaughan-Bassett's remaining three plants. Raises were frozen. In two years, the company's sales, production, and employment had all dropped 20 percent.

John Bassett saw the stack of TAA application papers on his desk, each representing one of his displaced workers, and he knew: It was going to take some new ideas and new energy to pull the company out of the morass it was sinking into. Something fun.

Fun, as in a new furniture line named after the biggest celebrity in American history. Fun, as in a blue suede sofa with fringe.

Fun, as in a recliner with room for a six-pack in the chair arm.

Fun, as in an April 2002 furniture market introduction featuring Burnin' Love mirrors, a Love Me Tender bed, and an armoire with Elvis Presley's signature in frosted glass on the door.

Why not? Lexington had Bob Timberlake, the artist who'd helped it design one of the bestselling collections in industry history. Hooker had Faith Popcorn, the author and consumer-trend forecaster. And Bernhardt had Martha Stewart—before she lied to federal government investigators.

John Bassett was already casting about for a celebrity license to call his own when his son Doug returned from a sales event in Tupelo, Mississippi, and announced that he'd been late getting there because it was the anniversary of Elvis Presley's death. Not only could he not get a hotel room in Memphis, but there was not a single rental car available to get him to Tupelo.

"Dad, they've shut down the whole city," Doug said.

And so the 2002 Vaughan-Bassett showroom at High Point was transformed into a miniature version of Graceland, with Elvis on the karaoke machine, rhinestone-studded outfits pinned to the walls, and employees wearing tinted aviator-style sunglasses (painted gold, with a line of holes running down each earpiece—and made in China, of course).

The glasses were such a hot item that when one middle-aged woman stepped onto an elevator and saw a salesman wearing a pair, she ripped them from his face. "I'm sorry, but I just have to have these!" she said, then bolted before the elevator doors closed. The company ran tapes of the King's concerts on a large-screen television, and more than a few women stood transfixed before it, some with tears streaming down their faces.

It was a beautiful, although unprofitable, distraction. Newspapers from Memphis to Germany covered the premiere of Vaughan-Bassett's Elvis Presley line of furniture. ABC let John talk about it on *Good Morning America*. And John Bassett says he'll never forget the sight of fifty-year-old women "bawling like they were fifteen-year-old girls!"

But Elvis people tended to buy Elvis records, key chains, watches, and bobbleheads. Not twelve-hundred-dollar suites of Elvis furniture. "It was like being next to a pot of gold, but you couldn't figure out how to get your hand in the pot," JBIII said. The line became the Edsel of the industry.

A regional sales manager phoned in from Elvis Week, a Memphis event the factory had sent him to following the line's premiere. "Bob, people who live in mobile homes are not gonna buy the suites," he said. At the end of the season, the collection was reduced to closeout status, with four-hundred-fifty-dollar beds retailing for two hundred dollars. As one retailer friend told Merriman, "I wouldn't give you fifty for it!"

It was a fabulous public relations success, as it introduced Vaughan-Bassett's furniture to stores that had never heard of the company. But the business took a one-million-dollar loss on the enterprise, a clunker that John Bassett came to call his glorious failure. "It was so bad, you almost had to stand back and admire it," he said. "What we learned was, Elvis people are fun, but they don't have a lot of money for furniture."

Even with her legal jam on the horizon, Martha might have been the more prudent choice.

Cardboard cutouts of Elvis still dot the landscape of the Vaughan-Bassett offices, not far from the last Hunka Hunka Burnin' Love mirror — gilt-framed and heart-shaped — which hangs above the office coffeemaker, around the corner from the decoupaged Elvis clock.

If JBIII was going to keep his business vibrant, he needed a better idea, a bolder move. Recycled celebrities, cost-cutting, and factory-tweaking — that had all been tried. What had never occurred to John, a lifelong Republican, was turning to the government for help.

Nobody remembers who at the American Furniture Manufacturers Association first came up with the idea. Some say it was Paul Toms, the chairman of Hooker Furniture. Others say it was Paul Broyhill, the retired magnate who'd run Broyhill Furniture before he sold it to Interco in 1980. (It's now part of Furniture Brands International.)

Furniture-factory workers were losing their livelihoods because of offshoring to China, just like the textile workers before them had. It was a fact. But was there any legal recourse to make it stop?

The furniture industry didn't have the corporate heft of, say, the Detroit automakers. But wasn't there a law on the books somewhere that might protect it from unfair and maybe even illegal trade?

Joe Dorn knew there was. He'd already successfully argued the nuances of the Tariff Act of 1930 on behalf of American producers of magnesium, who were being undercut by Chinese imports. He did it again for the makers of gray Portland cement, who alleged that the Mexican company Cementos Mexicanos (Cemex) was lowballing its cement in an effort to push American companies out of the market.

Dorn is a respected trade lawyer at the top-shelf King and Spalding, a multinational firm with trade headquarters at 1700 Pennsylvania Avenue—a block away from the White House. It's fair to say there are corners of Mexico and China in which Dorn is reviled. When Cemex CEO Lorenzo Zambrano met him in person for the first time in 2006, he greeted him with "You cannot be Mr. Dorn. You don't have horns!"

Dorn told me this story during an interview that lasted exactly one hour. (He was sorry I had driven more than four hours to talk, but he had clients, paying ones presumably, who were waiting for him.) We were seated at a long table flanked by high-backed leather chairs in a conference room that had a view of DC's bustling Lafayette Square. There was just a trace of his native North Carolina in his polite, measured speech. Asked if he'd ever traveled to China, Dorn deadpanned, "I'm afraid to go there."

Among the details the furniture makers learned from him at the 2002 AFMA meeting was that a coalition of American companies or their workers had every right in the WTO-governed universe to ask the U.S. Department of Commerce to investigate factories in another country for underselling, or dumping, as it was known. The practice of selling exported goods at artificially low prices designed to drive domestic producers out of business, dumping can also occur when exporters sell products cheaper in foreign countries than in their own. Dumping isn't illegal by WTO standards unless the domestic producers can prove harm—that is, show that the dumping has led to factory closings and higher rates of unemployment.

While American producers tend to prevail in two-thirds of antidumping cases brought before the U.S. International Trade Commission, the process is lengthy, complicated, and expensive. Just to commission an initial legal study would cost seventy-five thousand dollars, the lawyer told the furniture makers in a statement that was classic Joe Dorn: exact, understated, and lacking any whiff of emotion.

But the guys representing the industry in the room didn't need Dorn to provide the emotion. It was already there in spades.

Most of the furniture makers in the AFMA were now investing mightily in their own importing infrastructures — all those fax machines and interpreters, all those tasseled loafers on the ground in Dongguan and Shenzhen. If duties were imposed on China, it would result in their paying more for goods.

JBIII talked the manufacturers into ponying up money for the study. But six months later, when they reconvened to hear Dorn's report, most were importing even more.

"The last thing they wanted to hear was any news that China may have been breaking the law," JBIII said, recalling the way the audience response graduated from a low hum to near shouting as Dorn spoke — until he was no longer audible at all.

If people lost their jobs because of illegal race or gender discrimination, JBIII interjected at the meeting, how was that different from people losing their jobs because of illegal trade? Wasn't all of it illegal?

But the retailers will hate it, one CEO pointed out. "They'll put your picture in *Furniture/Today,* and they'll boycott you," he said. "They'll boycott all of us."

But what made the furniture makers so sure the retailers wouldn't skip all the middlemen and buy directly from the Chinese factories? That was already happening at Bassett Furniture. In 1999, Bassett and J.C. Penney had celebrated selling one billion dollars in furniture together with a big party in Dallas, near the company's Plano headquarters. When Penney complained the following year that Bassett's prices were too high compared with the imports', Bassett redesigned — or "value-engineered," as the marketing people called it — its bestselling Penney suites, slashing prices by as much as 33 percent.

262 • FACTORY MAN

Over the course of the next three years, Penney cut its Bassett orders drastically, replacing them with similar Chinese-made products until the Bassett line was entirely phased out. Later, Penney officials insisted they had dumped Bassett because of quality problems, not price—a claim Bassett CEO Rob Spilman disputes to this day.

"For years it was all about 'loyalty, loyalty'—and turned out, it was all just bull," said Joe Meadors, the retired Bassett sales executive who helped manage the J.C. Penney account for many years. "They said, 'We're goin' offshore; we're not gonna buy from you anymore.'"

At the AFMA meeting's end, as Joe Dorn was stuffing his papers into his briefcase, John Bassett pulled him aside and said he'd visit him in Washington if Dorn would finish his presentation. After they met, over the course of the next several months, John picked Dorn's brain about the process, calling weekly and learning about other cases brought on behalf of other clients, including the shrimp, magnesium, and polypropylene-bag industries.

To petition for a Commerce Department investigation, Dorn explained, JBIII would need at least 51 percent of his industry commit-ted to pursuing an antidumping case against China. Had John thought of the notion two years earlier, before imports had reached a critical mass, the support would have been a cinch. It wasn't quite the eleventh hour. But the tipping point, as Dorn explained it, was perilously close.

The dominoes tended to fall the same way in every industry hit by offshoring. "First, companies begin importing defensively from China, then they gradually start relying more and more on imports, and as you take the volume out of your U.S. plants, it makes the remaining U.S. volume less cost-effective," Dorn told me. "And it's a downward spiral from there." The earlier an industry organizes against unfair foreign competition, the likelier an antidumping coalition is to prevail.

Dorn wasn't sure John "could herd all the cats together," he said. "There were a lot of players, a lot of different voices that were independent. I had my doubts about whether it was even possible to bring together a coalition."

But Dorn was learning about John's propensity for legal pads and weekend telephone calls, not to mention his General Patton–style patter. JBIII wasn't Dorn's first client to travel covertly to an offshore factory — or send an entourage — to validate rumors of predatorily low pricing.

A lawyer's lawyer, Dorn had a career-long habit of working every Saturday morning at the firm, and Saturday mornings suited John Bassett fine. He made sure he had Dorn's direct office number.

The Chinese were about to feel the attack dog's bite.

In November 2002, Wyatt and Rose made their second trip to Dalian, with JBIII in tow, under the guise of quality control: they would peruse the Louis Philippe samples Dalian Huafeng had made for them, and, the company hoped, place an order.

This time, John Bassett saw it with his own eyes — the cinder-block buildings, the cold, crouching workers, the sky-high timber stacks. And because John was the top dog at Vaughan-Bassett, not just some presumably spoiled owner's son, manufacturer He YunFeng offered to meet with him personally to discuss plans for his burgeoning American Furniture Industrial Park. He even sent a driver to ferry them around the site.

John was used to dealing with Taiwanese businessmen who wanted to financially gore him.

He sat fairly speechless as He YunFeng, a Communist Party official on his way to joining *Forbes* magazine's list of the richest Chinese people, had the gall — or maybe it was just the new-to-capitalism naïveté — to describe how he intended to shutter every American bedroom-furniture factory, including John's.

No drinks were proffered; there was no back-slapping, no five-course meals.

Just these words, spoken by his stone-faced interpreter: Dalian

Huafeng intended to become the number one furniture maker in the world.

And this was exactly how: He YunFeng would sell the Louis Philippe for a hundred dollars because he considered that to be the "tuition" price of doing business in America—a loss he would have to take in order to capture the market share, he explained.

"He was not belligerent, but it was just like you were speaking to a judge," John recalled. "He was absolutely serious and confident in what he was saying."

Who's going to carry all this inventory? John wanted to know.

YunFeng's eyes went blank, John said. "And finally, he smiled, and his eyes lit up, and he told the translator, 'The American retailer will own the inventory.'

"And I said, 'Good luck with that.'

"It had never dawned on me until then that you're dealing with a bunch of Communists who have never had any competition whatsoever, and they're coming up with how they're gonna succeed right in front of you, and they actually think that every competing store in every community in America is going to carry the same suite of furniture," JBIII said.

"This guy even wanted to put the Taiwanese in southern China out of business, and those people were already hurting us. It was clear that this was a bigger threat than anything we'd been exposed to before."

Then He YunFeng looked at the grandson of Mr. J.D. Bassett, who actually had been the largest wood furniture maker in the world, and made an even bolder statement.

Close all three of your factories, he told him, and put the business of Vaughan-Bassett entirely in my hands.

Close his factories? Because a Chinese businessman wanted him to turn tail and run? Because this guy thought he could woo JBIII with fatter profits and promises to rid him of operational headaches like health insurance and the interference of all those acronymic regulatory agencies—EPA, OSHA, and EEOC—not to mention those pesky factory employees?

The conversation soon ended. That's when JBIII remembered the Taiwanese businessman saying, back in 1984, that Americans were all the same: *If the price is right, you will do anything.*

On the way out, the friendly sales manager asked Rose to help her buy a subscription to the trade publication *Furniture/Today,* saying she hoped it would help the Chinese understand the American industry. The Dalian Huafeng managers in northern China were confident, but they were still fairly naive about Americans and their cowboy capitalism. (Rose obliged—partly out of politeness, partly to keep up the ruse—and was later reimbursed.)

That naïveté would soon disappear, just as that forest of Russian timber near the construction site would disappear, turning into dressers and beds. The company had figured out how to export to Japan, after all. It would figure this out too.

Within a year, Rose heard from friends who were witnessing the metamorphosis of Dalian Huafeng. In reports she typed up for Wyatt in 2002 and 2003, her sources described one American buyer after another visiting its Liaoning factories—folks from Value City, Rooms To Go, Lewis and Sons, even Pat Bassett's Galax cousins from Vaughan Furniture. At least one American supplier sent two managers to live temporarily in Zhuanghe to teach the Chinese workers about American furniture and finishing systems, according to Rose's reports.

On the car ride back to Dalian, company lore has it that John Bassett looked over at his son Wyatt and invoked the name of Mr. J.D. Bassett. "My grandfather would roll over in his *graaaa-*ave," he announced, the story goes. He's repeated that line so many times since that neither he nor Wyatt nor Rose can remember if he really said it or not.

But people back in Bassett were saying it, he knew, every time another factory closed. He stared at the ceiling of the car, and he worried.

Back home, he picked up the nearest legal pad and got his top-shelf lawyer on the phone.

PART VI

19

===

Gathering the Troops

Ideally, you'd have every plant you own on a barge
to move with currencies and changes
in the economy.

—Jack Welch, CEO of General Electric

In its zygote state, the antidumping team consisted of the top-shelf lawyer, the brainiac son, the Glue of Everything (that would be the secretary Sheila Key, now a vice president), and the Taiwanese translator. John swears it was just dumb luck that his other son, Doug, now the company's sales and marketing chief, had joined Vaughan-Bassett in 1998, just as the Asian invasion was heating up. Looking back on the political backlash that was about to come from the big retailers, the Chinese factories, and their American importing arms and extend all the way to the hallowed halls of Washington, DC, one might think Doug Bassett's father had planned his return to the family business all along: prep school at the exclusive Episcopal High School, followed by his undergraduate degree from the University of Virginia, business school at Georgetown, then eight years of backslapping and stairwell negotiations on Capitol Hill for various Republican politicians and candidates.

If Wyatt came across as aloof, then Doug was the guy who buffed the team's edges, an iced-tea guzzler who knows it's as important to feed the media (and buy reporters drinks) as it is to bend an ear. If you're driving two hours for your first meeting at the factory, as I was in November 2011, Wyatt will have forgotten you're coming and will probably be too busy to talk. But Doug will call while you're en route just to make sure the roads are okay, even though there's not a raindrop or snowflake in sight.

He's sweeter than his dad and softer around the edges than his brother—at first glance, anyway. "I tell people, if you don't like Doug, there's no one in my family you'll like," JBIII said. His older son is savvy enough to know that it's okay to finesse a fact if it means he can get JBIII in front of an important audience. In 2009, President Obama proposed his $825 billion stimulus package, and it included COBRA changes that would have extended downsized workers' benefits for "up to forty years!" Doug recalled, which could have put Vaughan-Bassett and other manufacturers on the hook for millions.

"Dad read it that morning in the *New York Times,* and I called each of our senators—three Democrats and one Republican—and I said, '[Senator Jim] Webb's meeting with us at two, we can fit you in at one.' I fibbed a little. . . . We went up the next week, and eventually they came out with something we could support." A similar strategy was unleashed in the face of a power-company rate hike (which Doug got lowered, following a chat with the Virginia governor) and a new EPA emissions-regulation deadline (he helped set the strategy that led to a delay). He also helped restore hefty state funding for the High Point Market Authority. The North Carolina governor had tried to nix $1.65 million from the Market's 2013 budget, but Doug got forty-two North Carolina furniture-company presidents and CEOs to sign a letter he wrote as chairman of the authority. Published on the front page of several North Carolina newspapers, the letter pointed out that nine thousand North Carolinians still worked in furniture-making, retailing, and importing, representing revenues of eight to nine billion dollars.

To top it off, Doug was polite enough to let the governor announce the restoration of funds, which made it sound as if *he* were the one who'd saved the day. In the end, the Market wound up with $1.86 million, an increase over the previous year, which Doug called an "eminently fair compromise."

"Doug is very sales- and political-oriented. He knows how to get the most outta people," Sheila said. "Wyatt's very good at manufacturing and getting the most outta people here. If they don't agree, they work it out before it becomes a fight in front of anybody else."

Anyone looking back on the minefield JBIII had to navigate after meeting Joe Dorn and going eyeball-to-eyeball with He YunFeng might wonder how John ever managed to cobble together a majority of his industry. That person might also wonder what manufacturer turned importer in his or her right mind would join John's coalition for legal trade, a group whose actions, if all went according to plan, would culminate in boosting domestic production by placing duties on Chinese imports — robbing importer Peter to pay domestic Paul when the truth was that most economists and business schools and CEOs were cheering for Peter to find the cheapest labor he could, wherever he could find it. For the time being, with supply chains in southern China now fully operational, that place was China.

A businessperson looking back might want to examine how John Bassett had a knack for finding exactly the right person for the right job and then convincing that person to do the job exactly the way he wanted — through equal parts charm, brute coercion, and a mutual brand of loyalty that is perhaps only possible at a closely held, family-operated business run by a patrician CEO who happens to have a soft spot for the workers who made his family rich.

John may claim that he assembled his team by happy accident, but the plainspoken people of Galax viewed it as wily craftsmanship. "How many people do you know would think to send their kid to Washington after college so he could find out who you kiss up to and who you don't kiss up to?" a maintenance worker marveled.

"All that political spadework that Doug did, it was absolutely necessary," said lawyer Rick Boucher, a Democrat who was nearing the end of his twenty-eight-year career as a representative for Virginia's Ninth Congressional District, the western corner of the state, when Dorn was hired. While the U.S. International Trade Commission is supposed to be immune to politics, the commissioners "do take into consideration what other policymakers think," Boucher added.

"Doug really understands Capitol Hill, so he was up here all the time, getting letters written on their behalf. The thing about the Bassetts, they're not afraid to ask for something. But they're effective in the way they ask.

"What they ask for is always within the realm of the possible." And if what's possible isn't immediately evident, they have a way of making it so.

So Doug managed the politics. Wyatt disappeared into the arcane rules of the Department of Commerce and the International Trade Commission.

And John did what he does best, which is to pick up the phone and get people to do exactly what he wants them to do.

First, though, he called in his sons and his company controller, Doug Brannock. They huddled with plant manager Rodney, and Andy Williamson, the money guy John likes to keep nearby. ("Andy, what's the money today?" John hollers, and within seconds, Andy shouts the company's eight-figure savings-account balance for that day across the rickety partition wall.)

To hell with the dance card, John Bassett told his team. From here on out, they should imagine a different metaphor entirely, one that had nothing to do with Asian factories or hustler agents or pissed-off retailers. He took them to an imaginary desert island: There is one woman on it, and she's surrounded by twelve men. "I got news for you, boys!" he bellowed. "When you're the only girl left standing on an island with twelve men, you don't have to be good-looking; some*body's* gonna fall in love with you!"

If Vaughan-Bassett could be the last factory standing in the realm of midpriced wood bedroom furniture, he explained, beaming, it would prevail.

But privately, he was not so confident. He had no idea where the antidumping petition would lead. The company's stockholders were nervous, and many in the industry—including some of Vaughan-Bassett's biggest customers and best friends—were now thoroughly pissed.

"It feels like I'm walking through fog," he told his wife.

By the time Dorn—and the Dalian dresser—convinced John there was a case to be brought against the People's Republic of China, the blended strategy wasn't just some hot new business model. Importing was now close to becoming the dominant practice, raising the question: Was it even possible to get 51 percent of the industry on board? Lexington Home Brands and Furniture Brands were already importing one-third of their furniture from China. Ethan Allen Home Interiors had opened stores in Shanghai, Tianjin, and Urumqi and had plans to develop a chain of retail stores on the mainland. AkzoNobel, a Dutch-Swedish finishing supplier, was closing plants in the United States and Europe and opening three new factories in China.

Furniture Brands' Mickey Holliman had just closed the company's Thomasville plant, eliminating 425 jobs, a year after getting rid of 1,100 jobs in four factories with the closing of the Lane division in Altavista, Virginia. Holliman had just seen his company's net income plummet 45 percent. As he explained it to Wall Street investors, he was now investing ten million dollars in Asian logistics and quality control. The next plant closing took four hundred more jobs in Winston-Salem, North Carolina, but Wall Street cheered the closing, and Furniture Brands' stock price jumped to a record high of thirty-two dollars per share.

JBIII worked the phones constantly in early 2003, trying to drum up support for his fledgling American Furniture Manufacturers

Committee for Legal Trade. Several industry friends said they'd join, then immediately backed out after a retail customer or two — companies that were already importing much of their inventory — convinced them of the error of their ways.

"People had already gone to a lot of expense to set up buying teams in Asia. They thought they'd been playing by the rules, and they didn't see why the rules should change," said Jerry Epperson, the furniture analyst.

The worst thing that could happen to importers? The cheapest deals would come to a crashing halt. And not only that, but the duties collected from the most egregious of the dumpers would be funneled back to the American factories being hurt by the imports — meaning John Bassett and his ilk. That was thanks to a little-known piece of legislation called the Byrd Amendment, or the Continued Dumping and Subsidy Offset Act of 2000 (CDSOA), championed by a West Virginia Democrat, Senator Robert Byrd, who had quietly had it inserted into the Agriculture, Rural Development, Food and Drug Administration, and Related Agencies Appropriations Act of 2001 — without running it by any congressional committees that had experience with or jurisdiction over international trade.

The Byrd Amendment had been passed to the chagrin of the WTO and more than a dozen countries — several of which retaliated by immediately slapping duties on American exports. Senator John McCain called the Byrd Amendment "an almost-one-half-billion-dollar giveaway to U.S. corporations." Between 2001 and 2004, CDSOA funds provided over $1 billion to U.S. companies deemed injured by unfair trade. The biggest winners were makers of ball bearings, candles, and electronics, and the U.S. steel industry.

While his father worked on getting the 51 percent, Wyatt predicted the opposition would come in two phases: First, their detractors would make fun of them. Then, when it sank in what they were trying to do—stop the free-for-all to get the cheapest furniture the fastest—they were going to be mad as hell.

Sure enough, the opposition lined up to hire lobbyists and Washington lawyers of their own. The big names in retail—including Rooms To Go, J.C. Penney, Havertys, Crate and Barrel, and City Furniture—formed the Furniture Retailers of America and commenced pressuring their domestic suppliers not to join John Bassett's side.

"Several sent word that they weren't gonna buy from us anymore if we continued down that path," Doug Bassett recalled. "But in a lot of those cases, we'd already seen a three-million-dollar-a-year customer dwindle down to nothing. They'd already gone to a pure import model." In other words, these companies had no leverage with Vaughan-Bassett, because their orders were already zero.

Dorn had never seen a more complicated or vitriolic case involving such a disparate variety of interests and companies. (In the magnesium case, for instance, he had represented just one company.) Neither had opposing attorney John Greenwald.

Neither, it would turn out, had the ITC.

Lobbyists for the importers, retailers, and Chinese factories denounced the members of JBIII's coalition as old-school protectionists. As selfish opportunists looking to cash in. They were joined by a growing international chorus of free-trade proponents who claimed the Byrd Amendment violated the spirit of the WTO and wanted it repealed.

Coalition members didn't really care about keeping Americans off the unemployment rolls, the opposition said. They just wanted to cash their Byrd money checks.

By the time the dust came anywhere close to settling, at least fifty-three law firms were lined up to oppose JBIII's coalition, according to Dorn, and that included new law firms that spun off on their own as a result of this one case—and of the steady stream of legal bills it produced.

It was a heady time for Team John Bassett, and a pressure cooker too. If the coalition could sign up 51 percent of the industry, Dorn intended to file the largest antidumping case ever brought against the People's Republic of China, and it would be orchestrated from a mountain hamlet better known for barbecue and bluegrass than for international trade.

John went down his list, calling every furniture CEO he could and reminding them all of the generations of employees who'd worked for their families. Of the half a million American factory workers who'd lost their jobs because of offshoring in the 1980s and 1990s, 38 percent still hadn't found work, and one in five of those who had had taken a pay cut of 30 percent or more.

If China was refusing to play by the rules it had agreed to when it joined the WTO as a nonmarket economy—if it was really fueling its factories with deep subsidies and an artificially cheap currency—didn't the American factory owners owe it to their workers to find out if they were being wronged?

Legally, in fact, they did. There was a provision in the International Trade Commission rules stating that, in cases where the industry is divided, unionized employees can override management's opposition and file petitions of their own. If management remains neutral and the unions uphold the petitions, that counts as support. But that didn't mean much in the right-to-work South, where few factories were unionized.

So JBIII ran an end run around the free traders' defensive line. "The way he built the coalition was to go to these companies who were reluctant to join and to say, 'Boys, you better get in the wagon with me, or I'll make you wish you had,'" explained lawyer Tom Word, a longtime Vaughan-Bassett board member who spent decades representing the region's textile and furniture magnates. "He loves to play hardball."

The maneuver wasn't technically a threat. But John let it be known that newspaper ads could be taken out in furniture-factory towns informing employees of their right to join his petition whether management approved or not. *Ohhh ship*, indeed.

In Galax, he demonstrated how it could be done, calling together reporters from a hundred-and-fifty-mile radius to witness the signing of a support petition by the Galax workers, each of whom walked away with a T-shirt that said *I Voted to Save My Job.* It was a classic PR move — not necessary at all, because of course Vaughan-Bassett already supported the coalition JBIII had founded — but it was good for grabbing headlines.

Down the street, Vaughan Furniture had joined the petition-signing wave too, even though its managers were already poking around the factories in Dalian. Vaughan employees were working serious short time — one week on, one week off. "I signed because I'd like to keep my job as long as I can," thirty-nine-year-old Vince Brown told the *Greensboro News and Record.* "My bills each month add up to more than what I make."

By mid-July 2003, John had begged, badgered, and bullied fifteen factory heads into joining the coalition, including the CEOs of cousin companies started by his grandfather — Bassett Furniture, Stanley, Vaughan, and Hooker. Before long, though, the implications of siding with John Bassett, even if he was your uncle, became clear.

"We are trying to stand up for what we believe is proper," said Paul Toms, distant cousin and CEO of Hooker, the high-end furniture maker based in Martinsville. But six months later, after three of its five largest retail customers "expressed displeasure," as Toms told *Furniture/Today,* Hooker abandoned its support. Coalition alignment had also jeopardized relations with Asian sourcing partners, which were now providing 50 percent of Hooker's furniture. Lexington, then importing 60 percent of its furniture, pulled a similar about-face, as did Indiana-based Keller Manufacturing Company.

Retailer spokesman Mike Veitenheimer cheered the companies' withdrawal from the petition, joining a chorus of economists and business professors who saw the antidumping petition as bad economics, fraught with unintended consequences. "Instead of saving American jobs, as claimed by the petitioners, the supply disruption would lead to job losses in the U.S. for retail company employees," Veitenheimer said.

Those nefarious Asians, sniped Greg Rushford, a free-trade advocate and blogger who followed the petition controversy. "Here they go again…conspiring to sell American consumers the cheapest possible" goods. "The domestic petitioners are seeking prohibitive tariffs that would range from 158.7 percent to 440.9 percent. The petitioners have calculated how 'unfair' China is, down to the last decimal point."

But John Bassett realized that losing Hooker and a few others was the price of taking a stand. By that point, he had signed up thirty-one companies from seventeen states, spanning the country from California to Vermont—as well as five labor unions. He'd used the phone to gain the support of companies ranging from high-end hippie furniture makers in Vermont to good-old-boy hotel-furniture makers in Mississippi.

All had tossed and turned in their beds worrying about making payroll. All had had to lay people off.

Thanks to John's lifelong friendship with Steve Kincaid, who ran the case-goods division for La-Z-Boy, he also got the recliner giant to join his team. A third-generation furniture maker, Kincaid, then the AFMA president, accompanied John on a lobbying trip to the U.S. Department of Commerce.

"An official said to me, 'Well, Mr. Kincaid, we're not concerned about manufacturing jobs because you're really only talking about eight or so percent of the employment in the U.S. We think it's better for the consumer to have more disposable income by buying the cheaper Chinese goods,'" Kincaid said.

"What he was telling me was that, if I was going to Walmart to buy a T-shirt for ten dollars, that would be better than having people in Martinsville and Galax and Hudson making fifteen dollars an hour and supporting the local restaurants, insurance companies, and banks."

It was the same sophistry preached by Walmart founder Sam Walton, who claimed he could raise the standard of living by lowering the costs of retail goods. It was ironic, given that the only jobs many of the displaced workers in the small towns hollowed out by Walmart-championed offshoring could find were part-time, and sans benefits, in

In the first known picture of Bassett Furniture workers from 1902, W.M. Bassett (marked No. 17) is a wide-eyed eight-year-old perched (first row, far left) on a mish-mash of boards. His company cofounder father, J.D. Bassett Sr., is No. 13, and his cofounder uncle, C.C. Bassett, is No. 11, with daughter Mabel Bassett (later Hooker) in his lap. *(Bassett Historical Center)*

Before they were rich: Mr. J.D. and his daughter, Anne, on the family farm in Bassett, circa 1910. *(Bassett Historical Center)*

After he talked the railway into building a new line through his property — so he could sell them the lumber for the ties — J.D. Bassett Sr. transformed his front yard into a furniture factory, using wood from his plentiful lands and cheap labor from people who lived in the Blue Ridge foothills and longed to join the cash economy, including former slaves turned sharecroppers, 1914. *(Bassett Historical Center)*

In a show of burgeoning wealth, the Bassetts began wintering in Florida during the flu epidemic of 1918. Cofounders J.D. and C.C. Bassett with their wives, Pocahontas and Roxie (who were sisters), in the Florida Keys, circa 1920s. *(Bassett Historical Center)*

J.D. and Pocahontas Bassett's grand Victorian home, which matched the one occupied by his brother and company cofounder, C.C. Bassett. Pocahontas is perched on a trunk while two maids, presumably Mary Hunter and Gracie Wade (the live-ins documented in the 1930 U.S. Census), sit to the side on the lawn. (*Bassett Historical Center*)

"The Negroes made me," J.D. Bassett Sr. said of his progressive — and shrewd — decision to hire black workers at the founding of his company, when his Southern competitors relegated them to sawmilling and sharecropping. Black workers earned less than their white counterparts, and until the 1970s they worked in segregated departments, often in the dirtiest jobs, as shown here in a 1920s photo from a Stanley Furniture finishing department, or "rub room." *(The George Holsclaw collection, courtesy of Coy Young)*

John Bassett III was born during the epic flood of 1937, a storm so bad that the Red Cross pitched tents on the hills, and people sat atop railroad cars to inspect the rising waters as silt poured into their company-owned homes. Two of the four men pictured in downtown Bassett are clad in bib overalls, the typical factory worker's uniform. On the far left is town jeweler C.M. Stafford. *(Bassett Historical Center)*

Future kissing cousins Pat Bassett and John Bassett III are at opposite ends of the front row in this 1945 photograph of most of the furniture-making clan gathered in Galax, Virginia. Front row from left: Pat Exum (now Bassett), Stan Chatham, Pocahontas Bassett, John D. Bassett Sr., John Bassett III. Relatives present represented Bassett Furniture, Lane Furniture, Vaughan Furniture, Vaughan-Bassett Furniture, and Stanley Furniture. Jane Bassett (now Spilman) is fourth from the left, second row, and Mary Elizabeth Morten is fifth. *(Courtesy of John Bassett III, Pat Bassett, and Stan Chatham)*

Bassett, Virginia, was a boomtown in the post–World War II years, chock-full of stores, barbershops, movie theaters, and smokestacks (Old Town at right), nearly all of it now gone. During the Depression, the company reduced wages and hours — rather than lay anyone off. *(Bassett Historical Center)*

From horseback to hosting the queen: Virginia governor and Bassett in-law Thomas B. Stanley hosted Queen Elizabeth II and Prince Philip during a 1957 visit to commemorate the 350th anniversary of the Jamestown settlement. Photographed from left: Queen Elizabeth; Stanley grandson Hugh Chatham Jr.; Governor Stanley; grandsons Stan, Crockett, and Rob Chatham; Anne Pocahontas Bassett Stanley (in fur); and Prince Philip. *(The Anne Stanley Chatham collection of the Bassett Historical Center, courtesy of Stan Chatham)*

J.D. Bassett with his longtime chauffeur, Pete Wade, and fish caught near the family compound in Hobe Sound, Florida. When his sons teased him for never learning to drive, Mr. J.D. snapped: "I pay Pete 25 cents an hour so I can sit in the passenger seat and think about how to make more money." Pete was married to family maid Gracie Wade — the only one who raised her voice when John Bassett III left Bassett, the company and the town — following a family feud in 1982. *(The Anne Stanley Chatham collection of the Bassett Historical Center, courtesy of Stan Chatham)*

Bassett Furniture CEO W.M. Bassett in his namesake factory, which, many decades later, became the subject of another family-furniture tug-of-war. "W.M. Bassett was the best factory man of all. He had absolutely no personal ego," a salesman recalled. *(Courtesy of Mary Elizabeth Bassett Morten)*

Early white workers lived near the Smith River banks, and teamed up in groups of four or five to build boats together they could paddle across the Smith. Eventually, they walked to work on swinging bridges erected by the company. *(Courtesy of Steve Eggleston, © 1969)*

Pat and John Bassett were nationally recognized skeet-shooting champions in the early 1970s. The couple threw grand parties in their riverside home, and some workers said the pair reminded them of a Southern John F. and Jackie Kennedy. *(Courtesy of Pat and John Bassett)*

Wyatt Bassett, who would emerge as a key figure in his father's antidumping petition against China, went grouse-hunting with his father, John Bassett III, in the late 1970s. "He didn't even like grouse-hunting," his mother said. "He just always wanted to please his dad." *(Courtesy of Pat Bassett)*

Longtime Bassett Furniture CEO Bob Spilman was nicknamed S.O.B. — the joke was, it stood for Sweet Ole Bob — by his wife, Jane Bassett Spilman. He was the main reason John Bassett III left his namesake town for Galax, Virginia, and has long considered himself the family's black sheep. *(Photograph by Taylor Dabney, courtesy of Virginia Business magazine)*

Longtime family maid Gracie Wade was the only one to openly object when John Bassett III left his wife's family's furniture company in Galax after butting heads with his brother-in-law and boss, Bob Spilman, for decades. "It ain't right," she said, as she helped serve the family's Christmas dinner, which she continued, by tradition, well into her nineties. *(Courtesy of Pat Ross)*

Larry Moh, a Chinese native working in Taiwan, was among the first of the Asian furniture makers to capitalize on the new importing landscape. *(Wharton Magazine)*

John Bassett III, circa 2013. *(Photograph by David Hungate)*

The Vaughan-Bassett team that took on China, from left: J. Doug Bassett IV, John D. Bassett III, Taiwanese translator and consultant Rose Maner, company comptroller Doug Brannock, Wyatt Bassett, and vice president Sheila Key. *(Photograph by David Hungate)*

The nephew of John Bassett III and the son of Bob and Jane Spilman, Rob Spilman is now the CEO of Bassett Furniture Industries. J. Edwin Bassett (aka Mr. Ed) is pictured on the wall of the corporate offices, aka the Taj Mahal. *(Photograph by Jared Soares)*

Aftermath: A Trade Adjustment Assistance worker helps displaced Henry County worker Frances Kissee fill out her paperwork. Kissee lost six jobs in eighteen years to closures, the most recent in 2012 when the Martinsville call center she was working for moved operations to the Philippines. (Photograph by Jared Soares)

Aftermath: Once regal, C.C. Bassett's house on the hill has fallen into disrepair, along with most of the town. "It's a money pit," said current owner Carolyn Brown, who has trouble heating it in winter. Mr. Ed Bassett lived in the same home during the company's heyday, as did his wife, Ruby, who never refused to give food or money when her biracial brother-in-law appeared at her back door. (Photograph by Beth Macy)

Junior Thomas worked at Bassett Mirror Company, while his wife, Mary, worked at Bassett-Walker Knitting and as a housekeeper and nanny. Until Mary's death in November 2013, they lived together in a trailer in the community where most of the earliest black furniture workers lived, alternately named Chigger Ridge, Snot Hollow, Carver Lane, and Carson Road. "We made 'em what they had," Junior Thomas said. "We made 'em rich." (Photograph by Beth Macy)

Aftermath: Wanda Perdue lost her job when Stanley Furniture closed its Stanleytown plant in 2010, then struggled for years to find re-employment, even after she'd gotten her associate's degree. She asked the author to go to Asia to interview her replacement workers and explain "why we can't do that here no more." *(Photograph by Kyle Green, courtesy of the* Roanoke Times*)*

Aftermath: With nearly half of the region's workforce wiped out by globalization, the lines at the Community Storehouse food bank in Henry County form hours before the doors open. A conveyor belt from an abandoned textile plant is used to move the food along in boxes. *(Photograph by Jared Soares)*

Aftermath: "If you'd have told people in Bassett ten years ago that I'd be up here burying these plants today, they'd have said you were a complete fool," said Harry Ferguson, hired to bury the detritus remaining from a fire that destroyed Bassett Superior Lines in 2012. Once the most profitable furniture factory in the world, Bassett Superior Lines closed in 2007. It specialized in "pretty vanilla stuff the consumer no longer wanted," Bassett CEO Rob Spilman said, and was cavernously designed to furnish the GIs when they came home from World War II — not cheaply made hand-carved furniture from Asia. *(Photograph by Beth Macy)*

Walmart stores. Prices were lower, sure, but wages were in a race to the bottom too.

Kincaid remembers thinking, *I'm glad my father isn't alive to see this.*

In August 2003, John invited his industry colleagues to gather again—this time in a banquet room in a Greensboro hotel—to discuss another full-frontal attack. He needed lawyer money, a million and a half, at least. In North Carolina alone, more than forty furniture factories had closed in three years. Nationwide, more than a quarter of the furniture labor force, or thirty-five thousand workers, had already lost their jobs. Wooden bedroom imports were up 54 percent in the first half of 2003—more than in all of 2002. "You're in pain just like we're in pain," JBIII told the four hundred and fifty businesspeople gathered in the hotel. "If you want to help yourselves, we need your support."

Half the suppliers ended up donating, many of them anonymously, to avoid retribution from Chinese customers. "He put the pitch on me, and I gave him three thousand dollars, as small as I was," Garet Bosiger, the drawer supplier, said. "He was rallying everybody like a cheerleader and talking about Dalian."

Dorn told the group that the coalition had a fifty-fifty chance of winning duties, which could result in Chinese import prices increasing some 30 to 40 percent. Truth be told, though, King and Spalding had a better than .500 batting average. Dorn's firm had already won six out of seven antidumping cases against the Chinese, involving items as diverse as paintbrushes, cookware, and apple-juice concentrate.

When one supplier at the meeting asked why he should support the coalition at the risk of alienating the Chinese factories—which also bought his parts—John turned swiftly to the giant American flag he'd placed behind the podium.

"I'm going to give you the short answer," he boomed. "Because you're an American, that's why. Ladies and gentlemen, you were given your freedom, and you owe something to your country."

* * *

The International Trade Commission was an august body that was supposed to be bipartisan, with an even number of Republican and Democratic appointees. But it wasn't exactly like the U.S. Supreme Court, above the fray of political whims and party alliances. It was a group of human beings, most of them well connected and with friends in high places—including at the Department of Commerce, which would determine if and how much a particular Chinese company or importer was dumping.

For the next several years, JBIII would take his flag-waving show on the road dozens of times—to Rotary Clubs, coalition meetings, and Washington hearings. He gathered letters from politicians on both sides of the aisle. He got celebrities with Southern furniture-region roots—race-car driver Richard Petty and artist Bob Timberlake—to give their blessings in front of the media.

In a testimony before the House Ways and Means Subcommittee on Trade, filmed by C-Span, John Bassett drew an analogy between unfairly priced Chinese furniture and one of his hometown's specialties: moonshine. He took the eminent audience back to his Bassett youth, where bootleggers produced some of the finest and cheapest liquor around.

"It was illegal!" he boomed. "But when the ox getting gored by it was the federal and state government, they did something about it!"

The gallery chuckled.

"Very illustrative," a New Jersey congressman noted.

It was folksy, funny, and memorable, his delivery pitched to convey that he was a foreigner himself of sorts, one who'd just landed in Washington with a dispatch from the Real World.

"Every time he testified, he was completely undeferential," Boucher recalled. "He was very direct and absolutely unintimidated.

"When he got in front of a subcommittee, it was magic."

When Dorn filed the petition, in October 2003, 57 percent of the bedroom-furniture industry had signed on to the coalition. (Some companies, including Ethan Allen, remained neutral and were not computed in the tally.)

Furniture/Today reporter Powell Slaughter pored over the Department of Commerce and ITC websites, printing out everything he could find about the Tariff Act of 1930. Because China was a nonmarket economy, the Department of Commerce would have to use prices from a surrogate country—a non-Communist country with a comparable level of development, typically India or the Philippines—to determine the fair-market cost of the materials and labor needed to produce the furniture.

If the cost in the surrogate country was higher than the wholesale prices for Chinese-made goods, the difference between the two equaled how much the product was being dumped, and duties would be assessed accordingly—and retroactively. That meant that orders already placed for Chinese furniture could be hit with fees by the following spring.

Petitioners had to prove not only dumping but also domestic industry harm, but that was a piece of cake when you tallied up the job losses, with 28 percent of the entire domestic-furniture workforce eliminated over the past two and a half years. The factory-closing stories were by now so routine that Slaughter had recently taken an angry call from a source who accused him of forgetting the human cost of globalization by burying the latest factory-closing story on page 4.

"It's getting to be like a murder in New York City," Slaughter replied. The closings were so common that his publication barely deemed them news.

That's when it dawned on Slaughter: With Dorn's track record, it was wholly possible that John Bassett had just irrevocably moved the entire industry's cheese.

When Slaughter called the importers and Chinese manufacturers for comment, it was clear that several weren't taking the petition seriously. "I said, 'If they can get the ITC to tell Commerce to initiate an investigation, you might be looking at duties,' and people just laughed at me," Slaughter told me.

The beat reporter knew his sources well and didn't mind offering some behind-the-scenes advice.

"You better read the law," he told them.

The law didn't care if John Bassett had once imported 9 percent of his furniture (though he was now down to just 2 percent) or if Stanley was already importing much of its bedroom furniture from China. The law didn't care that La-Z-Boy now had forty-three employees managing import operations. When the opposition argued that placing duties on Chinese exports would not return jobs to the United States, the law didn't even bother to yawn.

If the petition struck opponents as disingenuous or hypocritical — that mattered not. The law especially didn't care that nine out of ten economists characterized the Tariff Act as "being a total departure from economic sense," as one scholar told me. "Jabberwocky economics would be the best way to characterize it."

Economic theory had nothing to do with this battle, Slaughter realized.

The Tariff Act of 1930 was what mattered most in deciding the case. If John Bassett won, the cheese was his to move wherever he damn well wanted.

By the time I interviewed John Bassett about the fracas, nearly a decade later, his tone had mellowed. He was all about not criticizing people for the tough business choices they'd made — at least, not publicly — and taking the high road, especially where retailers and relatives were concerned.

But the fiery tone of JBIII in the fall of 2003 was evident in the recording Rose Maner made of a speech he gave to the High Point Rotary Club. He led off by jabbing at President Bush for his refusal to get involved in the furniture case. Bush had issued tariffs of 8 to 30 percent on steel imported from Europe, Asia, and South America. "A lotta people didn't like it, and it was probably politically motivated," he told the group. "But we're bedroom furniture. I don't think it's that vital to the United States. And I don't think the president is gonna give us any protection."

The coalition wasn't in touch with the White House on the matter, but with the wars in Afghanistan and Iraq now in full swing—and America increasingly in debt to China to help pay for them—it was obvious the Bush administration wasn't a fan of angering the Chinese.

But the Tariff Act had been on the books for more than eighty years, and it didn't require congressional or presidential approval. "When China joined the WTO in 2001, they signed a contract that they would be a nonmarket economy for fourteen years," JBIII explained to the Rotary Club group. "What this means is...you don't know how they structure their profits. In fact, China has no SEC, no public reporting or disclosure rules, or financial statements you can see. China is a secret country, and I'll be very frank: The Chinese are wonderful, honorable and noble. They're hardworking, ambitious people. But their economy is set up with the most beautiful blend of entrepreneurship and communism."

He lauded the State of Alabama's recent efforts, via $253 million in incentives, to lure the country's first Mercedes-Benz plant to the town of Vance. Government support of industry was critical, he said, but in a system of legal trade, it was equally critical that government subsidies be transparent. "In China, there's no way to know what we're fighting against. So the Chinese never lose. They keep moving. It's like shadow-boxing. You can't hit somebody if you can't find 'em."

It was a fury of flag-wrapping showmanship that included the line "If you cut me to the marrow of my bone, it's red, white, and blue." (Another patriotism-slathered favorite: "I'm not an R or a D. I'm an A. For *American!*")

John Bassett wanted to be clear, he said: He was not asking for a handout. He just wanted the U.S. government to enforce its laws. He hoped, too, to motivate other manufacturers to rise to the challenge of foreign competition rather than close their factories and turn into importers. "One of our biggest problems is turning the attitude around in this country, making people believe in us again.

"Does that mean we will never close a plant? If we're inefficient, we will close a plant. But I want to be able to say to everybody in my organization...to look them straight in the eye and tell them that I did everything in my power to save their job. I want a free and fair playing field, and I'm willing to fight for it.

"I am *not* gonna turn tail and run."

The week before, he'd shared a similar sentiment with North Carolina senator Elizabeth Dole, who pledged to gather support in the Senate. Doug Bassett was already busy midwifing the Congressional Furnishings Caucus, a bipartisan group of twenty-seven congresspeople who represented furniture-heavy districts.

The clock was ticking. With millions working in its furniture industry, China was now the world's leading furniture exporter. And projections indicated that in just three more years, furniture would be China's number one export to the United States.

Any political strings that could be pulled should be, John told the High Point Rotary Club. A few weeks later, JBIII hoped to meet President Bush, and he planned to give him an earful—during the three-minute audience he'd be lucky to get—about how, as American citizens, "we deserve to have the law applied!"

A Republican-leaning independent and regular campaign contributor (mostly, but not exclusively, to Republicans), he got a mere twenty seconds with President Bush during a million-dollar campaign fund-raiser in Winston-Salem.

"Mr. President, we are the ones who have the antidumping campaign against Chinese bedroom furniture," John said, after having his photograph taken with Bush. "We'd appreciate your help."

"Contact the Commerce Department," Bush told him, shaking his hand and summoning the next donor in line. There was no hint of recognition, no "Thanks for your donation."

Still, that was a better response than the one T. C. Morgan received. A Republican and former vice president of the North Carolina Association of Furniture Manufacturers, Morgan had tried to arrange a meeting between Bush and some factory workers and executives, including the state manager for the textile workers' union. A few months before, Pillowtex had announced it was closing sixteen plants—including the one in Henry County's Fieldale, near Bassett—and eliminating 6,450 jobs.

"I actually thought it would be a good thing for the president to come meet with workers who have lost their jobs," union manager Anthony Coles told the *Charlotte Observer,* "rather than just meet with people who can afford a $2,000 dinner."

Bush had been happy to shake John Bassett's hand, and he even spoke with regional community college officials about job training. But a meeting with displaced factory employees could not be worked into his reelection-year schedule.

20

Mr. Bassett Goes to Washington

*By the time the judgment came down, there were
lawyers on the other side coming over to thank him.
They'd been wanting to start their own practices,
and they didn't know how they were gonna
do it—till this case came along.*

—JOHN'S DAUGHTER, FRAN BASSETT POOLE

The building that houses the U.S. International Trade Commission is all marble and reflective glass. It juts out onto Washington's E Street like the prow of a ship—rounded, confident, and impervious to the outside world.

ITC decisions hinge on six people, lawyers usually—three Democrats and three Republicans—whose job is to determine whether domestic industries are being unfairly harmed by imports that are dumped by foreign companies or by companies that are propped up by foreign government subsidies.

When President George Bush nominated West Virginia lawyer Charlotte R. Lane, a Republican and a former state delegate, to the commission in August 2003, it was unclear how much he knew about his new nominee. She was fifty-three, a former state utility commissioner, and, perhaps most important for the task at hand, the daughter of a factory worker.

Lane's father had worked as a custodian for the American Cyanamid plant at Willow Island for years, and as a child, she attended annual picnics and played with the other factory workers' kids. As she grew older and advanced up the tax-bracket ladder, it happened that she developed a passion for furniture, especially antiques and reproductions.

When Lane and some of her fellow commissioners ventured to Galax on a standard preliminary fact-finding tour, it wasn't the look of the mid- to low-end furniture at Vaughan-Bassett that caught her eye; it was the manufacturing details. When JBIII showed the touring delegation his factory and explained that the finishing process was what separated a moderately priced piece from a high-end item, the furniture devotee in her got excited.

To Lane, furniture was a lot more charming than magnets, plastics, or swimming-pool chemicals—subjects of some of the other antidumping cases on the ITC docket.

Furniture, you could get your arms around. You could touch it, tell a story about where it came from. Furniture was a kind of status symbol, like the BlackBerry John Bassett used to call people at all hours of the day and night.

Furniture was a snapshot of who you were when you bought it, how much disposable income you had, how you felt about the person you were buying it with.

"The wood itself, before you put on the finish, it was very substantially made, and it was good wood and good craftsmanship," Lane recalled of her Galax tour during a September 2012 interview in her Charleston, West Virginia, law office. (Like Joe Dorn, she gave me *exactly* one hour.)

JBIII showed off the equipment the company had bought as it embraced new "lean manufacturing" techniques. He had spent nearly

$40 million in the past five years on high-tech German and Italian routers and state-of-the-art kilns—a capital investment rate that was double his competitors'. The equipment allowed him to make furniture with fewer people, but he didn't immediately replace the people with the machines, he explained. He allowed attrition to do the work.

Before the tour, Lane said, she hadn't understood the full extent of his family ties to the smokestacks; knew nothing about the cousin companies inside the coalition and out. He had the famous Bassett name, of course. But more critical, JBIII had what Congressman Boucher had already witnessed inside the Beltway: that rare ability to simplify something complicated so that you laugh or shake your head—like his notion of comparing cheap Chinese imports to moonshine. ("You got to give people somethin' to re-*mem*-ba," John told me once, winking.)

With the commissioners gathered literally in his sawdust, the master showman was in an even better position than when he'd hauled the furniture into the Greensboro courtroom to defend himself against the Lexington trade-dress lawsuit. He had them exactly where he wanted them.

It was mid-2003, the preliminary ITC hearing would soon be on the docket, and there were things JBIII wanted the commissioners to know. He knew he'd inspired a deep animosity, not just from some of his relatives but also from some longtime customers. Jake Jabs, an aptly named Colorado retailer who had once been among his largest dealers, had canceled all Vaughan-Bassett orders the moment the petition was filed. Jabs logged about 150,000 air miles annually on buying expeditions, and he loved to search out remote, unknown factories—especially in China. When John chided the suppliers at his Greensboro meeting and told them they should support the coalition "because you're an American, that's why!" Jabs read about it in the press and immediately griped, "Nice political speech, John."

The gloves were off. Jabs told a *Furniture/Today* reporter that the coalition consisted of a "bunch of old North Carolina has-beens crying over spilt milk. It's a backwards, antiquated, dark-ages type of mentality that would even think of this."

The animosity troubled John Bassett, and when he shared that with Lane during the tour, it made a lasting impression. "The fact that he was so willing to go out there and fight for what was right in the face of so much opposition . . . it was so *personal* to him," she explained.

His genius, of course, was that he also managed to make it personal to *her*. When he pointed out the vacant factories near his own, she recalled the plant closings she'd seen in her home state. She remembered newspaper articles about desperate people arrested for stealing copper out of abandoned plants, just like in Bassett. She felt for him when he described the sleepless nights he'd spent—staring at the ceiling, worrying whether he was going to have to lay off people whose fathers and grandfathers had worked for his family.

During Lane's eight-year tenure, the ITC reviewed 192 claims of illegal foreign-trade practices, and domestic producers had prevailed sixty-nine times. When I asked why more domestic industries hadn't brought cases before the ITC when so many companies were closing factories and rushing overseas, she blamed legal fees and lack of awareness. "Many people don't even know the remedy is available. So by the time that people learn there's a venue at the ITC to bring a case, a lot of the injury has already occurred. It's very difficult for industries that are being injured by unfair competition to have the money for legal fees."

When Lane wagered that legal fees for a typical antidumping case ran "somewhere between a half million or a million or more," I almost did a spit-take with my coffee. Furniture analysts have suggested that the bedroom-furniture case has cost $5 million to $7 million, but several trade lawyers told me that $5 million was pocket change compared to the actual legal bills, which are still ongoing—though John and Wyatt refuse to divulge how much they've paid to Joe Dorn's firm.

John would rather talk about how the government made him display EEOC posters notifying workers of their right not to be discriminated against because of gender, race, age, or disability. But the government did nothing to inform those same workers about illegal trade as outlined in the Tariff Act of 1930 — something with potentially greater bearing on their jobs.

During a lobbying visit to the Small Business Administration in the fall of 2003, John chided the government for spending $33 million to advertise and market its newly redesigned twenty-dollar bill while doing virtually nothing to educate manufacturers about the recourse they might have against illegal trade.

"I can assure you, there's no one in my family that doesn't know how to spend twenty dollars!" he barked.

Powell Slaughter remembers the moment it hit him. He was sitting in the packed U.S. International Trade Commission hearing room, and he realized: all the good-old-boy backslapping that had been going on for generations in the industry, all the schmoozing dinners at Market, all that butter-squirting chicken Kiev — you could stick a fork in that now.

It was an exciting time to be a reporter for *Furniture/Today*, even though getting the players to reveal anything about their strategy had been "like pulling teeth," he said. He'd had no idea John Bassett had sent a Taiwanese interpreter turned investigator to Dalian, for instance. No idea that John had allegedly strong-armed his own nephew, telling Rob Spilman, "I sure would hate to see people picketing your factories" if Bassett Furniture didn't join the coalition, according to Rob.

Once Bassett was in the coalition, John reasoned, Stanley would have to join, or risk losing face in the community, since Stanleytown was literally next door to Bassett.

"You saw the two sides arrayed, literally on opposite sides of the courtroom...and you just kinda looked at people in that industry, so totally divided now, and you kinda went, *Wow.*"

The lawyers on both sides had never argued such a heated case, full of subterfuge and flamethrowing words like *extortion* and *fraud*. The fiery exchanges between Joe Dorn and his opponent at the November 2003 preliminary hearing featured surreptitiously recorded phone messages, the dramatic thud of a surprise-document throw-down, and the worst insult a fourth-generation American furniture maker like Rob Spilman could hear: that the Chinese made *better* furniture than Bassett Furniture Industries. (If Mr. J.D. had rolled over in his grave at that one, then Larry Moh was surely smiling in his. *Deliver a donkey, my ass.*)

The Chinese companies had cast their lot with another top-shelf Washington trade lawyer, John Greenwald, a Jim Belushi look-alike and a former Commerce Department official. Greenwald's father had been a lawyer and economist who spent his career helping to guide international trade policy for the United States, serving as a representative to the General Agreement on Tariffs and Trade, the post–World War II treaty regulating international trade and a precursor to the WTO.

Greenwald had argued both sides of the trade-dispute aisle, but in this case it was crystal clear that he was his father's son. Especially when the first thing he asserted during his opening remarks was that the petition was an out-and-out *fraud*.

It went downhill from there. Casting the petitioners as hypocrites who were themselves importing containers, Greenwald played a voice-mail message left by a salesman at Lea Industries (a subsidiary of fellow petitioner La-Z-Boy), advising a Rooms To Go manager not to worry about the antidumping case. If duties were leveled against the Chinese manufacturers, he would make sure the retailer could still buy the same products from him—via a factory in Vietnam, where duties didn't exist.

"We have been working on this backup...so the ugly stuff can't happen once you buy this furniture from us," the Lea salesman said on the recording.

"Now, I hope that Mr. Kincaid and the Bassett family and the Vaughan family have a sense of shame about the testimony they gave about third-country sourcing," Greenwald said. "That tape recording says in a nutshell what I wanted to say about the affirmatively

292 • FACTORY MAN

misleading nature of their testimony. It's business fundamentals, it's not dumping, that's driving the increase of imports from China and elsewhere."

The barbs about quality came next. Domestically produced Bassett Furniture was poorly made, the opposition argued, and its company executives were resistant to change. In the company's defense, Bassett CEO Rob Spilman told the commission that J.C. Penney had dumped the company in favor of Chinese imports, even after Bassett reengineered its products and slashed its prices by a third.

After which J.C. Penney's operations manager Jim McAlister leveled a torrent of grievances against its former vendor: Customer complaints had soared about Bassett Furniture defects. A quality audit of Bassett turned up a 50 percent defect rate—nicked finishes, for instance, and dresser drawers that didn't open smoothly. The defect rate on imports was only 1.9 percent, he said.

J.C. Penney had asked Bassett and others to come up with a corrective action plan to prevent further defects. "To this day, we have not received a corrective action plan from any of the domestic producers," McAlister said.

Rob Spilman all but called him a liar, reminding him that Bassett had won Penney's 1999 Supplier of the Year award. "Penney has never told Bassett that it had any concerns about our quality or service.... The only reason we have lost this business to imports from China is price."

Speaking for the newly formed Committee for Free Trade in Furniture, importer Bill Kemp showed two slides targeting what he called the "disingenuous stand by the petitioners because they are doing the same thing I am: importing furniture from other countries."

The first slide was one of Vaughan-Bassett's ads from *Furniture/Today* from the same series as the "Ohhh ship" caricature. This one had a man and a woman dressed in business suits, clutching briefcases and cell phones—and wearing gas masks. It had run in furniture-trade publications during the height of the SARS scare, with the kicker: "Is this how your buyers dress for work?"

"While I'm disturbed by the ad and it really bothered me, [along] with a lot of the people I work with in plants around the world, the point I would like to make about it is, in the left-hand corner there's a sign that says, 'Vaughan-Bassett Furniture, made in the USA,'" Kemp said.

Then came Kemp's punch line. His next slide featured a furniture carton bearing Vaughan-Bassett's logo and *Made in China* prominently written on its side. The photo had been taken years earlier, Wyatt said later, before the company slashed its imports to 1 to 2 percent. (In 2013, it did away with imports entirely.)

Kemp throttled the coalition's biggest public companies — Stanley and Bassett — by quoting from their own Securities and Exchange Commission filings. Stanley "continues to implement a blended strategy of combining its domestic manufacturing capabilities with an expanding offshore sourcing program... [that] will lower costs, provide design flexibility, offer a better value to its customer." Bassett Furniture reported to the SEC that it was embracing change in the industry "by reducing its domestic production of product that can be more efficiently sourced overseas."

Jeffrey Seaman, the CEO of Rooms To Go, then the nation's largest retail chain, said the petition was really about the loss of control — and profits — manufacturers felt when they realized "the retailers were smart enough to do it" themselves.

"So if you were Vaughan-Bassett, hypothetically, bringing in a bedroom [suite] for $1,000, reselling it to some of their customers... for $1,500 and that retailer sells it for $3,000, then you have another retailer who says, 'We don't need you, Mr. Vaughan-Bassett, to import for us. We'll bring it in, we'll pay $1,000 or $1,100 to import it and we'll sell it for $2,000' — well, the retailers selling for $3,000 are going to try to import it themselves."

In a follow-up hearing, Greenwald summarized his opposition by quoting from a 1960s British television program called *Beyond the Fringe:*

> It's a dark office in a war room. There is an elderly colonel who calls in an enthusiastic young lieutenant, Lieutenant Jenkins.... "Jenkins, we're going to drop you 300 miles behind enemy lines and we want you to attack the Germans from the rear." And Jenkins says, "Yes, sir. But why are we doing this, sir?"
>
> The colonel replies, "These are dark times, Jenkins, and what Britain now needs is a futile gesture."

Greenwald beseeched the commissioners not to interfere with globalization's natural economic course. "I hope you are not in the business of making futile gestures," he said.

Joe Dorn had spent too many Saturday mornings on the phone with John Bassett not to have his own gotcha moments carefully rehearsed and finely tuned. His first return volley was to point out that the Furniture Retailers of America, newly organized to oppose the petition, in no way represented all of the nation's furniture stores—or even a majority. As proof, he ceremoniously dropped letters from seven hundred retailers on the ITC table. They landed with a thud.

John Bassett had spent the past year calling many of the seven hundred stores, mostly mom-and-pops, and beseeching his sales staff to gather letters in support of the petition. They were now the bulk of his own customers—and the core of his VBX sales—and they were already being priced out of the market by container loads of furniture they were not themselves large or rich enough to buy.

Stick to the statute, Dorn reminded the commissioners. The statute asks the commission to consider the impact of imports on domestic producers as well as on American factories and American workers.

The petitioners had lost more than half of their operating income from 2000 to 2002. In three short years, sixty-eight bedroom-furniture plants had closed.

"Furniture Brands has been more hurt by imports from China than any member of our coalition, but they won't admit it," Dorn said. "They're afraid that those Chinese factories will cut them off if it does not oppose the petition," and that major retailers will stop buying from it for the same reason.

"Most importantly, Furniture Brands is afraid because it has bet the future of its company on dumped imports from China," Dorn said. "It cannot afford to tell Wall Street that its strategy is predicated on unfairly priced imports."

Dorn punctuated the point by introducing as evidence paperwork for eight applications for Trade Adjustment Assistance, representing eight of Furniture Brands' shuttered factories. "In each case, the Department of Labor certified the employees as eligible to receive adjustment benefits based upon a finding that increased imports contributed materially to their layoffs," he said.

The ITC, in other words, need look no farther than another branch of the federal government for proof that Furniture Brands' workers had been injured by Chinese imports.

After the first hearing, Dorn's firm had limousines waiting for JBIII and his crew. After the second, the coalition was faced with raising more money for legal fees, and to get back to Dorn's office, those same clients could either take a taxi or walk. On the way out of the ITC fortress, John Bassett smiled at Wyatt and asked what he thought of their top-shelf lawyer. Was he really worth all the money they were in the midst of trying to raise?

Father and son were strolling past the Smithsonian when Wyatt gave his answer. "If I were on trial for murder and I was innocent, I'd want Joe Dorn representing me."

But if he was guilty, he'd want John Greenwald on his team. Greenwald reminded Wyatt of his mother, Pat. As a child, when the family

296 • FACTORY MAN

arrived home on a Sunday night after a trip and found the pantry bare, Wyatt marveled at his mother's ability to fashion a remarkable meal out of toast and bacon with a sauce conjured up from stale cheese and a can of beer.

Years later, Wyatt laughed as he recounted this exchange with his dad. He was sitting at his Vaughan-Bassett desk, which was littered with wood samples and drawer hinges, components of a new suite he was helping design. (He had just returned from a powwow upstairs with engineer Linda McMillian, and he reeked of her Marlboros.)

Greenwald didn't have the Tariff Act on his side, Wyatt said, and yet he had still managed to fashion "forty-five minutes of very entertaining stuff.... It may not be legally sound, but has he whipped something out of nothing? You're damn right he has."

Within a month, the Department of Commerce initiated its investigation to determine whether the Chinese factories were truly dumping. In results released a month later, the ITC unanimously voted in the coalition's favor, pronouncing that domestic workers and manufacturers had indeed been injured by illegally dumped imports — something the people in Bassett could have shown them if anyone had bothered to look.

With the Byrd Amendment still intact, the Chinese dumpers were going to have to pay. But the preliminary duties assigned in 2004 were disappointing to JBIII and his sons: 14 percent, compared to the 35 to 40 percent Dorn had estimated.

But Dorn had a plan B that he believed would net the coalition its rightful due. The coalition had the right to participate in annual Department of Commerce reviews of the dumping margins. The process was as complicated as it was controversial, but, if successful, it just might level the playing field for the coalition. And it would very definitely bury Wyatt Bassett in spreadsheets and legal bills for many years.

21

Factory Requiem

Should I hate a people for the shade of their skin
Or the shape of their eyes or the shape I'm in.
Should I hate 'em for having our jobs today
No I hate the men sent the jobs away.

—James McMurtry, "We Can't Make It Here"

Just before the preliminary hearings, Bassett Furniture was on the verge of closing its Dublin, Georgia, plant, and Bassett CEO Rob Spilman prepared to deliver the news. The weekend before his flight to Georgia, he showed up at Joe Philpott's front door with a fifth of single-malt scotch.

"He said, 'I got bad news. Monday morning, we gotta close the damn plant,'" recalled Philpott, the retired senior vice president for manufacturing. "It was like drinking at a funeral," he said.

Henry County, once home to the largest percentage of manufacturing jobs in Virginia, now had the state's highest unemployment rate— 13.3 percent, three times higher than the state average. And the two executives were about to hold their first factory wake.

That week Joe Philpott's cousin bet him a hundred bucks that every one of the Bassett factories would be closed within five years. Philpott shook his head as he recounted the story, chuckling at his own naïveté. He had refused the bet. "You're crazy as hell," he told his cousin.

It was 2003. Bassett still had six plants in North Carolina and Virginia—including the company's cash cow, Bassett Superior, the one Philpott had managed himself for decades. His baby.

"I couldn't steal your money like that," Philpott had said.

But Rob wasn't so hopeful. He'd seen what they were up against in China with his own eyes. His first trip to China was as a Bassett Furniture vice president in 1994, back when some Asian managers still rode bikes and wore straw hats. On one of his subsequent thirty trips, he toured Dongguan from the back of Lacquer Craft executive Samuel Kuo's scooter. "He wanted to sell to me, and it was just mind-blowing how big this factory he was building was," Rob recalled. "We had big factories here, but this was three times the biggest factory I'd ever seen. There were so many workers huddled around the furniture, they were like *bees*.

"I thought, *My God, these guys are planning to take over the world,* which of course they were. They were like we were in the fifties and sixties," he said. "They were like my great-grandfather Bassett...and, man, do they *work*."

His father was incredulous when Rob reported back on the lack of safety measures in the Dongguan finishing rooms—no fans, no masks, nothing. Rob actually had a fondness for the smell of finishing material, but these fumes were so strong he had trouble catching his breath. "How do they stand it?" he had asked the plant manager, choking as he spoke.

"Spray two years and die," the manager said.

At which point there would be twenty more lined up to take the fallen worker's place.

"How you coming along with my nephew?" John Bassett asked me. Halfway through the writing of this book, I'd spent weeks camped out with my laptop and notebook in Bassett but had not once penetrated the Taj Mahal walls. So I wasn't coming along too well with his nephew. Still angry about a 2012 newspaper series on the aftereffects of globalization I'd written a year before, Rob ignored my first several interview requests.

Behind the scenes, a relative intervened on my behalf, pointing out that my book would be published regardless of whether he cooperated or not. That same relative (who asked not to be named) then coached me to e-mail Rob again and explain that, yes, this was my first book, and, no, I wasn't really a business writer, but I *had* won more than a dozen national journalism awards, as well as a yearlong Nieman Fellowship in Journalism at Harvard in 2010.

"He doesn't take you seriously," the relative said.

So, reluctantly, in an e-mail, I dropped the H-bomb.

A day later, Rob agreed to meet with me—for exactly one hour, preferably after his workday, the implication being that he would not waste work time on the likes of me.

When Rob gave me nearly three hours the first time we met, I understood immediately why industry insiders described him as being more likable than his mom, dad, and uncle *combined*. "I've been around a lotta heat my whole life," he said. "Hell, everybody can't be that way."

When he first became CEO, his dad called him regularly, never saying hello but simply launching into a tirade about some decision Rob had made, a tirade that usually began with "What in the *hell* were you thinking?"

Months into it, Bob Spilman caught his son on a bad day.

"Dad, are we friends?" Rob stopped him mid-rant.

"Uh...well...yeah, I guess we're friends."

"Look, Dad, as a friend, get off my fuckin' back!"

Astonishingly, once Rob stood up to his father, he did.

Rob described how the task of plant closing fell mainly to him when he became CEO in 2000. It was part of a wholesale strategy shift that favored imports and retail stores, but it resulted in the laying off of thousands. He had initially been optimistic about joining his uncle's coalition, hoping the antidumping duties might stave off the last of the plant closures—and maybe even keep the smokestacks humming at Bassett Superior Lines, by then the only furniture factory still operating in Bassett.

But unlike Vaughan-Bassett, Bassett Furniture was a publicly held company directed by a board filled with figure men, as Spencer Morten referred to them—high-powered CEOs who were a Who's Who of Southern commerce. "We've been a public company since 1930, with shareholders that have to get profits," Rob said. "At the end of the day, we are not a social experiment."

The first round of antidumping duties, or Byrd money, was disbursed to petitioners in 2006, and Bassett Furniture's share would amount to $17.5 million over the next six years. "The duties helped some, no question, but I felt like the horse was already out of the barn by the time they arrived," Rob said.

The ITC decision made the duties possible, but the ITC could not stipulate what the recipients of the cash had to do with the money. Bassett Furniture directed much of its Byrd money toward reinventing its retail operation, Bassett Home Furnishings. "A lot of it was perpetrated by the unfair advantage that the Asians had," Rob explained. "Our customers gleefully went over there [to Asia] and started buying directly from them so they could get it cheaper, just like Walmart's done.

"It wasn't our idea to change that model of prosperity we'd been operating under for decade after decade," he added. "The world changed. And it's been painful for us as a company to change. It's been emotionally taxing."

The evening after one of the plant closings, Rob called his school-age children together to watch the local cable-television news. The station was known for its populist bent, and Rob knew the story would make him look bad. He told them, "Forget your homework and sit down and watch this with me tonight because your dad's gonna get crucified."

His daughters cried, and his son was furious. Rob told them, "People are scared; they've lost their jobs. And I want you to realize what we've had to do, how serious this is. You'll hear about it at school. You've got to be sensitive to what's happening here. You've got to understand it and know y'all are fortunate kids. This is serious stuff."

Down in Dublin, retired plant manager Buck Gale felt sick to his stomach as he watched his former workers file out of the factory for the last time. Retired for two years, he'd had Bassett's Dublin plant earning seven-figure profits annually on his watch, surpassing even Bassett Superior Lines. Gale said he personally reinvented the production process for the low-end line of Bassett's products — only to be stymied by the company's new interest in higher-end products and its growing Ethan Allen–inspired retail program. (By 2003, Bassett Furniture had doubled its number of stores in five years, to 101.)

"Our product was priced so much lower than the other Bassett bedroom lines, it didn't blend with the image Bassett wanted," Gale said. "I wanted to, just pardon my French, kick somebody right in the damn teeth," he added.

Buck had grown up in Bassett and still owned property there. As a child, he'd worn John Bassett's hand-me-down clothes, passed down to his mother by John's mother at Pocahontas Bassett Baptist Church.

"They lost the fight, but they lost it not because of the factory workers in those plants. It wasn't nothing but *greed*," Gale said, so angry both times I talked to him on the telephone that he sounded near tears. Paul Fulton, the CEO who was supposed to be the placeholder until Rob Spilman grew seasoned enough to assume the mantle, had closed or sold off twenty-eight plants during his three-year reign.

Fulton eschewed the style of the old-line misters, who'd run the business as a model of efficiency — working weekends, sweating every detail, hiring people "who got up with the chickens and went to bed with the chickens," as Mr. Doug liked to say. He replaced them with marketing guys who emphasized short-term stock-market gains and

302 • FACTORY MAN

profit margins and gobbled up what the economists, bankers, and business schools were saying about creative destruction.

Retired now for twelve years, Gale said he loves Rob Spilman like a son. But he still wakes up every morning "tee-totally mad" over the factory closures, which he sees as an intentional failure to compete *and* a total disregard for the generations of factory workers who made the Bassett family and other shareholders rich. "Paul Fulton couldn't make a toothpick!" Gale shouted into the phone. "The little people were just used and abused."

Instead of modernizing and adopting lean manufacturing principles to keep its factories efficient, North Carolina State University furniture expert Steve Walker recalled, Bassett Furniture and others "took the easy way out. Barring some big effort on the part of the government to protect industry...if you were a public company, it was a whole lot easier to just shut 'em down and go buy the product."

Meanwhile, the smaller, privately held Vaughan-Bassett was pouring millions into new machinery to keep the plant efficient and up-to-date. It was a gamble, to be sure, as JBIII watched his sales plummet, going from $168.2 million in 2000 to $83.9 million in 2011, a period when the company received more than $21 million in Byrd money, most of which John funneled into computerized routers and kilns and a new rough end.

It wasn't a social experiment per se, as Rob Spilman might have put it. But with much of his personal wealth tied up in the business, JBIII had no choice but to fight to protect his family and company assets, his nephew and other industry watchers argue.

"If I had forty percent of my company's equity, and I had no brand name, and I only made one product—bedroom furniture—and my alternative is to close all my factories and import, that would be a death sentence for me," Rob said. "But if I wanted to keep the value I had in my private company, I would fight tooth and toenail, and get the U.S. government and whoever else I can think of to help me keep the value of my company.

"So everybody picked their poison."

In 2004, Rob Spilman still believed he could keep the last of his factories going—the Superior Lines cash cow. Asked to recount what his father thought of the closings that followed Bob Spilman's 1997 retirement, "He just said, 'I feel so sorry for you son of a bitches, I can't stand it. I was there when the easy money was made.' "

By that point, a rare form of leukemia had zapped the fire out of the hard-charging, expletive-dropping businessman, a man his son fondly called "the best ass-chewer in history." A man who had fully and inimitably articulated what he thought about everything and everybody, from his quirky corporate pilot to his cocky brother-in-law.

Like many of his underlings, I had a hard time grasping the essence of Bob Spilman. Was he a tough-guy genius motivated by the art of deal-making and loyal to his card-playing cadre? Or was he just a selfish narcissist, broken by his own lousy childhood and compelled to control the movements of everyone around him?

During my only trip to the Taj Mahal, when I asked Rob these questions, he chuckled and shook his head. "God Almighty, he was hard. But he did mellow as time went on," he said. "He had a charm about him that was endearing, and this extended to everyone from the guy pumping his gas to the Wall Street guy."

He then told two stories to illustrate his point.

The first was about a table-plant manager named Dick Rosenberg whose wife was a city girl and refused to live in Bassett; she made Dick return to their home in Atlanta on weekends, which irked Sweet Ole Bob to no end.

So much so that the CEO became positively obsessed with making sure that Rosenberg never left early on Fridays, even if he'd already put in well over forty hours that week. Spilman called Rosenberg's secretary every Friday afternoon at four to make sure he was still there. One Friday, Dick had already sneaked out when Spilman phoned and barked, "Where the hell's Rosenberg?"

When his secretary told him Rosenberg had left, Spilman made another call. He ordered Virginia State Police patrolmen to put up a barricade across the Virginia–North Carolina line to stop him. The troopers hauled the poor guy back to the Taj Mahal, where Sweet Ole Bob was standing in his office, making a big show of looking at his wristwatch.

"Well, it's five o'clock. Time to go!" he said, beaming. "Have a good weekend!"

The SOB was shrewd. He was funny—though usually at someone else's expense. And he was a master showman, as illustrated by a grand gesture Rob described him making at a High Point reception in the late 1990s.

Bob Spilman vented his rage about Chinese imports—on an innocent suckling pig. He picked up a carving knife, shouted "Larry Moh!," and stabbed the porcine centerpiece so hard the apple in its mouth quaked.

He was sick and tired of hearing Moh's name.

He may have been the puppeteer manipulating the factory closings, installing Fulton as his replacement until his son grew ready for the challenge. But the Spilmans were not the only factory men drowning in their scotch. The next people hit with pink slips were John Bassett's 385 workers in Sumter, the glit makers who had, over the course of almost two decades, added mightily to his company's profits. Until 2001, when the profits turned to losses. If the Chinese were hammering the wooden-bedroom-furniture market, they were positively killing the paper-on-particleboard sales. Why buy a printed product when you could now buy a wood one at the same price? Even the masses knew that much.

John Bassett closed the V-B/Williams plant in Sumter at the end of June 2004. To stop the hemorrhaging and keep the rest of his plants viable, he had no other choice. As he told a Sumter newspaper, "The government has determined China is cheating, but it's coming too late to save our Sumter plant."

Still, he worried about people like Roger Plock, a longtime maintenance man who couldn't afford to retire and was still healthy and eager to work. Who was going to hire a sixty-four-year-old in Sumter, especially with a job market already flooded by the closing of two nearby automotive-supplier plants that had moved operations to Mexico?

Twelve years had passed since Ross Perot warned Americans about the "giant sucking sound" of NAFTA. But people now saw firsthand that the fallout from all those trade-policy acronyms written years ago in faraway Washington, Doha and Uruguay eventually trickled down to small towns like Sumter, South Carolina, and Bassett, Virginia.

Back in Galax, the muttering reached new heights. So did the questions. Sheila Key, John's assistant, had to calm down nervous employees waiting to speak to him after their shifts. They wanted reassurances that the flagship Galax plant wasn't going down next.

"He wasn't sleeping at night," Sheila told me. "You could tell by looking that it was weighing heavily."

What happened next should have killed him. If you saw the photograph of his Lexus sedan, mangled from bumper to bumper, you'd wonder how he'd survived falling asleep on the Blue Ridge Parkway and crashing into a tree with only a sprained hand, bruising, and copious shards of glass embedded in his skin.

When he woke up moments after the impact, the airbags had all deployed. The first thing he noticed was the odor of cordite, the propellant that forced out the airbags, and it smelled exactly like hot shotgun shells. John Bassett was so tired and so embattled, so worried about angry retailers and legal fees and coalition members calling left and right, that it didn't occur to him that he had fallen asleep during his morning commute.

He thought somebody was trying to kill him.

PART VII

22

Million-Dollar Backlash

What happens is you see the sales start to trail off,
and usually one day they stop ordering from you.
You usually don't know exactly... who you've
been replaced by.

—WYATT BASSETT

By the time the retailers, importers, and furniture makers descended on High Point for the April 2004 Market, nobody was shooting at John Bassett. But as the usual crowd of seventy-five thousand descended on the furniture epicenter to browse showrooms and decide what to order for their stores, it occurred to him that his son Wyatt's prediction of mockery followed by anger had hit the bull's-eye. Some openly ridiculed him. Not only did many stop ordering from his factory, but several sported buttons emblazoned with a picture of a droopy-eared basset hound and the words *How big is your duty?*

Buyers were warmly welcomed at the new replica of Beijing's Forbidden City, erected by importer Lifestyle Enterprises, which was making no secret of where its furniture originated. Lifestyle was owned by Taiwanese-born William Hsieh, a friend and protégé of Larry Moh, and his company had contracted with factories across

Asia, with a concentration in Dongguan, to make its low-end promotional furniture.

This Forbidden City was a miniature showroom replica, just as John Bassett's Graceland had been, and it was every bit as gaudy, with sloped roofs, golden lions guarding the entrance, and smiling women decked out in embroidered Asian gowns. (The Peking duck, though, was surely a cut above Vaughan-Bassett's peanut butter, banana, and bacon sandwiches, an Elvis favorite.)

The antidumping petition turned out to be a boon for Lifestyle, which raked in the business that spring, its American-division CEO James Riddle said, recalling an über-popular $399 four-poster bed named the Emperor that featured leather inlays and hand-carved accents. "If anything, the controversy played to our favor," Riddle said. "The retailers looked instead for companies like us because we were a better value and highly promotional. They were so mad at John, they opened the door to us."

The retailers had progressed beyond anger now to a whole new stage: retribution. By June 2004, fifteen retailers across the country had dropped Vaughan-Bassett, wiping out some eight million dollars in orders.

They weren't using the word *boycott,* a Furniture Retailers of America spokesman claimed, though they did buy two-page ads that named every company listed on the petition, and *everyone* knew who the leader was, even if the ads didn't directly say so — the hound dog caricatured on the button: John Bassett. "Why are these companies asking to put their hands in your customers' pockets?" one ad said.

Even companies like Copeland, the Vermont furniture makers, were feeling the ire. Copeland Furniture had lost a quarter of its business to imports, and the Asians were knocking off the Frank Lloyd Wright designs that Tim Copeland, the company's founder, had paid big bucks to license, wholesaling them at prices that were a third below

Copeland's. Eventually Copeland laid off thirty employees, nearly a quarter of his workforce.

At Johnston/Tombigbee Furniture in Mississippi, CEO Reau Berry ended up delivering pink slips to over half his workforce. The third-generation Mississippi furniture maker had been visiting High Point all his life. Founded by his grandfather in 1932, the company had a Market showroom right above La-Z-Boy's, and Berry counted as friends retailers who'd been doing business with his family for forty years.

It was happening to everyone in the coalition. Half of Berry's customers dropped him, many without saying a word. Longtime friends and customers walked by his display at High Point and waved—on their way to the Chinese manufacturer's showroom next door. "When China joined the WTO, they took a nightstand I had for a hundred dollars, copied it, and sold it literally for fifty dollars," he said. "I can't compete against a government, especially a Communist government."

Berry was already importing some residential furniture from China in 2003 when an import agent working in tandem with the Chinese government threatened to cut him off if he supported John Bassett's coalition, Berry said. So Berry cut the agent off.

He overhauled his business model, dropping the residential furniture line. He made smaller cuttings of hospitality furniture instead, mainly for hotels and motels. Like upholstered furniture and kitchen cabinetry, hotel furniture is often custom ordered and therefore not as vulnerable to offshore competition.

Once a devoted Republican, Berry became such a vociferous and outspoken opponent of President George W. Bush's free-trade policies that his favorite publication, the London-based *Financial Times,* finally banned him from making any more comments on its website.

"I've sat here on the front end of this whole deal, and I may not be the brightest bulb, but I know that when my people don't have a job in Columbus, Mississippi, they're out of work forever," he told me. "There's nothing here for them to retrain for."

* * *

During both the fall and spring High Point Markets in 2004, the dueling sides hunkered down in separate quarters to strategize. The retailers and importers brainstormed ways to minimize the impact of the forthcoming duties, like setting up shop in Vietnam and Malaysia, as Lifestyle would soon do. (Bedroom imports from Vietnam, in fact, had already tripled during the first three months of 2004, according to the U.S. Customs Service.)

John Greenwald advised a packed house of three hundred that they needed to organize, and the Furniture Retailers of America spokesman followed up by explaining just exactly where they should send their checks. The FRA had already raised five hundred thousand dollars to fight the coalition, and it needed more. The opposition took out more trade-magazine ads, the general theme being that the petitioners were not only hypocrites who were themselves importing but also greedy protectionists.

FRA lawyer Bill Silverman accused petitioners of "making war" on retailers, decrying the preliminary decision to impose duties on dumpers. Silverman laid out the possible financial liabilities for all involved: years of annual investigations, the need for cash deposits paid ahead in anticipation of annual reviews, and continued legal fees.

The analyst Jerry Epperson told a *Furniture/Today* reporter that both sides were exaggerating the threat and overstating their arguments in an effort to raise more money for lobbying and legal fees.

When Keith Koenig, the CEO of Fort Lauderdale–based City Furniture, told the group that John Bassett's coalition was by and large "not the cutting edge, best and brightest in the industry," the crowd roared with cheers and applause. Koenig had been an old friend, golf companion, and longtime customer of John Bassett's. But he too canceled many of his Vaughan-Bassett orders.

Koenig described the worst possible result of the forthcoming investigation: If some of the seven Chinese companies being investigated by the Commerce Department were assigned high duties during the annual review process, it would significantly raise the cost of the imports for every furniture store in America. It could lead to an average duty of more than 20 or 30 percent, which would ultimately prohibit most of the Chinese bedroom-furniture factories from exporting to the United States.

"That imbalance would throw the furniture industry's supply chain on its ears, would not bring back any jobs to the United States, and would serve to provide [the few factories in China that had preliminarily been assigned low duties] with a near monopoly on bedroom furniture from China," he said.

"There's a neutron bomb in the parking lot."

From his Richmond office, Epperson meticulously tracked the shift to imports for his investment firm's database, and he attended all the meetings, pro and con. He wrote careful, evenhanded columns for *Furniture/Today* in which he predicted that duties would be "modestly inflationary for consumers."

The trade publication eventually hired him to write for its monthly Mandarin edition too. "I don't badmouth the Chinese," he told me, adding that he often included humorous tidbits about his early Asian forays — such as the speech he gave to Taiwanese businessmen in 1982. His translator had instructed the audience to laugh politely instead of actually translating Epperson's jokes, which the man didn't think the audience would understand.

Epperson conceded that John Bassett and his sons had every right to press their case: "A lot of these factories were getting rewards from the Chinese government," he said, including Dalian Huafeng. "Back then, they could sell with no profit at all and get a check back from their government as a thank-you for exporting."

That stopped with the start of the housing recession in 2008 and annual double-digit wage hikes in China. "Now they've shifted those rewards to high tech to raise the standard of living for their citizens," Epperson said.

That shift continues to prompt a small but growing reshoring movement as companies come back to the United States. New American GE and Caterpillar factories have gone up and there's even a new giant Ashley Furniture upholstery plant and distribution facility south of Winston-Salem, but there have been no major wood furniture-making endeavors in the mix. "Remember," Epperson said, "furniture has always been used as a way to educate agricultural workers on how to work indoors in a factory with heavy equipment."

Which is what Mr. J.D. did when he swiped the industry from Michigan and New York furniture makers. Who had swiped it from Boston's. Who had swiped it from England's. All of them in search of the cheapest labor and wood.

The free traders loved to remind the protectionists of this sweeping pattern. Globalization was imminent, and standing in its way was simply another futile gesture, a finger in a leaking dike.

In another rented room during the spring 2004 High Point Market, John Bassett gathered his bread-and-butter retailers, the mom-and-pop store owners with whom he had cast his lot; the same people who'd provided the seven hundred letters Joe Dorn had presented to the ITC with a dramatic thud.

John reminded them of his speedy VBX delivery program, then described his new ideas. One involved helping the retailers with advertising, and another was a new cooperative consumer-credit program he'd personally negotiated with a bank. "We call this the Triple Crown of retail," he said. "I'm going to birth you, feed you, and burp you!"

That sounded good to George Cartledge Jr., a second-generation retailer based in Roanoke whose eighteen-store Grand Furniture chain had been selling Vaughan-Bassett Furniture since John Bassett's father-in-law was in charge of sales, some fifty years before. Grand was big enough to import containers, and it managed its own store-credit program too. But the advertising assistance would now come directly out of the Vaughan-Bassett sales rep's commission, which resulted in a discount for the store.

More important, Cartledge admired how tirelessly JBIII worked — "At his age, he doesn't have to" — and the way saving the business was an all-hands-on-deck enterprise. Factory wages were frozen, including managers', and sales rep commissions slashed.

When Ashley Furniture asked Grand to join the FRA in opposition to John's coalition, Cartledge immediately refused. "We're not that concerned about whether the Chinese have to add another six or eight percent onto the cost," he said, even though Grand imports about 70 percent of its bedroom and dining-room inventory. Cartledge tries to sell as much made-in-America furniture as he can but worries the American consumer is already hooked on imports and what he calls "disposable furniture."

That trend has been buoyed by the surge in do-it-yourself decorating shows; catalogs like Restoration Hardware's and Pottery Barn's; and Super Bowl deals on Ashley recliners for $249 — for sale in your local grocery store, not to mention Walmart and Big Lots. ("If there's something wrong with that recliner, do you think Kroger knows how to fix it?" John Bassett snaps.)

No one buys a sofa with the idea of passing it down to kids and grandkids anymore, lamented Cartledge's son and the company president, George Cartledge III. Grand's number one upholstered-sofa color? Beige. "Because beige is a blank canvas. Consumers can take beige and put anything they want with it." Four to six years later, the younger Cartledge said, eight if they're lucky, the stained beige couch gets hauled to the curb — and the typical customer returns to do it all over again. As a *New York Times* writer recently observed, "You never hear children fighting over who gets the sectional."

Grand picked up most of the slack when the fifty-one-store chain Schewels Furniture cut nearly all its Vaughan-Bassett orders, according to Vaughan-Bassett sales rep Mike Micklem. In a last-ditch effort to maintain Schewels' business, John personally went to meet with Marc Schewel, the fourth-generation CEO, to hear him out.

"John was great," Micklem recalled. JBIII "let [Schewel] talk for longer than he normally listens to anyone," and he took copious notes in a rare (for him) show of tongue-holding. Though he often has a tin ear when it comes to workaday diplomacy, his hearing tends to sharpen when there's money at stake.

Schewel advised JBIII to read Milton Friedman's *Free to Choose* in a speech that would have made the *other* Friedman proud (Thomas L. Friedman, author of *The World Is Flat;* no relation). When the low-paying furniture jobs were among the last to go overseas, Schewel explained, Americans everywhere paid less for imported furniture, just as they had for shoes and clothes, creating a rise in living standards across the board.

In the case of his stores, imported bedroom suites were typically 20 to 25 percent cheaper than domestically made ones. Because of cheaper hand labor overseas, a decorative suite that would have cost twenty-five hundred dollars years ago now costs fifteen hundred dollars, a benefit Schewel likes to refer to as "a higher perceived value."

When Schewel was finished talking, John gave his perspective, and he focused on the part the Friedmans typically overlooked in their zeal to promote offshoring: the thousands of displaced workers who were too broke to benefit from globalization's consumer deals. "Look, the people who shop in your stores are the people we're trying to protect: the factory people," he said.

By the end, Marc Schewel and John Bassett were laughing and shaking hands—and agreeing to disagree. Schewel told me later it was the better value of the imports, not the antidumping fracas, that kept him from buying more Vaughan-Bassett furniture. (He still carries one Vaughan-Bassett group.)

"It was nasty, and to be honest, from a rep's standpoint, we just wanted it to be over," Micklem said. "You got so tired of going into stores and, whether they were for you or against you, that's all they were talking about."

What John Bassett never said publicly was that he believed the retailers were pocketing much of the profits rather than passing them along to their customers—a claim every retailer I interviewed vehemently denied. "John is full of BS," as Schewel put it. "I would say you could get a little higher markup initially, but pretty soon competition took care of that."

Schewel did weaken his argument when he added, "What difference does it make? Consumers were getting a much better deal even if dealers got a little higher markup."

Jake Jabs, who had once ordered two to three million dollars of furniture a year from Vaughan-Bassett, had a similar response, though he dropped his entire Vaughan-Bassett order. Probably some of those "smaller hillbilly North Carolina and Virginia retailers" did pocket more profits by selling imported furniture, he said. "But here in Colorado, we have a seventy percent market share, and we didn't get to have that by not giving people a value. We mark up goods thirty-five percent with everybody, whether they're domestic or import, whatever."

The political drama came to a crescendo that fall shortly after the preliminary duties began to arrive. Newspapers and *Furniture/Today* played the story down the middle, but many economists and politicos were as riled as the retailers. The Cato Institute called the case "the poster child for antidumping reform." Politicians were too easily cowed by the phrase *level the playing field* to wade through the complexities of the law, the libertarian think tank argued.

"The filing of this case was a tactical maneuver by one group of domestic producers that seeks to exploit the gaping loopholes of the antidumping law to get a leg up on its domestic competition," trade analyst Daniel J. Ikenson wrote. "This case is a perfect example of how porous antidumping rules are abused for commercial gain."

For John Bassett, the most surprising moment of all had nothing to do with duties or retailers and everything to do with another cheap Louis Philippe. This time, the knockoff was his own creation, and a Chinese manufacturer who felt he had dibs on the design didn't like it one bit.

The manufacturer and his lawyer visited John in the Vaughan-Bassett showroom at High Point and threatened to sue him for copying their suites.

"He said, 'Our Louis Philippe is very similar to your design,' and I said, 'No, it's not. It's *exactly* like your design, and I have every right to continue making it,'" John recalled.

Imagine the publicity: in the midst of sixty-plus American furniture factories shutting down because of Asian imports, a Chinese manufacturer was going to sue Vaughan-Bassett, one of the last domestic factories standing, because the company's executives had used their knowledge of trade-dress laws to knock off the guys whose knockoffs had been hammering them.

"What else you got?" John snapped, according to several Vaughan-Bassett managers who'd watched the exchange. "Because I'm not gonna waste my time talking about something this uninteresting.

"Go ahead, sue me!"

There was no denying it: He was already the bogeyman. Why not revel in it?

But his interactions with the Chinese weren't all heated. In the lobby outside a competitor's showroom, John noticed a scrum of Asian businessmen whispering and pointing at him. He imagined they were saying, *There he is, the man giving us all this trouble!*

He walked over, smiled, and introduced himself, extending his hand. They giggled and asked if they could have their photo taken with him—to show their friends and colleagues back home. Otherwise, who would believe it?

Flash went the cameras, and smiles all around. China's public enemy number one had become a tourist attraction.

* * *

Remember the five-point list? Number three was the call to constantly change and compete. John wasn't going to stop with the antidumping duties. Back in Galax, he gathered his designer, his sons, and their chain-smoking engineer, and together they took aim at their import-heavy competitors: Pottery Barn, Broyhill, Stanley, and the like. Before long, the sawdust was flying from a new Vaughan-Bassett suite called Cottage Collection. It had casual, modern lines and more finishes than the company had ever offered. It wasn't complicated, requiring little hand labor and minimal machine downtime. A store like Grand could offer it at two-thirds the price of a suite from the more upmarket Pottery Barn, with its stylized, higher-rent showrooms.

It looked at home in everything from a beach house to a country cottage. Colors ranged from creamy white to robin's-egg blue to dark cherry—the last one suggested by a finishing-room employee.

"You think it would look good in cherry, hell, make me a sample up!" JBIII boomed. While you're at it, he added, make one in oak, because the Asians have to import most oak from the United States, turn it into furniture, then ship it back, whereas we can get it right here. "Oak is one of the woods that's very hard to duplicate in the Far East," he said. "There's such a thing as Chinese oak, but it's got a face only a mother could love."

Then came a second new line of furniture. He called this one the Appalachian Hardwood Collection and premiered it with the ad-campaign slogan "We're not afraid to show our backsides." The ad featured him standing behind a turned-around dresser, so customers could see the authentic, solid-oak underpinnings in the back.

When a Philadelphia sales rep suggested a youth line for the Cottage Collection, the company introduced twin beds, bringing the offerings to six finishes and four bed sizes. A sales rep could now go anywhere in the country and sell the hell out of the Cottage Collection. Rustic oak appealed to the Midwesterners, pine was popular in Texas, and folks along the Outer Banks ate up the robin's-egg blue. The simple design made it a natural competitor against the imports because it required less labor, and the routers didn't require constant resetting.

"What you do is, you put on your business brain and you say, How can I compete in America?" JBIII repeatedly told me. "That's what this country needs to do more of, to get off its ass! Look, we do things football coaches do. We don't do things MBAs do. Don't make it complicated."

A smart factory re-creating its product line as a direct response to a competitor is no different from a team shifting its defense in the face of an opposing quarterback who can both throw and run. The Cottage Collection looked like the casual stuff the yuppies were ordering from Pottery Barn and Restoration Hardware, but with minimal labor and VBX delivery, it could be made faster and more efficiently. Which helped it become the company's bestselling suite for six years in a row.

In May 2013, JBIII spotted another hole in the defense when he learned of the bankruptcy and impending closure of a Kentucky-based importer of entertainment consoles. The company had been the only one of its kind east of the Rockies, and even though Vaughan-Bassett hadn't made those products in years, JBIII considered the closure and the booming flat-screen TV market and saw an opportunity.

A dealer had mentioned that he didn't like having to assemble the stuff coming in from Asia, and he didn't like that the imported consoles were available in only three finishes.

Never mind that JBIII would be having back surgery that summer, and never mind that he'd have to buy all new machinery if the company suddenly shifted to offering consoles and tables. (Wyatt was also working on their new line of occasional tables, which had been among the first products to be offshored. "The smaller guys we cater to, they can't bring in containers of these," he said.)

By the time the Kentucky factory closed, Vaughan-Bassett's salesmen were pitching stores with the new products, which were pre-assembled and available in six colors. And they could ship them out within forty-eight hours. "Nobody's turned me down yet," Micklem said in August 2013. "Our dealers saw that it was an easy thing to add to their orders, and it's going gangbusters."

John Bassett might have been flipping China the bird, but he knew enough not to blast the American retailers. Not for the record, anyway. In an article that appeared in the *Wall Street Journal* in the summer of 2004, Jake Jabs skewered John, but John said nothing personal about Jabs in response; he merely described what his factory was doing.

"We took the high road and never criticized anybody for their choices," he and Doug and Wyatt all told me repeatedly, as if reading from a family-authored playbook. All the change that roiled the industry—the laid-off workers, the lost customers, the severed friendships—was painful for everybody involved, they said.

The high road looked lofty in print. But anyone who'd heard JBIII's desert-island speech—about the lone girl on an island with twelve restless men—had to know there were a few other motives at work. If the dust settled and he managed to be among the very last furniture-factory men left standing in America, there was a chance he might win back the angry retailers who had dropped him.

23

Copper Wires and Pink Slips

*Some bones broken will forever be weak. They will
ache and cause pain. The best we can hope for is
acknowledgment. What drives me crazy is when
people don't want to acknowledge!*

—U.S. POET LAUREATE NATASHA TRETHEWEY ON THE
IMPORTANCE OF DOCUMENTING PAINFUL HISTORIES

Between 2001 and 2012, 63,300 American factories closed their
doors and five million American factory jobs went away. During
that same time, China's manufacturing base ballooned to the tune of
14.1 million new jobs.

That "giant sucking sound" predicted by Ross Perot ended up being
less like a freeway sinkhole and more like a slow-motion collapse. And
the media grew bored with the long-drawn-out story, as it often does.
The U6 unemployment rate, which includes both the unemployed
and the underemployed, continued to hover in the 14 to 15 percent
range, but the political will to fix it seemed to fade along with the
media's interest.

"The Byrd Amendment is so complicated that most reporters don't
really understand it, but it's hugely important," said Richard McCormack, the coauthor and editor of *ReMaking America* and the editor of

Manufacturing and Technology News, a trade publication. "Or they write about outsourcing one time and think they've covered it."

National news outlets, many of them funded by Wall Street and retail advertisers, allowed the narrative of globalization to be hijacked by multinational corporations and mainstream economists, McCormack believes. "It's very, very sad that these people have just stayed on their theoretical high horse while the country's gone completely bankrupt because we make so little here of what we actually purchase," he said.

Or as Harvard labor economist Richard Freeman told me, after a long rant about how the wealthy have gotten almost all the benefits of free trade, "Most economists don't know any real people. And, please, you can quote me on that!"

Yet in the small towns of Martinsville and Bassett, where the Families had actively fought off the development of a diversified economy—to keep the wages depressed—unemployment *was* the prevailing story, with the highest rates in the state. And people were wondering: What good did it do to have access to cheap consumer goods if you had no money to buy them?

Even globalization guru Tom Friedman, writing in *The World Is Flat,* briefly acknowledged the agony caused by offshoring: "When you lose your job, the unemployment rate is not 5.2 percent; it's 100 percent."

Friedman's 5.2 percent is much closer to the unemployment rate in Bethesda, Maryland, where he lives in an 11,400-square-foot mansion with his heiress wife. But it comes nowhere close to capturing the truth of Martinsville and Henry County's double-digit unemployment and the problems that result, from the increasing need for food stamps and free school lunches and Medicaid to the rising rates of teen pregnancy and domestic violence.

The Washington insiders may live in cushy suburbs like Bethesda, but five hours away a person driving into Bassett today will pass by trailer parks and a plethora of the small, old-fashioned nursing facilities called rest homes. Going south from Roanoke to Bassett, those in the know will drive very slowly on the curvy four-lane highway as they navigate the speed trap at Boones Mill. They'll wind their way through Clearbrook, where in 2008 a twenty-four-year-old Iraq veteran suffering from PTSD and depressed about his lack of viable job prospects opened fire on county police after a low-speed chase—forcing officers to shoot him dead. There's a makeshift memorial by the side of the road: a gravel-filled cinder block adorned with an American flag and a cross on which his father has written *USAF* and his son's name, Micah Sword, in Sharpie marker.

These small-town stories rarely made their way into the *New York Times* or the *Washington Post*. Small media outlets and regional papers like the one I write for still cover every factory closure and every new release of unemployment figures, but our resources have dwindled drastically with the Internet explosion. Besides, smaller media have never had the authority or the scope, to say nothing of the resources, to follow what happens at the WTO.

Driving through Henry County now, you wouldn't guess that it had once been the state's industrial powerhouse, a place that launched governors, Fortune 500 CEOs, and Speakers of the House. In 1963, a *Roanoke Times* reporter swooped into Martinsville to write a three-part series about the industrial boomtown, which was then boasting an unemployment rate of less than 1 percent. Bassett Furniture was sinking two million dollars into its new Taj Mahal offices at the time. Stanley Furniture and American of Martinsville were expanding to the tune of a million dollars each, and DuPont was adding a twenty-eight-million-dollar addition onto its nylon yarn plant, already a behemoth tucked into a five-hundred-acre horseshoe bend of the Smith River.

"This is the town where you can joke about unemployment," the series began. "A restaurant man needs some counter help. 'What we need around here,' he says, 'is some unemployment.'"

By the time I arrived in 2012, almost half a century later, the region that had once boasted 42,560 jobs now had just 24,733. Nearly half the workforce had been axed by globalization. While most of the vanished jobs had been related to furniture or textiles, gone with those factories were dozens of diners, industry suppliers, and mom-and-pop shops. Replacements tended to come in the form of Dollar Trees, Family Dollars, and check-cashing stores. Worse, sometimes there were no replacements at all, just empty storefronts. The unemployment rate was by far the state's highest, hovering between 15 and 20 percent. One in three families in Martinsville received food stamps, and three of every . four public-school students qualified to receive free or reduced-rate lunches. No one was joking about unemployment now.

But the reality of displacement cannot be conveyed with simple numbers. There are some life-affirming success stories among the rolls of the laid-off, to be sure. Few are more inspiring than the eighth-grade dropout who spent twenty-three years doing piecework in a textile mill and then went to college after she was laid off. And she kept on going to college—until she had settled herself and her family firmly in the middle class. In a decade, Kay Pagans went from not knowing how to turn a computer on to teaching technology classes.

Buoyed by TAA retraining funds, waitressing work, and a husband with a steady paycheck, she went to Patrick Henry Community College when Bassett-Walker Knitting (then called VF Knitwear) closed in 1999. By the time she was fifty-five, she was a professor there whose job was to mentor displaced workers, teaching them to use computers, helping with remedial math, and generally holding their hands. "I tell my story because I think it's important for them to see that there is life after death," she told me. "But they're scared. They're absolutely petrified.

"There are some people who are not capable of doing what I did, whether it's a mental block or maybe the math. What do you do with those people beyond saying, 'Everybody's gonna go to college and get a better job,' especially when there aren't many jobs to retrain for?"

Pagans is an outlier, having made her higher-education strides at a time when college access for poor people was diminishing at record rates—and that was *before* the start of the worst recession since the Depression. "I was going to college at age forty, and I was petrified," she said. "But I knew it was now or never, my one chance to do something different."

The large majority of dislocated workers don't take advantage of the federally funded programs Pagans used to educate herself. When I asked several why, most of them cited the TAA clause requiring them to attend school full-time—a foreign concept to people who joined assembly lines the moment they turned eighteen, have mortgages to pay, and have neither the confidence nor the math skills that remaking oneself requires.

Whither those long-term unemployed? That was the question that had first sent me and my photographer friend Jared Soares to Martinsville, and trying to answer it felt a lot like trying to bottle smoke. You can interview people at one of the state's workforce development centers, but that's only a snapshot of who's applying for unemployment or TAA benefits on a particular day, and it doesn't take into account the growing ranks of people on disability. The people who've stopped looking for work aren't at the workforce centers either, nor are the people whose benefits expired long ago. Also missing are the legions who have ephemeral jobs they drive to outside the area, which now account for nearly half the region's 25,414-person workforce.

The ones who had money to relocate have mostly already gone— the DuPont chemists and accountants, the midlevel factory supervisors. The remaining population is smaller, poorer, grayer, and more diverse. For the first time in Martinsville's history, the 2010 census recorded more blacks and Hispanics than whites.

There's no one place to see the satellite view of displacement because, as Columbia University psychiatrist Mindy Fullilove explained, laid-off workers are, by definition, displaced. "When a factory closes, networks become fractured, and people can't find each other," Fullilove said. "Their old methods of communicating have disappeared."

People seem to disappear, like scrap lumber tossed into a factory hog.

Remember the moment in *The Wizard of Oz* when the film turns from black-and-white to Technicolor? There were days when it felt like I was watching that process—in reverse. During my nearly two years of reporting this story, first for my newspaper series and then for this book, I tried to capture a sense of what used to be and what remains by walking around—sometimes without seeing another soul—and by driving.

I rode with a variety of people, from politicians to ministers to activists; from teenagers to retirees. I took notes while Henry County assistant prosecutor Wayne Withers drove my car, pointing out churches where copper pipes had been ripped out and homes where burglars were caught stealing opiates and antianxiety drugs.

We drove past sad old strip malls and parking lots riddled with weeds, vacant except for a guy hawking sports jerseys from the trunk of his car. We drove by the abandoned call center that was supposed to reemploy hundreds of the displaced workers and did so, beginning in 2004—before it shut down, eight years later, and moved offshore to the Philippines.

"I see a lot of people in court now for fighting with their wives," Withers said. "People who were middle class before they lost their jobs. I didn't used to see that."

In the warm months, I saw yard sales, one after another, some tucked into snaky corners of rural back roads. "People's taking their furniture and just putting it on their front lawns, deciding between eating, paying their light bill, or getting their medicine," a retiree, Mary Thomas, told me.

Then there were the feel-good tours, the admonishments for me to be positive, to keep my journalism light. "Don't make it sound like we have tumbleweeds rolling through downtown," Martinsville mayor Kim Adkins pleaded. And yet when I asked her to estimate what she believed to be the actual unemployment rate—counting both official unemployment enrollees and those whose benefits had long since expired— without hesitating, she said one-third.

Allyson Rothrock purposely avoided the depressing parts as she drove me around the region in her Volvo station wagon. The director of a community foundation called Harvest, created in 2002 with the $152 million sale of Martinsville's public hospital, she insisted the area had to move beyond its past in order to flourish again. But few people were immune to the effects of the current economy, she conceded, her eyes welling with tears as she recalled her husband's layoff from his job as a factory middle manager—and their subsequent divorce. People were so stressed that the owner of a small business approached her in the office parking lot in tears one night, begging for a loan so he could make payroll.

Harvest had pumped millions into raising high-school-graduation rates, boosting college attendance, and bumping up tourism—all designed to buttress the most important goal of all, luring in new business, preferably high-tech or high-skilled manufacturing. Rob Spilman was personally organizing funding for community college interns to learn to operate Bassett's computerized machinery. "We don't need guys to run Google around here, but we need capable, competent people," he said.

Rothrock drove me to several Harvest-sponsored projects, including a nine-million-dollar state-of-the-art soccer complex; the region's first baccalaureate-offering college, the New College Institute; and a gleaming greenway along the Smith River with bike-borrowing stations and kayak put-ins.

"You can't move the river to China!" she exclaimed.

There was a palpable, almost raging disconnect between the happy and employed tour guides and the unemployed people I found on my own, many of whom saw Harvest as an instrument of the well-to-do, an extension of the same executives who had shut the factories down.

Many of the laid-off people were reluctant to talk to me. Some canceled appointments for interviews, nervous that being quoted in the newspaper might keep them from being called in for an interview or would endanger the part-time jobs they were lucky to have.

One whispered that she supplemented her unemployment checks by taking in a boarder and baking cakes—her sister took the cakes to work to sell by the slice—but she worried her benefits would be reduced if I used her name. A credit union manager who was replaced by an ATM when her branch closed in 2011 was now running a consignment store downtown. After the layoff, she grieved harder than she did when her forty-seven-year-old husband died of a heart attack, six years before. "Because I knew that an organization was in control of my layoff. Whereas with my husband, that was at least God's doing," she said.

The first couple of times I asked John Bassett to meet me in his namesake town, he refused, saying he feared I'd make it appear that he was gloating about his hometown's demise. Was I the snake he needed to kill and stretch out to see how long and dangerous I was?

We sparred nearly every time we spoke. One observer, listening to the verbal ping-pong, nervously asked us if we'd still be speaking by the time the book was published. It was a fair question.

"Don't worry, we do this all the time," he said.

I'd wanted a tour of John Bassett's Bassett—the barbershop where he'd gotten his first haircut, the storefront cubicle where his brother-in-law had demoted him, the plethora of smokestacks (a few still there, others only a memory) that bore his family's name. I'd seen it myself many times, but now I hoped to see the outcome of globalization through his eyes, to understand what he felt as he remembered Bassett's more prosperous days.

In June 2012, he finally agreed (as long as I agreed not to take pictures). We met in the parking lot that was once part of his grandfather's legacy, the First National Bank of Bassett. Now a Wells Fargo branch, the square brick building sits in the shadow of the Bassett Furniture headquarters, home to the only parking lot in town that's still full of cars.

At the time, Bassett CEO Rob Spilman wasn't talking to me. (This was months before he'd consented to two long interviews and several phone and e-mail fact-checking sessions.) My March 2012 Harvest story had explored how the foundation had become a flashpoint for long-simmering racial tensions; how it had built a soccer complex in a white community and then, after the recession hit, reneged on its promise to build a basketball arena in the historically black district. "The Harvest Foundation is entwined with the good old boys like roots around a pipe," local NAACP president Naomi Hodge-Muse had said.

Critics argued that Harvest ignored the plight of those hit hardest by the shuttered factories. They also believed it was infected with old-money cronyism — as evidenced by the fact that Rob Spilman was now chairman of the Harvest-funded New College Institute board. (Spilman has since directed Bassett Furniture's foundation to donate $200,000 toward a new NCI building that will house programs in advanced manufacturing, health care, and entrepreneurship.)

"We are never going to be exactly like we once were, but we're rebuilding now with Harvest and NCI," Rob had said at the time. "And it doesn't do us any good to cry in our beer."

I'm certain he didn't intend to sound cruel. But he seemed to have no idea how that statement might come across to people who were still suffering, still looking for work. It was not unlike being deaf to the demands of students at a college for the hearing-impaired.

"Cry in our beer?" shouted Lisa Setliff, a laid-off Stanley Furniture worker turned community college student. "I want to tell him, you're lucky you've got beer to cry in!"

It was a muggy June morning in the Appalachian foothills. JBIII and I began our tour by leaving the Smith River and driving into the kudzu-covered hills. The meandering country route eventually landed us atop a hill at the Bassett family cemetery.

If the living Bassetts wouldn't talk to me, we would start with the dead.

JBIII parked his Lexus at the bottom of the cemetery drive. We stepped around the barricade that blocked the road, walked past the No Trespassing sign, and made our way up the steep private road. Under a canopy of lichen-covered oaks and Virginia hardwoods, we first paid our respects at the cemetery centerpiece: J.D. Bassett's marble mausoleum, adorned with a simple stained-glass cross.

When we reached the top of the mausoleum steps, the doors swung open easily.

It was time, finally, to meet the misters—J.D. and his brother C.C.; their respective sons, W.M. and Ed. Their coffins had been stacked, along with their wives', in separate burial vaults. Descendants and distant relatives encircled them, some housed in a second mausoleum that was built after the first one had filled. In the grass along the periphery stood the markers of long-ago line workers whose families had lacked burial plots as well as the money to buy them, whereupon Mr. J.D. had kindly said, Sure, put them here.

Birds chirped and trilled. JBIII was limping a bit, having had foot surgery a few months before at New York's Hospital for Special Surgery, the country's number one orthopedics hospital and the place where people like A-Rod go when they need better bones.

"You see?" he says, stretching his arms out with a half smile. "You came up here and you were still under the smokestacks of Bassett."

Until, one by one, those smokestacks fell.

"You wanna see what happens to industrial America when you don't do what you're supposed to do?" John Bassett asked, then told me to turn my recorder off.

It's a sentiment he repeated throughout the tour as he alternated between anger, sadness, and an uneasy understanding of the choices his relatives made; between holding his tongue and saying what he really thought.

"It was gut-wrenching for everyone," he told me for maybe the thirty-fourth time, and finally I got what he was saying: He might have won the battle to keep his Galax factory chugging along, but this hometown tour was painful. "You have to remember, I haven't driven through these streets in fifteen years," he said.

Mr. J.D.'s Victorian home had been razed long ago; C.C.'s home (occupied later by his son, Mr. Ed) was still standing, but it was in such disrepair that the man who lives there now called it a money pit and said his family could barely afford to heat it. (We met a year later when he and his sons were fixing the brick wall at the end of the driveway, not far from the cement stairs that had carried the cofounder from his hilltop mansion to work. The wall had been smashed by a drunk driver who'd slammed into it — in a stolen car.)

On the outskirts of Bassett, John and I stopped at the home he and Pat lived in when their kids were small, checked out the gardens (now overgrown) and the barns where he kept Cindy and Jill, the grouse-hunting dogs. "This house used to be so beautiful," he said of the four-bedroom, four-bath white-brick home. They had named it Riverside, set as it was on twenty-four acres that abutted the Smith.

But now rusted gutters hung askew, and a volunteer locust sapling sprouted from a mossy-tiled roof. It was unclear if the house was abandoned or if the people who lived here just couldn't afford to keep it up.

Driving through the center of town, he tried to bring alive the place he once knew — he pointed out where the hotels and boardinghouses had been, the diners and the retail stores, the movie theaters where blacks once had to sit upstairs.

Across from a shuttered Bassett outlet store, we paused to look at a large rectangle of manicured grass with a chain-link fence surrounding its perimeter. It was sterile, newly erected, and downright jarring in its perfection.

Rob Spilman had been tasked with leveling the original Bassett Furniture factory, aka Old Town, years after his father had closed it, in

1989, and it was Rob who ordered the creation of the manicured grass where Old Town once stood.

"It's a community improvement gesture," his cousin Jeb Bassett, a company vice president, told the *Martinsville Bulletin* when the factory was demolished in 2009. "It's not very motivating to come to work every day and look at the remains of a partially demolished factory."

Down the road at J.D. plants Nos. 1 and 2, the first factories John Bassett ran, subcontractors wearing HAZMAT suits were cleaning up arson rubbish with shovels and backhoes—pushing bricks into piles, dumping piles into refuse containers. A few weeks before our tour, Silas Crane, thirty-four, was sentenced to prison for accidentally setting it on fire while stealing copper wires. The fire destroyed not only much of the abandoned factory but also hundreds of thousands of dollars in charity goods that were being housed there by a nonprofit.

A subcontractor hauling away the debris told us we were on private property, and trespassing was not permitted.

"I ran this plant for twenty-five years," John argued.

But the worker shook his head and pointed to the road, and we left as directed without saying another word.

Some companies handled the closings with more sensitivity than others. As we drove past Martinsville's Hooker Furniture, which closed its flagship plant in 2007, I described my interview with fifty-one-year-old Lane Nunley, who was Hooker's sample man for fourteen years, the man responsible for turning the designers' drawings into wood. I told John about the pride Lane took in his work, how he'd recalled former chairman Clyde Hooker Jr. calling every employee by name and the way the old man tearfully looked each worker in the eye the day he closed the Martinsville plant.

"It was devastating. It was almost like going to a funeral for everyone you knew," Lane had said. "But Hooker was fair to us. They always did treat you like you meant something to 'em."

As a tribute to the employees, the high-end furniture maker had even let North Carolina filmmaker Matt Barr document the final shipment of furniture made in the plant for a documentary called *With These Hands*. When it premiered, in 2008, hundreds of former workers turned out to watch it. They even presented Clyde Hooker, by then retired, with a refurbished factory steam whistle.

Hooker had been a seven-year-old boy when his father built the plant in 1927, with Bassett family backing, and the day the factory opened, young Clyde got to blow the steam whistle heralding the very first shift.

"There was a standing ovation, and people were crying," Matt Barr told me. "I don't think they held the closing against him, because he had always treated them so well. They understood he wasn't the bad guy; globalization was the bad guy."

CEO Paul Toms, Clyde Hooker's nephew, acknowledged the workers' pain, telling the filmmakers, "I feel like we've let folks down."

Nunley had made eighteen dollars an hour at Hooker, plus benefits and profit-sharing. His work was so meticulous that a headhunter representing a Chinese factory had offered him a training job overseas. ("Training my friends' replacements? No way," Lane told the man.) By the time I met him, in 2012, he had used TAA funds to earn a certificate in auto-body repair.

Now he worked in Stoneville, North Carolina, where he earned nine dollars an hour and didn't have health insurance. "I haven't been to the doctor in three years," he said. "If I get the flu or something, I ride it out and use home remedies instead."

When Nunley was between jobs, he'd worked briefly for American of Martinsville, a hotel-and-motel-furniture maker that closed without warning in 2010, eventually filing for bankruptcy. Most employees didn't know about the closing until they arrived at work on Monday morning to find the doors locked and only a security guard to deliver the news. Many of the 228 laid-off workers also lost weeks of vacation pay they were owed.

John pulled into the American of Martinsville parking lot, where we were greeted by an ironic antique: a crooked sign telling long-gone job seekers where to drop off their applications. John Bassett sighed.

"It's depressing when you think about what was and what is," he said. "We had to close a lot of factories. I've closed some factories myself." The moment felt rare—uncurated and unguarded. And it brought forth the primary focus of JBIII:

"But we didn't have to close 'em all."

On our way back to my car, we passed through Fieldale, once home to the sprawling Chicago-based Fieldcrest Cannon (later Pillowtex Corporation), which operated twenty-one fabric mills across the Southeast and Mid-Atlantic. Fieldcrest towels were such a symbol of Henry County prosperity that Virginia House Speaker A.L. Philpott used to pass them out to every member of the Virginia General Assembly, adding a special light blue set for the lieutenant governor—to match his wife's eyes.

Closed in 2003, the plant that once employed a thousand rug and towel makers was now the site of a church-based food bank, Victory International Ministries. That seemed a fitting end to our tour.

Only it wasn't quite.

A few days later, JBIII called. He'd just talked to his relatives in Bassett, and it seemed there was a reason Mr. J.D.'s mausoleum doors were so easy to open during our tour. Neither of us had noticed anything missing, but thieves had removed every bit of brass and bronze from the factory founder's tomb—doorknobs, vases, ornamental grillwork, window covers. Apparently, they'd tried to steal the doors too, but they were too heavy to lift.

At Stoneleigh, the mansion that former governor Bonce Stanley had built as his faux-English trophy castle, the copper downspouts had also been stolen. "So they've raided a cemetery, they've set a closed factory on fire, and they're taking this stuff to dealers because commodities are now very high," John told me on the phone.

"Are people bitter?" he had asked me, weeks before.

Lots of people I met were bitter, including Samuel Watkins, a sixty-year-old who'd worked at Stanley Furniture in Stanleytown as a molder operator for thirty-four years. His next job, at a Martinsville semi-custom cabinet plant called MasterBrand Cabinets, lasted ten months before the factory closed in September 2012, putting 335 out of work. I happened to run into Samuel one sultry day in August 2013, the same week the Associated Press announced new data showing that four in five American adults will face poverty during their lifetimes. It was one of the first national news articles I'd read that directly connected growing poverty to the increasingly globalized economy and the destruction of factory jobs. A month earlier, MIT professor David Autor coauthored a study pointing out more concerning statistics: that for each year low-wage American factory workers were exposed to competition from Chinese goods, their wages fell 2.6 percent more than higher-wage factory workers', and disability rates in hard-hit towns like Martinsville were up by as much as 30 percent. "The people who argue that trade is just great for everyone, that argument is inaccurate," Autor told me.

The brunt of globalization's blow had clearly been borne by low-income American workers, and finally even the scholars and Washington journalists were catching on to that fact, something Samuel Watkins could have told them four years ago. He had no idea I was a journalist writing a book about the effects of globalization, but he nonetheless pulled me aside during a chance encounter and positively spilled the hurt, bitterness, and shame he'd experienced in the ranks of the unemployed. When Watkins told his caseworker at the Virginia Employment Commission he was struggling to find full-time work, "She told me to get a grip. She said I wasn't gonna make thirteen ninety an hour no more," he said.

"As a society, we goin' back," he added. His wife, a sixty-one-year-old former furniture worker, was in the process of applying for federal disability benefits. They'd already gone through their retirement nest egg, and Samuel was now mowing lawns and working as a gardener for $8.50 an hour six days a week. He had no health coverage and had recently maxed out his credit card to have an infected tooth pulled. He hauled his tools and gas around in the back of a dented 1999 Ford Explorer.

Without question, people were still bitter. And some had progressed to a stage beyond bitterness.

Some were desperate—enough to commit arson, enough to steal from the dead.

24

Shakedown Street

*Just as a good airplane pilot should always be
looking for places to land, so should a lawyer
be looking for situations where large amounts
of money were about to change hands.*

—Kurt Vonnegut, *God Bless You, Mr. Rosewater*

In 2007, Rob Spilman took another bottle of scotch to the home of Joe Philpott, the longtime Superior boss.

"Joe, I got some bad news," he said, and Philpott knew what was coming: They were about to hold another factory wake. The last furniture factory in Bassett, the storied Bassett Superior Lines was about to close.

"I cried like a baby," Philpott told me. "I loved those people. Look, if I go to Food Lion now, I see four and five people I know, and we'll hug and kiss. Black and white. Tears will still roll up in my eyes."

Four years earlier, back when the Dublin plant fell, Philpott's cousin had bet him a hundred dollars that every one of the Bassett factories would be closed within five years. Philpott hadn't taken the bet. It had sounded preposterous: A town named Bassett with no Bassett factories?

But even though Bassett Furniture had received $1.54 million in antidumping duties in 2006—designed to buoy its domestic production and protect jobs—the company was now being driven by imports, stores, and custom-assembled domestic products. With a 10 percent increase in imports from 2006 to 2007 and more increases to come, the giant, aging bedroom-furniture plants were being rendered obsolete.

It was official. Bassett was still a company town, to be sure, as Rob Spilman proved to his shareholders and the directors of his board. But it was no longer a factory town.

There were still men and women—designers, marketing people, executives—going to work in the Taj Mahal, though twenty-five of the one hundred and thirty office employees, recent hires mostly, now commuted from Greensboro and other less depressing locales. But no more low-end furniture barreled down the Superior Lines conveyor belt. No more sawdust flew. No more chuckalug, as workers called the zooming conveyor belt that had been the cash cow, able to push through two hundred nightstands in a single hour.

Today, the only Bassett-area factory making anything has a random-sounding holdover name—Plant No. 11, a nine-million-dollar structure in the Patriot Centre, a Martinsville industrial park. John Bassett calls it an assembly plant, not a real factory, a claim his nephew vehemently disputes. The two are friendly, though Rob doesn't relish it when old ladies approach him at family weddings and exclaim, "John Bassett, you have not changed a bit!"

Sawdust may not exactly fly in Plant No. 11, but there are 102 employees who do, custom assembling and finishing casual dining furniture made partially from imported components to the specifications of the customers. What used to require the work of sixteen women is now managed by an Italian-made robotic finishing machine operated by two employees. Products that used to take six to eight weeks to produce now leave the plant within ten days.

Together, men and machine apply the company's trademarked Indurance, a heat- and scratch-resistant finish. The mass-production chuckalug perfected at Bassett Superior is long gone; individual pieces of furniture are now quasi-designed inside a Bassett store by the end consumer, who uses a store computer to choose from forty-two colors and a thousand fabrics. "We can make just one single piece if we want, then switch [the machine] out," Rob Spilman said enthusiastically. "And we can have it to her house in thirty days."

Bassett relies on those lean manufacturing principles at its upholstery plant in Newton, North Carolina, where 450 workers clustered in work cells use computer-controlled routers to build upholstered sofas and chairs using pre-cut imported fabric. Between its eighty-nine stores and corporate offices, Bassett employs fifteen hundred people and sold $321 million worth of furniture in 2013 — roughly two-thirds of what it sold at its peak. That decline mirrored the overall industry's as first globalization then the worst housing market correction in sixty years sliced furniture sales roughly in half. When money is tight, a new dresser can wait. "When things changed, you had to get more nimble," Rob said.

The company now partners with HGTV, which airs national commercials touting its HGTV Home Design Studio at Bassett. Its signature service is sending a Bassett store consultant to a customer's home to redesign an entire room. *Makeover* is an HGTV-friendly buzzword, as are the *big reveal* and the *validator*—or the breadwinner, who presumably writes the check. A documentary-style video running on a loop inside the stores spotlights a made-in-America ethos, featuring interviews with furniture workers at the company's two remaining plants and Rob Spilman talking about his family's furniture heritage, including his great-grandfather Mr. J.D.

"We have totally re-architected this thing," Rob said as he walked me through the Martinsville plant in 2013, a few weeks before the company announced a 31 percent increase in quarterly sales. "It was like trying to change a tire while driving down the interstate at seventy miles an hour."

With retail, which now accounts for two-thirds of overall sales, behind the wheel. "Our stores were telling us we needed better finishes, more high-end furniture, and so that's really why we were running out of places to sell promotional furniture that came out of Superior Lines," Rob said. "The old plants were all big, cavernous, and designed to do a lot of volume," predominantly bedroom furniture. But Bassett's bedroom furniture, now all imported, makes up just 16 percent of Bassett sales.

"The endgame was to sell furniture, Bassett Furniture, not Bassett bedroom furniture," he said. And the stores really were helping the bottom line.

. In the unincorporated company town, the company ultimately came first, just as it always had.

What the endgame should have been is a matter of opinion, of course, and the opinions in Bassett, Virginia, play out predictably, with a dual narrative that tracks mostly along labor/management lines. But even retired vice president of marketing Joe Meadors, the ultimate company man, believes Bassett Superior could have continued making bedroom furniture profitably—if the stockholders had been willing to wait out the recession. "They were raising Cain at the meetings," Meadors said. Quarterly dividends, once about twenty cents per share, were cut at the height of the housing recession, in 2009 and 2010, then restored in late 2011.

The company could have been in worse financial straits than it was, with 10 percent annual revenue declines for three of the years between 2003 and 2007. But it had invested $51.7 million in hedge funds, which had produced millions to defray the losses on the company's balance sheet. "If you lose money selling couches and chairs, how can you pay your investors a hefty dividend?" *Fortune* magazine asked. "You play the markets."

Bassett's 46.9 percent share in High Point's International Home Furnishings Center had kicked in another six-million-dollars-plus in earnings. The company's IHFC investment was "the greatest thing Dad ever did for the shareholders," Rob said. It allowed the company to survive its transition from manufacturer to retailer—in the middle of a recession.

In 2011, the company sold most of its interest in IHFC, netting $74 million in the $275 million sale. That allowed Bassett to dole out $21.5 million in dividends and retire $7 million of common stock the following year.

The line workers I talked to seem to have no notion that the decision to switch to retail, pushed by a silver-tongued consultant in 1997, had played any role in the demise of their jobs.

Were they bitter? John Bassett had wanted to know. Yes, but they seemed to heap most of their ire first on the nebulous, distant enemy—*fucking Chi-Comms!*—and next on the federal government for not being more like Japan and Germany, with policies that protect industry and encourage jobs.

Followed by Rob Spilman, who accepted millions of dollars in anti-dumping duties and closed damn near all the factories anyway. It was that or perish, in his view. "I personally think that if we had just stayed in the open market and not done retail, I'm not sure we'd be here today as a company, period. We had to get control of our distribution to survive as a company," he said.

"We had great big factories that were built to furnish the GIs when they came home from World War Two." They'd specialized in fast cuttings of "pretty vanilla stuff the consumer no longer wanted," he added, not hand-carved products from Asia.

In the words of Lee Gale, a former Bassett manager, "Rob struggled to balance the value of those who knew the industry and those who didn't, and he mostly relied on people from the retail side. He didn't understand the passion that the line workers who lived in the community had to keep Bassett Furniture successful."

So the work of people like Minnie Wilson and Maxine Brown was deemed obsolete and old-fashioned, like the smokestacks drawn on the retail consultant's collage. Wilson had bumped from closing to closing, starting out in the finishing room of the W.M. plant in 1990. She was raising her grandchildren by the time W.M. closed, when she was shifted to Superior Lines, as many of the best employees were.

When Superior closed too, she limped along on unemployment benefits, the three weeks' of severance pay that was supposed to reward her seventeen-year tenure, and, finally, Social Security. It took her three years to find a part-time job, but she did: handing out coupons and food samples at Walmart.

Unemployment depressed her, especially coinciding as it did with her grandson's deployment to Iraq. He'd joined the army at eighteen, a month after Superior closed. "There was just no place left for anybody to go for a job," Wilson said.

In March 2012, demolition workers were in the process of razing the factory when a spark ignited the building. The storied Speed Lines — that place where they were once *printin'* money — went up in flames, as the J.D. plant had done a year before, and it took the abandoned table plant next door down with it.

Asthma prevented former Superior worker Maxine Brown from going to watch it burn as so many others in the community did, parking their cars and pickup trucks across the road from the plant and getting as close as they were allowed.

Her husband, Wallace Brown, who'd worked at the table plant for thirty-five years, rushed to witness the conflagration, as if paying his respects. He had moved his family from West Virginia to Bassett in 1967, back when work was so plentiful that if you left your house to apply for a job in the morning, "You might as well take your lunch bag with you 'cause you were gonna get a job," his wife recalled.

False rumors had been circulating that the Superior Lines bricks were being cleaned off and shipped to China, Maxine told me. "China could get our jobs, our timber, our whole nine yards. But when the building caught fire, I thought, *At least that's one brick you won't get!*

"It hurt," she said, "like a friend passed away. You had worked for thirty-some years with your friends in that building and now, poof, it's gone. It was like losing your home."

The Browns were nearing retirement age when the factories closed, able to draw Social Security benefits before their unemployment ran out. Their offspring weren't so lucky. "Every one of our factories now, they're gone, so our children and our grandchildren keep having to leave to find work," she said. Five grandchildren joined the military, four of them deploying (without serious incident) to Afghanistan and Iraq.

One grandson, back from an eighteen-month tour, took out student loans to get a certification in mechanics. But unable to find work in the region after graduating, he moved to Washington, DC—not unlike the way his grandparents had fled their depressed West Virginia mining community to come to Bassett.

About the only thing Maxine and Wallace Brown have left of Bassett is a piece of furniture, the kind of thing the Spilmans and Bassetts would never allow in their homes: a chest of drawers Maxine helped fashion in Superior's rough end. She also has a table from the J.D. plant that had been slightly marred during production, marked as a cull, and discounted. "One of my kids said I should get rid of that table, but I said no, I want it. It's a keepsake to me, and I can look back on that and say, 'I helped 'em make it.'"

Joe Meadors, the retired vice president, returned to the factory, by now a demolition site, in the summer of 2012. He had begun his career selling for the company's table plant, and he wanted a commemorative brick—before the backhoes took them away.

The end of Bassett Superior Lines played right into the hands of the companies that opposed John Bassett's petition. At the five-year sunset review hearing, held in 2010, opposing lawyers stressed that many of the companies employing blended strategies had pocketed millions in Byrd money, only to close their factories anyway.

Hypocrites, the lawyers called them. "Even as the [antidumping] order was entering into effect, Bassett and the La-Z-Boy companies were shutting down U.S. plants and turning to imports for the bulk of their supply," John Greenwald pointed out.

JBIII had even mothballed his Elkin, North Carolina, plant a year earlier, citing the housing recession as the culprit and saying his goal was to reopen when the economy rebounded. Though he kept some Elkin employees on, shifting them to nearby warehouse operations, four hundred Elkin workers lost their jobs.

After the hypocrite card came the Vietnam card, an argument designed to point out the many unintended consequences of the 1930 Tariff Act, the maneuverings that resulted in the biggest winners being alternative foreign exporters. Slap duties on Chinese bedroom imports, critics said, and most bedroom factories will move to Vietnam. During the first ITC hearing, in 2003, the lawyers had predicted it would happen, and it had.

Greenwald and the other opposing attorneys described how dozens of Taiwanese operators had closed down their Chinese factories to avoid the duties—and then moved to Vietnam, where labor was even cheaper (eighty dollars a month per worker, compared to a hundred and seventy dollars in China) and duties didn't apply. A furniture industry that had been booming in Indonesia before China joined the WTO was now roaring back.

But the big headline of the sunset hearing, reported everywhere from *Furniture/Today* to the *Wall Street Journal* to the *Washington Post,* centered on something called settlement payments. This was not originally part of Joe Dorn's plan B, his strategy to make sure the initial low duties assessed by the Department of Commerce—which some in the coalition suspected were politically motivated, as a bow to the bankrolling Chinese—were significantly upped.

Dorn had told JBIII that the annual administrative reviews would help bring the duties in line with what his earlier research had shown: that many Chinese companies were dumping at a rate of 35 to 40 percent.

The process works like this: Every year the coalition (and any other U.S. bedroom manufacturer) can petition the Department of Commerce to investigate Chinese factories they suspect are dumping to assess what a company's individual dumping margin should be. Commerce Department officials fly to China and delve into the records of the two or three companies believed to be the worst offenders.

The remainder of the factories on the list are assigned new duty rates calculated as an average of their dumping margins, based on their self-reported responses to questionnaires. Each company being reviewed supplies reams of data that permits Commerce to determine how much its labor, overhead, and materials actually cost. Since China is a non-market economy, the Commerce Department uses the Philippines as the surrogate country—initially, it used India—to value each item's cost.

The process is complicated and convoluted. The most important thing to understand is this: Very few Chinese factories want to be on that review list, and nobody wants to be at the top of it. Most want to retain the average duty rate, assessed in 2005, of 7.24 percent, viewing it as the cost of doing business with America.

Annual audits are "unbelievably painful, tedious, time-consuming, and [the outcome] could change your rate," one Chinese factory owner told me. "It's your legal costs, your time, the duties you pay, how you structure your business in terms of what you sell in the U.S.... People hate uncertainty the most, and if your rate changes, that affects all of your future business. It definitely makes a huge impact."

The alternative? Write King and Spalding a five- or six- or even seven-figure check and have your name withdrawn from the list of potential reviewees. All of which gives the keepers of the list—Dorn's lawyers, working with Wyatt—an extraordinary amount of power in the deal.

One competing Virginia furniture executive whose company adopted imports early on (and closed all its factories) was angry about the reviews and even angrier about the settlements. "I like Wyatt, but he's employing numbers to target Chinese furniture makers as part of the private settlement racket that the antidumping action has become," he said.

Both the Chinese CEO and the Virginia executive agreed to be quoted only on the condition that I not print their names or the names of their companies. They like Wyatt, sure, but they are wary of the threat of higher duties, which they perceive him as controlling. They're also troubled by the lack of transparency—even though all settlements are reported, confidentially, to the ITC.

"It would not help us going forward, and may subject us to even more work by the petitioners after highlighting this," the Chinese executive explained in a follow-up e-mail.

To JBIII and his fellow coalition members, the settlements remain the best method—given the bureaucratic and imperfect system they're forced to operate in—to ensure the worst dumpers get audited or reviewed. But the people testifying against the coalition at the sunset hearing didn't see it that way.

"Clever shakedowns," a lawyer representing the retailers called the payments.

"An extortion racket," railed one Georgia retailer who'd opened a small hand-carved bedroom-furniture plant near Shanghai but closed it amid uncertainty over the duties. Leslie Thompson told the commission she couldn't afford to hire legal counsel to handle her Department of Commerce review and, at the end of a lengthy process, she ended up being slapped with a 30 percent duty. She might have been exempt from subsequent reviews, as she told the ITC commissioners, but only if she could persuade Dorn's firm to get her company off the administrative review list. She recounted a phone call between her and Dorn:

"What can you do for me?" Dorn had said, according to her testimony. Dorn said he didn't remember the call. "I don't fault her for not understanding the procedure; it's very complicated," he told me later. He also emphasized that the American court system encourages private settlements in commercial litigation.

Lawyer John Greenwald floridly compared the negotiations to the Catholic Church's medieval practice of selling indulgences. He's represented some of the larger Chinese factories, which he said pay as much as $500,000 to get off the list; the bigger a company, the more it pays. "To a Chinese company, it is absolutely worth seven figures, if they're big enough, to settle" and avoid the risk of being slapped with a higher duty. "The Chinese as a whole are much happier with this system than the alternative," Greenwald said.

In a ninety-minute interview at his Pennsylvania Avenue Washington law office, John Greenwald switched between praising John Bassett's genuine concern for American workers and criticizing the unintended consequences his petition had provoked. He was also stymied by the ITC, which, following the sunset review hearing in 2010, voted six to zero—again—in the coalition's favor.

Once more, Joe Dorn had the law solidly on his side, the main questions being: Are the Chinese still dumping? And would the domestic industry be injured if the dumping order went away? In another slam-dunk, Dorn proved the answer to each question was yes.

Greenwald picked up the dog-eared copy of the Uruguay Round Agreements Act sitting on his desk and read from the amended Title VII of the Tariff Act of 1930: *In examining the impact of prices and volume of imports, the commission shall evaluate all relevant economic factors which have a bearing on the state of the industry.*

"What I fault the commission for was not understanding what this case really did," Greenwald told me. "It did two things. It shifted enormous production from China to other places in Asia; that's undeniable fact.

"Second, it turned into a money machine for the law firm King and Spalding."

It also ultimately kept a handful of privately held companies from closing or moving offshore, he conceded, and one of them was John Bassett's, which no longer imports furniture at all. "But I do not believe that anybody from the public companies [within the coalition], from

La-Z-Boy to Stanley to Bassett [Furniture], cared about anything other than their stock price, and they thought this might be a short-term fix."

The country of Vietnam should erect a statue in JBIII's honor, Greenwald said. "I actually like John Bassett. He has a good, courtly Southern charm about him, and if you look at the cast of characters in the domestic industry, he has more integrity than most. He's trying to save jobs, not figure out how to take his own plant to China.

"John became the bogeyman man in the industry, and it wasn't fair. Because he genuinely cared about his workers, and he cared about the communities.

"He was trying to save what was left of American furniture. It just didn't quite work out the way he hoped."

Tell that to the workers in Galax, where John Bassett was on the cusp of turning into a folk hero. People approached him at gas stations and restaurants and thanked him for fighting so hard. One resident, a retired furniture worker, wrote a poem that began:

You have to admire old John Bassett.
For the town of Galax, he's an asset . . .

Recognizing him in a restaurant recently, a retiree who'd once sold lumber to Bassett Furniture interrupted an interview we were having to applaud him for his efforts in Washington. Tourism officials in Galax talked about erecting the world's largest bed. College business classes invited him to be a guest lecturer and deliver his five-point speech.

"I could kiss John Bassett," said Naomi Hodge-Muse, the NAACP leader. "I'm just so proud there's still one Bassett who has that under-standing that you are responsible for your community, and you don't just turn around and walk away!"

But in the furniture industry, especially among certain retailers, the uproar over the duties cemented Bassett's status as an outlier and an outcast. As Jake Jabs put it, the Chinese factories that received the

350 • FACTORY MAN

lowest duties, Lacquer Craft and Markor International, were the ones that had the money to pay the lawyers to do the paperwork for them.

"The smaller, hand-carving factories we were buying from...they got zapped with two hundred percent duties," said Jabs, CEO of American Furniture Warehouse. "They didn't have the attorneys, couldn't speak English, couldn't do the paperwork."

City Furniture CEO Keith Koenig had a similar story about a Dongguan factory he frequented. It was run by hard-charging entrepreneurs—"cowboys," he called them. "Little wild men!" But cowboys make bad accountants, and, when the company muffed its response to the Department of Commerce questionnaire, the factory ended up with a 198 percent duty. "They dropped bedroom furniture entirely, and now they're supplying tons of [other furniture] to Costco," Koenig said. More than fifty companies ended up with similar duties and found themselves scrambling to relocate or reconfigure their offerings sans made-in-China bedroom furniture, he said.

Among those who stopped exporting to the United States was the maker of Casa Mollino, a garish, hand-carved, four-poster-bed bedroom suite that Jabs liked so much he put it in his own home. Many factories started emphasizing dining and living room furniture—since the coalition covered only wooden bedroom furniture—shifting their bedroom exports to Europe and other parts of Asia. Jabs himself ordered more imports from Vietnam.

In the manufacturers' rush to set up quickly in Vietnam, a few efforts flopped—including one Taiwanese company that built a dormitory alongside its factory. The owners hadn't known that most Vietnamese workers weren't migrants, as the Chinese had been, but lived close to the factories in villages with their families—a cultural faux pas that would have been anathema to Larry Moh.

"Because of this petition, you can feel the animosity against Americans in China now," Jabs said. "And what we don't need is the Chinese pissed off at us."

A first-generation American with a Russian-born mother and a

Polish-born dad, Jabs, eighty-three, had traveled to more than fifty countries and bought furniture from thirty of them. His take on globalization was a free-trader's long view: He argued that under the trade-friendly policies birthed by the Marshall Plan and agreements such as GATT, the world experienced an unprecedented rise in the standard of living and an increase in world peace. "It's hard to be an enemy with someone you're doing business with," he said.

While he gave John Bassett credit for reinvesting in his factory, JBIII and "all those North Carolina hillbillies just don't realize that it's a global world, that free trade helps people, and that isolationism hurts both the country and the consumer," Jabs said.

Keith Koenig agreed, though as a longtime friend and golfing companion of John Bassett's — as well as a Southerner — he'd never put it so bluntly. He used John's own language instead: "The antidumping duties just moved the cheese from China to Vietnam, which hasn't put John in a less competitive environment one bit. Everybody just figured out how to get around what they've got to do. The lawyers have benefited the most; they've gotten very rich," Koenig added, referring to settlement payouts and legal fees. "And who paid that premium? Well, the American consumer did."

Most of the economists I interviewed for this book — neoclassicists whose writings dominate the mainstream political discourse on economics today — said the same thing. Harvard's N. Gregory Mankiw has argued that antidumping duties hurt the poor most because price increases on necessities make up a larger percentage of their spending. He cited University of Oregon economist Bruce Blonigen, who bemoaned the unintended consequences of antidumping petitions — the settlements, for instance; and the unnatural incentive a company might have to perform poorly just before joining a petition.

When I spoke to Blonigen, he implied that the benefit to John Bassett's seven hundred workers in Galax in no way made up for the slightly higher prices American consumers now paid for bedroom furniture. Antidumping law is "a poor policy for helping these folks out," he said. "In reality, we shouldn't be making bedroom furniture any-more in the United States. Shouldn't we instead be trying to educate these workers' kids to get them into high-skilled jobs and away from what's basically an archaic industry?"

There was no hint of sympathy for the likes of former Superior workers Minnie and Maxine. To most economists, factory work was a throwback. It was still okay to work in health care, retail, recreation, insurance, hotels, and haircuts. But it wasn't cool anymore to actually make stuff.

Gary Hufbauer of the Peterson Institute for International Econom-ics analyzed the antidumping disputes between the United States and China, and using figures supplied by the Department of Commerce, he calculated that the amount of duty money paid per saved factory job was $800,000.

"What happens is you take the increased dollars American consum-ers have to pay to Sears or Kmart or Walmart for their tires, or what-ever item it is, and divide it by the number of jobs. Where does that money actually go? It typically goes to the company, not the workers."

But the companies who actually use the Byrd money for its intended purpose—to keep their factories going—make sure that, indirectly or not, it *does* go to the workers: it keeps them employed. And the econo-mists who dismiss manufacturing as too low-tech to merit a spot in the United States' advanced economy forget that American companies have also lost much of their capability to make high-tech products. As journalist Richard McCormack pointed out in *ReMaking America,* in 2012, there were 1.75 billion cell phones made in the world—and not one was manufactured in the United States.

"The United States became a superpower because of its embrace of all manufacturing," he wrote. "China has become a world power by following a similar path."

Few economists have bothered measuring the drag on local econo-mies brought on by Chinese imports or the cost borne by taxpayers in terms of unemployment benefits, food stamps, and disability, but MIT professor David H. Autor is one of those few. We all get slightly cheaper goods as a result of imports, to the tune of between thirty-two and sixty-one dollars per capita, he noted in a groundbreaking 2011 paper. But the benefits of trade are shallow and widespread, while the disadvantages are concentrated and long term for those displaced.

He argued for better-designed job-training programs that would help people rejoin the labor market and acquire skills and prevent them from exiting the workforce, as so many people do in import-slammed areas. According to his calculus, in places like Martinsville, the increase in disability payments alone is a whopping thirty times greater than the increase in TAA participation.

"People get desperate. They can't get work, but they need some source of income," Autor told me, explaining how Social Security disability now functions as the de facto insurance program for many of the long-term jobless who suffer from hard-to-verify ailments such as back pain and mental-health disorders. "I'm in favor of assisting people to adjust. Unfortunately and unintentionally, though, our biggest program now [for helping them] is our disability program, and it's the worst—a permanent exit from the labor force."

As late as the beginning of 2012, there were still millions in Byrd monies that had been collected but not yet dispensed, much of it tied up in appeals. Assessed duties are appealed with such fervor that funds can sit in reserve as long as seven years before the money is paid out.

But the Byrd money collection pipeline was nearing its end. In 2006, back when few economists were calculating the costs of trade in human terms, Congress killed the Byrd Amendment due to mounting political pressure from several U.S. industries, the GAO, and the WTO, which found that the Byrd Amendment violated its rules. The Byrd Amendment was "WTO-incompatible" and "therefore must go," said Pascal Lamy, the European Union trade commissioner, who argued that importers were being punished twice by handing over the duties to American firms making the competing products.

With the repeal of the amendment, Chinese factories found to be dumping would still have to pay duties, but eventually those duties would stop going to the injured domestic producers and would be funneled directly into the U.S. Treasury instead. ·

How soon the repeal would actually take effect was still a matter of intense negotiation, and, as usual, JBIII wanted a say in the matter. He met with top aides to Speaker of the House Dennis Hastert and Senate majority leader Bill Frist.

In the spring of 2007, John Bassett was tasked with speaking on behalf of the industries that had filed successful antidumping petitions. Of all the CEOs representing industries from shrimp to ball bearings to magnesium and cement, the group members had chosen the persistent, slow-drawling furniture maker from Galax to plead their case.

U.S. trade representative Rob Portman was in Geneva at the time, so his assistant led the meeting, detailing—for a solid forty minutes— the concerns of each country that had opposed the Byrd Amendment and how most wanted it repealed, pronto. Especially China. (During Portman's thirteen-month tenure as trade rep, America's trade deficit to China rose by almost $228 billion.)

JBIII had a page full of notes on his legal pad, and he had been practicing his remarks in the shower for days. But by the time he was given the floor, there was just ten minutes left.

An astute observer looking down on the scene would have noticed the red creeping into John Bassett's face. That person would have noted the eye rolls, the nervous up-and-down bouncing of the heel and the knee, the pocket change clinking against the silver money clip, the frequent checks of the pocket watch—a gift from his wife, engraved with a favorite line from his favorite movie, *Casablanca: The fundamental things apply.*

John Bassett had some fundamental things he wanted to say now, and he was furious that his time was nearly up.

He picked up his legal pad, turned it over, and slammed it on the table. Then he asked the audience members to turn around and look behind them—to the American seal displayed on the door. Joe Dorn looked as if he might faint.

"What country do you represent?" JBIII asked the lawyer from the trade representative's office.

Um, the United States, he said.

The ass-chewing commenced: "We've been here forty-five minutes, and you haven't mentioned our country once. Listen, you are not paid to look after these other countries; you're paid to look after us."

When the staffer objected, saying, "No one's ever talked to me like this before," JBIII cut him off.

"Well, *somebody* should have, sir. China has its own trade rep, and I'm quite sure that person is capable of looking after China. *Yo'* job is to look after us."

The two of them disappeared into a back office, and a compromise was shortly announced. The Byrd Amendment monies would be extended an additional nine months.

"It was a bunch of money, by the way," JBIII said later of the Byrd money extension checks. "But we had to get smack in their face."

Like so many Washington deals involving trade, the closed-door exchange was not reported in the media. Although manufacturing had taken the biggest hit in the history of the country, with five million jobs eliminated in a single decade, very few articles connected offshoring to the decline of the working class. Or to the number of people receiving food stamps—which had tripled between 2000 and 2012, easily topping the number of newly created jobs.

The principles espoused by Friedman and the free-trade cheerleaders always got top billing. None of which was news to Wyatt Bassett. After the 2012 company Christmas potluck, I asked him about the economists' criticism of his family's decade-long battle to keep its flagship factory going. Sitting at his spreadsheet-papered desk, Wyatt shrugged his shoulders and half smiled. "Everybody should just be an economist, I guess?" he said.

"If somebody wants to predatorily kill your industry and take market share, that's fine as long as the consumer can get it a little cheaper? But what happens when they destroy your industry and then raise prices thirty percent once all your factories are gone?

"Our issue is, let's separate the fair and legal competition from the cheaters; to us there's a difference. Should the Chinese be allowed to devalue their currency? . . . And where does all this money come from to educate everyone?"

He threw his questions out rapid-fire, his mouth struggling to keep pace with his brain, which had clearly mulled over the academic arguments many times before, always defaulting to the same images: his crotchety dad striding through the factory in his New Balance tennis shoes (made in Massachusetts; he'd checked), complaining about too much machinery downtime, and asking Shirley Johnson (the hot-glue lady, they called her) about her grandkids. Real people, in other words.

Wyatt was cordial, though not exactly relaxed during our interviews— except when his wife called to tell him to pick up burgers on his way home, or when Sheila interrupted to ask which *Nutcracker* performance he wanted to attend. (Doug's daughter was playing a mouse in the Winston-Salem holiday production.) His khakis were worn, with strings hanging from the hems, and cinched by a preppy, embroidered belt (pink, with blue whales).

When I asked the line workers about him, one woman told me he used to come across to the factory workers as being "stuck up." She was near retirement and therefore had nothing to lose when she confronted him one day and said, "You act like you're better than we are."

Wyatt started laughing and told her he'd try harder to talk to people, which he did — though frankly, he seemed more at ease among the spreadsheets. ("Wyatt's actually a hoot, if you can get him to relax," his mother told me.) I watched him lead one management meeting in the fall of 2012 while his dad sat along the periphery, straining not to speak except when his opinion was sought. Wyatt was confident and firm, interrupting managers who didn't have their facts lined up, at one point barking, "What *else* haven't we done?"

He was more open than I thought he'd be about navigating the settlements, something neither John nor Dorn had divulged to media, both of them offering the standard "no comment" to trade publications and national business reporters. When I ventured that the process sounded almost like *Moneyball* with furniture, Wyatt brightened, as if I were finally, after all these months of interviews, speaking his language.

"I *love Moneyball*," he said. "The book and the movie."

Maybe Wyatt was Paul DePodesta, the money-crunching assistant GM and the man upon whom Jonah Hill's character in the movie was based. In Michael Lewis's bestselling book, Oakland Athletics' general manager Billy Beane accomplishes a rare thing in Major League Baseball: He creates a killer team on a bargain budget. In the movie, computer spreadsheets designed by Hill's character, a Yale economics graduate, become scouting tools, a statistical means of ferreting out the best players nobody's ever heard of, on the cheap. On his way to a near miraculous winning season, Beane does things nobody else in the business would do, like moving a catcher to first base and ignoring his seasoned scouts in favor of advice from the upstart Yalie.

If furniture is the baseball in this story, Wyatt is the brains behind the dugout, spreadsheeting and conferring with his dad, or in the movie's case, Billy Beane (played by Brad Pitt). JBIII is the general manager, the guy who would actually move a lumbering catcher to shortstop — or spend millions taking on China — if he thought it would keep his organization intact.

What father and son pull off isn't a game changer in the annals of global business, but to the home team back in Galax, it's a grand slam.

The annual furniture playoffs known as the settlement payments begin in February, just as the Chinese factories turn their cost data into the Commerce Department. Dorn's trade lawyers sift through the information, trying to figure out if the Chinese have accurately filled out the questionnaires or if they're trying to game the system—choosing the cheapest plywood or mirror glass, for instance. (They're less likely to appear as dumpers if they use, or claim to use, the lowest-priced raw materials.)

New information comes in throughout the months-long process, including the quantities of furniture shipped by Chinese factories, measured both in container loads and in dollars, the prior year. The King and Spalding lawyers calculate dollars per container load, then rank the companies on a list. Typically, the company with the least amount of dollars per container is dumping the worst.

But higher-end furniture must be adjusted for, as must the amount of furniture sold by the company the preceding year so the lawyers can scope out irregular pricing trends. Throughout the year, if a coalition member spots a piece of furniture in a store that seems uncommonly cheap—another Dalian dresser, say—the coalition lawyers make a note to look at that company's figures when the next customs report comes out. "You have to keep your ear constantly to the ground," Wyatt said.

Around the first of February, the phones at King and Spalding start ringing. This is the time when lawyers representing dozens of Chinese companies begin their settlement negotiations with the firm. According to Wyatt, if a company's settlement offer is too high, it can backfire. "If a guy calls in and says, 'I'm gonna pay you a half million to get off this thing,' he obviously has something to hide," and Wyatt and the lawyers confer again about whether that company should be on the administrative review list. Maybe that company gets moved to the top of the list—especially if its figures are markedly lower than the previous year's. Maybe, as new offers trickle in, more evidence of large-scale dumping appears, and the list reshuffles again.

Some Chinese factories have been found to be funneling, or illegally shipping their furniture under the name of another, lower-duty factory or importer. "Say it's a guy who's shipped twenty million dollars the year before, then he shows up with one million, and you're pretty confident he's funneling," Wyatt explained. "But you know he's not going to end up as one of the two or three mandatory respondents" chosen for the Commerce Department audit, because there's already strong evidence that at least that many companies are dumping worse. (Mandatory respondents are the two or three factories suspected of most egregiously dumping furniture into the American market.)

As Wyatt put it: If that guy offers him a settlement that would pay for, say, two months of legal fees—and Wyatt and Dorn already know his factory isn't at the top of their list—why not accept his settlement offer, knowing that they'll take a hard look at his numbers again next year? By which he means: Don't let the perfect stand in the way of the good.

For four months, Dorn and the other attorneys reshuffle the spreadsheet as new offers and information stream into the firm. "You've got a half dozen lawyers representing sixty-some Chinese companies," Wyatt said. "In addition to our list, other U.S. companies submit their own lists, and some Chinese companies have asked to be reviewed," hoping to have their previous duties lowered.

"It's like playing a board game," Wyatt said, "and you're moving the tiles. You're trying to get this tile over here, and yet there are all these tiles in the middle" that need adjusting before you can make the desired move.

By the end of May, the firm of King and Spalding submits the winnowed-down list to the Commerce Department, which then sets out to review the mandatory respondents.

It's *Moneyball* meets Connect 4 meets card-counting at the blackjack table, all of it played with millions of non-Monopoly dollars. And it's perfectly legal. Dorn had checked first, of course, noting that out-of-court settlements had been common in prior cases involving the shrimp and cement industries, not to mention in 90 percent of American commercial litigation. "I think trade lawyers in general tend to be unimaginative and uncreative by not doing more settlements," said Dorn.

* * *

While some Chinese furniture makers claimed the payments became a replacement income stream for coalition members after the Byrd money petered out, Wyatt insisted that "substantially all" the settlement money has gone to fund the coalition's legal expenses. "I can absolutely understand why the other side is upset," Wyatt said. "One of the ways they could've killed us was financially, if we couldn't have continued to collect money to fight" for the annual reviews.

"Now, not only do we have a way to fuel it, hell, it's coming from them! And they are the ones who came to us offering it! I'm sure it grates like hell on 'em, that they're essentially funding our side."

The settlements have become the de facto method for making sure the ITC order gets enforced—a convoluted, indirect way to ensure that at least *somebody*, even if he is billing by the hour, is minding the back room of the global store. The settlements pay for the King and Spalding lawyers to sort through the surrogate-country figures, raise questions with the Commerce Department about suspected funnelers, and sift through every document filing and every appeal.

They pay for them to file Freedom of Information Act requests and hire private investigators to walk the docks and ferret out funnelers who are cheating at the ports. With Doug Bassett's help, the lawyers lobby public officials to force compliance among factories and importers that still haven't paid their duties. According to Dorn, the uncollected duties amount to $369 million, much of which is still owed to the petitioner companies.

"The amount of uncollected duties is astronomical," said Bonnie Byers, an economist at King and Spalding who's worked on the bedroom-furniture case for years. Some companies with outstanding duty bills disappear, only to reemerge in another location with a different name. "Then what you want to find out is whether they have assets in the U.S. that we can go after," she said.

All in all, the firm employs five people who work the case year-round, which is why the bills are so large.

"If we are taking money to support and enforce the ITC order, our intentions are clear: We want it to be enforced so we don't have dumping from China," Wyatt insisted. "Would [critics] prefer we go on a vacation [with the money] instead? To enforce the order, we have to stay in the game."

Greenwald estimated the case has so far generated fifty to sixty million dollars in legal fees for lawyers on both sides of the battle. JBIII bristled when I mentioned those figures, then dismissed Greenwald's claim and demanded that I not put Greenwald's numbers in the book. Months earlier, though, he had described a dinner party he'd been to, during which a "lady lawyer" guessed that the coalition paid out some fifty thousand dollars a year in legal fees. "She was off by at least fifty to a hundred to one!" he exclaimed. "People have no idea how slow the wheels of justice are, and the millions upon millions we've spent in legal fees every year."

All in all, using the liberal end of JBIII's estimate (five million dollars a year), Dorn's fees were not a bad investment, considering the coalition companies walked away with $292 million in antidumping duties. Now channeled to the U.S. Treasury instead of the petitioners, the duties continue to cut into Chinese wooden bedroom-furniture imports, which have declined more than 70 percent, from $1.85 billion in July 2006, when the ITC order was first initialized, to $538 million as of June 2013. Three-quarters of the almost two hundred Chinese companies submitted for administrative review have been assessed duties higher than the initial 7.24 percent, Wyatt Bassett pointed out, underscoring both the effectiveness of the order and the hunch that sent JBIII to Dalian in the first place: Many Chinese factories were cheating.

"I feel good about our work," said the former ITC commissioner Charlotte Lane. "At the sunset reviews, we can tell if the orders are working or not, and we found generally that most of them were."

When I asked why so many furniture makers closed their factories anyway, she wasn't sure. The petition was filed late in the game, she offered, the housing recession added more stress to an already struggling industry, and it's hard for Americans to compete with countries where companies don't have stringent environmental regulations or health-care costs to maintain—to say nothing of the labor-cost differential or claims of currency manipulation.

"One of the things I heard over and over from all the domestic industries—and I was there eight years—was that American companies can compete against anybody as long as the playing field is level," Lane said.

Among the most egregious dumpers put forth for review was Dalian Huafeng, which received a whopping 41.75 percent duty, applied retroactively to its 2009 shipments, Greenwald said. That helps explain why its owner, He YunFeng—who's on the Chinese equivalent of *Forbes'* four-hundred-richest-people list—cut back his American exports and closed his American warehouses.

He YunFeng now manufactures mainly for China's emerging middle class, he told a *Furniture/Today* reporter, citing as his reasons the antidumping duties and the elimination of Chinese government incentives to export. Multiple requests to interview Dalian Huafeng managers for this book, submitted to the company's Washington attorney, were ignored.

Asked how he felt when Dalian Huafeng was zapped with such a large duty, John Bassett called it "totally anticlimactic," coming as it did after scores of hearings, meetings, and testimonies. It was now some eleven years after he'd first gone eyeball-to-eyeball with He Yun-Feng and his hundred-dollar dresser.

Making furniture in America now relies as much on lawyers and settlements and private eyes manning the docks as it does on sawdust. "It should not be this laborious," he said, sighing. "But it is."

The Byrd checks arrived in stacks, due to some arcane rule prohibiting the federal government from writing million-dollar checks.

"You'll get [something like] twelve checks for $999,999.99, and then one check for $2.13," John Bassett told me one afternoon at his Roaring Gap home.

"You couldn't make it up," his wife, Pat, said, shaking her head.

"Well, you know what, they haven't bounced," he deadpanned.

Vaughan-Bassett invested $23 million of the money in new plant equipment, contributed 10 percent of it to its employee profit-sharing plan, and used some of it to start a companywide free health clinic for families. The money saved upwards of seven hundred jobs in Galax, which, in turn, as some have argued, have saved the town. It allowed Vaughan-Bassett to go from not being in the top five wooden bedroom-furniture producers in the country a decade ago to being number one now.

The economists may cry foul, and the Chinese may protest.

But as John Bassett put it, his voice rising: "Our critics have never had to stand in front of five hundred people, like I have, and tell 'em they're not gonna have a job. And watch women cry because they don't know what's gonna happen to their families or how they're gonna feed their children. This is *not* like picking up a telephone from your office on Wall Street and saying, 'Close factory number thirty-six down in Alabama.' These are people we look in the eye every day!"

PART VIII

25

Mud Turtle

*I guess we traded our jobs for somebody somewhere else in
the world to have a better life, I don't know.*
—SAWMILLER TIM LUPER

In 2006, John Bassett tasked controller Doug Brannock with putting a lid on the factory's rising health-care costs. Even with the company paying 75 percent of each of the workers' premiums, half the workforce couldn't afford to join the plan and went without insurance entirely. The ones who did have it didn't go to the doctor unless they were very sick, trying to avoid the twenty-five-dollar co-pay. Some employees with high blood pressure went without their medication because they didn't think they could afford the pills.

JBIII worried about that. He gave Brannock three months to negotiate something with the company's insurer and a local internal medicine practice, and what Brannock came up with was an entirely new concept: At a cost to the company of $350,000 a year, the Vaughan-Bassett Free Clinic would offer weekday afternoon and Saturday hours to accommodate both the first and second factory shifts (so workers who weren't too sick could still nab their attendance bonuses). It was located off-site, several blocks from the factory, part of an already existing clinic with a nurse-practitioner on staff and a doctor on call.

From preventive checkups to sick visits, anything that didn't require the expertise of a specialist was covered at no charge to the employee, without any deductibles or co-pays. Workers' family members also had access at no charge— "Even my mother if she wants to go can go, as long as there's an opening for her," Brannock said—because the company has already paid a captive rate for the slots. A list of three-dollar generic drugs available at Walmart made its way into every employee's hands.

Shirley Johnson, aka the hot-glue lady, started taking her blood pressure medicine for the first time in years. And health-care costs associated with the regular medical plan plummeted, as most workers opted to use the free clinic regularly, which decreased the need for expensive acute-care visits and more than made up for the $350,000 clinic cost. In the spring of 2013, the company's manufacturing technology director Jim Stout found out he'd had an undetected heart attack through a routine screening at the factory offered to all employees. Several tests later, he learned he'd been walking around with an 80 percent blockage in two of his coronary arteries. He was in surgery within the week to prevent another, more serious attack.

"It would not have been caught without the screenings. I had just been chopping wood and felt a little tired. But I'd thought it was just age," he said. "I could have died."

Health-care costs don't go down immediately under the new plan, Stout pointed out, which is why so few employers think to try it. "It takes a year to eighteen months to see the effects [on the insurance claims] of preventive care. But John doesn't get nervous about things like that.

"He has a belief, and he follows through."

Before the clinic opened, some of the young factory workers had never been to a doctor in their adult lives, and Stout wasn't the only one saved by a clinic test. Costs to the company, which spent $1.45 million annually on health care, remained flat even though insurance rates grew 12 percent to 20 percent annually over the same period nationwide.

But that wasn't what drove the decision to start the clinic, John Bassett and his sons insist. They were worried about their workers and their workers' families not going to the doctor, and *someone* needed to act.

JBIII had already tangoed with the CEOs of Winston-Salem's Baptist Hospital and Blue Cross and Blue Shield of North Carolina a year earlier, after a newspaper reported that the two entities were locked in a reimbursement dispute that had the potential to prevent twenty-five thousand patients—including his workers—from using the region's number one hospital. "Sheila, get them on the phone!" he'd barked over the partition from his conference-room table turned desk.

As Doug Bassett tells it, his father gave both executives an old-fashioned, Bassett-style ass-chewing. "I don't care what the details are, but the two of you are acting like children. I have seven hundred employees, and what you're doing now could affect three thousand lives. You two settle it by the end of the day, or I'll settle it."

By the end of the day, a press release was drafted: the companies were still at an impasse, but Vaughan-Bassett employees would not be affected by the dispute.

"He called 'em up and talked to them like they were the naughtiest fourth-graders he'd ever seen," Doug recalled. "It was a classic John-Bassett-solved-in-a-day."

When I asked JBIII about the dustup, he quoted Shakespeare's Brutus, who said he loved Caesar but killed him anyway because he loved Rome more. His point being: America didn't have enough leaders who loved the country more than their individual interests. "Who's gonna speak up for these people if we don't?" he said. "You think somebody down there running a ripsaw is gonna call the chairman of Blue Cross? Oh *hell* no!"

It was paternalism at its finest, not unlike Mr. J.D. telling the racist doctor to pack his bags. Someone had to tell those boys what their job was.

* * *

There was just one problem with the Vaughan-Bassett Free Clinic. Though every employee was strongly encouraged to get a free preventive physical, several dozen refused to go, nearly all of them men. Many were smokers who didn't want to be lectured. Some feared they had diabetes—or worse—and didn't care to know.

A few clung to stubborn libertarian beliefs, like the chain-smoking sample engineer Linda McMillian who thought the company was playing Big Brother and resented the intrusion into her private life. "People are too obsessed with their health," she told me. "I don't go to the doctor unless I feel bad."

Doug and Wyatt were baffled. They asked personnel managers to assure those who were refusing the annual physicals that federal privacy laws prevented their bosses from seeing the results. "They thought, *The company wants to know what I'm doing on the weekends,*" Brannock said of the sixty who flat-out refused.

So JBIII grabbed the list of noncompliant employees and said, "Why don't you let me handle this?"

He picked up his legal pad and composed a letter to the offending employees. If thirty days passed and the workers still hadn't submitted to the physical, he threatened to rescind *their families'* use of the free clinic.

He instructed Sheila to mail the letters that Friday afternoon, strategically timed for Saturday receipt—and told her to address the letters to the men's wives. "I let Mama take care of it!" he boasted. "I let Mama put a finger in their face!"

By Monday afternoon, fifty-three men had signed up for physicals. They reminded John of toy soldiers, standing in a line that stretched out the clinic doors. Two of the men learned they had diabetes and thanked him, eventually, for making them go.

There are many sayings among the country people who live in and around Galax, among the families who've been sawmilling and fiddling and wood culling for generations. Several of the sayings have to do with furniture and factories, a holdover from when furniture was by far the region's main enterprise, before five of the six Galax plants fell. "We had a good Market" meant the orders poured in after the semi-annual High Point show. Chances were, workers would therefore not be on "short time" and might even get to work "five and a half days" with time-and-a-half pay for Saturday morning.

There was another saying you heard a lot back in 2008, when Vaughan Furniture Company—which had once employed 2,200 people—closed its last plant in Galax, even though the factory had just received $3.3 million in antidumping duties. "The plant closing is not the fault of the employees of Vaughan Furniture Company," said CEO Bill Vaughan, who blamed it on the "continued popularity" of imports among his customers.

The company had recently built a new corporate office on the outskirts of town, a three-story brick structure that was now a command center for its importing efforts and its forty employees. (Internet connection? Check. Fax machine and factory turned warehouse? Check. Extra office space that can later be used as rental property? Check.)

"Why'd they build that right before they shut everything down?" town historian John Nunn said, echoing the question on everyone's mind. "I think the Vaughans panicked, and fear makes you think, *If everybody else is doing the same thing, they must be right.*"

The Vaughans were so impressed by the cheap Chinese furniture, especially the ornate high-end stuff, that they didn't anticipate any issues with the retailers, explained retired Vaughan sales executive John McGhee. "The thought at first was, *We'll get an even bigger profit margin if we go high-end,* and we all just went gaga for the prices," he recalled.

But eventually Vaughan's retail customers did the same calculations, and they started flying to China themselves. "The Chinese had sucked us into buying the furniture and teaching 'em how to make it," he added—the one thing the retailers could not have done.

"And who got hurt? We got hurt!" he said. "The Chinese more or less slit our throats."

* * *

Bill Vaughan, now a lawyer in Galax, declined to be interviewed, writing in an e-mail that he didn't "have any wish to rehash old news."

Those still spinning from the closings are rehashing it, though. As sawmiller Tim Luper of nearby Fries put it, "The Vaughans were still making [some profit] at those Galax plants and decided to close them anyway, and people who depended on that work were mad.

"But they've learned that John Bassett will wait till he's down to his last dime [of profit] before he closes Vaughan-Bassett. He's like a mud turtle that lives in a creek. If you get bit by one, it won't let loose till the sun goes down. Mr. Bassett is just like that. He'll hold on to the end."

Luper has become a kind of mud turtle himself, working to keep his business viable in the wake of Galax's furniture-factory closings. He mills lumber for log homes now, mostly vacation getaways for people who don't need to take out mortgages. He had to invest thousands in new equipment so he could produce the wood for tongue-and-groove flooring—at the same time the price of the lumber plummeted because demand was so low.

Among the displaced thirteen hundred furniture workers in Galax, those in their fifties and sixties had the toughest time recovering from the closings. Luper has friends his age who mow grass, clean homes, wash cars, and make crafts and foodstuffs—anything to manage until their Social Security kicks in. A minister and food-bank operator told me she's counseled a handful of folks who are camping out in the woods.

A Facebook yard-sale page created by a twenty-nine-year-old hotel night auditor gets visited by nearly everyone in the town of seven thousand. In January 2013, it had more than eleven thousand members, counting residents of surrounding counties, and featured house-cleaning and clothes-washing services for as little as four dollars an hour. One continuing controversy involves members who try to resell drink mixes, power bars, and canned goods that have been donated to them by a local charity. "Is that right or wrong? It's not for me to say," moderator

Jessy Shrewsbury told me. "Some people are just very desperate for money to pay their bills."

A combined United Way and Goodwill program trains workers over fifty for job placement, and tourism in the quirky mountain town has risen by a third in the past three years, thanks to a strong focus on authentic music and crafts (including furniture woodworking) and nature trails. There's a funky cowboy-boot-shop-and-history-museum combo near the outskirts of town, the main attractions being a stuffed two-headed calf enshrined in a glass case, Carhartt jackets, and Frye boots.

The fiddlers' convention—known by old-time musicians all over the world as simply Galax—now attracts forty thousand visitors each year, and Galax is also home to Virginia's most visited state park as well as the state barbecue competition. Virginia's number one barbecue maker gets a trophy topped with a slot for a real fiddle or banjo—winner's choice—that's crafted by local luthier Tom Barr, who runs a music store downtown in the old barbershop space where the famous Hill-Billies got their start. The region some call "the rooftop of Virginia" counts a half a dozen acclaimed instrument makers, in fact. Guitar god Wayne Henderson of nearby Rugby made Eric Clapton wait ten years for his Henderson, and many of the staff musicians at the Grand Ole Opry play guitars built by Galax luthier Jimmy Edmonds. "You're dealing with a town where a good fourth of the population plays!" exclaimed Joe Wilson, the folklorist.

On Friday nights you can hear that music live on *Blue Ridge Backroads,* a WBRF FM radio program, or see it in person at the restored Rex Theater downtown. There's a throwback diner called simply the Grill where the bill on most meals, no matter what you order, comes to exactly five dollars. An elderly black shoe cobbler named Slim is training Jorge, who runs the Hispanic barbershop next door, to do shoe repair so Jorge can take over Slim's duties when he retires.

Still, 40 percent of Galax residents qualify for food stamps; two-thirds of the town's schoolchildren are on free or reduced-rate lunches; and nearly a quarter of the population lives in poverty. "It's terrible to admit this to a news reporter, but Galax has the fifth-highest crime rate in Virginia," said Galax police chief Rick Clark, noting that Mexican drug cartels have a presence in the area. Galax is "out of sight, out of mind, and they can keep a low profile," he said, and it's also near two interstates, making it a prime staging area for distribution.

"People didn't get rich here, but they were able to make a living, have a garden, and maybe raise their own pork," Clark added. "Now the tragedy is, our best and brightest that used to stay here before don't stay. Now you work for the city, the hospital, or Vaughan-Bassett Furniture, and that's pretty much it."

As Luper, the sawmiller, put it, "I guess we traded our jobs for somebody somewhere else in the world to have a better life, I don't know."

Wilson, the folklorist from the nearby former cotton-mill town of Fries, agrees. Named a Living Legend by the Library of Congress and a National Heritage Fellow by the National Endowment of the Arts, Wilson has never met John Bassett, who doesn't socialize much in Galax beyond daily shop-talk lunches with his sons at the County Line Café, a blue-plate-lunch diner where he likes to think he's paying homage to the many lunches his father and uncles had with Mr. J.D. (sans Miss Pokey's after-lunch "naps").

But as the creative genius behind several recent developments in and around Galax—the Crooked Road musical heritage tour, for instance—Wilson understands Appalachia's place in the world better than most. And he believes John Bassett's boldness will be remembered for generations.

"The people who did these quick moves, they were looking at the bottom line in the next two or three years. But John had faith in the workers here. He had faith in these mountains and the trees that grow on them," Wilson said. "Free trade really meant that no one was looking out for the little people....He was bright enough to know that what was going on with [globalization profits] was just temporary, and our government was going along with it, and he had to nip some of that in the bud."

As the folks in Bassett like to put it: Little John got the last word.

26

The Replacements

*I want you to see what they do in Indonesia and explain
to me why we can't do that here no more.*

— WANDA PERDUE, DISPLACED STANLEY
FURNITURE WORKER

From Bassett to Martinsville to Galax, every Virginia furniture factory founded with the help of Mr. J.D. Bassett near U.S. Route 58 fell victim to the 58 virus except one: Vaughan-Bassett. Even Stanley Furniture, which hauled in the largest portion of antidumping duties by far—$80 million—closed its flagship Stanleytown plant at the end of 2010. Two years later, it moved its corporate office from Stanleytown to High Point, eliminating forty-five more local jobs and consolidating offices with its newly renovated showroom. (It maintains two Henry County warehouses, which together employ about seventy.)

Though it still imports adult furniture from Indonesia and Vietnam, Stanley adopted a new kind of blended strategy in 2011: At the same time it closed the Stanleytown plant, the company pumped $8 million in Byrd money into new equipment for its aging plant in Robbinsville, North Carolina, reshoring—or bringing back to the United States—its Young America children's line. The change was prompted in part by a string of crib recalls that had roiled the industry, most involving Chinese imports (though Stanley's biggest voluntary recall of cribs, involving its 2nd Nature Built to Grow cribs, were made in Slovenia).

Stanley flipped what it made domestically, betting that nervous upper-middle-class parents (and doting grandparents) would be willing to spend more on made-in-America baby cribs—eight hundred dollars versus four hundred dollars for a near identical imported crib. The American-made cribs are Greenguard-certified by an independent public-health nonprofit that monitors air quality and chemical emissions, and they come in more than one hundred finish choices, from surf blue to chili pepper.

Stanley also named Micah Goldstein, a Dartmouth-educated MBA, as its chief operating officer. Goldstein, forty-three, had previously managed the manufacturing of hydraulic-equipment trailers and cardboard boxes. He knew a lot about lean manufacturing but virtually nothing about furniture, and what he did know about the industry didn't impress him. "The world-class companies ask the workers for advice. But in furniture, the families had always dictated how things were done," he said.

The Ivy Leaguer seemed a fish out of water in rural North Carolina. The day I rode from Asheville to Robbinsville with Stanley marketing director Neil MacKenzie, Goldstein had Neil bring him a soy latte from the Asheville Starbucks. It was no longer warm when we arrived two hours later, of course, but a cold Starbucks beat the weak coffee offerings of the Robbinsville McDonald's any day.

Goldstein was energized by the challenge of rebooting the old Robbinsville factory, which had been a Burlington carpet plant before the company bought it in the early 1980s. State-of-the-art equipment allowed him to reduce the number of lumber cutters in the rough end from forty-two to eleven. The efficiencies were part of a downsizing strategy that shrank the workforce from 460 to 340 (due to attrition, Goldstein said, not layoffs, which have not occurred there since 2007).

Flat-screen TV monitors hang from the ceiling, allowing workers to track every piece of wood and maximize lumber yield. Part of a new $3.5 million rough end, the technology is coordinated by a twenty-something high-school grad, Chase Patterson, whom Micah refers to as "mission control."

He plucked Chase out of the packaging department because Chase wasn't afraid of new technology, and had him trained by the Germans who'd made the machinery. In a booth overlooking the factory floor, Chase manages orders and inventory with the help of three computer monitors and a headset. Highly skilled workers here earn $32,000, while the average Stanley production worker makes $26,000, and the best among them are recruited to join Goldstein's Continuous Improvement team.

"People were skeptical at first," said CI team member Al Jones, recalling longtime workers who were upset when their staple guns and screwdrivers were moved. "But now that everybody's in survival mode, they realize there's no other option. There's no plan B left here in Robbinsville," as Stanley Furniture is the largest employer for miles around. People in Graham County, home of North Carolina's highest unemployment rate, now understand: The skinny MBA toting the tepid soy latte may very well be their best hope for making it in America.

I thought of displaced Stanley worker Wanda Perdue, who was still searching for her plan B more than a year after we'd met. Despite the Herculean effort it took for her to get her associate's degree, paid for by TAA funds (she was also helped along by a softhearted math tutor who was once a displaced worker herself), Wanda, fifty-eight, was still looking for full-time work almost three years after her Stanleytown plant closed, cobbling a living together on part-time Walmart work and her husband's disability check. After thirty-seven years with Stanley, she no longer had health insurance and could afford only store-brand foods and cheap cuts of meat. She had to be practically dying before she went to a doctor, as paying a doctor's bill meant her utilities wouldn't get paid on time.

The most scarring event in her unemployed life so far? The day she swallowed her pride and called a Smith Mountain Lake church to ask if she could use its food bank.

"Sorry, you're out of our jurisdiction," the secretary informed her.

"I might be out of your jurisdiction, but I'm not out of the Lord's jurisdiction," she said, then she thanked the woman and hung up.

Wanda had asked me to follow her story all the way to Surabaya, Indonesia, where her replacements now worked, not in a single factory but in ten separate facilities, all Indonesian-owned and subcontracted through Stanley and various competitors, including Pottery Barn, Bassett, and Ethan Allen.

She seemed genuinely curious about the Asians who'd replaced her and her Stanley brethren, part of the three hundred thousand American furniture workers who'd lost their jobs to offshoring—first in China, then in Vietnam, and now, following the cheap-labor waltz, to the world's most populous Muslim country. I was curious too.

Were the Indonesians' lives better than hers? Did they struggle to feed their families, go to the doctor, send their children to school? And what exactly did her old bosses at Stanley do on the other side of the world?

Coaxing Stanley to let me tour the factories where its adult furniture is manufactured took several months. I began asking in the spring of 2012, which was lousy timing—it was soon after the mass suicides to protest working conditions at the Foxconn factory in the Chinese city of Wuhan. Micah Goldstein made it clear: He didn't want a story about working conditions in Indonesia. "We don't own the factories there," he said repeatedly.

When I landed in Surabaya in March 2013, I had already Skyped with Stanley's vice president for Asia operations, a British-born factory man named Richard Ledger whose career perfectly mirrored the arc of globalization in the developing world. He'd met his wife in the Philippines in 1997, back when the furniture workers he supervised there were earning twenty-five dollars a month. In 2005, he ran logistics from white-hot Dongguan, China, where migrant laborers worked seven days a week, lived in dormitories, and earned eighty dollars a month.

In 2008, when rising labor rates in China cut into profits, Stanley sent Ledger to Vietnam. Though the company still contracts with factories in Ho Chi Minh City (from an office staffed by fifteen employees), the bulk of its adult furniture is now made in and around Sidoarjo, outside of booming Surabaya. Indonesia has a centuries-old history of furniture-making, government-managed mahogany forests, and labor rates that are among the lowest in the world.

How does Ledger live in Indonesia? In a golf-course community, with a chauffeur on call and medical needs that are taken care of by a quick flight to Bangkok, where his two youngest children were born. He also has two armed guards outside his home at night, posted there following a frightening late-night break-in. When his chauffeur drove us into the Shangri-La Hotel Surabaya plaza for lunch one day, guards checked the undercarriage of the SUV we were riding in for bombs, as has been standard practice in upscale hotels since the 2002 Bali bombing, which killed 164 international tourists.

I thought of Rob Spilman recalling his first trip to Indonesia several years earlier, before there were any five-star hotels designed to cater to Western businessmen. With the Bali bombings fresh, Rob said he had slept in his clothes and barricaded his hotel-room door at night with a dresser.

The first time I interviewed Ledger, in 2012, an Indonesian furniture worker was earning about a hundred dollars a month. By the time I landed in Surabaya, a year later, the national minimum wage, owing to a cluster of strikes in Jakarta, was neck and neck with Vietnam's. A worker now made around a hundred and eighty dollars a month.

Stanley's importing office is in a booming suburb called Citra Land, which bills itself, aspirationally, as the Singapore of Surabaya. It's staffed by a couple dozen yellow-polo-shirt-wearing engineers and logistics people, including two Filipinos who engineer parts for the furniture designs that are e-mailed to them from the High Point corporate offices. They all work late so they can Skype across the twelve-hour time difference. During the day, they troubleshoot problems in the ten factories where their products are made.

Most sit in a row of computers surrounded by glass vases filled with calla lilies. The place is run by a highly efficient office manager named Dini who reminded me of Sheila (both stylishly approaching middle age and married to their work, although Dini commutes on a motorbike while Sheila drives a much cushier Acura).

I accompanied American-educated Indonesian Jim Febrian, Stanley's thirty-year-old sourcing supervisor, as he hopped from factory to factory, consulting his smartphone constantly and relying on his driver to maneuver through the narrow rural byways and around the occasional rickshaws — not to mention the throngs of motorbikes, some with entire families heaped on top. Every afternoon it poured, giving the steaming countryside, still dotted with rice paddies, the aroma of wood fire and wet dog.

Jim's driver was a cheerful twenty-something named Eko Hadi. The company had hired him away from the Shangri-La Hotel, where he had been a bellman, because, as Jim explained, he was friendly and spoke a little English, sort of. ("Are you taking us to the hotel?" I asked when he met us at the airport. "Yes," he said. "Or should we go to the Stanley office and see Richard first?" "Yes," he replied.)

Motorbikes are the hot economic indicator of Indonesia, which has been growing annually by 6 percent. You can get one for fifty dollars down, and the motorbike is usually a rural Indonesian's first credit purchase. Sometimes workers double up on a single motorbike to commute to work, not unlike the original Bassett workers' building and sharing rowboats to get across the Smith River.

In the office, Dini and Jim were accustomed to Westerners in general and Virginians in particular. But that wasn't the case inside the factories; I was the first white person many of the line workers had ever spoken to at Multi Manao, a sprawling, twenty-five-hundred-worker factory where Stanley furniture is made alongside pieces for Pottery Barn, West Elm, and Pier One. Employees clustered around benches and worked several people to a chair, mostly sans conveyors or machines, which reminded me of photographs the Bassett barber had given me from Stanleytown circa 1925. I spoke to a field hand turned ripsaw operator named Kusnun Aini who had ridden his motorbike to the factory. Aini, forty-three, used to earn forty dollars a month working a farmer's rice fields.

Elok Andrea, twenty-six, had taken a similar path, though this was technically her first paying job. She'd been a subsistence farmer working a tiny family-owned plot of rice and corn but had recently been hired on to feed boards into a rough-end saw. She's now able to send her six-year-old to school; that wasn't possible before, she said, as tuition is thirty dollars a month. "She wants to send her to college one day," the Indonesian translator said, clapping her hands in approval.

Asked why she prefers factory work to farming, Elok said, "Here, we work under a roof." There's a free clinic on-site if she gets sick, as well as a hut for after-lunch prayers.

In a state-of-the-art factory an hour away, Panca Wana was fulfilling an order for Ethan Allen, its largest customer, according to managers there, though it also makes furniture for Lexington, Stanley, Century, and several other American-owned brands. The factory is owned by an Indonesian real estate mogul who thinks nothing of dropping $700,000 on an Italian-made router. Without question, numerous people in the industry said, it's the most modern furniture factory in the world.

"When everyone else here is employing two hundred carvers, he's buying machines," Ledger said. "He loves machinery, and he knows it's not wise just to rely on cheap labor."

The legions of villagers who apply to work at Panca Wana take psychological tests designed to gauge their stability and critical-thinking skills, Panca Wana's quality-control manager Allen Jubin told me. A North Carolina native, he worked stints for Broyhill, Kincaid, and Henredon before moving to Asia, first China and then Vietnam.

He golfs regularly with the growing number of North Carolina and Virginia furniture expats, most of whom inhabit a realm that is not quite American and not quite Indonesian. One of Jubin's golf buddies, for instance, is Jerry Hall, an affable forty-five-year-old who heads quality control for Stanley. During Hall's nine years of Asia-hopping, he's never once driven his own car. He's learned to love spicy food, except at breakfast, and he maintains homes in both Vietnam and Indonesia. Hall likes the golfing better in Indonesia but prefers the food in Vietnam, where it's possible to order his native chicken-fried steak and gravy via his computer and have it delivered to his apartment door in Ho Chi Minh City—in thirty minutes.

After the Bali bombings, Hall swore he'd never go to Indonesia, and that was before he knew about Febrian's family home in a Christian enclave on Sulawesi being burned by Islamist radicals in 1996. But now that Hall lives here part-time, not far from Ledger in Citra Land, he prefers Indonesia.

"I really miss biscuits," he told me. Never married, he worried about his eighty-eight-year-old father, who lives in rural Virginia. He wished his dad would learn to Skype on the iPad he bought him for Christmas. Stanley's Filipino engineers, who see their families a few times a year, shared similar feelings about being so far from home.

Wanda Perdue might still be looking for full-time employment, I thought, but at least she has her family nearby.

Though talk of reshoring manufacturing is heating up—and companies like Ford, Apple, GE, and Caterpillar are bringing some production back to the United States—economists and furniture analysts alike doubt that low-skilled furniture-making will ever be what it once was in America. The exceptions? Niche markets like high-end furniture, hospitality, upholstery, and cabinetmaking, all of which tend to rely on made-to-order specs.

The exceptions also include the few companies that never moved offshore to begin with, such as Vaughan-Bassett, Mississippi's Johnston/

Tombigbee, and a growing number of small, Amish furniture-making enclaves. The last, predominantly in Ohio, Pennsylvania, and Indiana, capitalize on their own version of low-cost labor—their families and children. (My retailer buddy Joel sells several Amish-made lines and says 60 percent of his inventory is now American-made.)

In October 2011, a North Carolina furniture maker named Bruce Cochrane tried to ride the reshoring wave, resurrecting a high-end furniture factory that had been in his family for four generations. He grabbed both headlines and accolades, including an invitation to sit next to Michelle Obama at the president's State of the Union address. Lincolnton Furniture lasted little more than a year before Cochrane closed it, citing the slow economy, price competition with Chinese imports, and unanticipated costs to retrofit the old plant.

I asked Ledger and Hall how they had handled the political hot potato that was the antidumping petition. They supported John Bassett's efforts, they said, but found it expedient not to inquire about the details. "To be honest, I just never asked about it," Hall said. "I wanted to always be in a situation where if a factory owner [in Asia] brought it up to me, I could honestly say, 'I don't know.'"

Ledger predicted during my 2013 trip that Indonesia had a "good ten years" before the cheap-labor dance sends furniture-making on the move again in the developing world. "Indonesia has two hundred and forty million people, and you gotta feed 'em somehow," he added.

Jubin, who was working in China when the petition was filed, called it "a bunch of horse hockey" that did nothing but spur furniture-making in Vietnam, Malaysia, and Indonesia. "A lot of people made a lot of money off it, but nobody got their jobs back as far as I know."

When I ventured that workers at several American plants were able to *keep* their jobs, he dismissed the petition anyway, saying the bulk of furniture-making was still destined to move to countries with cheaper labor.

The mud turtle and his seven hundred workers apparently didn't count, nor did the twenty smaller furniture-making petitioners from Mississippi to Vermont.

"Furniture may come back to the U.S. but it will be much smaller and much leaner, and it may not happen in our lifetime," Jubin insisted.

Furniture-making returning to the United States was not a scenario any of the Indonesian line workers I spoke with wanted to entertain. At a factory called Romi Violeta, barefoot men etched designs onto mirrors for Neiman Marcus, and a few lumber sorters also working shoeless stood amid splintery piles of lumber culls. Workers crouched on the floor to carve and distress pieces for Stanley that combined wood, metal, and leather. It was over a hundred degrees inside the factory, but the only person sweating seemed to be me.

A particular piece they were working on looked similar to a Stanley piece I had admired at the High Point trade show a year earlier. Stanley's Atlanta-based public relations consultant had been guiding me through the company's showroom when she stopped to elaborate on the distressed heirloom-cherry sideboard with leather straps and brass handles that retailed for $2,079. "We want it to look like you found it in an antique market in Paris," she said.

It took flying to Indonesia to figure out exactly how that furniture was antiqued. To artificially age the wood, Romi's marketing manager told me, workers keep it for months at a time in pools of disaster mud, a dark sludge that flows from a nearby mud volcano. The volcano was caused by a natural-gas drilling accident in 2006 that killed fourteen people and displaced thirty thousand. (The well operator claimed, falsely, that the eruption was prompted by an earthquake.)

The process gives the wood a richer hue and pocks it with holes drilled by insects that live in the mud. "It was weird to us at first, messing up good furniture on purpose," a Romi sample engineer who goes by the single name of Fachrudin said, shrugging. "But if that's what the Americans want…"

When I asked Fachrudin if he ever thought about the Appalachian workers he had effectively replaced, he abruptly answered no. Then he giggled nervously, not wanting to appear impudent.

"What I do worry about every year is the future of this factory," he offered. "I worry that someone somewhere else, somewhere cheaper, will start to make furniture, and that will be that for us." In the office the next day, Dini said a very similar thing.

At Panca Wana, managers were already replacing some workers with machines, and the minimum wage was predicted to increase another 20 percent nationwide by the end of the year. Exactly where would the next jobs land?

Where would the globe-trotting Appalachian hardwood go next, and would the drilling-induced mud that it marinated in be far behind? It was a globalized world indeed, down to the Sidoarjo bugs etching those tiny scratches and dings.

Ten months after my trip, in January of 2014, Ledger said Indonesia's minimum wage had risen again, to two hundred dollars a month. With an impending election, he worried about possible political instability. The company was considering beefing up efforts in Vietnam again, but capacity there was finite, he told me, and many Vietnamese factories were now busy supplying China's growing middle class. The Chinese "pay well, are less picky, and the logistics are easier to manage," he said.

Furniture-making would leave Indonesia much sooner than ten years, he now believed, predicting the reshoring of furniture jobs to America, only this time with higher-skilled lean manufacturing and increased technology. "Hopefully the Stanleys and Bassetts of the world have managed to hold onto their factories so they are able to take full advantage," he said.

The two sure bets? First, that the Stanley stamp on the back of that sideboard could not begin to document its provenance. And second, that soon after we returned from Asia, my cell phone would ring.

"How fast were they running?" John Bassett wanted to know.

It was the same question he'd asked after I visited the Robbinsville factory several months before. He and Goldstein are friendly competitors, touring each other's plants and swapping ideas about machinery.

I hadn't clocked the Robbinsville lines with a stopwatch, but they seemed to be running fine, I reported.

"Remember this," he said. "You only make money when the sawdust is flying, not when you're messing around setting up your machines."

When I ventured that the Robbinsville factory looked higher tech than Vaughan-Bassett's, at least to my untrained eye, his hackles went up, and that already booming voice had my cell phone vibrating in my hand. "Listen, we know where every piece of our inventory is at any time. We don't have to look at a damn row of computer monitors to know what we have."

The next time I visited Vaughan-Bassett, the mud turtle was on the move, and he was throwing around his favorite word: *alacrity.* He was positively obsessed with speed and volume, upping productivity in every corner of his plant. "I wanna change people's attitudes about manufacturing in this country," he said, unleashing a breathless torrent of JBIII-isms. "Before I die, I'd like to have made a little bit of an impression."

And: "Everybody thinks all the great ideas come outta MIT, but let me tell you, there's a great deal of innovation that comes off the factory floor."

And: "If we close everything, that innovation's gonna move to wherever the factory is. We gotta invest in America instead of derivatives!"

And: "Sooner or later we've got to turn and face our enemy again. I did it, and you know what I found out? They're not as damn tough as everybody thinks they are."

It was the fall of 2012, and he'd just turned seventy-five.

He said he planned to semi-retire at the end of the year, though he grew antsy any time he left the factory for more than a few days. (The

Vaughan-Bassett middle managers got more phone calls when he was in Florida and not there to witness things firsthand.) Barring some kind of disability, he finally conceded, the only way he'd ever completely retire was "if they take me out behind the lumber stacks and shoot me."

Meanwhile, he intends to drill poster-board point number three into every employee he can reach: *Be willing to change and improve, again and again and again.*

That fall he hung mirrors in his machine room, and not so the ladies could check their lipstick. Workers weren't feeding panels through the gang saw fast enough for him. The housing market wasn't rebounding fast enough either. Orders were down, and, human nature being what it was, employees understood that if they worked too quickly, they might soon be on short time.

JBIII had to do something to speed the panel-cutting along. The machine feeder had long relied on the person tailing the machine to signal with a wave before passing the next panel through. So he hauled in ten-dollar mirrors and had them suspended from water pipes on the ceiling. The mirrors allowed the machine feeder to anticipate the hand-off sooner, speeding up the process some 20 percent.

Next he tackled the three Italian-made five-axis routers, purchased to the tune of $1.2 million. Rather than spend a fortune on computer monitors, as Stanley had done, JBIII had an electrician screw Walmart wall clocks onto the side of each one.

At the start of each shift, the clocks began ticking the seconds off every time the machine was reset or otherwise not spewing sawdust. It was his commonsense (read: "cheap") answer to measuring machinery downtime.

If the clock counter showed one of the three routers drastically behind the other two in production by the end of the day, then the guy operating that machine had to get eyeball-to-eyeball with Wyatt or JBIII. An added incentive to keep the line moving along: every person passing by that machine could look up and see exactly how much progress was or wasn't being made.

The operators rolled their eyes about it, yes, but they were not surprised. "He's very much beloved by the people on the floor," said Jim Stout, the manufacturing technology director. "But they also know that every now and then he's gonna come through and boost things because he's a Bassett, and the Bassetts have always done that kind of thing."

Production levels went up substantially when the three machine operators began competing with one another, as John had known would happen. It was the old grouse hunters come to life again. The method was not unlike the time he'd convinced his wife to give up cigarettes, a case he'd been pleading for several years: He and Pat were attending a middle-aged relative's wedding to a much younger bride. As the trophy bride sauntered down the aisle of the church, lean and tan and wrinkle-free, John leaned over to Pat and whispered, "After you die of lung cancer, I'm gonna get me one of those." Two days later, she put down her cigarettes for good.

He was a pain, yes, and maybe even "an asshole," as his competitors liked to say. But few workers grumbled aloud because they understood: he really was the last factory man standing, and he was doing everything he could think of to save their jobs, from hanging mirrors from the rafters and providing free doctor visits to telling the Chinese just exactly where they could put their hundred-dollar dressers.

"We spend all this time training our guys on computers, but you know what? They can't stop my simple wall clock once it gets hooked up," he said. "I hate to go back to sex again. But some things people have been doing the same way for a long time, and you know what? It's still pretty good!"

27

"Sheila, Get Me
the Governor!"

*When John reinvented his company, it was almost like he
became first-generation again.*

—Doug Bassett Lane, Mr. J.D.'s great-grandson
and former executive of Lane Furniture (now part
of Furniture Brands)

I n his khaki pants and sweater vest, the aging patriarch climbed atop
the creaky conveyor belt. He was beaming with his cat-pouncing
grin, a smile that could only be described—in Galax, anyway—as
tee-totally victorious. He was about to announce the reopening of the
Webb Furniture plant next door, a factory that had closed in 2006,
eliminating three hundred jobs.

Over the next three years, he said, he would invest eight million dollars to upgrade the old plant and would rehire some 115 of the town's
1,300 displaced furniture workers in an enterprise he was calling Vaughan-
Bassett II. Now he was not only the largest employer in Galax but also the
largest manufacturer of wooden bedroom furniture in America.

A podium had been hauled in for the announcement, a microphone
installed, and chairs lined up for the politicians and the press. Boxed
lunches were on hand for the media (Doug's idea) as well as for the

Vaughan-Bassett workers (John's), who got both chicken sandwiches and the gift of not having to clock out for lunch.

The region's movers and shakers sat before John Bassett and his sons in rows of folding chairs arranged like church pews. Beside them stood hundreds of Vaughan-Bassett workers clad in denim and T-shirts and flannel, the whole tableau dwarfed by a giant American flag that had been tacked behind them on the cabinet-room wall. Along the periphery stood millions of dollars' worth of high-tech machinery—much of it Byrd money–funded—and rows upon rows of dressers, nightstands, and beds.

Few people understood how many hurdles John Bassett's team had jumped to bring this announcement to fruition: the last-minute strings pulled to nab state and city economic-development incentives plus the $200,000 in tobacco commission funds (via a program that promotes economic growth in tobacco-dependent communities using proceeds from the national tobacco settlement). He wanted the money not so much because he needed it but because it gave a stamp of legitimacy to what he was trying to do.

Few knew about the phone calls to the governor, who was in South Carolina campaigning for Mitt Romney at the time. The sixty-six text messages Doug Brannock exchanged with state senator Bill Stanley to make it all happen after Brannock very casually mentioned at the end of one manager meeting, "Well, I guess it's too late to get any grants."

"You've got to be fucking kidding me!" John Bassett had snapped.

Brannock had momentarily forgotten poster-board lesson number one: *If you don't think you'll win, you will lose.*

For the next eight days, every official or economic developer with any ties at all to the region received the full-on Bassett, the battle plan being *tenacity* + *speed* = *victory*. "Guys, we've got to move with a-*la-cri-ty!*" he barked.

JBIII hadn't even voted for Senator Stanley, a Republican from Franklin County, having been friends with his opponent, the incumbent, most of his life. But during the fall 2011 campaign, Stanley had stopped by Vaughan-Bassett for the requisite tour and poster-board speech. He promised John Bassett he would help protect his interests if he got elected, even if he didn't get John's vote.

After which JBIII peered over his glasses and agreed to support him if he won — as long as Stanley (no relation to the furniture makers) left him his personal cell phone number, and "not the one with some little ole eighteen-year-old girl answering the phone."

John Bassett doesn't forget promises, and he never loses a phone number (because, well, he gives it to Sheila). When he called in his Bill Stanley chit, he barked at the newly installed senator, "Are y'all gonna sit on your asses in Richmond, or are you gonna get it done?"

And: "Be sure the governor's here so he can take all the credit."

What normally takes the machinations of state government two or three months was nailed in eight glorious, debate-filled days. The senator got to witness what the management team at Vaughan-Bassett had learned years ago from the Taiwanese translator turned spy to the controller who reinvented corporate health care: People like being part of a live-wire organization. Some even like working for someone for whom *cain't* is the only dirty word. As Garet Bosiger put it, "He may be an asshole, but when he's *your* asshole, that's a very good thing."

At the podium, John Bassett III leaned into a microphone that his booming baritone didn't need. It carried across the lumber stacks, past the congressman and the state senator, past the sanding-room employees. It echoed through the high-tech machinery he'd bought with the money he got from standing up to the Chinese, from beating them *fay-ah and squay-ah*.

He'd lowered his prices, reengineered every inch of his manufacturing process, and hadn't hesitated to have a penalty called when he learned what the international trade laws could do for him up in Washington.

And because he'd given the middle finger to China, Vaughan-Bassett was in a position to expand as soon as the economy started growing again.

This time he quoted billionaire investor Warren Buffett: " 'If you wait for the robins to come back and you wait for the dogwoods to bloom, you're too late.'

"Guys, this is January," he said in a speech only the most churlish of cynics could have denounced. "The robins aren't here, and the dogwoods ain't blooming. But come April, we will be *hee-ah*."

The move wouldn't exactly save Galax, which has always had more industry diversity than its furniture-making cousin company towns to the east. But without Vaughan-Bassett as the corporate backbone, the town's other employers—including a mirror and glass company called Consolidated that used to make mirrors for the region's furniture makers but now specializes in hurricane- and bulletproof glass—might not have stayed or prospered. An upholstery factory, Mississippi-based Albany Furniture, might not have opened in one of the old Vaughan plants, community leaders say. And the giant Lowe's and Walmart would have had a hard time making it without the infusion of cash from those factories' workers.

Galax without Vaughan-Bassett?

"It would look like Martinsville," said Bill Webb, head of the Virginia Employment Commission in Galax.

"It would look like Bassett," said Ray Kohl, the Galax tourism director who wants to display the world's largest bed as a tourist attraction, not unlike the world's largest dresser in High Point or Thomasville's world's largest chair.

There were other precedents for the world's largest bed. In 2009, Bassett Furniture had erected a twenty-foot-tall Mission-style chair, dubbed the Big Chair, in Martinsville's uptown. Built in 2002 in celebration of the company's hundredth anniversary, for seven years it toured the country to herald the opening of Bassett Furniture stores before it found its "final resting place... right here in the seat of the furniture industry," as Rob Spilman put it at a press conference.

He'd donated it for use in the region's new Deep Roots heritage tourism campaign, whose organizers installed it beside the abandoned American of Martinsville offices. That was two years after Bassett Furniture closed its last factory in Bassett and a year after American and Stanley

Furniture closed their nearby factories' doors. When the chair went up, the region counted 3,000 people employed in furniture. By 2013, that figure was down to 651, most of them office and warehouse workers.

"If they threw a giant sweatshirt over the chair, it would complete the picture," said Tripp Smith, a Martinsville food-bank volunteer. He shared that sentiment in a letter to the *Martinsville Bulletin,* writing: "I feel we should have the uptown chair monstrosity dismantled, packed up in a box and shipped to China. I'm sure we could find an empty container headed that way." (The three-ton chair was eventually taken down for repairs, and a decision was later made to "retire it," the newspaper reported in February 2014.)

Smith's comment was meant as snark. But in fact, Smith's dig was prescient: Within two years, the number one export at the Virginia Port Authority was logs and lumber. The number one import? That very same wood making its way back across the ocean to Virginia as dressers, tables, and chairs stamped with the names Bassett, Stanley, Hooker, and Vaughan.

JBIII doesn't need to erect the world's largest bed to ensure his legacy. His factories—and the others he helped save with his coalition—speak for him. Reau Berry, the sole owner of Mississippi-based Johnston/Tombigbee, took the $13 million he received in Byrd money and bought equipment that allowed him to hasten his manufacturing lead time and craft a piece of hotel furniture in twenty-four hours instead of two weeks. He also paid vendors and other bills.

"If Senator Byrd is not in heaven when I get there, I'm gonna be very disappointed," he said. "That money allowed me to compete with China, and it saved my factory," which employs a hundred and fifty people, down from four hundred at its peak, Berry added. "We're not getting rich, but we're not going out of business either. And every dollar I pay somebody—whether it's through my payroll or to a vendor—you can multiply it by seven.

"The real value in manufacturing is creating a community where cash flows. If the American people only realized what's taken place, they wouldn't ever buy anything from Walmart again."

John Bassett's rhetoric is less charged, more politically considered. When it comes to his relatives who went the other way or to the retailers who bailed on him, he tends to keep his mouth shut. He's been three steps ahead of most of them all along anyway.

Take the winter of 2013, one decade after the fracas began. Business was sluggish, and short time was rearing its ugly head. The company had made $25 million in profits in 2012, which was exactly what it had netted from its last stack of Byrd money checks. It broke even, in other words, though its balance sheet was solid, with shareholder equity of $114.5 million.

A segment of John's opposition, led by Ashley Furniture, was in appeals court suing to get a portion of that money, arguing that even though the company had opposed the coalition at the ITC, it had still been making furniture domestically when the petition was filed, and, based on its First Amendment right of free speech, it deserved a portion of the already distributed funds. The case was tied up in federal appeals court, and JBIII had his top-shelf lawyer in Washington on the clock. "It's all about the money, you know," he said. "The lawyers all get paid by the hour, and they like to keep it all rolling along."

As a safeguard against an appeal ruling that might not go his way, John had socked most of his last stash of Byrd money away in CDs—in case he had to return some of it. "You never know how long a snake is till you kill him and stretch him out," he said, again.

Then he went back to work. He dispatched himself, Doug, and Wyatt to different sections of the country. In one thirty-six-hour span, the seventy-five-year-old hit South Dakota, St. Paul, and Salt Lake City, drumming up business and getting eyeball-to-eyeball with retailers who had been criticizing his stand against imports for years.

His own salespeople were competent, he said. "But there's nothing that can replace somebody with the name Bassett sitting in front of you."

Some, like Keith Koenig of City Furniture, placed orders for the first time in years. Some met with him but held firm. "We're just not gonna buy from him," Jake Jabs told me after JBIII's visit. "I like him. He's a personable guy. But we're still mad."

Others were nudged by necessity more than sales pitch. A New York retailer declined to place a rush order with VBX in the wake of Hurricane Sandy, saying a cheaper product was already on its way from Asia. When that container load arrived, all twenty bedroom suites were adorned with black mold (it's the tropics in Indonesia, after all), and an order for ninety Cottage Collection suites was then placed.

"I can put 'em on a truck tomorrow for you," JBIII told the retailer. "We have a lot of things in Galax, Virginia. But we don't have black mold."

As for that five-point poster he used to trot around with him, the one mashed in a backroom closet next to an old cardboard cutout of Elvis? It's now on PowerPoint, operated by a young IT employee at Vaughan-Bassett whenever he gives one of his talks—by one of the "people who iPad" so he can spend his time thinking about making money instead.

The five points can be culled down to five simple words: Fight harder than everybody else.

The sales pitch always begins with a little soft sex because, in his words, "Soft sex always sells."

Thus begins the retelling of the go-to tale for the retailers: *Imagine you're the only woman stranded on a desert island, and you're surrounded by a dozen men...*

He's told that story so often now that eliciting laughs from the listener is like breathing to him. It's like that one nightly cocktail he allows himself as he and Pat watch Brian Williams on the *NBC Nightly News* at top-decibel level (because his ears are shot from all those decades of grouse hunting and all that tinkering on furniture-factory floors).

The desert-island pitch is classic John Bassett because it's folksy and dumb-like-a-fox. As one of the salesmen he calls regularly on Saturday afternoons put it, "His real gift is his uncanny ability to make you believe you're an idiot if you don't see things the way he does."

"*When you're the only girl left standing on an island with twelve men, you don't have to be good-looking,* some*body's gonna fall in love with you!*

The desert-island pitch is usually a slam dunk with retailers, as solid a beginning as being born in the middle of an epic flood with a silver spoon in your mouth, a chauffeur on standby, and the hospital bill already paid by your millionaire grandpop.

Not only is Vaughan-Bassett the last girl left standing on the island, she just happens to be good-looking too. That girl can put a wrinkle in a blouse.

Though he'd never say it to a retailer, he added another flourish when he told me the story, yet again, a few days before the Vaughan-Bassett II press conference. Five hours away, President Barack Obama could talk all he wanted about bringing manufacturing back from Asia. He could even pluck the North Carolina furniture maker Bruce Cochrane from the crowd and sit him next to the First Lady—not knowing that Cochrane's efforts to reboot his family's furniture-making efforts would fail a year later, alas.

"But when you never went cheap with some other woman down the street," he told me, peering over dusty glasses, "you don't have to come drag-assin' back."

At the start of my research for this book, I pictured tagging along as John Bassett III went grouse hunting. That didn't happen; his bad back prevents hunting. Besides, as he put it, trash-talking, even if he could still hunt, he doubted I was fit enough to keep up with him.

Golfing was also out of the question because he knew and I knew that a nongolfer wouldn't dream of taking a swing at any of the exclusive clubs to which he belongs.

The closest I got to one of his golf courses was the stroll I took along the Roaring Gap course one autumn day with Pat and their rescued beagle mutt, Elvis. Most of the magnates had already retreated to their warmer-climate homes for the winter, but Pat, then seventy, stuck around because her best friend lives next door. And because John drives everyone crazy when he's away from the factory more than a few weeks.

Asked how she puts up with his sharp tongue and relentless focus on work, she said, "Well, I just am crazy about him. And when I can't stand it anymore, I turn around and go to Florida." With Elvis in the passenger seat, his snoot on the console, she makes the eleven-hour drive solo in her Mercedes with only one bathroom stop.

She pointed to a stand of pines where she and John regularly crouch during evening strolls around the golf course, playing hide-and-seek. "It does feel kind of silly, hiding from a dog," she admitted drolly.

They share an earthy, borderline randy sense of humor, joking repeatedly about the erotic romance novel *Fifty Shades of Grey*—which Pat devoured and liked so much that she even bought the cookbook parody, *Fifty Shades of Chicken*.

The factory man and I were friendly, but our exchanges were often fraught. During one heated fact-checking session, he argued so vociferously against the inclusion of some wealth-related facts that I felt like the line worker in Mount Airy who'd just had the stool kicked out from under him.

Within forty-eight hours of the argument, though, he'd sent flowers and apologized for berating me. He did assist greatly in the reporting of this book, pulling strings to help me land several hard-to-get interviews, including with several people he knew might not say positive things about him.

His wife was quick-witted and warm, inviting me twice to stay at the family's Roaring Gap estate. Pat Bassett cooked while I sparred with her husband in the kitchen, the place where he builds a fire at five every morning and then sits to read newspapers from around the globe. She listened in on some of our interviews, interrupting to translate his long-winded business lectures, intuiting when I was confused and offering a better explanation.

My requests to sit in on Vaughan-Bassett board meetings and sales calls were met with a curt no. It would make people uneasy; it was *gauche* of me even to have asked. When I inquired about the new furniture designs two months prior to their unveiling at the spring Market, JBIII acted like I meant to expose the company's trade secrets, even though my book wouldn't be published until a year *after* the 2013 trade show.

Mostly, he called me on the phone, never once saying hello when I picked up. Sometimes he yelled at me; other times he made me laugh. Every now and then I asked a question and he answered it with no spin or emotion attached.

He called whenever he felt like it. Weeknights and weekends. During my last day of Christmas vacation ("Well, if I'm talkin' to you, then I'm workin' too!"). During early-evening hikes up Mill Mountain with my husband and my dog ("Why you breathin' so hard?"). While he was thick-tongued and on postoperative painkillers two days after having surgery on his back ("I'm already bored").

One Monday morning, I'd left my cell phone in another room of my house and didn't hear it ring — only to return to four missed calls from his Hobe Sound home and a message, left at 8:14 a.m. "Well, I see yo' sleepin' in today" began the scolding, booming voice.

But in all the calls, not once did he break the time-honored code: Not once did he speak ill of his lifelong nemesis, the brother-in-law who pushed him into doing the big things his grandpop had hoped he would — only not at Bassett Furniture. When Bob Spilman died in 2009 at eighty-two, his family organized two funerals, one in Martinsville and one in Richmond. John was one of the few people who attended both — but not, he insisted, "to make sure he was really dead," as some industry watchers have suggested. He went to support his sister.

It was up to me to notice that, during a spring 2012 High Point Market dinner lauding JBIII as a pillar of the industry, his immediate family milled around with the three hundred guests, including folks from competing furniture companies, industry analysts, and some retailers who'd dumped him ("They acted like I had BO!"). But no one else from the Families came to pay tribute. (Rob Spilman and Jeb Bassett did attend his 2013 induction into the American Furniture Hall of Fame, which is considered the pinnacle of industry achievement.)

There are people in the industry, including some members of his extended family, who believe he took China to the mat because he loves fighting more than he loves his Galax factory workers. The most cynical among them say he's fueled by regret that he missed his chance to cash out in the mid-1990s—when he could have taken the company public, before the domestic industry tanked. (JBIII vehemently denies that claim.)

"We haven't used his tactics," said Roxann Dillon, the eighty-year-old granddaughter of C.C. Bassett, speaking about Bassett Furniture and referring, dismissively, to the antidumping case, even though the company joined the coalition and walked away with $17.5 million in duties. "John Bassett didn't have all these stockholders to keep happy; his was a family-owned thing with very few shareholders.

"Get your facts right," she snapped.

There are others who just as vehemently believe he saved a factory and a town not only because it was good business but also because it was the right thing to do. Members of both camps were in the room that night.

The event emcee was Marc Schewel, the retailer who'd cut his Vaughan-Bassett orders drastically when imports became available at a better price. He began by calling JBIII an "entrepreneur, survivor, independent thinker, unstoppable barn burner; the signature domestic furniture manufacturer for whom made in America is not a slogan, it's a credo.

"But I did a little behind-the-scenes investigation," Schewel continued. "And I found out that John's suit was made in India, his shirt in Sri Lanka, his tie in Thailand, his shoes in China, his television set in Korea, his watch in Switzerland, his eyeglasses in Germany..."

Ba-dah-bum. The event began with Schewel's barbs and ended with John Bassett describing a stranger approaching him at a Galax gas station a week earlier and thanking him for keeping the town afloat. "There's a snap again in people's steps," he said of the community. "It's their confidence coming back. People actually believe there's a place for them again in the global environment."

* * *

His sons may not have inherited his fiery charisma, but when John Bassett dies, most people in Galax believe they'll carry his legacy forward. They wouldn't dare close the factory, one former manager said. "They're afraid Daddy'll come back and haunt 'em!"

He'll be buried in the graveyard next to the church at Roaring Gap, he told me on the day of our hometown tour. We had stopped at the Martinsville cemetery to see his parents' graves. On one side were the headstones of his parents' best friends, the childless couple next door. In a far corner of the family plot stood the tombstone of a woman named Mazie Opal Sizemore Lawson. John didn't know who Mazie was—someone whose family apparently lacked a plot to bury her. But, like Mr. J.D. before her, his mother had told the woman's family, *Sure, put her there under the dogwood tree.*

Approaching the other side of his parents' graves, I spotted the headstone of Robert Henkel Spilman. "He's right beside your parents?" I marveled.

"Right," he said. We stood there in silence for a few seconds. Birds chirped. Squirrels darted about.

Then he told me the story of another awards ceremony, one held in 2008 to honor his nephew Rob. John had written a letter in support of Rob's nomination for the American Furniture Manufacturers Association's Distinguished Service Award. The extended family had gathered to support him, including his father, Bob Spilman, who was ailing but not disabled at the time.

"Bob was very nice to me, and I thanked him, and then he started to talk about what could have been, and I said, 'Bob, let's not get into this. It was probably my fault as much as it was yours.'"

It was too late for apologies, too late for what-ifs. It was the last time they saw each other, and if John Bassett had had no intention of hashing out the past with his brother-in-law, he certainly wasn't going to hash it out four years later with me.

The Smith River Twitch

I had crossed a line into a region where the past was still felt to be alive and where the ghosts of the past still governed events.

—HENRY WIENCEK, *THE HAIRSTONS*

During one of my last trips to Bassett, I finally went on a tour with Bassett Historical Center librarian Pat Ross, whose family had landed in town shortly after Mr. J.D. got his start. Her grandfather was the one who made all the lights in town blink when he flipped the switch on his power hog of a boiler.

More than anyone I interviewed for this book, Pat wanted me to get the story exactly right, to honor the workers as well as the pioneer owners. "It's history," she said every time I banged up against an uncomfortable truth. "If you dig it up and it's true, it's your job to tell it."

Pat was seventy years old and still ran the center as a volunteer, even though she'd officially retired a year before. Volunteers bring in chocolate most days, and whenever anyone makes the forty-minute trip to Danville to shop, they stop at the Midtown Market, a store known for its chicken salad (the key being fresh chicken, minimal mayo, no eggs).

Tubs of chicken salad appear in the center's kitchen like manna, gifted by volunteers for hungry researchers and reporters alike.

It was Pat's daughter, Anne Marie, who wrote the history of Mary Hunter, Mr. J.D.'s maid and the namesake of Mary Hunter Elementary School, when she was in the seventh grade. Anne Marie had interviewed Gracie Wade, Mary Hunter's successor as the family maid, for the project. Nearing ninety at the time, Gracie was still serving the Spilmans' Christmas dinners, still gardening her little patch of Carver Lane. She liked to place the walker her grandchildren insisted she use inside her wheelbarrow, then wheel the contraption over to her vegetable plot. That way, if the kids paid a surprise visit, she could grab it and pretend to have been using it all along.

John Bassett caught Gracie doing that once shortly before her death. During his infrequent trips to Bassett, usually for Bassett Mirror board meetings, he never failed to stop by Gracie's house to hug her, and he never failed to leave without handing her "a little piece of money," as he called it.

"Listen," he told me, "when I go up to the pearly gates and Saint Peter says to me, 'Who do you know here?' the first person I'm gonna tell him is Gracie because I know she'll put in a good word for me."

A place like Bassett takes time to pin down. It's a welter of geography and history, of barbed wire and blue heron, of crumbling brick behemoths and tiny hillside trailers that, astonishingly, somehow still stand.

It takes patience to pinpoint the soul of any community, and if one is very lucky, the benefit of someone like Pat Ross, who, month after month and layer after layer, helped me really see the effects of globalization on her beloved hometown, down to the streetlight that illuminates the center at night. Ever since Bassett Furniture stopped providing the town's communal lighting, residents have solicited donations to pay for it—at a cost of $720 per pole per year—though some businesses gave up and had their lights removed from the poles.

When I finally got around to asking Pat for a tour of Bassett, I'd already seen it from a disparate set of passenger seats. I'd been chauf-feured around town in Spencer Morten's phlegmy-sounding Mercedes diesel and in my own Subaru with Junior Thomas behind the wheel—he still prefers driving over riding after all these years. I'd stood atop the roof of my car while seventy-year-old barber Coy Young clutched my ankle to keep me from falling with my camera onto the railroad tracks, all to re-create the ghost-town version of a downtown Bassett postcard from the bustling 1930s.

It was May 2013, and Pat had something she wanted me to see near her home. As she drove, we passed her alma mater, John D. Bassett High (class of 1960), now a medical-records storage facility owned by an old classmate who opens the former gym to senior-citizen walkers two mornings a week. (He also runs food and clothing banks out of the school.) We passed the little company homes, some now rented out to visiting trout fishermen or NASCAR fans flocking to see the Martins-ville Speedway race. The winner of Martinsville, as it's known, still leaves with a coveted regional symbol: a Ridgeway grandfather clock. The clocks, though, are no longer made in the Henry County hamlet of Ridgeway.

They're made in China, like most everything else.

Halfway to our destination, Pat drove to an African American cem-etery behind a black church next to a recycling center that was once Mary Hunter Elementary. I'd been wanting to see Mary Hunter's grave for months. Pat waited in her car while I walked along the weed-choked rows and fallen-down headstones. I found plenty of Hairstons, Finneys, and Barbours, but no Mary Hunter, alas.

Rosella Johnson had not been quite three years old when she died in 1920. *Gone but not forgotten,* read her headstone, which was lying on its back, covered in vinca vine and sticks.

Seeing the grave of Reverend Moses E. Moore (1866–1929), I thought of the solace so many Reconstruction-era furniture workers must have taken in their churches and in the promise of the afterlife. The reverend's parents had grown up enslaved on Henry County plantations, his mother's last owner being George DeShazo, his father's, Betsy Moore. By 1920, he was a fifty-six-year-old mulatto furniture worker living in Horsepasture who ministered on the side and lived in a rented farmhouse with a wife and six kids.

I got goose bumps when I realized I'd probably already seen his photo in the early Old Town picture (it was the only area furniture factory then operating in the region). He was likely one of the lighter-skinned black men standing in the back row, wearing overalls and holding a hat.

His lichen-covered headstone was unencumbered and dignified, with a Holy Bible sculpted into the top. At the bottom, in a half-cursive font, it said: *Earth has no sorrow that heaven cannot heal.*

It was a glorious May day, and Pat and I watched men in their waders fishing in the middle of the rippling Smith. We found our destination across from Pat's house, on a ridge overlooking the town.

Harry Ferguson was about to get on his backhoe. He was a factory undertaker now, hired after the HAZMAT-suit wearers and demolition guys left Bassett Superior Lines. It was Harry's job to put what was left of it underground.

The concrete and bricks had already been hauled here by truck — some forty-five thousand tons in all — so a landowner (and distant Bassett relative) could use it as fill for the ravine behind his house. The rough end of Superior Line's rough end would be . . . to extend a wealthy man's lawn.

"If you'd told people in Bassett ten years ago that I'd be up here today burying this plant, they'd have said you were a complete fool," Harry said.

Grass seed would be sown once Harry got the ground leveled, as had already happened at the Superior site. Rob Spilman told me he wasn't sure what the company would do with all the new expanses of lawn created by the factory demolitions. The company was already allowing town volunteers to hold a weekly farmers' market in the old train depot, and the grass at Old Town would host the fall Bassett Heritage Festival. Perhaps the land behind Superior, with its proximity to the Smith, would tie into the county's growing system of greenway trails and boat put-ins. "Maybe we can make this a quaint little cool destination someday and use it to tell our own little brand story," Rob said, reminding me of one of the Harvest Foundation's economic-development mantras:

You can't move the river to China!

Two weeks later I found myself drifting toward the Smith. There had been a drenching rain the week before, and upriver, the Philpott Dam was in power-making mode. I floated on a side creek for about thirty seconds before my boat hit the Smith, and the gentle paddle I'd envisioned turned into white-water rafting instead. My guide was Jim Franklin, seventy-three, a float fisherman who'd run the Bassett particleboard plant for thirty-four years.

He named the abandoned factories that were still standing as we swiftly passed them. He pointed out where he'd personally hauled some of the concrete and brick from Bassett Superior and Old Town, placing the chunks just so on the riverbank to stave off erosion.

He canoed, I kayaked, and when the river wasn't rushing and demanding our full concentration, he told me stories under a canopy of sycamores and scrub trees that teemed with wildlife. A Canada goose roamed the riverbanks with her trio of goslings. A great blue heron tracked our moves, swooping ahead every few minutes before landing on a new surveillance perch. The air temperature was sixty-four degrees, the water its usual forty-two, which is why people fish in the Smith but rarely swim, and why the trout find it ideal.

My full-immersion baptism in the Smith came right after we rounded the bend near the old Stanley Furniture factory and found a giant tree limb blocking most of our passage. Jim paddled expertly through a narrow channel on the left. I made the critical mistake of hesitating, which put me in exactly the worst position—parallel to the log—before the current slammed me against it.

The underwater plunge was as bone-chilling as it was abrupt. After being trapped for a moment between the tree and the kayak, I emerged coughing then clawed my way through the icy waters to Jim's canoe. We rode out the rest of the rapids together—him inside the boat and me out, with my arm hooked over the bow. "You're fine now," Jim reassured me. "You're fine."

Before long, I wasn't fine. My feet were numb, and fear of hypothermia sent me scrambling for the steep, muddy bank, which was cloaked in poison ivy.

Jim continued downstream, helpless to stop his canoe in the rushing river. "I'll meet you up on the road!" he shouted, disappearing around a curve.

Scratched and shivering, I emerged from the woods about ten minutes later near a Stanleytown strip mall, behind a Family Dollar store. My Ray-Bans and ponytail holder were submerged in the river, along with my dignity, and when I appeared from the brush with matted hair, ripped pants, and muddy sandals, the woman taking out the store trash was startled. I looked mad, like some poor meth head who'd stumbled out of a newspaper mug shot. She shook her head.

"I'm not gonna ask," she said unhelpfully, and hustled back inside.

Pat Ross picked me up at the CVS next door, bringing blankets, and before long we tracked down Jim, who had a small posse of old factory guys searching for me along the river. They'd lassoed the kayak before it floated too far downstream, and Jim even rescued my drenched reporter's notebook from the riverbank, the scrawl inside still legible somehow.

The people of Bassett wanted their stories told.

The executives could drive through town with their blinders on—some of them commuting from across the state line—but the people of Bassett placed commemorative bricks on bookshelves and heaved chunks of factory foundations atop riverbanks. They built their own little monuments to a way of living that had vanished in a decade, one smokestack at a time.

Their world was *not flat*, and they wanted a witness to it. Someone to describe the creeping small-town carnage created by acronyms like NAFTA and WTO and an impotent TAA, all of it forged by faraway people who had never bothered to see the full result of what globalization had wrought.

Which is how a relative stranger ended up making three separate visits to search out Mary Hunter's grave. It had taken several phone calls on Pat Ross's part, but finally she found someone who knew exactly where to look: on the other side of the church, up a steep bank covered in weeds and fraught with chiggers and snakes.

Pat waited worriedly by the car while I climbed the bank and whistled to signal that I was okay. Five minutes into the climb, I spotted the rusty wire fence that surrounded Mary Hunter's grave. It was the ornate, old-fashioned kind, with crinkly wires twined together in a scalloped edge along the top. One of the four sides was collapsed and tilted inward toward the stone, as if leaning on a crutch.

Recent rains had painted a dry crust of mud along the bottom of the gray marble stone, which was adorned with engraved daisies flanking her name near the top. The *u* in *Hunter* was thick with the labor of mud dauber wasps who were building a new home.

Beneath her name and date of death, tucked into an overgrown cemetery that was maybe a mile from Mr. J.D.'s pilfered mausoleum, the inscription on the tombstone read:

In memory of Mary Hunter
A faithful servant of
Mr. & Mrs. J.D. Bassett Sr.

This was American history, forgotten in these Blue Ridge foothills and buried amid another invasive Asian import: a sprawling bank of kudzu.

* * *

Several weeks earlier, I had asked for my own brick from the Bassett Superior burial ground. Harry Ferguson pulled one out of his stack and, with some degree of ceremony, chinked off the mortar before passing it to me carefully, the way one might hand over a sleeping baby or a rising loaf of bread. He knew and I knew that this piece of molded red clay didn't begin to represent the world of furniture-making from the Smith River banks to the Sidoarjo mud.

But it was warm from the May sun, and it was solid, and, by and by, when Harry looked me in the eye, neither of us said a word. We just knew: There were people out there who would crawl on their bellies like a snake if it meant they could bring it all back.

Acknowledgments

This book began with a set of images that were found, nurtured, and documented by photographer Jared Soares, who not only noticed what most everyone else simply drove by but actually stopped and got to know some of the five million people who had lost their jobs to globalization. The stories I wrote to accompany Jared's photographs were originally developed under the direction of my *Roanoke Times* editors Carole Tarrant and Brian Kelley, with support from managing editor Michael Stowe and publisher Debbie Meade. *Factory Man* grew directly out of that series.

My agent, Peter McGuigan at Foundry Literary + Media, shaped every element of this book with gusto, smarts, and good humor, with help from his colleagues Bret Witter, Matt Wise, and Kirsten Neuhaus. Included in the cadre of journalists, authors, and friends who cheered, read drafts, or offered wise counsel at key points along the way were Roland Lazenby, Ralph Berrier Jr., Andrea Pitzer, Jeff Howe, Gary Knight, Martha Bebinger, Alissa Quart, Annie Jacobsen, Jim Steele, Mary Bishop, Margaret Newkirk, Shankar Vedantam, Marcela Valdes, John Beckman, Bond Nickles, Leigh Anne Kelley, Josh Meltzer, Katelyn Polantz, Gemma de'Choisy, Kevin Sites, Lisa Mullins, Audra Ang, Joe Wilson, Jordan Fifer, Stephanie Klein-Davis, Mike Hudson, Darcey Steinke, Sue Lindsey, Sharon Rapoport, Will Fletcher, Dan Crawford, Aida Rogers, Joe Stinnett, Jonathan Coleman, Evelio Contreras, and Clay Shirky.

At Little, Brown and Company, executive editor John Parsley shepherded every sentence of this book with a rare blend of curiosity, skepticism, and kindness. Other phenomenal Little, Brown supporters include Malin von Euler-Hogan, Sarah Murphy, Amanda Brown, Fiona Brown, Tracy Roe, Michael Pietsch, Judy Clain, Jayne Yaffe Kemp, Helen Tobin, and Miriam Parker.

For travel, financial, and other assistance—like getting me to Asia and back—I'm tremendously thankful for the generosity of the Ochberg Society for Trauma Journalism (special thanks to Deirdre Stoelzle-Graves, Dr. Frank Ochberg, and Jeff Kelly Lowenstein) and to the Lukas Prize Project, a collaboration of the Columbia School of Journalism and the Nieman Foundation for Journalism at Harvard (with special thanks to Lisa Redd, Gene Foreman, Bob and Nancy Giles, Shaye Areheart, James Geary, Ellen Tuttle, and Ann Marie Lipinski). I'd also like to thank the Virginia Center for the Creative Arts for residency support.

Huge hugs to friends and relatives who fed me along the way and must have grown tired of listening to my furniture tales—but were *usually* too polite to say so—including Chris and Connie Henson, Angela Charlton, Jenna Swann, Chet Weiss, Ed and Katherine Walker, Betsy and Gerry Bannan, Frances and Lee West, Jean and Scott Whitaker, Sarah Macy Slack, Tim Macy, Chris and Bill Landon, Barbara and Frosty Landon, and Chloe Landon. Lezlie and Keno Snyder at Parkway Brewing Company in Salem, Virginia, deserve a hoppy shout-out for launching their own made-in-America collaboration in celebration of this book: Factory Girl Pale Ale. My sons, Max and Will Landon, were usually patient with my lack of cooking and were always handy with a hug when I needed one.

This non–business writer was schooled in furniture-making by many experts: Joel Shepherd, Mike Micklem, Jerry Epperson, Steve Walker, Art Raymond, Joe Meadors, Buck Gale, Spencer Morten, Rob Spilman, David Williams, Reuben "Scotty" Scott, the late Bob Merriman, and the generous Indonesian Stanley Furniture crew of Richard Ledger, Jim Febrian, Jerry Hall, and Dini Martarini. Heartfelt thanks—and re-employment hopes—go to Stanley's Robbinsville workers, who learned in April 2014 that their factory would soon close.

As an interloper writing about an industry that has long been the purview of business and trade-publication beat journalists, I owe a great debt to past and current reporters at *Furniture/Today* (especially Powell Slaughter, Thomas Russell, and Clint Engel), the *Wall Street Journal* (Timothy Aeppel and James R. Hagerty), the *Martinsville Bulletin* (Ginny Wray and Debbie Hall), the *Roanoke Times* (Megan Schnabel, Duncan Adams, George Kegley, Jeff Sturgeon, Matt Chittum, and the truly fabulous Ben Beagle), the *Galax Gazette* (Chuck Burress), and *Virginia Business* magazine (Estelle Jackson). I'm also grateful to the American Furniture Hall of Fame for sharing their oral histories, as well as to Michael K. Dugan, whose *Furniture Wars* became one of my most dog-eared sources.

Roanoke historian John Kern's research on early African American workers at Bassett Furniture was incredibly helpful, as was Dorothy Cleal and Hiram H. Herbert's *Foresight, Founders, and Fortitude: The Growth of Industry in Martinsville and Henry County, Virginia.* Leslie T. Chang's *Factory Girls: From Village to City in a Changing China* schooled me on the human side of offshoring from the other side of the globe. For context on racial complexities in the southern Piedmont—and in America—there is no finer book than Henry Wiencek's *The Hairstons: An American Family in Black and White.*

I'm grateful for materials shared from the archives of Pat and John Bassett, Richard Stanley Chatham, Desmond Kendrick, Rob Spilman/Bassett Furniture, John Nunn, John B. Harris, Naomi Hodge-Muse, Doretha Estes, Coy Young, and, especially, the Bassett Historical Center. For snacks and for extending a true sense of community to me, no one was kinder than lifelong Bassett residents Mary and Junior Thomas, who never let me drive unassisted across their tiny bridge. Mary passed away on November 19, 2013, at the age of eighty-one, and her jam-packed funeral was truly and tee-totally glorious. Speakers marveled about her *Let's Make a Deal* purses ("She had whatever you needed in that thing") and her home remedies—especially her secret cure for taking the sting out of a burn, which she could do both in person *and over the telephone.* ("You could just feel the fire comin' outta you.")

In the category of Librarians and Clerks Who Rule: Bill Bishop at the U.S. International Trade Commission helped me navigate the thousands of documents stemming from the bedroom-furniture anti-dumping case. Belinda Harris at the *Roanoke Times* unearthed old photographs and stories and helped tally the layoffs. Spencer Johnson at the Martinsville–Henry County Economic Development Corporation waded through stacks of data on changing workforce patterns, as did Ray Kohl in Galax. Volunteers and staffers at the Bassett Historical Center were welcoming enough to let me take up most of a room in the summer of 2012. The best fact-checker and census-comber award goes to BHC director Pat Ross, with props to her plainspoken assistant Anne Copeland, who grimaced when she saw me drenched and shivering in the wake of my Smith River plunge. Cloaked in Pat's blankets, with Pat's car heater on high, I knew Anne would come gawk at me in the center parking lot, and, sure enough, out she strode with both eyebrows raised. "Well, now you pretty much *have* to dedicate the book to her, don't you?" she said.

At Vaughan-Bassett Furniture, Wyatt Bassett spent many hours going over the intricacies of the antidumping case with me, and Doug Bassett, Doug Brannock, Jim Stout, Joyce Phillips, Rose Maner, Pat Bassett, and especially Sheila Key shared many insights. For his three-hundred-plus phone calls at all hours of the day and night—and for that inimitable, booming voice that never once began with "Hello, this is John"—thank you, John Bassett III. You weren't the easiest person to talk to, but you were always interesting and you were often fun. And not just anyone can explain the intricacies of grouse hunting and Chinese currency manipulation, and tell a dirty joke—all in the same breath.

To all the unemployed and underemployed former factory workers who poured out their hearts—especially Wanda Perdue—consider this book yours.

Lastly, to the updraft beneath my armpits and for every single thing, thanks to my husband, Tom Landon.

Notes

Prologue: The Dusty Road to Dalian

Interviews: John Bassett, Wyatt Bassett, Rose Maner

The largest migration in human history: By 2008, 130 million Chinese people had moved from the country to the cities, according to Leslie T. Chang, *Factory Girls: From Village to City in a Changing China* (New York: Spiegel and Grau, 2008). By 2010, that figure was 150 million workers, according to Yuyu Chen, Ginger Zhe Jin, and Yang Yue, "Peer Migration in China" (NBER Working Paper Series, vol. w15671 [January 2010]). In 2012, nearly 160 million migrant workers were living in China's cities ("The Largest Migration in History," *Economist*, February 24, 2012).

Chapter 1: The Tipoff

Interviews: Naomi Hodge-Muse, Bernard "Bunny" Wampler, Joel Shepherd, Jared Soares, Wanda Perdue, Kay Pagans, Delano Thomasson, Mauri Hammack, Octavia Witcher, Mary Redd, Wayne Withers, Marcia Bailey.

Jared Soares's work on Martinsville: http://jaredsoares.com/index.php?/project/martinsville/.

Top-down coverage of the financial crisis: "Covering the Great Reces-sion," Pew Research Center's Project for Excellence in Journalism, October 5, 2009.

Most millionaires per capita: Undocumented but widely held local belief and often repeated in Virginia media, from the *Martinsville Bulletin* to *Blue Ridge Outdoors* to the *Richmond Times-Dispatch*.

Unemployment figures: Virginia Employment Commission and Mark Heath, Martinsville–Henry County Economic Development Commission, interview with the author, February 9, 2012.

Crane's crimes: Crane pleaded guilty and was convicted in June 2012, sentenced to one year and one month in prison, and fined nearly $970,000: Alison Parker, "Silas Crane Pleaded Guilty in Court Wednesday Morning," June 13, 2012, WDBJ7.com.

Property- and drug-related crime: Henry County assistant commonwealth's attorney Wayne Withers described an increasing number of cases involving copper thefts from abandoned factories and even churches. Shoplifting and drug-related break-ins were also on the rise.

Cedar hope chests: At its peak in the 1960s, the Lane Company, based in Altavista, Virginia, operated seventeen factories in five states. Its promotional mini-cedar-chest program was once so popular that nearly two-thirds of young women graduating from American high schools received certificates for them.

"It's the Real Love-Gift": http://www.ebay.com/itm/1948-Lane-Cedar-Hope-Chest-Wanda-Hendrix-vintage-2pg-ad-/150536985049?pt=LH_Default Domain_0&hash=item230cb419d9.

"creative destruction": Joseph Schumpeter (1883–1950) coined the term to describe the free market's messy way of delivering progress. He called capitalism "the perennial gale of creative destruction."

The World Is Flat: The benefits of globalization appear on page 143 of Friedman's *The World Is Flat* (New York: Picador, 2005); he is quoting a study by Morgan Stanley that was originally reported in *Fortune* magazine on October 4, 2004.

Background on Grimes Manufacturing: Sarica Manufacturing Company, a circuit-card assembly supplier for Honeywell based in Urbana, was started by former Honeywell employees when Honeywell announced it was going to begin outsourcing the circuit boards. Sarica employs ninety workers, according to Urbana economic development coordinator Marcia Bailey.

Chapter 2: The Original Outsourcer

Interviews: Pat Ross, Jane Bassett Spilman, John Kern, Mary Elizabeth Morten, Spencer Morten, John Bassett, Pat Bassett

The history of Bassett: Bassett, Virginia, was built on land that was known as Horsepasture before the magisterial districts were divided in the late 1800s. Bassett land is now part of the district of Reed Creek.

Mr. J.D. buying the little kids ice cream: Recounted in a 1935 letter by Mabel Coleman of Mayodan, North Carolina, on file at the Martinsville–Henry County Museum. She wrote to him for a school assignment, asking him to buy her a bike for Christmas. It's unknown whether he bought the bike, but he did save the girl's letter.

Flood description of J.D. Bassett: Howard White, longtime plant manager who grew up in Bassett and started working for BFI in 1939; interview with the author, July 30, 2012.

Description of flood scene: Malcolm Donald Coe, ed., *Our Proud Heritage* (Bassett, VA: Bassett Printing Corporation, 1969).

Slave population: According to 1840 census figures, Henry County had 2,852 slaves, which was 41 percent of the population. One in four Virginians owned slaves, and the largest slave owner in the state — as well as one of the largest in the South — was Henry County's Samuel Hairston, whose family owned 1,600 slaves on several tobacco plantations according to Henry Wiencek's remarkable book *The Hairstons: An American Family in Black and White* (New York: St. Martin's Press, 1999).

"Race is entwined": John Kern, interview with the author, June 15, 2012.

Hairston pronunciation: Beth Macy, "Lingering Racial Divide Clouds Foundation's Efforts," *Roanoke Times*, March 18, 2012.

Patrick Henry's presence in the county: "Martinsville & Henry County — Historic Views" (Martinsville–Henry County Women's Club, 1976).

Nonwhites as new majority: From the 2010 U.S. Census, the first census in which whites were a minority in Martinsville. The Hispanic population is 3.9 percent.

Land begetting more land: Detailed in Anne Bassett Stanley Chatham, *Tidewater Families of the New World and Their Westward Migrations* (Austin, Texas: Historical Publications, 1996), 627–30.

Largest slaveholding state: In 1860, Virginia had 490,865 slaves, accounting for 31 percent of its population. See "Slavery in Virginia: A Selected Bibliography," edited by David Feinberg (Library of Virginia, 2007).

John Henry Bassett's two young slaves: Chatham, *Tidewater Families,* and the 1860 Henry County slave schedule.

John Henry Bassett's holdings: 1860 Henry County slave schedule and census records.

Protecting the family assets: Chatham, *Tidewater Families.*

Role model of relentlessness: J. L. Scoggin's description of J.D. Bassett's work ethic in the *Bassett Journal,* 1932.

Mr. J.D.'s ambition theorized: Chatham, *Tidewater Families,* 665.

Role of plug tobacco: In 1900, four tobacco factories made chewing tobacco in the city, according to "Martinsville & Henry County—Historic Views."

Moonshining practices in southwest Virginia: Henry County is directly south of Franklin County, which inspired Matt Bondurant's novel *The Wettest County in the World* (New York: Scribner, 2008) and the subsequent film *Lawless,* about illegal moonshining activities in the region.

How the town of Bassett got its name: "Memories of Grandma and Grandpa Bassett," recorded by Mary

Elizabeth Bassett Morten and reprinted in Chatham, *Tidewater Families.* According to the original post office deed, the town was initially called Bassetts (with an *s*), and the original postmaster was John Henry Bassett, not his son.

J.D. Bassett as a young adult: "Big Oaks Prompted Industry," *Martinsville Bulletin,* 1964.

Casket-selling business: J.D. Bassett obituary, *Martinsville Bulletin,* March 1, 1965.

Splitting four hundred rails a day: Ann Joyce, "J. D. Bassett Sr. Notes His 92nd Birthday," *Martinsville Bulletin,* 1959.

Miss Pokey and the founding of Bassett Furniture: John Bassett III, Pat Ross, Jane Spilman, Mary Elizabeth Morten, and various grandchildren, interviews with the author.

First North Carolina furniture makers: Thomas Wrenn organized the High Point Furniture Company in 1888, and by 1900, High Point claimed twelve furniture makers. Bernhardt Furniture began in Lenoir, North Carolina, in 1889, and Lexington Furniture in Lexington, North Carolina, in 1901, according to John James Cater, "The Rise of the Furniture Manufacturing Industry in Western North Carolina and Virginia," *Management Decision* 43 (2005): 906–24.

Lots of timber but no roads: Account of Mary Elizabeth Morten in Chatham, *Tidewater Families,* 675.

J.D. Bassett selling his brothers on becoming partners: Dorothy Cleal and Hiram H. Herbert, *Foresight, Founders, and Fortitude: The Growth of Industry in Martinsville and Henry County, Virginia* (Bassett, VA: Bassett Print Corporation, 1970).

J.D. bossing Reed Stone around: Chatham, *Tidewater Families,* 666.

Work ethic of early factory workers: Historian Liston Pope noted that workers "took it for granted that all members of the family would work as early as possible…and began notoriously large families, even surpassing the immigrants who populated the East with a plentiful supply of workers"; see Liston Pope, *Millhands and Preachers* (New Haven: Yale University Press, 1942).

Selling price of first Bassett Furniture: Cleal and Herbert, *Foresight, Founders, and Fortitude.*

Initial designs of Bassett Furniture: From Bassett corporate history and Rob Spilman, interview with the author, May 2, 2013.

Demand for mass-produced furniture: Cleal and Herbert, *Foresight, Founders, and Fortitude.* "By offering cheaper labor costs in a union-free environment and abundant capital, the South enticed hundreds of textile mills to move," wrote Michael K. Dugan, a retired industry executive and business professor, in *The Furniture Wars: How America Lost a Fifty Billion Dollar Industry* (Conover, NC: Goosepen Press, 2009).

J.D. Bassett's money for his children: Spencer Morten, interview with the author, June 29, 2012.

Hardscrabble workers: When the original Old Town plant caught fire in December 1917, the entire town formed a bucket line to the Smith River, but the heat was too intense and the factory burned to the ground. The company rebuilt the building—in brick—immediately. *Henry Bulletin* stories, 1918.

Five hundred employees: *History of Virginia,* entry on John D. Bassett Sr.

(Chicago and New York: American Historical Society, 1924).

The South as a dominant furniture-making region: Cleal and Herbert, *Foresight, Founders, and Fortitude.*

"I pay Pete twenty-five cents": John Bassett, interview with the author, April 26, 2013.

J. D. Bassett Jr.'s exclamation upon having a son: Recollections of Minnie Lane Bassett, J.D. Bassett's granddaughter, recounted in Chatham, *Tidewater Families.*

Letter from John D. Bassett Sr. to John D. Bassett III: Dated June 14, 1938, the letter now hangs on JBIII's Vaughan-Bassett office wall in Galax, Virginia.

Chapter 3: The Town the Daddy Rabbits Built

Interviews: John Bassett, Tom Word, Frosty Landon, Ward Armstrong, Bernard "Bunny" Wampler, Spencer Morten, Joe Philpott, Jerry Epperson, Robert Jiranek, Jane Bassett Spilman, Sonny Cassady, Bettie Alley

Factory coping strategies during World War II: Among the Southern furniture companies that limped through the war years, Bernhardt Furniture Company made airplane parts, and the Kittinger Company built PT boats, according to Michael Dugan in *The Furniture Wars: How America Lost a Fifty Billion Dollar Industry* (Conover, NC: Goosepen Press, 2009).

Hams instead of bonuses: Dorothy Cleal and Hiram H. Herbert, *Foresight, Founders, and Fortitude: The Growth of Industry in Martinsville and Henry County, Virginia* (Bassett, VA: Bassett Print Corporation, 1970).

"**Mr. J.D. had personally surveyed**": Bettie Alley, interview with the author.

Bonce Stanley's puppetry: This was documented for decades by *Roanoke Times* journalist Frosty Landon, who—full disclosure—is my husband's uncle. When Stanley died, in 1970, Frosty, a young editorial writer, opined that "the Stanley years would go into the history books as a shameful period that, by design or otherwise, crushed anti–Byrd Organization forces (Democrat and Republican) by raising, in Biographer [J. Harvie] Wilkinson's words, 'false hopes for an eternity of segregation.'" Frosty's stinging observations—published almost before Stanley's body had grown cold—had the Families of Henry County lighting up the newspaper publisher's phones. It resulted in Frosty's being transferred to the newsroom, where he manned the night copy desk for years before he managed to work his way back up the editorial ladder.

Virginia's circumvention of *Brown v. Board of Education:* The term *massive resistance* was coined by Senator Harry Byrd, who said: "If we can organize the Southern States for massive resistance to this order I think that in time the rest of the country will realize that racial integration is not going to be accepted in the South" (*"Brown v. Board of Education:* Virginia Responds," exhibition, Library of Virginia, 2003).

Governor Stanley's announcement of massive resistance: See WDBJ7.com civil rights archives, August 1956.

J.D. Bassett wasn't brilliant: Bernard "Bunny" Wampler, interview with the author, August 24, 2012.

Family squabbles: Spencer Morten, interview with the author, echoed in

Cleal and Herbert, *Foresight, Founders, and Fortitude*, 49–51.

Martinsville real estate magnate: Heck Ford's great-grandfather Colonel Joseph Martin led the area's Colonial forces during the Revolutionary War (and gave Martinsville its name). Ford began selling real estate at twenty-one, and by thirty he had brokered the deal that lured in the region's first textile plant, according to Cleal and Herbert, *Foresight, Founders, and Fortitude*.

Origin of W.M. Bassett factory: Spencer Morten, interview with the author.

$1.5 million sold in 1929 by the W.M. plant: *Thirty Years of Success: A History of Bassett Furniture Industries* (Bassett, VA: Bassett Furniture Industries, 1932).

Ernst and Ernst brought in to inventory assets: Cleal and Herbert, *Foresight, Founders, and Fortitude*, 51.

"just build another plant": Found in the archives of Desmond Kendrick at his Martinsville–Henry County Museum; written by Crawford Remsen in the early 1930s, publication unknown.

Conveyor-belt lessons: Wilson was executive vice chairman of the War Production Board. He later served as the secretary of defense under President Eisenhower.

"*printin*' money": Joe Philpott, interview with the author, June 29, 2012.

$1 million of furniture sold in a month: Documented in a photograph at Martinsville–Henry County Museum, archived by Desmond Kendrick.

Waterfall furniture description: Jerry Epperson, e-mail to the author, and paper, "The Forty Year Styling Study with a Review of Changing Merchandising

Concepts," *Furnishings Digest,* February 2002.

Price of waterfall: Ozzie Osborne, "Family-Owned Firm Has Had Many Good Years of Business," *Roanoke Times,* July 31, 1983.

Strengths of designer Leo Jiranek: Robert Jiranek, interview with the author, September 17, 2012.

"you're only the damn crumb": Oft-repeated story recounted by Carolyn Blue in an interview with the author.

"Daddy Rabbits" reference: Thomas O'Hanlon, "5,350 Companies = a Mixed-Up Furniture Industry," *Fortune,* February 1967.

No Bassett furniture in Jane Spilman's home: Jane Spilman, interview with the author, June 18, 2012.

Perle Mesta: Known as the original "hostess with the mostest" for her lavish Washington, DC, political society parties, Perle Mesta was an American socialite and the U.S. ambassador to Luxembourg from 1949 to 1953.

$33 million in annual sales: Bassett Furniture Industries corporate history, 1952; the number of employees comes from Cleal and Herbert, *Foresight, Founders, and Fortitude,* 55.

$6 million in factory modernizations: Ozzie Osborne, "Family-Owned Firm Has Had Many Years of Good Business," *Roanoke Times,* July 31, 1983.

Chapter 4: Hilltop Hierarchy

Interviews: Junior Thomas, Mary Thomas, John Redd Smith Jr., John Kern, Jane Bassett Spilman, Pat Ross, Coy Young, Spencer Morten, Mary Elizabeth Morten, Howard White, Carolyn Blue, Mary Herford, John McGhee, Naomi Hodge-Muse

Nabs: Southern slang for the Nabisco-made packets of orange peanut-butter crackers and other cellophane-wrapped snacks.

Tobacco to textile: When R. J. Reynolds acquired many of the Martinsville tobacco companies and relocated them, the town's fathers had enough money to turn the old tobacco plants into textile mills, according to "Martinsville & Henry County—Historic Views" (Martinsville–Henry County Women's Club, 1976) and local historian John Redd Smith Jr.'s interview with the author, December 11, 2011.

Black working conditions: John Kern, "Bassett Historic Context," Roanoke Regional Preservation Office, interviews conducted 2008–2010.

Blacks excluded from work in North Carolina plants: Blacks in North Carolina were relegated to the lower-paying lumberyards, according to Bill Bamberger and Cathy N. Davidson, *Closing: The Life and Death of an American Factory* (New York: W. W. Norton, 1998), 31.

Black worker versus white worker pay: Pay stubs found at the Bassett Historical Center showed a white worker making twenty-two cents an hour around the same time.

Pay disparity in 1960s: John Kern, interview with the author.

Employment of black women: *Fayette Street, 1905–2005: A Hundred-Year History of African American Life in Martinsville Virginia* (Fayette Area Historical Initiative and the Virginia Foundation for the Humanities, 2006). Though white women and some African American men worked in the first two Jobbers plants, black women weren't hired until the opening of Jobbers' third plant, located in a building the locals dubbed Pneumonia Hall because of its single woodstove.

J.D. Bassett's advice to hire blacks: John Kern, "Jim Crow in Henry County, Virginia: 'We Lived Under a Hidden Law,'" lecture delivered at Virginia Forum, April 16, 2010.

Mary Hunter's disability: Oral history gleaned by Bassett family servant Gracie Wade for a school research paper by Mona Clark and Anne Marie Ross, "In Search of Mary Hunter," collected in the archives of Bassett Historical Center, 1978.

Naming of Mary Hunter Elementary and Mary Hunter's age: Jane's father, John D. Bassett Jr., known as Mr. Doug, was chairman of the Henry County school board when Mary Hunter Elementary was built, according to interviews with Jane Bassett Spilman and Pat Ross. Mary Hunter's reported birth year ranges from 1861 to 1868; it was recorded differently from census to census. "Mary Hunter School," a history on file at the Bassett Historical Center that documents the $40,000 gift, was written by John B. Harris, who was the first principal of Mary Hunter Elementary.

Jane Spilman's maid: Account of Dorothy Menefee's relationship with the Bassett family relayed in author interviews with Carolyn Blue and Mary Herford, August 14, 2013; Jane's gift of house to family servants confirmed by Rob Spilman.

Children of furniture cofounder and maid: Interviews by the author with several Henry County residents past and present, including Naomi Hodge-Muse, whose father was a Bassett family chauffeur and whose grandmother was a Bassett family cook; Coy Young; Pat Ross; Spencer Morten; Mick Micklem; and Junior and Mary Thomas.

Henry "Clay" Barbour obituary: *Martinsville Bulletin,* December 12, 1993.

Not shunned but not invited to dinner: Coy Young, interview with the author, July 6, 2012.

Ed Bassett getting Carver Lane finally paved: Junior Thomas, interview with the author, January 28, 2014.

"The Negroes made me": The recording of J.D. Bassett Sr. saying this was destroyed when Spencer and Mary Elizabeth Morten's house burned, but both of them reported the quote, word for word, in separate interviews. "I never heard the word *nigger* in our house," Mary Elizabeth added.

Boats built by workers to get across the Smith River: Howard White, interview with the author.

Mary Hunter's exclamation at seeing the beach sand for the first time: This story is recounted in Anne Bassett Stanley Chatham, *Tidewater Families of the New World and Their Westward Migrations* (Historical Publications, 1996), by the author's brother Tom Stanley, the son of T.B. and Anne Bassett Stanley.

Description of Jane and father checking on the factories: Jane Bassett Spilman, interview with the author.

Chapter 5: The Cousin Company
Interviews: John Nunn, Howard White, Pat Bassett, John Bassett, Nelson Teague

Galax poaching: Galax is sold for more than a dollar a leaf in the international floral trade, part of an illegal $200 billion global natural-products industry, according to the National Park Service.

Hillbilly music origins: Blue Ridge Music Center and Sarah Wildman, "On Virginia's Crooked Road, Mountain Music Lights the Way," *New York Times,* May 20, 2011.

"the area was growing so fast": John Nunn, interview with the author, July 26, 2012.

Early outreach from town to business investors: *Galax Gazette,* rotogravure special section, 1937.

Original lots sold in Galax: Ed Cox, golden anniversary souvenir booklet "Pioneers, Ghosts, Bonaparte and Galax," 1956.

Black population still comparatively small: U.S. census estimate, 2011, shows blacks make up 6.7 percent of the Galax population.

Early businesses served multiple purposes: The post office housed a school, a casket company, and a furniture store. The Chevrolet dealership sold Frigidaires and offered electrical-wiring installation in homes, according to John Nunn and Judith Nunn Alley in *Images of America: Galax* (Charleston, SC: Arcadia, 2010).

Need for furniture post–Civil War: David N. Thomas, "Getting Started in High Point," *Forest History* 11 (July 1967).

Decline of furniture factories in the Northern states: William Stevens, *Anvil of Adversity: Biography of a Furniture Pioneer* (New York: Popular Library, 1968).

Northern furniture makers' inability to keep up with the times: Frank E. Ransom, *The City Built on Wood: A History of the Furniture Industry in Grand Rapids, Michigan, 1850–1950* (Ann Arbor: University of Michigan, 1955).

Bassett Furniture's careful money-management style: Howard White, interview with the author.

Wyatt Exum's rescue story: The movie *Fighter Squadron,* starring Robert Stack and John Rodney, is said to be loosely based on Wyatt Exum's dramatic World War II rescue per Pat Bassett, interview with the author, August 2, 2012.

Exum's Silver Star: Ibid.

Difference between working in Bassett and Galax: Ibid.

Mao Tse-tung's Great Leap Forward: Dennis Tao Yang, "China's Agricultural Crisis and Famine of 1959–1961," *Comparative Economic Studies* 50 (2008): 1–29.

Suicides off tall buildings in Shanghai: "High Tide of Terror," *Time,* March 5, 1956.

Taming of the Smith River: Since its completion in 1953, the Philpott Dam has prevented an estimated $350 million in flood damage, per the U.S. Army Corps of Engineers, Wilmington district.

John Bassett's wild behavior in college: Nelson Teague, interview with the author, August 13, 2012.

Washington and Lee's mock-convention history: Nikki Schwab, "At Mock Convention, Washington and Lee Students Showcase Their Uncanny Knack for Picking Presidential Candidates," *U.S. News and World Report,* January 17, 2008.

Mr. Doug took his car away as punishment for bad grades: Nelson Teague, interview with the author.

Chapter 6: Company Man

Interviews: Pat Ross, Coy Young, Joe Meadors, Mary Elizabeth Morten, Jerome Neff, Bernard "Bunny" Wampler, John Bassett, Bob Jiranek, Spencer Morten, Colbert "Mick" Micklem, Betty Shelton

Company growth under W.M. Bassett: When Bassett announced the opening of a new fifteen-acre, two-and-a-half-million-dollar Bassett Table plant, the *Henry County Journal* boasted, "There was no architect nor contractor for the mammoth new plant. W.M. Bassett himself...designed and superintended the job" (*Henry County Journal*, November 7, 1957).

Five hundred Bassett-owned homes: Bassett homes rented for a quarter a room a week, and deductions for rent and power were taken out of employee paychecks, according to worker interviews and Jerry Bledsoe, writing in the *Carolina Cavalier*. For twelve dollars a year each, white employees could also use the $386,000 community center built by W.M., which included a pool, playground, and bowling alley. Smaller separate facilities were later built for black workers (*Martinsville Bulletin*, June 10, 1960).

Selling the excess power: Barber Coy Young and longtime sales manager Joe Meadors, interviews with the author, August 16, 2012.

W.M. Bassett's trademark fedora and his relationship with employees: Mary Elizabeth Morten and Jerome Neff, interviews with the author, August 6, 2012 (Morten), and April 24, 2013 (Neff).

Company size in late 1950s, early 1960s: "Bassett: Furniture Giant of Virginia," *Commonwealth*, December 1961. "Bassett Deals in Mass Production for the Mass Market," Milton J. Elliott wrote. He quoted Mr. Doug as saying, "We produce more than 2,000 rooms of furniture a day and hope to keep it that way." (A 1959 article in the *Virginia Record* had a different number; the claim

there was that Bassett was sold in 35,000 stores.)

W.M. Bassett's bonds with workers: Pat Ross, interview with the author, July 26, 2012.

W.M. Bassett's death: "Death of W.M. Bassett Mourned Throughout Va.," *Martinsville Bulletin*, July 18, 1960.

Meeting of Bob Spilman and Jane Bassett: Bunny Wampler, interview with the author, August 27, 2012.

Bassett men impressed with Spilman: Spencer Morten, interview with the author.

J.D. Bassett's hospital home: Asked why J.D. Bassett Sr. lived in the hospital for so many years, Junior Thomas, who still chauffeurs Bassett family members around, said, "He wanted curb service, head to toe!"

Annual birthday fishing outing: J.D. Bassett's grandson Doug Bassett Lane, a former Lane Furniture executive turned fishing-supply retailer, strongly disputes my assertion that his grandfather may not have caught the fish. Told that the man was wearing a three-piece suit in the picture, he insisted, "I don't care; he caught it!"

J.D. Bassett Jr. instructed to be friendlier: Jane Bassett Spilman, interview with the author.

The largest furniture maker: *Fortune*'s O'Hanlon called it the second-largest, behind Broyhill Furniture, but conceded that Bassett seed capital accounted for one-eighth of the entire industry's volume (factoring in the cousin companies and spinoffs) (Thomas O'Hanlon, "5,350 Companies = a Mixed-Up Furniture Industry," *Fortune*, February 1967).

"$60 MILLION IN 60 YEARS": *Home Furnishings Daily*, July 19, 1961.

World's largest chair: The chair shipped from Bassett to Washington in 1958 while J.D. Bassett's son-in-law Thomas B. Stanley (Uncle Bonce) was governor of Virginia.

Company's hottest-selling collection: Bassett's bread-and-butter line was the Mayfield, an Early American design that "blends with America's new times and desires but represents all the grace and charm of our heritage," according to an advertisement.

Defining the furniture belt: O'Hanlon, "5,350 Companies."

State-controlled industrialization in China: Wayne M. Morrison, "China's Economic Rise: History, Trends, Challenges, and Implications for the United States," Congressional Research Service, September 5, 2013.

Mao's order to melt down furniture and other household items: Benjamin A. Valentino, *Final Solutions: Mass Killing and Genocide in the Twentieth Century* (Ithaca, NY: Cornell University Press, 2004).

Mr. Doug's treatment of Mr. Ed: Bob Jiranek, interview with the author.

Chapter 7: Lineage and Love

Interviews: Pat Bassett, Jane Spilman, John Bassett, Bernard "Bunny" Wampler, Joe Meadors, Fran Bassett Poole, Spencer Morten, Mick Micklem, Delano Thomasson

J.D. Bassett's sexual escapades: Story related by Bunny Wampler, who heard it directly from Mr. J.D.'s grandsons George Vaughan and Tom Stanley Jr.

Hollins College history: Ethel Morgan Smith, *From Whence Cometh My Help: The African American Community at Hollins College* (Columbia: Uni-

versity of Missouri Press, 1999). The school is now called Hollins University, and it's acclaimed for its fine-arts curricula, particularly its creative writing, theater, and dance.

Shenandoah Club history: The Shenandoah Club was a white men's club that didn't admit women, blacks, or Jews until the late 1980s; Justin McLeod, "Woman Who Helped Change Roanoke Club's Racist History Is Retiring," WDBJ7.com.

Mao Tse-tung's exaltation of communism: "Red China: The Arrogant Outcast," *Time*, September 13, 1963.

Wharton School graduate Larry Moh: Wharton School at the University of Pennsylvania alumni magazine (2007).

Company's overarching emphasis on sales and employment: Joe Meadors, interview with the author.

J.D. Bassett's house falling into disrepair: Mary Jane Osborne, interview with the author, May 15, 2013.

Never-married company secretary: Georgia Witt recalled in a 1966 newspaper article, "You came here to work and that's what you did, six days a week, ten hours a day." At the time, she had been with the company more than fifty years, had the number one parking space, and had no plans to retire.

J.D. Bassett's obituary: "John David Bassett Sr. Leaves Great Heritage to Our People," *Martinsville Bulletin*, March 1, 1965.

Chapter 8: Navigating the New Landscape

Interviews: Anna Logan Lawson, Coy Young, Jane Bassett Spilman, Bill Young, Frank Snyder, Mick Micklem, Spencer

Morten, Howard Hodges, John Bassett, Bernard "Bunny" Wampler

Gallaudet University controversy: *New York Times* stories, March 1988; Jace Lacob, "ABC Family's 'Switched at Birth' ASL Episode Recalls Gallaudet Protest," *Daily Beast,* February 28, 2013; "A New President Signs on a Gallaudet as Deaf Students Make the Hearing World Listen," *People,* March 28, 1988.

Jane Spilman's invitation to join the Gallaudet board: Rob Spilman e-mail with the author, January 27, 2014.

Aftermath of the controversy: Ben Beagle, "Gallaudet Decision Defended," *Roanoke Times,* March 17, 1988.

County deputies driving Bob Spilman to Market: Bob Spilman, interview with E. L. Briggs, American Furniture Hall of Fame Foundation Oral Histories, April 4 and 7, 2005.

Bob Spilman's cost-cutting acumen: Frank Snyder, interview with the author, September 21, 2012.

Flexibility to make big acquisitions: SEC records; Thomas O'Hanlon, "5,350 Companies = a Mixed-Up Furniture Industry," *Fortune,* February 1967; and Estelle Jackson, "Sweet Ole Bob: The Furniture Industry Is No Game for Patsies," *Virginia Business,* February 1987.

"so many damn plants": Bob Spilman, interview with E. L. Briggs.

Chapter 9: Sweet Ole Bob (SOB)

Interviews: Frank Snyder, Mauri Hammack, Naomi Hodge-Muse, Reuben Scott, Garet Bosiger, Bob Merriman, Howard Altizer, Joe Philpott, Jim Philpott, Junior Thomas, Bill Young, Coy Young, James Riddle, Rob Spilman, Jerry Epperson, Carolyn Blue

Segregated factory departments: Bassett wasn't alone in its discriminatory practices. According to a 1998 analysis by Harvard sociologist Frank Dobbin, at the time, just 20 percent of American employers had established affirmative-action policies. By 1976, more than 80 percent of large firms had equal-employment policies, according to the Bureau of National Affairs.

First to make alcohol and "do it legal!": Dwayne Yancey, "Hey, Sugar, She's No Average Republican," *Roanoke Times,* October 20, 1991.

Naomi Hodge-Muse family: Her husband, William Muse, got his Imperial Savings and Loan federal insurance during the Nixon administration—via a connection with a White House cook (Naomi Hodge-Muse, interview with the author, September 18, 2012).

Nixon's redwood-sapling symbol: "Richard Nixon, Remarks Upon Returning from China, Feb. 28, 1972," from the archives of the University of Southern California–China Institute.

Mr. Ed worked at fourteen: Bassett Furniture was found to be guilty of violating child-labor laws as far back as 1915, when it was fined twenty-five dollars (Bureau of Labor and Industrial Statistics, State of Virginia, 1916).

Spilman's feet on John Bassett's desk: Garet Bosiger, interview with the author, November 22, 2012.

"My brother-in-law is still a child": Bob Merriman, interview with the author, November 26, 2012.

Lunchtime poker with Bob Spilman: Frank Snyder, Howard Altizer, and Joe Philpott, interviews with the author, November 27, 2012 (Altizer).

"Bifold" doors: Bill Young, interview with the author, July 25, 2013.

Spilman's charitable deeds: Jim Philpott, interview with the author, October 15, 2012.

Prisoners on work release in factory: Joe Meadors, interview with the author, September 12, 2012. He said some of the prisoners were such good workers that the company hired them after they got out of prison.

Bob Spilman on union-busting: Bob Spilman, interview with E. L. Briggs, American Furniture Hall of Fame Foundation Oral Histories, April 4 and 7, 2005.

Barbs exchanged between Bob Spilman and Smith Young: Estelle Jackson, "Sweet Ole Bob: The Furniture Industry Is No Game for Patsies," *Virginia Business*, February 1987.

Increasing output just to break even: Frank Snyder, then secretary of the BFI board, interview with the author.

Chapter 10: The Mount Airy Ploy
Interviews: Reuben Scott, Brent Carrick, Ruth Phillips, Russ Ashburn, Mick Micklem, George Fricke, Eddie Wall, John Bassett, Pat Bassett, Duke Taylor, Sherwood Robertson, Frank Snyder, Bob Merriman, Howard Hodges, Linda McMillian, Spencer Morten, Jerry Epperson

Mount Airy plant closing: Bassett closed the plant in November 2005, putting three hundred out of work (*Furniture Today*, July 23, 2006).

Bassett textile plant sold for an eight-figure sum: In 1984, Bassett-Walker Knitting Company was sold for $293 million to VF Imagewear, which was then Henry County's largest

employer, with 2,300 workers. It closed in 2001, a year when 91,000 American textile workers lost their jobs.

Executive office layout: Over coffee at a Bassett Forks McDonald's in September 2012, retired lawyer Frank Snyder drew me a sketch of the Taj Mahal suites before and after John Bassett's stint in Mount Airy.

Chapter 11: The Family Elbow
Interviews: Frank Snyder, Claude Cobler, John Bassett, Jane Bassett Spilman, Jerry Epperson, Spencer Morten, Bernard "Bunny" Wampler, Junior Thomas, Joe Meadors, Howard White, Pat Bassett

"To get rich is glorious": The quote is widely attributed to Teng Hsiao-p'ing, but there's no proof he actually said it (per Evelyn Iritani, "Great Idea But Don't Quote Him," *Los Angeles Times*, September 9, 2004).

Offshoring model pioneered at Taiping Handbag Factory: Recounted in Leslie T. Chang, *Factory Girls: From Village to City in a Changing China* (New York: Spiegel and Grau, 2008).

Growth of Chinese exports: Ding Qingfen, "Evolving Export Strategy," *China Daily*, June 1, 2011.

American occasional tables to become extinct: "Bassett Expects No Business Increase," *Roanoke Times*, January 5, 1985.

Wages in China and the United States: Estelle Jackson, "Sweet Ole Bob: The Furniture Industry Is No Game for Patsies," *Virginia Business*, February 1987.

Record sales of $301 million: "Bassett Reports Sales and Income Gains," *Roanoke Times*, December 30, 1981.

Cause of death was pneumonia, not choking: Chuck Burress, "Crib Deaths Haunt Bassett," *Roanoke Times and World-News,* December 10, 1978.

Stinging rebuke for crib deaths: Jack Anderson, "Baby Cribs Investigated," syndicated column, April 30, 1980; Jackson, "Sweet Ole Bob."

Warning posters issued: U.S. Consumer Product Safety Commission news report, February 1980 and February 1984.

$1 million cost to company to send warnings: Mag Poff, "Bassett Beginning Campaign to Warn of Dangerous Cribs," *Roanoke Times,* February 14, 1980.

Nine deaths associated with cribs: U.S. Consumer Product Safety Commission news report, revised June 21, 2001.

Spilman has "*got* to know": Gregg Jones, "A Long Slowdown? Bassett Furniture Chief Strives to Minimize the Effects of Recession," *Roanoke Times,* March 14, 1982.

Press coverage of John Bassett's move to Galax: "Bassett Resigns Posts," *Martinsville Bulletin,* December 29, 1982.

Chapter 12: Schooling the Chinese
Interviews: Jerry Epperson, Laurence Zung, Michael Moh, Joe Meadors, Michael Dugan, Buck Gale, Jim Philpott, Paul Fulton, Steve Kincaid, Joe Philpott, Tom Word, Reuben Scott, Richard Bennington

"A businessman setting up shop": Quote from a 1977 *Economist* article recounted in "End of an Experiment: The Introduction of a Minimum Wage Marks the Further Erosion of Hong Kong's Free-Market Ways," *Economist,* July 15, 2010.

17 percent of the Chinese population in cities: United Nations Development Programme, *Rapport mondial sur le développement humain 1999* (Paris: De Boeck Université, 1999), 198.

American embargo and government attitudes toward China: Martin Jacques, *When China Rules the World: The End of the Western World and the Birth of a New Global Order,* rev. ed. (New York: Penguin, 2012), 176. The United Nations imposed a similar Cold War embargo on China in 1951. The United States didn't recognize the People's Republic of China as the legitimate China until 1979.

China was half a century behind Virginia: By the 1950s, for the first time in Virginia's history, most Virginians lived in towns, cities, or suburbs, as people moved from farm to factory. Charles F. Bryan Jr., "Manufacturing a New Virginia, One Box at a Time," *Richmond Times-Dispatch,* June 17, 2012.

Moh borrowed $80,000 to start his business: Lee Buchanan, "Man of the Year: Laurence Moh," *InFurniture,* December 2002.

Wage differentials: Bureau of Labor Statistics figures, "International Comparisons of Hourly Compensation Costs for Production Workers in Manufacturing," 1997.

Imports "will be with us forever": George Kegley, "Bassett Upgrades Products, Enters Motel and Office Markets," *Roanoke Times,* February 5, 1987.

Factory closures in 1986: Ibid.

Estelle Jackson, "Sweet Ole Bob: The Furniture Industry Is No Game for Patsies": *Virginia Business,* February

1987; and Jim Philpott, interview with the author.

A family-controlled industry: Michael Dugan, *The Furniture Wars: How America Lost a Fifty Billion Dollar Industry* (Conover, NC: Goosepen Press, 2009), 17.

Conglomerates acquired furniture companies: James Flanigan, "Merger Mania Strikes Again in Furniture Field," *Los Angeles Times*, February 27, 1987.

Raiders mainly pursuing high-end furniture makers: "Bassett Denies Takeover Rumors," *Roanoke Times*, September 9, 1988.

Sales down from previous year: American Association of Furniture Manufacturers data, quoted in George Kegley, "Furniture Outlook Drab, Prospects Worst in 35 Years, Bassett Stockholders Told," *Roanoke Times*, February 8, 1990.

Chapter 13: Bird-Doggin' the Backwaters

Interviews: Pat Bassett, John Bassett, Tom Word, Garet Bosiger, Hope Antonoff, Jerome Neff, Bob Merriman, Eddie Wall, Sheila Key, Spencer Morten, Joyce Phillips, Duke Taylor, Bernard "Bunny" Wampler, Jill Burcham, Joe Meadors, Joe Philpott, Linda McMillian

Dick Cheney: *Daily Show* correspondents and others mocked the absurdity of a sitting vice president shooting a seventy-eight-year-old friend in the face while hunting quail that had been raised in a pen and were released mere seconds before they were shot.

Bassett couple's hunting prowess: Pat Bassett was named to the 1973 All-American team by *Sports Afield* magazine in recognition of her being one of the top ten women gunners in the country. In one statewide competition she hit 99 out of 100 shots, according to "Bassetts Are Top Guns," *Martinsville Bulletin*, March 3, 1974.

Company losses in 1982/1983: Vaughan-Bassett Furniture Company financial statements, December 3, 1983.

George Vaughan's lobbying for highway: John Vaughan, interview with Roy Briggs, American Furniture Hall of Fame Foundation Oral Histories, November 26, 2001.

Chapter 14: Selling the Masses

Interviews: Garet Bosiger, John Bassett, Bob Merriman, Wyatt Bassett, Laurence Zung, Michael Moh, Hugh McLarty

Business prospects for selling paper-on-particleboard furniture: Tom Word, *The Price of Admission: Reflections on Some Personal Heroes* (self-published, 2011).

Civil War heritage of Sumter region: Sumter was home to Potter's Raid, a series of battles that happened after the war ended (but before word of its ending reached the town). Sumter was also an hour away from Columbia, which was burned by Union troops in 1865, an event that still resonates as an act of Northern malice, especially in the South Carolina midlands.

Webb Turner's rise and fall in furniture: Michael Dugan, *The Furniture Wars: How America Lost a Fifty Billion Dollar Industry* (Conover, NC: Goosepen Press, 2009), chapter 9.

Borax as slang for flashy, cheaply made furniture: The term derives from furniture acquired by saving Kirkman's Borax Soap wrappers, according to Richard R. Bennington, *Furniture Marketing: From Product Development to Distribution* (New York: Fairchild Publications, 2004).

Sumter wages: Garet Bosiger, interview with the author; Galax wage information came from Doug Bassett and industry average from Steve Walker, furniture expert at North Carolina State University.

Background on the Market: The semiannual trade show occurs in April and October in High Point, North Carolina. Sales representatives and sales managers try to win orders for placements of the new goods in stores nationwide while retailers try to get access to as many lines as possible without ceding valuable floor space (as described in Dugan, *The Furniture Wars*).

Vaughan-Bassett's sales figures: By 1996, the company was selling $108 million and had a net annual income of $5.7 million, according to the Vaughan-Bassett Furniture Company annual report, 1996.

Fears about NAFTA: Anthony DePalma, "Clear Today; Tomorrow, Who Knows?; Culture Clash," *New York Times*, January 2, 1994.

Asian work ethic: Richard Burkholder and Raksha Arora, "Is China's Famed 'Work Ethic' Waning?," Gallup, January 25, 2005.

Cowboy capitalism: China joined the International Monetary Fund and the World Bank in 1986 and was granted observer status in GATT in 1982. In the early 1990s, the American brand of capitalism exerted growing influence there, and was heightened by the collapse of the Soviet Union and the growing dynamism of Silicon Valley; see Martin Jacques, *When China Rules the World: The End of the Western World and the Birth of a New Global Order*, rev. ed. (New York: Penguin, 2012), chapter 11.

Chapter 15: The Storm Before the Tsunami

Interviews: Garet Bosiger, John Bassett, Pat Bassett, Wyatt Bassett, Tim Prillaman, Michael Moh, Doug Bassett Lane, Joe Meadors, Warren Zirkle, Bob Merriman, Bernard "Bunny" Wampler

Hurricane Hugo damage: "Hurricane Hugo Today Would Cause $20 Billion in Damage in South Carolina," *Insurance Journal*, September 22, 2009.

Hurricane Hugo severity: Jesse Ferrell, "Remembering Hugo from 1989," AccuWeather.com, September 22, 2011.

Container lines building larger ships: Heightened competition among ports and the economics of global shipping are detailed in Marc Levinson, *The Box: How the Shipping Container Made the World Smaller and the World Economy Bigger* (Princeton, NJ: Princeton University Press, 2006).

Popularity of Victorian Sampler: From closing arguments in the case *Lexington Furniture Industries v. Vaughan-Bassett Furniture Co.*, in the United States District Court for the Middle District of North Carolina, June 3, 1996.

Size of Lexington Home Brands: Scott Andron, "Lexington Furniture Loses Lawsuit," *Greensboro News and Record*, June 6, 1996.

Size of Masco: In 1996, Masco sold a majority stake in the furniture and fabric companies that made up its home furnishings division for $1.1 billion (Jay McIntosh, "LifeStyle Value Plummets," *Furniture/Today*, November 4, 2001).

Deconstructing the Lexington suite: Wyatt Bassett, interview with the author, December 18, 2012. Court transcripts indicate Lexington's suite sold for 32 percent more than Vaughan-Bassett's.

"nullify our whole design program": Doug Bassett Lane, interview with the author, October 8, 2012. Doug Lane is the son of Minnie Bassett Lane (John's sister), who was the daughter of a Bassett CEO and the wife of a Lane CEO. Lane recorded the quote from his uncle Edward Lane Jr., a longtime executive with Lane Furniture, as he lay dying in a Roanoke hospital in 2004.

Leo Jiranek's fending off of Lane lawsuit: Joe Meadors, interview with the author.

Lexington's patent-pending claim: Scott Andron, "Furniture Copying Still Unclear," *Greensboro News and Record,* June 9, 1996; and Wyatt Bassett, interview with the author.

One dollar in damages: The judgment was later overturned when the judge ruled that the jury couldn't properly award punitive damages without also awarding actual damages. Vaughan-Bassett had not presented a firm figure on how much Lexington's unfair competition cost in terms of lost sales ("$1 Judgment Against Company Overturned," *Greensboro News and Record,* July 24, 1996).

Chapter 16: Trouble in the 'Ville

Interviews: John Bassett, Wyatt Bassett, Spencer and Mary Elizabeth Morten, Rob Spilman, Joe Philpott, Paul Fulton, Joe Meadors, Coy Young, Dave Phillips, Mike Micklem, Ralph Spillman, Frances Kissee, Buck Gale

"giant sucking sound": The phrase was coined in 1992 by presidential candidate Ross Perot during his debate with President George H. W. Bush and Governor Bill Clinton. Perot opposed NAFTA and predicted it would lead to jobs being shipped to countries where young workers would be paid minimally by companies that could operate without regard to employee health or environmental controls. Transcript available at http://www.nytimes.com/1992/10/16/us/the-1992-campaign-transcript-of-2d-tv-debate-between-bush-clinton-and-perot.html

CalPERS proposal to separate positions of CEO and chairman: "CalPERS Seeks to Divide Top 2 Posts at Bassett," *Bloomberg News,* May 13, 1997.

"little more than a claque of the CEO's cronies": John A. Byrne, "The Best & Worst Boards: Our New Report Card on Corporate Governance," *Businessweek,* November 25, 1996.

Bob Spilman's efforts to keep the Market in High Point: "Natural Born Leader," *High Points,* March 1997.

Bob Spilman's contributions to the Port of Virginia: Al Roberts, "The Men Who Put the Port on Track," *Virginian-Pilot,* November 26, 1990.

Paul Fulton's influence: Douglas C. McGill, "At Sara Lee, It's All in the Names," *New York Times,* June 19, 1989.

Imports making up a third of all wood furniture sold in America: Scott Andron, "Furniture Imports the Talk of Market," *Greensboro News and Record,* May 3, 1998.

J'Amy Owens's marketing acumen: "Sales Guru to the Stars," *Inc.,* October 1999.

Bassett Furniture strategizes to court women buyers: James R. Hagerty, "Showing Furniture Makers the Softer Side," *Wall Street Journal,* July 18, 1999.

Closing of W.M. plant: Ginny Wray, "Bassett to Close City Plant," *Martinsville Bulletin,* May 22, 1997.

Bassett Furniture tries to cut its losses: Megan Schnabel, "Bassett Takes a $19.6 Million Beating in 1997," *Roanoke Times,* January 10, 1998.

Apparel and textile job losses: Nearly a million were lost between 1976 and 1996, primarily due to the growth of imports; technological advances in transportation, communication, and production; and the worldwide search for markets, according to Mark Mittelhauser, "Employment Trends in Textiles and Apparel, 1973–2005," *Monthly Labor Review,* August 1997.

Local reaction to W.M. plant closing: Ginny Wray, "Amid Shock, Few Expected Plant Closing," *Martinsville Bulletin,* May 22, 1997.

Bassett Furniture sales in decline: In 1996, Bassett reported a net income of $18.5 million on sales of $450.7 million, according to Schnabel, "Bassett Takes a $19.6 Million Beating."

Twenty-eight Bassett Furniture factory closures over three years: Megan Schnabel, "Bassett Furniture Industries Has a New Chief Executive Officer, But He's an Old Hand at the Company," *Roanoke Times,* March 29, 2000.

TAA participation rates: Government Accountability Office Studies, and Beth Macy, "The Reality of Retraining," *Roanoke Times,* April 22, 2012.

Cost of razing the W.M. factory: Jessie Weston, "Plant Razing Tops $840,000," *Martinsville Bulletin,* March 11, 1998.

Unemployment rate in Martinsville: Jeff Sturgeon, "Hampton Plant Cuts 120 Jobs," *Roanoke Times,* December 30, 1999.

Chapter 17: Stretching Out the Snake

Interviews: Wyatt Bassett, John Bassett, Linda McMillian, Allen Farmer, J. "Doug" Bassett IV, Tim Prillaman, Bob Merriman, Pamela Luecke, Doug Brannock, Rose Maner

Chinese view of Americans' work ethic: James McGregor, "Advantage, China," *Washington Post,* July 31, 2005.

Increase in Chinese imports from 2000 to 2002: U.S. International Trade Commission, public conference, November 21, 2003. Domestic producers of bedroom furniture increased their imports from a level equivalent to 6 percent of their domestically produced shipments in 2000 to a level equivalent to 19.6 percent of those shipments in 2002, according to *Wooden Bedroom Furniture from China: Preliminary Hearings Before the U.S. International Trade Commission,* 17 (January 2004).

Vaughan-Bassett's sales dive as result of imports: Profits sank from $14 million in 1999 to $6.4 million in 2000, according to Wyatt Bassett.

Closing of Bassett's veneer plant in Burkeville: Allen Farmer, former veneer plant manager, interview with the author, November 13, 2012.

Vaughan-Bassett's and other companies' sales decline in 2001: Figures from public SEC statements, compiled and presented at furniture suppliers' meeting, Galax, Virginia, July 30, 2001.

J.D. Bassett plants closure: Duncan Adams, "Bassett Furniture to Eliminate 280 Jobs," *Roanoke Times,* November 29, 2000.

Two million copies of the Chinese-language edition of the WTO rule

book sold: Thomas Friedman, *The World Is Flat* (New York: Picador, 2005), 137–39.

Genesis of Vaughan-Bassett Express: Jim McIngvale, Thomas Duening, and John Ivancevich, *Always Think Big: How Mattress Mack's Uncompromising Attitude Built the Biggest Single Retail Store in America,* (Chicago: Dearborn, 2002).

Robert E. Lee's greatest victory in the Civil War: Robert Cowley and Geoffrey Parker, eds., *The Reader's Companion to Military History* (Boston: Houghton Mifflin, 1996).

$1.2 million of pretax profits: "Furniture Veterans Bear Witness to How Trade Spats Split Industries," *Wall Street Journal,* June 17, 2004; importing details from Wyatt Bassett, interview with the author, December 14, 2012.

Kuo's videotaping at Vaughan-Bassett: "Furniture Veterans Bear Witness."

China's treatment of Taiwan: The one-China policy had its origins in 1949, when Chiang Kai-shek moved the seat of his defeated government to Taiwan; Chiang and Mao Tse-tung each insisted that his government was the only legitimate government of China and that it had authority over both the mainland and Taiwan. Though Taiwanese businessmen maintained strong economic ties to China, few Taiwanese citizens wanted to come under Beijing's harsh Communist rule. China has long regarded Taiwan as a renegade territory.

Taiwanese factories moving to the mainland: Sheryl WuDunn, "Taiwan's Mainland Efforts Widen," *New York Times,* April 14, 1990.

Chapter 18: The Dalian Dance Card
Interviews: Rose Maner, Wyatt Bassett, John Bassett, Doug Bassett, Frank Tothill, Michael Moh, Joyce Phillips, Sheila Key, Joe Dorn, Joe Meadors

Furniture imports increase again: Denise Becker, "Chinese Imports Talk of Market," *Greensboro News and Record,* October 17, 2002.

Furniture job losses tallied: Edward Cone, "Against the Grain," *Baseline* 21 (August 2003): 55–57.

Larry Moh's location for fiberboard business: The Chengdu Economic and Technological Development Zone was approved as a state-level development zone in February 2000, sixteen years after Dalian's.

Industrialization of Leshan: The first foreign-based company was Motorola, which built a semiconductor plant there in 1995 ("Motorola Leads Foreign Investors in Development of Western China," China.org.cn, March 28, 2001).

Opening of Larry and Michael Moh's FFDM: Powell Slaughter, "China Plant Impresses Retailers: FFDM Has Eye on $100M Mark," *Furniture/Today,* December 1, 2002.

Bo Xilai's ascent in party politics: Dexter Roberts, "A Princeling Who Could Be Premier," *Bloomberg Businessweek,* March 15, 2004.

Corruption scandal: Jamil Anderlini, "Bo Xilai: Power, Death, and Politics," *Financial Times,* July 20, 2012.

Bo Xilai's wife in jail for murder: David Barboza, "As China Official Rose, His Family's Wealth Grew," *New York Times,* April 23, 2012.

Russian companies accused of illegal logging: "Attention Wal-Mart Shoppers," Environmental Investigation Agency, 2007 report. The practice was confirmed by undercover EIA investigators; see Raffi Khatchadourian, "The Stolen Forests: Inside the Cover War on Illegal Logging," *New Yorker*, October 6, 2008. Several months later, Walmart announced it would investigate its suppliers more rigorously and joined the Global Forest & Trade Network, according to "What Not to Buy at Walmart," May 17, 2011, cbsnews.com.

Growth goals of Dalian Huafeng: Research Office of Provincial Township Enterprise Bureau of the People's Government of Liaoning Province, "The History/Growth/Development of Dalian Huafeng Furniture Co., Ltd.," *Liaoning Daily*, August 9, 2003 (translated by Rose Maner).

Factory dormitory size: "Ju Qian (Capable) Furniture Factory Report," China Labor Watch, April 2007.

Dalian Huafeng's plans: Testimony of Wyatt Bassett, U.S. International Trade Commission, public conference, November 21, 2003. Summary of Vaughan-Bassett's injuries caused by imports: Testimony of John Bassett, U.S. International Trade Commission hearing, November 9, 2004, available at usitc.gov.

Bob Timberlake: Richard Craver, "Designer Will End Ties with Company," *Winston-Salem Journal*, December 11, 2012.

Joe Dorn's earlier Cemex case: The antidumping petition resulted in a 58 percent duty on Cemex imports; see David P. Baron and Justin Adams, "Cemex and Antidumping," case study, *Harvard Business Review* (January 1, 1994).

J.C. Penney's dumping of Bassett Furniture: Testimony of Rob Spilman,

Bassett Furniture CEO, U.S. International Trade Commission, public conference, November 21, 2003.

J.C. Penney alleges price was not the cause of dropping Bassett: Testimonies of Rob Spilman and of Jim McAlister, operations manager of quality and sourcing for J.C. Penney, U.S. International Trade Commission, public conference, November 21, 2003.

Chapter 19: Gathering the Troops

Interviews: Doug Brannock, Wyatt Bassett, John Bassett, Sheila Key, Rick Boucher, Doug Bassett, Joe Dorn, Steve Kincaid, Powell Slaughter, Rose Maner

Jack Welch's views on offshoring: Quoted in "Where America's Jobs Went," *The Week*, March 18, 2011.

Market's state funding restored: Travis Fain, "McCrory Shifts—No Cuts for High Point Market Funding," *Greensboro News and Record*, April 2, 2013.

Boucher's influence in Washington: In 2007, Congress.org ranked Rick Boucher as the tenth most powerful member of the U.S. House of Representatives. In 2010, he lost his seat to Republican Morgan Griffith, a defeat analysts attributed to his support for his party's cap-and-trade energy bill and growing conservatism in the coalfields.

Domestics companies' importing statistics: Cited in the antidumping petition and Greg Rushford, "The Yankee Trader," *Rushford Report* (December 2003).

Furniture Brands' losses: Jon Hilsenrath, Peter Wonacott, and Dan Morse, "Competition from Imports Hurts U.S. Furniture Makers," *Wall Street Journal*, September 20, 2002.

Furniture Brands' investments in Asian plants: Dan Morse, "In North Carolina, Furniture Makers Try to Stay Alive," *Wall Street Journal,* February 20, 2004.

Origin of Byrd Amendment: Tudor N. Rus, "The Short, Unhappy Life of the Byrd Amendment," *New York University Journal of Legislation and Public Policy* 10 (Winter 2007): 427–43.

Retaliatory duties brought against American exporters: "Issues and Effects of Implementing the Continued Dumping and Subsidy Offset Act," United States Government Accountability Office, September 2005.

Political unpopularity of the Byrd Amendment: The European Union and eight other countries challenged the authority of the Byrd Amendment in 2001, saying it "clearly flies in the face of the letter and spirit of the W.T.O. law," according to Elizabeth Olson, "U.S. Law on Trade Fines Is Challenged Overseas," *New York Times,* July 14, 2001.

Displaced factory workers not faring well: Based on the work of economist Lori Kletzer of the University of California, Santa Cruz, published in "Globalization and Its Impact On American Workers," University of California, Santa Cruz, and Peterson Institute for International Economics, written as preconference paper, "Labor in the New Economy," May 2007 (revised).

Workers pledge support of antidumping petition: Denise Becker, "Workers Rally in Fight Against Chinese Imports," *Greensboro News and Record,* July 30, 2003.

Paul Toms's initial support of petition: Denise Becker, "Furniture Industry Looking to D.C.," *Greensboro News and Record,* July 16, 2003.

Hooker abandons support of petition: "Chinese Furniture Faces U.S. Tariffs," *Wall Street Journal,* June 17, 2004.

Other companies abandon support of petition: Amy Dominello, "The Committee Battling Against Chinese Furniture Loses Two Manufacturers But Gains One," *Greensboro News and Record,* September 10, 2003.

Supply disruptions predicted: Powell Slaughter, "Hooker Exits Antidumping Group; Five Others Join," *Furniture/Today,* February 22, 2004.

Petitioners ridiculed for picking on China: Rushford, "The Yankee Trader."

Factory employment figures referred to by Steve Kincaid: Nearly twelve million Americans, or 9 percent of the workforce, are employed directly in manufacturing, according to the National Association of Manufacturers and the Bureau of Labor Statistics, 2012.

Sophistry preached by Sam Walton: George Packer, *The Unwinding: An Inner History of the New America* (New York: Farrar, Straus and Giroux, 2013), 104–5.

Bedroom imports continue to climb: Powell Slaughter, "Lawyers Tip Hands on Antidumping," *Furniture/Today,* December 14, 2003.

John Bassett pressures suppliers to sign on: Powell Slaughter, "Suppliers Urged to Support Petition," *Furniture/Today,* August 17, 2003.

"Because you're an American": Ibid.

Thirty-one companies in petition: Powell Slaughter, "Antidumping Clears Hurdle," *Furniture/Today,* December 14, 2003.

"like a murder in New York City": Powell Slaughter, "We Should Acknowledge Human Cost of Imports," *Furniture/Today*, June 29, 2003, and Powell Slaughter, interview with the author, January 28, 2013.

La-Z-Boy employees dedicated solely to importing efforts: Amy Martinez, "As Layoffs Mount, Import Relief Sought," *Raleigh News and Observer*, August 27, 2003.

"Jabberwocky economics": Gary Clyde Hufbauer, Reginald Jones Senior Fellow at the Peterson Institute for International Economics, interview with the author, January 24, 2013.

Tariffs on steel imports: The WTO ruled the steel tariffs were illegal, and Bush eventually lifted them, after twenty-one months, citing an improving economy and cost-cutting efforts by domestic steel makers. Elizabeth Becker, "W.T.O. Rules Against U.S. On Steel Tariff," *New York Times*, March 27, 2003.

John Bassett's speech: Speech delivered at the High Point Rotary Club, October 16, 2003.

Incentives to lure Mercedes to Alabama: "Ten Years After Mercedes, Alabama Town Still Pans for Gold," *Savannah Morning News*, October 9, 2002.

Engineering of Congressional Furnishings Caucus by Doug Bassett: Powell Slaughter, "Antidumping Petition Filed," *Furniture/Today*, October 31, 2003.

China the world's leading furniture exporter: Jim Morrill and Tim Funk, "Job Losses Strain Loyalty of Bush Allies," *Charlotte Observer*, November 7, 2003.

Furniture likely to become China's number one U.S. export: John Bassett testimony, U.S.-China Trade Relations, House Ways and Means Committee Subcommittee on Trade, February 15, 2007, transcript available at http://www.c-spanvideo.org/videoLibrary/transcript/transcript.php?programid=170038.

Chapter 20: Mr. Bassett Goes to Washington

Interviews: Charlotte Lane, Fran Bassett Poole, Joe Dorn, Wyatt Bassett, John Bassett, Jake Jabs, Rob Spilman, Powell Slaughter, John Greenwald

Vaughan-Bassett embracing lean manufacturing: Wyatt Bassett testimony, ITC hearing, November 9, 2004; figures compiled based on financial records in "Furniture Veterans Bear Witness to How Trade Spats Split Industries," *Wall Street Journal*, June 17, 2004.

"North Carolina has-beens": Clint Engel, "Retailer Views Mixed on Antidumping Effort," *Furniture/Today*, August 17, 2003.

ITC's vote tally for and against domestic producers: William Bishop, Hearings and Meetings Coordinator, U.S. International Trade Commission.

Estimate of legal fees for antidumping petition: Jerry Epperson, furniture analyst and investment banker, interview with the author, June 19, 2012.

Government spending to advertise new twenty-dollar bill: Betsy Streisand, "Need Change for a $20 Bill? Call Hollywood," *New York Times*, September 28, 2003.

John Bassett III telling Rob Spilman that his factories could be picketed if Bassett refused to join

coalition: Rob Spilman, interview with the author, May 2, 2013.

Statements from preliminary hearing: Culled from transcripts, U.S. International Trade Commission, public conference, November 21, 2003.

Jeffrey Seamans explaining company's practices: Ibid., 234.

"the business of making futile gestures": Transcripts from the U.S. International Trade Commission hearing, November 9, 2004.

Operating income losses and closures tallied: "Petitioners' Final Comments," memorandum to the U.S. International Trade Commission, prepared by King and Spalding, December 7, 2004.

Chapter 21: Factory Requiem

Interviews: Joe Philpott, Rob Spilman, John Bassett, Buck Gale, Paul Fulton, Steve Walker

Record unemployment in Henry County: "October Unemployment Rate," *Roanoke Times,* December 6, 2003; statewide rate from the Bureau of Labor Statistics.

Lack of safety precautions in Chinese factories: Bob Spilman, interview with E. L. Briggs, American Furniture Hall of Fame Foundation Oral Histories, April 4 and 7, 2005. Confirmed in Rob Spilman's interview with the author.

Number of Bassett Furniture stores: Testimony of Rob Spilman, U.S. International Trade Commission, public conference, November 21, 2003.

V-B/Williams plant closing: Krista Pierce, "Furniture Plant Closing Its Doors," *Sumter Item,* June 29, 2004.

Chapter 22: Million-Dollar Backlash

Interviews: Wyatt Bassett, James Riddle, Keith Koenig, John Greenwald, Tim Copeland, Reau Berry, Jerry Epperson, John Bassett, George Cartledge Jr., Mike Micklem, Marc Schewel, Jake Jabs, Jim Stout, Hope Antonoff

Wyatt Bassett on the gradual process of being dumped by a retailer: Wyatt Bassett testimony, U.S. International Trade Commission hearing, November 9, 2004.

Description of Lifestyle's Forbidden City at Market: "Furniture Veterans Bear Witness to How Trade Spats Split Industries," *Wall Street Journal,* June 17, 2004.

Sales losses after being dumped by angry retailers: "Chinese Furniture Faces U.S. Tariffs," *Wall Street Journal,* June 17, 2004.

Furniture Retailers of America's ads: Ibid.

"not the cutting edge": Clint Engel, "Antidumping Issues Aired at Market," *Furniture/Today,* May 2, 2004.

"There's a neutron bomb": Clint Engel and Powell Slaughter, "Retail Groups Says Antidumping Costs May Rise," *Furniture/Today,* October 14, 2004.

Double-digit wage hikes in China: Chinese wages rose 10 percent a year between 2000 and 2005 and 19 percent a year between 2005 and 2010, according to Harold L. Sirkin et al., "U.S. Manufacturing Nears the Tipping Point," *BCG Perspectives,* March 22, 2012; https://www.bcgperspectives.com/content/articles/manufacturing_supply_chain_management_us_manufacturing_nears_the_tipping_point/.

Reshoring movement: According to "Coming Home," *Economist,* January 19, 2013, most of the multinationals bringing production back to the United States cited as their reasons the rising wages in Asia and the discovery of the hidden costs of moving production far away from corporate offices. See also Rana Foroohar and Bill Saporito, "Made in the USA," *Time,* April 22, 2013.

Lack of couch staying power: Steven Kurutz, "Analyzing the Couch," *New York Times,* February 27, 2013.

"porous antidumping rules are abused for commercial gain": Daniel J. Ikenson, "Poster Child for Reform: The Antidumping Case on Bedroom Furniture from China," Cato Institute, June 3, 2004.

Lumber and furniture movement at the Port of Virginia: Virginia's number one export is lumber; its number one import is furniture, much of it crafted from the exported logs and lumber, according to Jeff Keever, senior deputy executive director of the Virginia Port Authority, interview by May-Lily Lee on *Virginia Conversations,* WVTF Public Radio, August 3, 2012. In 2013, the top Virginia export was soybeans, followed by logs and lumber, according to the Governor's Conference on Agricultural Trade, March 6, 2014.

Chapter 23: Copper Wires and Pink Slips

Interviews: Richard McCormack, Lee Gale, Kay Pagans, Wanda Perdue, Coy Young, Spencer Johnson, Mindy Fullilove, Wayne Withers, Mary Thomas, Kim Adkins, Allyson Rothrock, Rob Spilman, Frances Kissee, Kim Wheeler, Octavia Witcher, Mary Redd, John Bassett, Lane Nunley, *Matt Barr, Jane Bassett Spilman, Larry Brown, David Autor, Richard Freeman*

"Some bones broken will forever be weak": Quoted in Allison Glock, "Natasha Trethewey: Poet in Chief," *Garden and Gun* (October/November 2012).

63,300 factories closed: Richard McCormack, ed., *ReMaking America* (Washington, DC: Alliance for American Manufacturing, 2013).

Poor media coverage of unemployment: Jason Linkins, "The Media Has Abandoned Covering the Nation's Massive Unemployment Crisis," *Huffington Post,* May 18, 2011.

Acknowledging unemployment caused by offshoring: Thomas Friedman, *The World Is Flat* (New York: Picador, 2005), 264.

Unemployment where Friedman lives: Peter Newcomb, "Thomas Friedman's World Is Flat Broke," *Vanity Fair,* November 12, 2008. In March 2013, the unemployment rate in Bethesda, Maryland, was 4.9 percent.

Veteran with PTSD who committed suicide by cop: Beth Macy, "A War Within," *Roanoke Times,* October 23, 2011.

Martinsville/Henry County once very prosperous: Ben Beagle, "Boom Wipes Out Unemployment in Henry County," *Roanoke Times,* February 24, 1963.

Job-loss numbers: Number of jobs in 1990 were almost double the number in 2010 in Martinsville and Henry County, according to "Labor Market Statistics—Quarterly Census of Employment and Wages." The Martinsville unemployment rate was 21.9 percent in January 2010, according to the Virginia Employment Commission.

Data for free/reduced lunch in Martinsville: Virginia Department of Education statistics, http://www.doe.vir ginia.gov/support/nutrition/statistics/ free_reduced_eligibility/2011-2012/ divisions/frpe_div_report_sy2011-12 .pdf.

Harder for poor people to go to college now: According to Stanford sociologist Sean F. Reardon, the achievement gap between rich and poor children born in 2001 was 30 to 40 percent larger than for those born twenty-five years earlier (quoted in Joseph Stiglitz, "Equal Opportunity, Our National Myth," *New York Times*, February 16, 2013).

Henry County's commuting workforce: Spencer Johnson, "2010 Commuting Patterns in Martinsville-Henry County," Martinsville–Henry County Economic Development Corporation, provided by Johnson in e-mail to author, February 15, 2013.

Martinsville now a majority-minority community: 2010 U.S. Census data compiled by Beth Macy, "Lingering Racial Divide Clouds Foundation's Efforts," *Roanoke Times*, March 18, 2012.

StarTek jobs in Martinsville offshored to the Philippines: Beth Macy, "The Reality of Retraining," *Roanoke Times*, April 22, 2012, and Amanda Buck, "Trade Act OK'd for StarTek," *Martinsville Bulletin*, February 29, 2012.

Small-business man begging for Harvest funds to make payroll: Macy, "Lingering Racial Divide."

Rob Spilman admonishing people not to "cry in our beer": Ibid.

Dismantling of Old Town factory: Ginny Wray, "Bassett Furniture Relic Coming Down," *Martinsville Bulletin*, August 27, 2009.

J.D. plant arson: Alison Parker, "Henry County Man Sentenced for Starting November Fire at Bassett Furniture Warehouse," WDBJ7.com, June 13, 2012. Crane was sentenced to one year and one month in prison and fined $970,000.

American of Martinsville's abrupt closing: Duncan Adams, "228 Lose Jobs in Henry Co. After Factory Shuts Down," *Roanoke Times*, April 28, 2010.

Fieldale history: Dorothy Cleal and Hiram H. Herbert, *Foresight, Founders, and Fortitude: The Growth of Industry in Martinsville and Henry County, Virginia* (Bassett, VA: Bassett Print Corporation, 1970).

Importance of textile industry to Virginia: "Henry County Presents Towels to Legislators," *Roanoke Times*, March 2, 1962.

End of textile industry in region: Jamie C. Ruff, "Pillowtex Closing 16 Plants, One in Virginia—Files for Bankruptcy," *Richmond Times-Dispatch*, July 31, 2003. Pillowtex closed all sixteen of its plants, ending jobs and benefits for 16,450, including those in Henry County.

Closing of MasterBrand: Debbie Hall, "MasterBrand Cabinets to Close Here," *Martinsville Bulletin*, August 3, 2012.

Four in five Americans will live in poverty: Hope Yen, "AP Exclusive: 4 in 5 in US Face Near-Poverty, No Work," Associated Press, July 28, 2013.

MIT study: William Mauldin, "China Imports Punish Low-Wage U.S. Workers Longer," *Wall Street Journal*, July 22, 2013.

30 percent increase in disability: David Autor, interview with the author, October 1, 2013. Autor was also featured in "Trends with Benefits," *This American*

Life, March 22, 2013, available at http://www.thisamericanlife.org/radio-archives/episode/490/trends-with-benefits.

Chapter 24: Shakedown Street

Interviews: Joe Philpott, Rob Spilman, Lee Gale, Minnie Wilson, Maxine Brown, Charlotte Lane, Joe Dorn, John Greenwald, Wyatt Bassett, Jake Jabs, Keith Koenig, John Bassett, Richard Ledger, Bruce Blonigen, Mark Drayse, Gary Hufbauer, Shirley Johnson, Bonnie Byers, Doug Bassett

Bedroom plants rendered obsolete: Rob Spilman, interview with the author, and Heath E. Combs, "Duties Often Reinvested," *Furniture/Today*, April 22, 2007.

Bassett Furniture sales on the upswing: In February 2013 Rob Spilman said the company was on track to sell $300 million in 2013.

Bassett Furniture sales growth: Jay McIntosh, "Bassett Rebounds to Profit as Sales Soar 31% in 1Q," *Furniture/Today*, April 8, 2013. The company grew 22 percent in fiscal year 2012, Rob Spilman said.

Bassett Furniture's hedge-fund investments: Roddy Boyd, "Furniture Company or Hedge Fund?," *Fortune*, February 29, 2008.

Vagaries of Bassett Furniture dividends: Quarterly stock dividends went to a more modest five cents per quarter following the IHFC sale, according to Rob Spilman.

Countries that protect domestic industries: Germany and Switzerland have sophisticated apprenticeship programs, and Germany and Japan have policies that protect industries and encourage innovation; see Donald L. Barlett and James B. Steele, *The Betrayal*

of the American Dream (New York: PublicAffairs, 2012). Nobel Prize–winning economist Michael Spence cites the benefits of Germany's salary and wage limits and worker protections in *The Next Convergence* (New York: Farrar, Straus and Giroux, 2011).

John Greenwald's hypocrite claim: *U.S. International Trade Commission in the Matter of Wooden Bedroom Furniture from China*, October 5, 2010, http://www.usitc.gov/trade_remedy/731_ad_701_cvd/investigations/2009/wooden_bedroom_furniture/PDF/Hearing%20(review)%2010-05-2010.pdf.

Elkin plant closing: Devetta Blount, "400 Out of Work, Vaughan-Bassett Furniture Closing Elkin Plant," WFMY News2, Devetta Blount, Dec. 1, 2008. The factory rehired fifty employees the following year for its factory and distribution center.

Companies seeking countries other than China to import furniture: Andrew Higgins, "From China, an End Run Around U.S. Tariffs," *Washington Post*, May 23, 2011.

Georgia retailer phone conversation with Joe Dorn: U.S. International Trade Commission sunset review (2010): 193–99, available at https://edis.usitc.gov.

Dormitories not needed alongside every Vietnam factory: Richard Ledger, vice president of importing for Stanley Furniture, interview with the author.

Antidumping laws are bad economics: N. Gregory Mankiw and Phillip L. Swagel, "Antidumping: The Third Rail of Trade Policy," *Foreign Affairs* (July/August 2005).

Cost of antidumping duties per job saved: Gary Clyde Hufbauer and Jared C. Woollacott, "Trade Disputes Between

China and the United States: Growing Pains So Far, Worse Ahead?" Peterson Institute for International Economics Working Paper, December 13, 2010.

Not a single cell phone is made in the United States: Richard McCormack, ed., *ReMaking America* (Washington, DC: Alliance for American Manufacturing, 2013), 20.

Concentrated disadvantages of trade: David H. Autor, David Dorn, and Gordon H. Hanson, "The China Syndrome: Local Labor Market Effects of Import Competition in the United States," *American Economic Review* 103 (March 2011): 2121–68; available at economics.mit.edu/files/6613.

Byrd Amendment "must go": Paul Meller, "WTO approves sanctions on U.S.," *New York Times*, September 1, 2004.

Duties collected now go into U.S. Treasury: Since the Byrd Amendment was repealed by Congress in 2006, with implementation effective October 1, 2007, the collected duties have gone into the U.S. Treasury, not to the petitioner companies; see Paul Blustein, "Senators Vote to Kill Trade Law," *Washington Post*, December 22, 2005. California representative Bill Thomas, a Republican, got the repeal attached to the Deficit Reduction Act of 2005.

America's trade deficit with China: U.S. Census Bureau, "Trade in Goods with China," www.census.gov/foreigntrade/balance/c5700.html#2005.

Tripling of food stamps, shifting of jobs from manufacturing to retail: McCormack, *ReMaking America*, 30–31.

90 percent of commercial litigation: Bureau of Justice Statistics, Federal Tort Trials and Verdicts, 2002–2003, as quoted by trade lawyer Kenneth J. Pierce in a memorandum to Joe Dorn.

Amount of duties collected: Joe Dorn, interview with the author, December 19, 2012.

Decline of Chinese imports: Wyatt Bassett, interview with the author, August 6, 2013, and Charlotte Lane, interview with the author, September 17, 2012. The decline was also documented in "U.S. Furniture Imports Slump In 2013," published in the *Import Genius,* citing the Timber Network's "Market Report," July 2, 2013.

Closing of Dalian Huafeng's American warehouses: Heath E. Combs, "Great River Trading Closing U.S. Furniture Warehouses," *Furniture/Today*, July 21, 2011.

He YunFeng's focus on emerging Chinese middle class: Clint Engel, "U.S. Buyers See Potential, Challenges at Dalian Show," *Furniture/Today*, June 24, 2007.

Chapter 25: Mud Turtle

Interviews: Tim Luper, Shirley Johnson, Doug Brannock, John Bassett, Jim Stout, Doug Bassett, Linda McMillian, Sheila Key, John Nunn, Tim Prillaman, Jessy Shrewsbury, Ray Kohl, Jill Burcham, Susan Clark, Joe Wilson

Brouhaha between hospital and insurance company: M. Paul Jackson, "Doctors' Practice Tries to Ease Fears, Blue Cross–Baptist Clash Has Worried Some Patients," *Winston-Salem Journal*, April 22, 2005.

Vaughan Furniture employment: John Vaughan, "History of Vaughan Furniture Company," reprinted in Galax History online at galaxscrapbook.com, June 30, 2012.

Press release on closure: "Vaughan Furniture to Close Galax Plant," *Carroll News,* March 19, 2008.

Tourism up by a third: Ray Kohl, interview with the author, March 29, 2013.

Blue Ridge Backroads: The show is also available at www.blueridgecountry98 .com.

Social services figures in Galax: Susan Clark, Galax's Department of Social Services director, interview with the author, March 29, 2013. According to the Virginia Department of Education, 62 percent of Galax schoolchildren qualified for free or reduced-rate lunches.

Chapter 26: The Replacements
Interviews: Micah Goldstein, Chase Patterson, Al Jones, Neil MacKenzie, Wanda Perdue, Richard Ledger, Jerry Hall, Rob Spilman, Dini Martarini, Jim Febrian, Elok Andrea, Kusnun Aini, Allen Jubin, Bruce Cochrane, Katie O'Neill, Fachrudin, Kristanto Siswanto, John Bassett, Jim Stout

Stanley Furniture domestic employment: Debbie Hall, "Stanley Holds Last Local Annual Meeting," *Martinsville Bulletin*, April 19, 2012.

Stanley's switching crib production from offshore to domestic: Timothy Aeppel, "A Crib for Baby: Made in China or Made in USA?," *Wall Street Journal*, May 21, 2012.

Crib recalls: "Stanley Furniture Recalls Cribs Due to Entrapment Hazard," *Home Furnishings Business*, June 2008.

Stanley's layoffs in Robbinsville: "Stanley Will Lay Off 200 at N.C. Plant," *Furniture/Today*, December 17, 2006.

Indonesian economy: I. Made Sentana and Farida Husna, "Indonesia's Economic Growth Slows," *Wall Street Journal*, February 5, 2013.

New Ashley plant opening in North Carolina announced: Based in Arcadia, Wisconsin, Ashley Furniture, the world's largest retail brand of home furniture and accessories, is investing $80 million in a new upholstery-manufacturing and import-distribution center in Advance, North Carolina; see Rana Foroohar and Bill Saporito, "Made in the USA," *Time*, April 22, 2013.

Niche markets stand a better chance of being domestically made: "Here, There and Everywhere: Special Report on Outsourcing and Offshoring," *Economist*, January 19, 2013.

Resurrection and fall of Lincolnton Furniture: Cameron Steele, "Lincolnton Company, Praised by Obama for Bringing New Jobs, Closes," *Charlotte Observer*, January 4, 2013, and Karen M. Koenig, "Lincolnton Furniture Shuts Down," *Woodworking Network*, January 4, 2013.

Cause of disaster mud pinpointed: "Scientists Blame Drilling for Indonesia Mud Flow," NBC News Asia-Pacific and Associated Press, June 11, 2008.

State of furniture making in Indonesia in early 2014: Richard Ledger, interview with the author, January 28, 2014.

Chapter 27: "Sheila, Get Me the Governor!"
Interviews: Doug Bassett Lane, John Bassett, Bill Stanley, Doug Brannock, Sheila Key, Tim Prillaman, Ray Kohl, Susan Clark, Tripp Smith, Reau Berry, Wyatt Bassett, Keith Koenig, Jake Jabs, Mike Micklem, Pat Bassett, Marc Schewel

Economic incentives: Beth Macy, "Vaughan-Bassett to Add 115 Jobs," *Roanoke Times*, January 27, 2012.

Unveiling of big chair in downtown Martinsville: Debbie Hall, "Big Chair Is at Home," *Martinsville Bulletin,* September 20, 2009.

Furniture employees in Martinsville/Henry County: Virginia Employment Commission, Quarterly Census of Employment and Wages, third quarter, 2012.

Same wood coming back across the ocean: Jeff Keever, director of Virginia Port Authority, *Virginia Conversations,* WVTF Public Radio, August 7, 2012.

Shareholder equity value: Vaughan-Bassett Furniture Company annual report, 2012.

Litigation over Byrd Amendment duties: Nick Brown, "Byrd Amendment Doesn't Hurt Free Speech," Law360.com, October 29, 2010.

Update on Ashley case: In August 2013, the United States Court of Appeals for the Twelfth Circuit voted two to one against Ashley and in favor of the petitioners, ruling that companies had to have voted for the petition in order to lay claim to any of the Byrd money funds.

Epilogue: The Smith River Twitch
Interviews: Pat Ross, Harry Ferguson, Rob Spilman, Jim Franklin, John Bassett

Traditional parting gift for the winner of Martinsville NASCAR race: Fast Freddy Lorenzen won the first Martinsville clock in 1964 when he ousted Richard Petty and Junior Johnson, according to Ryan McGee, "The Timeless Victory: A Victory in Martinsville Means the Most to NASCAR Trophy Lovers," ESPN.com, accessed January 2, 2014, http://sports.espn.go.com/espnmag/story?id=4011608.

Ridgeway clocks made in China: Grand Furniture executive George Cartledge III, interview with the author, May 24, 2013.

Reverend Moses E. Moore's parents: Gleaned from the Henry County Cohabitation List, recorded in February 1866, when the government sent a Freedmen's Bureau official to each county in Virginia to record blacks by name. If the man of the household took his common-law wife to the courthouse—enslaved blacks had not been allowed to marry—the marriage was then legalized on a list that included information about prior slave ownership. Only a handful of Virginia's county cohabitation lists survive. In 1976, Henry County's was found in a dumpster outside the Martinsville jail by a part-time Bassett librarian and given to a black educator to transcribe, according to Pat Ross and recounted in Henry Wiencek, *The Hairstons: An American Family in Black and White* (New York: St. Martin's Press, 1999), 176–80.

Mulatto furniture worker: As described in Wiencek, *The Hairstons,* 18, quoting Squire Hairston on his mulatto forebears: "They were born from the masters by the kitchen women. They would take our mothers and get children just like they wanted to."

Fall festival now held at Old Town: Beth Macy, "Bassett Is a Factory Town—but with No More Factories," *Roanoke Times,* September 13, 2013.

Index

BACK BAY · READERS' PICK

Reading Group Guide

FACTORY MAN

How One Furniture Maker Battled Offshoring,
Stayed Local — and Helped Save an American Town

by

BETH MACY

A conversation with Beth Macy

What prompted you to write this book?

In 2012, I wrote a newspaper series about the aftereffects of globalization on nearby factory towns, inspired by the work of a photographer friend, Jared Soares. He'd been documenting the region in and around Martinsville, Virginia, home of the highest unemployment rate in the state, for more than a decade.

Early on in my reporting, I stumbled upon an unlikely hero, a third-generation factory owner who'd given China the middle finger in a court of international trade, fighting to keep his 700 workers in nearby Galax, Virginia, employed. Revered by his workers and reviled by his competitors, John Bassett III (JBIII) was a storyteller's dream, and you could plot the whole course of one industry through his family, tracking it to Asia and back. When I heard there was also a family feud involved, my story Spidey sense kicked into high gear. As my agent enthused, "Holy crap, Macy. You've found *Moneyball*—with furniture!"

Factory Man *shows the arc of furniture making from rural Virginia to China to its current perch in Indonesia. How did you do your research and reporting?*

It was a lot of material to wrestle with, and I went at it methodically, mapping out a timeline and beginning with the dramatic moment in China in 2002, wherein JBIII confronts a Chinese furniture maker whose $100 dresser is threatening to take down the entire American furniture industry. From there I went back to the formation of Bassett

Furniture in 1902 and advanced the story forward to today—through race and labor relations complexities, corporate power grabs among Bassett family members, and the various furniture companies' response to globalization, aka "the Asian invasion."

I'm not a business writer, so the economics learning curve was initially steep. But ultimately that helped me by giving me fresh eyes. I wanted the book to be accessible for non–business readers, too, and I kept it more focused on people than numbers. I talked to displaced workers and managers alike. I interviewed furniture industry experts, economists, and historians as well as Asian factory operators, line workers, and logistics people. I also talked to babysitters, barbers, bricklayers, and ambulance drivers.

I pored over documents at the U.S. International Trade Commission and talked to lawyers on both sides of the battle. I ventured to bedroom furniture factories in Indonesia at the request of a laid-off worker in Virginia who wanted me to explain exactly why she'd lost her job and what her replacements' lives were like. One person led to another in my hunt for new material. Then I began connecting the timeline dots with the stories I'd collected. It was 110 years' worth of material to wrangle, with complex economic threads and family and factory feuds that I compare to *Mad Men* in the mountains—with moonshine instead of martinis.

What made you think John Bassett III's story was worthy of a book or otherwise emblematic of America's role in world trade?
What he'd pulled off was big, bold, and counterintuitive: He'd orchestrated the filing of what was then the largest antidumping petition against the People's Republic of China—and won. And he'd done it from tiny Galax, Virginia, a town better known for bluegrass and barbecue. The tale sounded fascinating from the moment I first heard about it, but like all stories, the deeper you dig, the more complicated and layered it gets.

Your mom was a displaced factory worker and you grew up in a factory town. Do you think your background was an asset in your reporting?

For whatever reason, my "superpower" has always been that I'm good at establishing trust quickly with all kinds of people. I'm genuinely interested in understanding their stories, especially if it's a story I haven't heard before, and most especially if that story sheds light on a complex social issue.

My ability to connect stems from empathy; people sense that my heart is 100 percent in my work, and that's something you can't fake. I grew up poor, the daughter of the town drunk and a tough-as-tar mom who soldered airplane lights and kept our family going. I learned early on that there are no easy heroes or obvious antagonists in life, and I learned it watching my mom haul my drunk dad out of a bar on Friday night, before he drank his paycheck away and the grocery money was spent. What my background has always underscored for me is this: Marginalized people deserve a witness. In this case, the displaced workers were just waiting for someone to come along and describe the creeping small-town carnage created by acronyms like NAFTA and WTO, all of it forged by faraway people who had never bothered to see the full result of what globalization had wrought.

How does this book touch on some of the untold aftereffects of globalization?

I try to show the effects on the line workers, beginning with the 1980s, when Asian middle managers first appeared in the Virginia factories to watch them work—without any hint that they would eventually be replaced on the other side of the world. As pink slips proliferated in factory towns across America, people struggled to feed their families, picking up under-the-table odd jobs and maxing out credit cards and, if they were lucky, working part-time at Walmart.

Sure, blue jeans and bedroom suites got a little cheaper to buy, but if you had no income, what good did that savings do for you? I also took a hard look at Trade Adjustment Assistance, a decades-old federal program that was supposed to provide retraining for the dis-placed—but is largely unworkable for a variety of reasons outlined in my book. Disability rolls ended up soaring instead, as did property and drug-related crime. The Bassett family mausoleum was even pillaged by desperate people looking to resell brass and copper fixtures on the black market.

What do you think a "factory man" needs to make it in America today?

That's a really complicated question, and it grew more complicated as my story's layers unfurled. Rob Spilman, the CEO of Bassett Furniture, a public company since 1930, would tell you that his job was to keep the company going and his shareholders happy—and, to that end, he succeeded. "We are not a social experiment," he said.

On the other end, Rob's uncle, John Bassett III—who chairs the smaller, privately held Vaughan-Bassett—had other motives at play. He was fueled not just by his desire to show his relatives back at Bassett Furniture just who the real factory man was but also to stick up for his 700 workers in Galax, families who had toiled for generations to help make his family rich. JBIII gives a speech he calls his "five points for competing in the global marketplace," which is all about being relent-less on matters large and small, from making 2 a.m. phone calls to company managers, to buying multimillion-dollar Italian-made machinery with proceeds from the anti-dumping battle, to hiring a Taiwanese interpreter-turned-spy to keep track of goings-on inside the Chinese factory walls.

It took a character with an outsized ego—and millions of dollars, paid to Washington lawyers—to prove that the American government and the World Trade Organization weren't policing global trade the way they promised they would. No one was minding the back room of the new global store; for me, that was the biggest takeaway of this book.

Do you have a business background? How much did you have to learn, and how did you go about doing it?

I like to take a statistic or a trend, then find the people who are most affected, then work my way up to explain how they got to where they are—and what the official response to that condition is. When the food stamp cuts were being debated in 2013, I hung out in food pantries for days. Writing about the impact of the recession on families between 2008 and 2011, I attended unemployment support groups and interviewed families who were doubling up in living spaces to stave off homelessness. I visited a laid-off construction worker and others living off the grid—growing their own food, trading knitting for tax preparation and digital equipment for horse manure.

I don't think of myself as a business writer; I need an editor to double-check my math! So I read a lot of economics books and ran my drafts past business professors, and I read (most of) *The Economist* every week!

On the other hand, "real" business reporters would not have viewed John Bassett III's story through my lens. They had already written him off as an outlier, whereas I saw his story as the perfect vehicle for showing what's happened in boardrooms and boiler rooms across America.

In* Factory Man, *you describe remarkable stories from displaced factory line workers, retired middle managers, and senior executives. How did you get reluctant interviewees to talk to you so openly?

I prepare for tough interviews as much as I can, but I've learned that if you go into them with a spirit of transparency and convey your desire to be fair, people usually open up. "You know a lot about us," one reluctant CEO said at the end of a two-hour interview. He'd made me wait almost a year before he consented to the interview.

So polite persistence and genuine curiosity won the day—as well as the luxury of having all that time to gather new material, all the while hoping he'd eventually let me in. As Robert Caro has put it, "Time equals truth."

What surprised you most during the course of writing this book?
Just how rich the material was, from the corporate pilot who landed without landing gear, to the maid who wore two girdles at once (to prevent being groped by her boss), to cousins marrying each other partly to keep the wealth in the family. Not to mention the undercover trip to Dalian, China, to find that $100 dresser—with the aid of a cheerful Taiwanese spy!

I used to think business writing was all stock market reports and soybean futures and really boring stuff. But the world of *Factory Man* was fascinating to me. It was a juicy entrée into the modern financial history of our country. And you couldn't make it up.

What's your relationship like with John Bassett III, and what did he think of the book?
It's complicated! There's genuine affection there and genuine annoyance—on both sides. I've known him for three years now, and we've talked on the phone probably a thousand times. He had no editorial control over the book, and parts of it initially shocked and hurt him. We had a come-to-Jesus meeting about it during which no emotion was left unexpressed, and we didn't talk for several days.

But he embraces the book now. He calls it "a cross between *Gone With the Wind* and *Peyton Place*," giving me no credit at all for my economics and legal legwork. He likes to give me "fatherly advice," as he calls it, which typically involves him wheedling me to attend furniture-store speaking functions when I need to be home working on my next book, which is due soon. The day critic Janet Maslin put *Factory Man* at the top of her 2014 Favorite Books list, he called to say, "Just re-*mem*-bah: The higher the monkey climbs up the tree, the more it shows its ass." That's his fatherly advice!

What's your next book about?
It's called *Truevine*, named for the rural Virginia sharecropping community where it begins. Around 1900, two African American albino

brothers named George and Willie Muse were sold to the circus, where they eventually became stars of the sideshow. Set against the backdrop of the circus and the Jim Crow South, the book centers on their mother's efforts to win back their freedom. Like *Factory Man,* it mines themes of race, greed, and exploitation, using one outlier story to illuminate raw truths about the broader world.

Beth Macy's recommended reading

Books that influenced the writing of *Factory Man*

Factory Girls: From Village to City in a Changing China,
Leslie T. Chang

From the ground up, this journalist chronicles the largest migration in human history, documenting the heartaches and triumphs of young rural women migrating to China's cities, trying to do right by their families and experiencing the growing pains associated with entering the working/middle classes. I read this book and notated it, and then, during all the car trips back and forth to Bassett, I listened to the audiobook in my car.

The Hairstons: An American Family in Black and White,
Henry Wiencek

An astonishing social history of race in the southern Piedmont region of the United States, told through a single family (black, white, and mulatto) grappling to understand the legacy of slavery and its contemporary relevance. Lots of Henry County references here, including a great anecdote about the salvaging of marriage records for former slaves recorded by the Freedmen's Bureau — from a Martinsville, Virginia, courthouse dumpster.

The World Is Flat: A Brief History of the Twenty-first Century, Thomas L. Friedman

The classic proglobalization tome. I get that Friedman was reporting on new and exciting developments in the world. He even tipped his hat, briefly, to the effects of offshoring back home. In many ways, *Factory Man* was my response to Friedman's book. It takes a longer and more critically nuanced view of globalization, with special emphasis on overlooked rural America, where unfettered free trade was not the "win-win" that politicians promised it would be.

The Unwinding: An Inner History of the New America, George Packer

The *New Yorker* writer's illuminating take on America's recent economic history, told through a series of portraits of hardworking Americans and corporate greed-heads, in the style of John Dos Passos. The giant Bassett chair in Martinsville even makes a guest appearance.

Mountains Beyond Mountains: The Quest of Dr. Paul Farmer, a Man Who Would Cure the World, Tracy Kidder

The journalist's profile of Dr. Paul Farmer's work in Haiti is a portrait of a fascinating (and fiery tempered) do-gooder, interspersed with telling exchanges between the interviewer and the interviewee and woven with spot-on narrative and surprisingly complex social/medical/business analyses. Kidder is a master portrait painter. By the end of the book you've learned so much about the world by following one complicated person's actions in it.

Questions and topics for discussion

1. What surprised you most about the course of offshoring in America?
2. Which character in the book did you most identify with, and why?
3. Now that you've read *Factory Man*, how important is it to you that you buy made-in-America products? Do you feel differently from the way you did before you read the book?
4. What role did retailing play in the loss of some 300,000 American furniture jobs?
5. How was the movement of furniture jobs from Virginia and North Carolina to Asia different from when those same jobs moved to Virginia and North Carolina from Michigan and New York a century before?
6. How did the status of publicly held (rather than privately held) companies factor into executives' decisions to offshore production to Asia?
7. What role did the family feud play in John Bassett's decision to fight the offshoring trend?
8. Why do you think Beth Macy included a chapter on race relations in the Jim Crow South in a book about the furniture industry? How did it deepen your reading of other events in the book?
9. Other than filing the antidumping petition, what strategies did John Bassett employ to keep his Galax, Virginia, factory going?
10. What lessons might workers—and owners—in other industries draw from his experience?

11. Do you agree with the economist who said we shouldn't be making furniture in America, that we should instead focus on industry that is better-paying and higher-tech?

12. What parallels does Beth Macy draw between the lives of displaced Virginia workers and the furniture makers she met in Indonesia?

13. Do you think policy makers, economists, and politicians have a responsibility to address the reshoring of manufactured goods to the United States?

14. What does the government owe to trade-displaced workers in terms of retraining, education, financial aid, and so on?